AF553679

ENCYCLOPAEDIA OF EDUCATION FOR LIVING TOGETHER -3

CURRICULUM FOR LEARNING TO LIVE TOGETHER

By

Dr. Digumarti Bhaskara Rao

M.Sc., M.A., M.A., M.Ed., Ph.D.

Dean, Faculty of Education

Member, Academic Senate

Ex-Chairman, Board of Studies in Education

Member, Research Advisory Committee

Acharya Nagarjuna University

D-43, S.V.N. Colony

Guntur - 522 006 (India)

DISCOVERY PUBLISHING HOUSE PVT. LTD.

NEW DELHI-110 002

First Published - 2005

Reprinted - 2018

ISBN: 978-81-7141-848-0 (Set)

ISBN: 978-81-7141-991-3

Published by:

DISCOVERY PUBLISHING HOUSE PVT. LTD.

4383/4B, Ansari Road, Darya Ganj

New Delhi-110 002 (India)

Phone: +91-11-23279245, 43596064-65

Fax: +91-11-23253475

E-mail: discoverypublishinghouse@gmail.com

sales@discoverypublishinggroup.com

web: www.discoverypublishinggroup.com

Printed at:

Infinity Imaging Systems

Delhi

FOREWORD

The development and reform of school curricula is an ongoing preoccupation for educational authorities in all countries. The approach of the new millennium has given new urgency to efforts by governments to provide all citizens with access to quality education, at least for the basic level, while improving and widening access to secondary education. More than ever before, governments are being called upon to equip children and young people through education with the capacity to lead meaningful and productive lives in a world of bewilderingly rapid and complex change. Existing curriculum content and pedagogical methods are increasingly being called into account, as pupils leave schools ill-prepared for the world of work and adulthood, unready and unmotivated to carry on learning throughout their lives. The meaning and role of education, of teaching and learning, are constantly being redefined in an effort to meet the real needs and demands of individual and society.

The implication of globalization for societies around the world is at the heart of present concerns to improve and upgrade education systems. While globalization is often defined primarily in terms of its economic dimensions, the Report to UNESCO of the International Commission on Education for the Twenty-first Century—the *Delors report*—sees the most important consequence of this complex phenomenon to be its socio-cultural and ethical dimensions. It draws attention to the growing interdependence and interrelationships between peoples and cultures the world over: 'the far-reaching changes in the traditional patterns of life require of us a better understanding of other people and the world at large today; they demand mutual understanding, peaceful interchange and indeed harmony'.[1] However, the report stresses that 'learning to live together'—one of the pillars of education—will only occur through the possession of self-knowledge and understanding, and appreciation of one's own origins and culture.

It is now widely recognized that designing a curriculum is mainly a national concern, normally shared between educational protagonists at the central, local and school level. The principle of subsidiarity suggests that curriculum issues should not be addressed at the supranational level. Indeed, experience shows that, until quite recently, international exchanges and co-operation in curriculum development were limited, being restricted to professional associations of curriculum specialists. However, two recent trends have contributed to bringing international attention to bear on curriculum matters:

1. The globalization of economies and societies raises a new challenge, requiring the adaptation of educational content to meet both national demand and international concerns;
2. The diversification of actors, both national and international, involved in the delivery of education (in particular with the growing use of information and communication technologies—ICTs), as illustrated by the significant share of non-formal education, have resulted in the emergence of new concepts and norms for educational content; as indicated by such terms as the 'common core', 'universal values', 'basic life skills', etc. Once again, this means sharing responsibility for educational content, as well as presenting us with new opportunities for international co-operation.

It is against this background and in an effort to respond to the numerous contemporary concerns about the content of education, that the International Bureau of Education (IBE), designated as the UNESCO institute responsible for strengthening the capacity of Member States in curriculum development, is focusing its new programme activity on the adaptation of the content of education to the challenges of the

---

1. Delors, J., et al. *Learning: the treasure within*. Paris, UNESCO, 1996, p. 22. (Report to UNESCO of the International Commission on Education for the Twenty-first Century.

twenty-first century. The IBE's programme is divided into two components: (i) integrating the concern of living together into the content of education; and (ii) adapting the content of education in order to cope with some of the challenges raised by a globalized world.

The IBE programme of co-operation in 'research and studies', 'training and capacity building'; and 'the exchange of information and expertise' is based upon two major assumptions:

(a) Although different Member States of UNESCO have very uneven and heterogeneous experiences in the design and adaptation of their educational content, there is room for beneficial exchanges between countries;

(b) Although there are some common views on how to address the demand that content should be modified, a great deal remains to be done to improve the process of adaptation.

The approach to implementing the programme followed by the IBE is based on the assumption that the programme proposes to include: (a) an international platform of information on educational content; and (b) a number of regional and sub-regional co-operation projects. The preparation of such programmes is carried out through regional workshops.

This sub-regional workshop took place in 1999 in New Delhi to cater to the concerns of South and South-East Asia. The purpose of the workshop was:

(a) To collect information about the status of educational content in the region—a 'fact-finding' exercise;

(b) To encourage the assessment of experiences, both among Asian countries and a selected number of countries from other parts of the world; and

(c) To explore and map out some areas for potential co-operation among the participating Member States.

Two key phrases of the IBE's new programmes were incorporated into the umbrella theme of the course, which was The adaptation of content to the demands of the globalization and the need for learning to live together.

This publication is a compilation of the various presentations made during the workshop. Both through the diversity of topics covered and the list of issues raised, it offers a rich and varied picture of the challenges facing Asian countries seeking to adapt educational content to meet the social demand of the coming decade.

The IBE would like to thank all of the contributors, both from the participating countries and from other parts of the world, who have shared their information and experience during the workshop. Indeed, the distinction between 'faculty' and 'participants' proved to be of little relevance in this workshop, where all contributors learned from each other.

On behalf of the International Bureau of Education, I would like to express our deep appreciation to the Government of India—and in particular to the Central Board of Secondary Education—for its generous support of the workshop. India both financially supported and hosted the meeting and contributed significantly to the debates and to enriching the information shared among the participants. Finally, I should mention with thanks the financial and intellectual contribution of the Deutsche Stiftung fur internationale Entwicklung, which ensured the success of the workshop.

Jacques Hallak
Assistant Director-General,
Director of the IBE.

PREFACE

Education is gearing towards preparing individuals to live in together since ancient times. However, the notion of 'learning to live together' is clearly shaped only very recently by the UNESCO's International Commission on Education for the Twenty-first Century. The Commission emphasized that education had a treasure within and developed a vision of education for the 21st century based on four pillars namely Learning to know. Learning to do, Learning to be, and Learning to live together. The first three pillars are essential for the sound development of persons, communities or individual nations, but the fourth pillar, learning to live together, is of a different, more global nature: its omission may result in the annihilation of all educational, cultural, health and developmental efforts through war, terrorism, deterioration of resources, pandemics, etc.

The theme for which the UNESCO convened from 5 to 8 September 2001 in Geneva the 46th session of the International Conference on Education (ICE), organized by the UNESCO's International Bureau of Education, was "Education for All for Learning to Live Together: Contents and Learning Strategies—Problems and Solutions".

The ICE brought together over 600 participants from 127 countries, including in particular 80 ministers and 10 vice-ministers of education, as well as representatives of inter-governmental and non-governmental organizations. The themes of ICE are very relevant all over the world with regard to the necessity and complexity of living together as well as to the role and limitations of education in this respect.

This book, Learning to Live Together, is in four volumes, namely, Volume 1: International Conference on Learning to Live Together, Volume 2: Globalization and Living Together,

Volume 3: Curriculum for Learning to Live Together, and Volume 4: Science Education for the Contemporary Society. This multi-volume book will make all the partners of education aware of the entire spectrum of learning to live together and involve them in making the 'learning to live together' a reality.

I am very much grateful to Ms. Cecilia Braslavsky, Director of the UNESCO's International Bureau of Education and Secretary-General of the 46th Session of the International Conference on Education for her kind co-operation in this academic endeavor. I am thankful to Mr. John Fox, Head of the Publications Unit of UNESCO-IBE for according me the permission to reproduce the material from various documents that appeared in this book. I am thankful to all the contributors and editors of various documents incorporated in this book. I am also thankful to the UNESCO's International Bureau of education, UNESCO, Indian Ministry of Human Resource Development, Indian Central Board of Secondary Education, Ministry of Education of Cuba, Caribbean Network of Educational Innovation for Development, Organization of Ibero-American States, The Oman National Commission for UNESCO, UNESCO-Principal Regional Office for Asia and the Pacific, Thailand Ministry of Education, and The Chinese National Commission for UNESCO.

Sai Soudha
D-43, S.V.N. Colony
Guntur-522 006
Andhra Pradesh
India

Dr. D.B. Rao

CONTENTS

PART 2
Management of Curriculum Change and Adaptation

Part 1

Curriculum Development for Learning to Live Together

* The final Report of the Sub-regional Seminar on Curriculum Development for Learning to Live Together: The Caribbean Sub-region held in Havana, Cuba. © International Bureau of Education.

Introduction

Cecilia Braslavsky

The International Bureau of Education (IBE), the Caribbean Network of Educational Innovation for Development (CARNEID) and the Ministry of Education of Cuba, jointly organized a sub-regional seminar on the theme of 'Curriculum Development for Learning to Live Together' in Havana from 15 to 18 May 2001. The Organization of Ibero-American States (OEI) also contributed financially to the meeting. The seminar brought together twenty Member States of UNESCO-CARNEID, namely: Antigua and Barbuda, Anguilla, Aruba, Bahamas, Barbados, Belize, British Virgin Islands, Cuba, Dominica, Dominican Republic, Grenada, Guyana, Haiti, Jamaica, Netherlands Antilles, St. Kitts and Nevis, St. Lucia, St. Vincent and the Grenadines, Suriname, and Trinidad and Tobago. The number of participants totalled twenty-six, made up of senior officials from the Ministries of Education—mainly curriculum development officers, a number of whom specialized in subject areas related to the themes of the seminar. There were also four primary school principals specially invited by CARNEID.

This collaborative initiative between the IBE and CARNEID began in 1999 following a survey carried out by the IBE into curriculum development needs at upper primary and secondary levels in the Caribbean sub-region. Interest was expressed by Caribbean Member and Associate Member

States, as well as by the heads of UNESCO offices in the Caribbean to develop follow-up activities with the IBE on issues related to peace education. The curriculum development seminar in Havana was the result of these proposals, and of the IBE's interests in renewing a networking relationship with the region in close association with CARNEID. The IBE, as the UNESCO institute traditionally responsible for recording, monitoring and reporting on educational innovations worldwide, was involved in the establishment in 1979 of CARNEID, one of UNESCO's networks of educational innovation for development.

The seminar was also organized as a preparatory meeting for the forty-sixth session of the International Conference on Education (ICE), held in Geneva from 5 to 8 September 2001. The principal issues addressed during the seminar were related to the three themes selected for Discussion Unit I of the ICE, namely: (i) *Citizenship education: learning at school and in society,* (ii) *Social exclusion and violence: education for social cohesion,* and (iii) *Shared values, cultural diversity and education: what to learn and how*? These issues were considered by UNESCO-CARNEID and the participating countries to be of primary concern for Caribbean societies in the current climate of rapid and uncertain change in the region and wider world.

The seminar consisted of a number of lecture presentations by Caribbean and non-Caribbean experts, followed by plenary discussions and workshops which explored aspects of the themes and looked at practical ways of implementing them in the school curriculum. Experts were selected from both within and outside the region so as to provide a diversity of approaches and viewpoints, with three of the presenters basing their contributions on their own practical experiences of educating for citizenship and social cohesion. These contributions were balanced by more theoretical presentations by other experts. The workshops that followed also adopted a variety of approaches, with two experts in each case working jointly on the specific theme to which they had been assigned. The workshops included practical activities involving one-to-one listening exercises, role play, and drawing up of curricular approaches. In addition, Cuban specialists also made two presentations on the themes of 'Educational diagnosis' and 'Quality and equity in education' (see Annex).

The seminar programme also included visits to three schools—primary, secondary and special education (for visually impaired students)—housed within a large educational complex.

In bringing together curriculum specialists from across the linguistically and culturally diverse region, the seminar allowed for the exchange of information on national or sub-regional curricular approaches to issues of common concern. Even among the English-speaking countries, which traditionally share much in common, there was the opportunity for discovering new initiatives taking place in other CARICOM (Caribbean Common Market) states. The experience in Cuba provided participants with a practical experience of 'living together' and of learning to appreciate the cultural diversity of this small region.

The reports and materials submitted by participants indicate that most of the countries of the region have developed curricula pertaining to citizenship education and related issues, such as human rights. However, effective implementation of such curricula remains the crucial challenge for all countries. Innovative programmes such as the 'Changing the Culture of the Classroom Project' and 'Pathways to Peace' hold much potential for increasing the focus in education systems on learning to live together as an integral dimension of school curricula throughout the region.

Participants and experts made a number of proposals for strengthening the teaching and learning of the issues in the curriculum, and for promoting them as an integral part of the ethos of the school, the education system and wider society. The IBE and UNESCO-CARNEID intend to consolidate their work with the countries of the region in the area of curriculum development for citizenship education, providing what support they can for the various initiatives that have already been undertaken.

Section 1

Curriculum Development for Learning to Live Together

2

Synthesis of Country Reports and Responses to the Questionnaire

Isabel Byron

As preparation for the seminar, participants were requested to submit reports on the curriculum development process in their countries, with particular reference to the presence in the curriculum of the seminar themes. Participants were also asked to answer a short questionnaire relating to the inclusion of the themes in the curriculum in their countries. For reasons of relevance and space, this synthesis will focus on those aspects of curriculum development relating to the themes of the meeting and the broad concept of 'learning to live together'. The three themes examined in detail were the following: *Citizenship education: learning at school and in society; Social exclusion and violence: education for social cohesion*; and *Shared values, cultural diversity and education: what to learn and how?* These were the three sub-themes for Discussion Unit I of the forty-sixth session of the International Conference on Education (ICE).

Introduction

The themes of Discussion Unit I of the ICE were generally considered by participating countries to be priority areas of concern for schools and the wider society. The Caribbean region, whose nations are classed mainly among the world's small states, is experiencing numerous social challenges common to many other parts of the world. A number of these have emerged in recent years due to the rapid developmental changes taking place both within and outside the region. Rapid change in small permeable societies has had varied impact. While much has been positive in bringing a higher standard of living to many, and increased exposure to the outside world, it has also resulted in greater inequality within the population and brought a number of related problems, many of which particularly concern or impact upon children and young people. This, consequently, has serious implications for education systems and institutions in the region.

The labour market has become increasingly competitive with more skills and academic qualifications required for employment in many sectors. As in other societies, young people entering the labour market are expected to be more flexible, polyvalent, adaptable to new situations, resourceful, and able to relate well to other people and other cultures, among other attributes.

Lifestyles in the region are increasingly materialistic and individualistic, with resulting disintegration of traditional family/community structures and values. Many of the fragile economies of the region have suffered badly over the past three decades from the combined effects of globalization, natural disasters and mismanagement, with growing rates of poverty among their populations. There is growing movement of peoples (some of it illegal) between the various countries of the region and from further afield, resulted in a greater mixing of cultures and lifestyles. These various developments, among others, have resulted in rising rates of violence and crime, and anti-social behaviour more generally, including growing domestic and school violence. In addition, there has been periodic or continuous political instability in some countries, which has led to severe disruption of peace, further deterioration in the quality of life, and challenges the prospects for future stability and cohesion.

The countries of the region have experienced a common history of colonization, plantation economies, slavery and indentured labour, followed by the struggle for independence and national and regional identity. Out of this commonality, a Caribbean culture and identity have been formed, but with considerable diversity existing both within and between countries, based on the individual histories of each island/country and the heritage of the European colonizer, specific geographical location and features, demographic patterns and trends, political and socio-economic development. The dominant culture has been that imposed by the European colonizers, although this has been adapted to a hybrid Caribbean culture composed of elements of the many peoples who came to the New World. In countries such as Guyana, Trinidad and Tobago, Suriname and Belize, with very multicultural societies, separate ethnic groups (descendants of African, Indian, Chinese, Indonesian, European and Amerindian peoples) have retained many aspects of their traditional cultures and religions. While this diversity enriches the culture and way of life of these nations, it has also created racial tensions and conflict, posing great threats to stability and well being in some of these countries. Furthermore, with increased migration between the countries of the region and from further afield, populations even in the smaller islands, which tended to be much more homogenous, are becoming increasingly diverse.

A number of country reports referred to these various challenges to the growth and maintenance of peaceful, cohesive and prosperous societies, recognizing the key role of education in offering a solution to such problems. There is a general concern within education systems in the sub-region to adapt the school curriculum to current and future societal needs through changing both content, and methods of delivery and assessment. Some countries, like Trinidad and Tobago, Belize, the Netherlands Antilles and Barbados, are undertaking comprehensive reforms of primary or secondary education or both, others like Jamaica, St. Kitts and Nevis, St. Vincent and the Grenadines, and Grenada, are reforming key aspects of their curriculum or have recently done so.

Traditionally, European culture dominated education, but over the past three decades Caribbean educators have made increasing efforts to design curricula to cater to local needs and realities, reflecting Caribbean experience. The

Netherlands Antilles and Suriname made specific reference to ongoing efforts to reform the curriculum so as to make it more relevant to the reality of Antillian culture, the former curriculum remaining patterned on that of the Dutch education system.

Reports indicated the intention of Caribbean governments and educators to use the medium of the school to foster and reinforce values for citizenship among young people (see Box 1). Reforms include efforts to revise *content* to meet the diverse social challenges which threaten democratic processes, social cohesion and harmonious co-existence. Also, a number of innovative approaches to the teaching/learning *process* which should facilitate the acquisition of values and skills for citizenship have been included in reform packages and are being implemented in some countries.

Box 1: Concepts of citizenship

The various country reports identified diverse elements as comprising the concept of citizenship within their specific education systems and societies. For many it includes the possession of patriotism and national pride, and respect for authority, law and order. Access to and an understanding of democracy is felt to be central to the notion of citizenship: the awareness of and willingness to exercise both one's rights and responsibilities in society, and to participate actively in development and in furthering the common good. The ability/capacity to pursue gainful employment is specifically mentioned in some reports to be both a right and a duty of citizens. For a number of countries, the ability to think critically and independently, to exercise sound judgement and to be capable of making choices, are also considered essential aspects of citizenship. Haiti's citizenship education curriculum includes the concept of freedom, and with learning how to use this right meaningfully. Also considered of importance are respect and love for the family, respect for the equal rights of others, empathy for fellow humans, adherence to a moral and ethical code, and tolerance for, and appreciation of, difference in others. Some countries referred to the need for students to become intelligent consumers or to learn to lead healthy lifestyles. The capacity for lifelong learning is also cited by some as a quality needed for effective citizenship. A number of countries indicated that citizenship may be expanded to include the formation of a Caribbean or Latin American identity, with a few referring to the idea of global citizenship.

Goals/Policy Approaches

Caribbean governments have publicly stated their commitment at regional as well as national level to fostering the values implicit in the themes of the seminar. In 1997, CARICOM heads of government formulated a profile of the 'new Caribbean citizen' whom they wish their education systems to form (see Box 2). The elements of this profile encapsulate the themes examined in the seminar, clearly denoting an acknowledgement by governments of the central role formal education is felt to play in the transmission and reinforcement of values for personal, national and regional development. The Organization of Eastern Caribbean States (OECS) has also undertaken an education reform initiative which, as a collaborative venture among its seven member states, 'purports to set an example in regional collaboration and co-operation to the rest of the Caribbean and in the process, strengthen Caribbean identity and ideals' (Report from Dominica, p. 2).

Box 2: Profile of the ideal Caribbean citizen

The 'new Caribbean citizen' must:

- Be imbued with a respect for human life;
- Be emotionally secure with a high level of self-confidence and self-esteem;
- Regard ethnic, religious and other diversity as a source of potential strength and richness;
- Be aware of the importance of living in harmony with the environment;
- Have a strong appreciation of family and kinship values, community cohesion, and moral issues including responsibility for and accountability to self and community;
- Have an informed respect for cultural heritage (Report of Barbados, p. 5).

Common to educational goals is the aim to promote the all-round development of students, enabling them to acquire the qualities, skills and knowledge they need to become responsible, active citizens and lifelong learners, leading fulfilling lives. Policy documents describe education as a vehicle for fostering democratic citizenship at the national level. In some cases, it is also portrayed as a means of promoting a sense of belonging to a regional/global community (see Box 3).

Box 3: Goals for citizenship education

- '[to prepare] youth to become active citizens who will become a caring and compassionate people and who, as lifelong learners, will continue to improve the quality of life for themselves and others' (Report of Bahamas, p. 5);
- '[to] promote an understanding of the principles and practices of a democratic society' (Report of Trinidad and Tobago, p. 11);
- 'schools should prepare students for life so that they may adapt effectively to technological changes, and furthermore pro-actively participate in the social, economic and political activities of the country' (Report of Belize, p. 3);
- 'Foundation-based education is aimed at instilling in the young child knowledge, insights, skills and values which lay a foundation for his/her personal development and optimal participation in society' (Report of Netherlands Antilles, p. 5);
- '[to] promote collaboration and brotherhood between Dominicans and knowledge and practice of participatory democracy as a means of coexistence, allowing all citizens to exercise the right and the duty to participate actively in decision-making for the common good'... '[to] promote an attitude which favours solidarity and international co-operation based on a just economic and political order, peaceful coexistence and understanding between peoples' (Report of Dominican Republic, p. 5).

The goal of social cohesion is implicit in these and other stated principles. Active participation as a citizen in society implies possessing a sense of belonging, being accepted by others and having a desire to contribute to the common good. A few countries (Belize, Netherlands Antilles) referred directly to the inclusion in their education policy documents of the 'Four Pillars of Learning' concept defined in the Delors report, which includes 'education for learning to live together'.

Education is also seen as a means of transmitting values felt to be common to the society as a whole, or to the universal human experience (see Box 4). The idea of shared values is implicit in goals which speak of the fostering of national identity and pride, or of promoting regional identity. It is also present in the listing of such qualities as honesty, fairness, civic and personal responsibility, concern/respect for others, respect for the environment, industriousness, etc., which seek to promote the well being of all. Values considered to be common may be transmitted through all subjects and through the hidden curriculum. However, those subjects usually considered to be of particular importance in this regard are those in the social sciences, such as social studies, history, moral and religious education, health and family life education. These are discussed in the section on content.

Box 4: Shared values and social cohesion

A good example of education being used to promote the concept of shared values and social cohesion is found in Haiti's goals for citizenship education: 'Education for human rights and citizenship, through the acquisition of basic values and principles which structure and direct relations between the diverse groups of citizens within the Republic ...Education for sociability through the knowledge and internalization of the principal norms on which society is built, permitting citizens to develop attitudes and social behaviour which will lead to peaceful coexistence, education for social ethics through the popularization of the principles which allow the pupil/citizen to develop a sense of duty towards himself and others' (Report of Haiti, p. 4).

The General Law of Education of the Dominican Republic states that education is based on a number of values including Christian, ethical, aesthetic, community-spirited, patriotic, participatory and democratic, with the aim of harmonizing collective and individual needs (Report of the Dominican Republic, p. 4).

Goals for social studies in St. Lucia include: helping 'students develop attitudes, values and habits that are consistent with [those] of a democratic and humane society' (Report of St. Lucia, p. 9).

In Jamaica, goals for social studies aim at teaching about shared Caribbean historical experience and developing skills needed for communal, national and world harmony, and importantly, teaching students that values do conflict (Report of Jamaica, p. 6).

Many cited principles and goals also address the issue of educating for an appreciation of difference and the promotion of peaceful coexistence among peoples. In recognition of the multicultural nature of many Caribbean societies and of the tradition of migration from Caribbean societies to many parts of the world, education policy acknowledges the need for students to learn to exist harmoniously with others at home and abroad. Education is seen as having a role in promoting cohesion through the recognition of diversity, including, for at least some countries, an awareness of and appreciation of the diversity of religious faiths (see Box 5).

Box 5: Education principles and goals for cultural diversity

- '[Promote] an appreciation of and respect for different people and cultures and a commitment to justice and equity for all' (Report of Belize, p. 4);
- '[Foster] a belief in the value of the differing gifts and aptitudes of individuals and in the importance of these differences in an interdependent society ... an appreciation of the significance and value of the rich diversity of the Bahamas and its people, and of the responsibility of the educational process to reflect and respond to that diversity with tolerance and understanding' (Report of Bahamas, p. 6);
- 'provide opportunities for all students to develop an understanding and appreciation of the diversity of our culture' (Report of Trinidad and Tobago, p. 9);
- 'acquaint the pupils with all other cultures [in Suriname] so as to advance acceptance, appreciation and respect towards one another' (Report of Suriname, p. 6);
- 'Foster patriotic consciousness, both personal and social, in relation to identity and national sovereignty, starting from the strengthening of the elements of national culture and the valorizing of the indigenous and the vernacular; avoiding all types of exclusion and recognizing all races, indigenous, Hispanic, African Creole and all others, in the context of the promotion of solidarity, justice and freedom, and through the development of the self-esteem of all citizens' (Report of the Dominican Republic, p. 8).

Content

All countries indicated that their curricula contain various elements relating to the themes of the seminar. For the majority, related issues are taught primarily through the subjects of Social Studies/Social Sciences and Health and Family Life Education (HFLE). These are offered at both primary and secondary levels in most countries, although often only in the lower years of secondary school. As with the broad educational goals referred to above, specific goals or learning outcomes for social studies curricula from a number of countries indicate that considerable importance is attached to the acquisition of knowledge and values for active citizenship, social cohesion and intercultural understanding (see Box 6).

Box 6: Selected outcomes for the social studies curriculum in Jamaica and Trinidad and Tobago

JAMAICA

Students should be able to:

- demonstrate belief in the democratic process;
- demand their rights and exercise their responsibilities as citizens in a democratic society;
- appreciate the physically and mentally challenged as equal members of the society and recognize their contributions;
- examine the impact of different ethnic/racial groups on [the] culture and assess the extent of their influence;
- develop a sense of responsibility for the consequences of their actions and act with regard for the rights, life and dignity of persons in the family, community, nation and the world;
- recognize the bond that all Caribbean people share, regardless of natural or man-made boundaries;
- recognize and respect cultural differences, and display tolerance for people of other cultures;
- develop values and skills needed for personal, family, community, national and world harmony;
- appreciate that interdependence is necessary for human group survival (Report of Jamaica, p. 6).

TRINIDAD AND TOBAGO

Students should be able to:

- empathize with the values and perspectives that guide the behaviour of people from different cultures and understand that all cultures contribute to the advancement of the human experience;
- respect and act to preserve the fundamental principles and ideals of democratic society at all times;
- respect and act to preserve human rights at all times;
- show respect for and pride in themselves, their community, nation and region;
- demonstrate an attitude to community living in which they recognize their place and role in the advancement of the human experience in real and concrete ways (Report of Trinidad and Tobago, p. 16).

Numerous areas taught in social studies curricula cover issues related to the themes of the seminar. Programmes may contain a specific citizenship education component, such as the Barbados curriculum at secondary school level. Modules include: Heritage, Citizenship and the Constitution, Social and Negotiating Skills, Entrepreneurship, Conflict Resolution, Comparative Religions, Unions and the Workplace. Similarly, the social studies programme of the Bahamas includes a thematic area entitled 'Responsible Citizenship' (see Box 7).

Box 7: The Social Studies curriculum of the Bahamas

Included in the goals outlined for Social Studies are:

- *empowering young citizens with knowledge and understanding of their own country;*
- *promoting the democratic processes;*
- *fostering concern for environmental conservation;*
- *encouraging regional co-operation;*
- *inculcating values, self esteem and tolerance.*

Primary school students are taught about the socio-economic and political features of Bahamian society, while secondary school students learn about the rules that govern it, the roles of citizens (from both a national and global perspective), and ways to evaluate and respond to moral issues. The secondary school curriculum is divided into broad thematic areas, namely, (1) Personal and Social Issues (Making Moral Decisions, Relationships/Career Planning, Protecting the Physical and Social Development); (2) Values for Productive Living (Reproductive Health/Violence Prevention, Christian Ethics, Keeping the Democratic Process Alive); and (3) Responsible Citizenship (Family Patterns/Parenting/Budgeting, Christian Perspective on Personal and Social Issues, Bahamian—The International Citizen).

In addition, a combined Social Sciences Curriculum Module programme is presently being developed including a combination of religious education, life skills, environmental issues and violence prevention (Report of the Bahamas, pp. 7, 8, 10).

In other countries, a number of themes/topics address diverse aspects of these broad issues. In St. Lucia, students in social studies learn about, among other areas, 'the relationship between rights and responsibilities'; 'rights, duties and responsibilities of children and citizens'; 'interdependence of people and countries of the regions of the world; democratic versus non-democratic behaviour' (Report of St. Lucia, p. 10). In St. Kitts and Nevis, primary school students follow topics such as 'How our government works', 'Our civic responsibilities', 'the Caribbean', 'Communities all over the world', with specific values identified to correspond to the topic in question. Thus, for 'How our government works,' values include: *importance of democracy, participation, making choices, accountability*; and for the topic, 'Caribbean', values include: *tolerance, respect and appreciation of cultural diversity, appreciation of our Caribbean neighbours* (Report of St. Kitts and Nevis, pp. 9, 11). Haiti has recently launched a citizenship education component within the broader programme 'Education for Society'. Elements include human rights education, knowledge of political, legal and social institutions, social responsibility, social ethics and critical thinking. Specific themes taught are *identity, rights and duties, culture, solidarity, security, justice, freedom, equality, state and democracy, culture of peace* (Report of Haiti, p. 6).

Health and Family-Life Education (HFLE), which is a new addition to the curriculum of most of the countries of the English-speaking Caribbean, includes a focus on life skills. These include skills in decision-making, problem solving, creative and critical thinking, effective communication, interpersonal relationships, self-awareness, empathy, coping with stress, negotiation, refusal, assertiveness. In the Bahamas, a number of additional programmes are offered within the scope of the HFLE curriculum including: Character Education, Self-Esteem Promotion, AIDS Prevention Education, Adolescents Reproductive Health Education Project, PACE — a comprehensive programme for student mothers, and SECOND STEP — a violence prevention programme.

Other subject areas through which issues of citizenship and related areas are taught include Religious, Moral or Values Education (sometimes a combination of these three), Human Rights Education, Career Education and also though the medium of Guidance Counselling (see Table 1). In 1998, Guyana launched Human Rights Education (HRE) in schools after a four-year preparatory phase. Seven other countries of the region have used the Guyanese initiative as a model for the development of a Caribbean Teachers' Manual on HRE for Citizenship which was launched in Trinidad and Tobago in 1999.

Table 1: Subject areas through which themes of seminar are taught[1]

Country	Subject		
	Social Studies	HFLE	Other
1	2	3	4
Antigua	✓	✓	✓(Moral education)
Bahamas	✓(primary, secondary)	✓(primary, secondary)	✓(Religious studies—primary, secondary)
Barbados	✓(primary, secondary)		✓(Religious and moral education—primary, lower secondary)
Belize[2]	✓(primary)	N/A	N/A
BVI	✓	N/A	✓(Religious instruction)
Cuba		✓	✓(Citizenship education)
Dominica	✓(primary, secondary)	✓(primary)	N/A
Dominican Republic	✓(primary, secondary)		✓(Integrated humanistic and religious education, cross-curricular approaches—primary, secondary)
Grenada	✓	✓	✓(Religious education)

Table 1: (Contd...)

1	2	3	4
Guyana[3]	N/A	N/A	✓(Human rights education)
Haiti	N/A	N/A	✓(Citizenship education—primary, secondary)
Jamaica	✓	✓(primary, lower secondary)	✓(Religious education—primary secondary, Guidance and counselling—lower secondary)
Netherlands Antilles	✓(primary, lower secondary)	N/A	✓(Spiritual education, Social development—primary, lower secondary)
St Kitts and Nevis	✓(primary)	N/A	✓(Moral and religious education—primary, secondary)
St. Lucia	✓(primary, secondary)	✓	
St. Vincent and the Grenadines	✓(primary, secondary)	✓(primary, lower secondary)	✓(Counselling—lower secondary
Suriname	N/A	N/A	N/A
Trinidad & Tobago[4]	✓(secondary	✓(secondary)	✓(Moral and values education—secondary)

1. Information is included only for countries presenting reports to the seminar and is based on those reports.
2. Belize only reported on primary education.
3. Guyana only reported on human rights education.
4. Trinidad and Tobago only reported on secondary education.

N/A: Information not available.

With regard to education for appreciation and understanding of cultural diversity, some countries (Bahamas, Belize, Grenada, St. Vincent and the Grenadines) mentioned the recent introduction of foreign language teaching (Spanish and/or French) at primary level, indicating that this was a means of strengthening children's capacity for intercultural understanding.

Concern to balance academic content with affective and social development was expressed in the reports. Barbados outlined the social and emotional learning (SEL) content which it plans to integrate into its curriculum. It includes values, self-management, problem solving, decision-making, communication, conflict resolution. For other countries, this concern is clear in the new focus on the teaching of skills and attitudes, and the efforts to introduce new teaching methods, described later in this synthesis.

However, reports from St. Vincent and the Grenadines and Dominica both observed that there was a need in their curriculum for more structured and co-ordinated programmes for citizenship education. 'It is quite evident that despite the effort to focus on social issues there is need for a functional and effective programme in citizenship education. Many stakeholders have been clamouring for the introduction of civic education in the school's curriculum' (Report from St. Vincent and the Grenadines, p. 10). Problems related to the implementation of curricula are discussed later in this synthesis.

Extra-Curricular Programmes

A number of extra-curricular programmes which aim at teaching principles of good citizenship and fostering values or peaceful coexistence were mentioned. In St. Lucia, student councils at secondary school level have been established. St Vincent has introduced a Drug Abuse Resistance Education Programme (DARE) for the 10-12 year old age group. It is a programme collaboratively delivered by the police force and classroom teachers. In Grenada and Antigua an extra-curricular programme 'Young Leaders' teaches citizenship skills through community projects. Haiti also referred to collective school community programmes.

In Barbados, two programmes seek to extend students' experience and knowledge of arts, history and culture. Personal Empowerment through Arts and Creative Education (PEACE) seeks to integrate values education through use of the performing arts. A programme entitled Cultural and Historical Exposure for Kids (CHEKS) is also offered. Suriname's Bigi Brasa project trains youth to practise cultural skills for the purpose of transferring these to other young people. Trinidad and Tobago referred to involvement in the UNESCO Associated Schools Project.

The Bahamas listed a number of extra-curricular programmes focusing on the specific themes including:

- *I'm Special Programme (Primary)* which promotes positive attitudes and behaviours in students through the provision of positive peer mentors. Activities encourage pride in self by allowing students to achieve some measure of success.
- *The Associated Schools Project,* which provides activities to make students aware of the importance of working together and improving their thinking, attitudes and actions.
- *Second Step Violence Prevention (Primary-Junior High)* which is designed to reduce impulsive and aggressive behaviour in children and increase their level of social competence. It teaches skills such as empathy, impulse control and anger management.
- *Behaviour Modification Programme,* which teaches students about coping with negative peer pressure/ crises (Bahamas, reply to questionnaire).

Mention was also made of more traditional programmes such as Student Christian Movement Clubs, Community Service Projects, Social/Civic Clubs (Girl Guides, Boy Scouts), with some countries referring to sports/physical education programmes as a means of teaching values of teamwork and solidarity.

Teaching/Learning Methods and Approaches

Many countries indicated efforts to introduce a number of new approaches into the classroom, in line with contemporary educational trends. Many of these, if effectively applied, could assist in the development of skills and attitudes for the practice of citizenship and the strengthening of social cohesion, as well as cater more equitably to the diverse learning needs of students. Trinidad and Tobago's social studies curriculum advocates that teaching methods reflect democratic practice, with students being allowed to participate in decision-making with regard to the organization of learning activities. Belize refers to efforts to create a friendly, caring classroom environment for children so that they feel a sense of belonging and develop positive attitudes towards school along with a desire for lifelong learning. Barbados's social studies curriculum at primary level includes opportunities of collaborative project work and community based activities which aim to promote a better understanding and appreciation of the multicultural society.

New approaches are primarily based on a constructivist, child-centred theory of learning. Gardner's theory of multiple intelligences is also shaping teaching policy in some countries. New teaching/learning strategies mentioned include activity-based learning, project-based activities, class discussions, group work and co-operative learning, peer teaching, role play, establishment of closer links with the occupational sector and the community, recognition of children's prior learning (gained outside the school setting).

Some reports (Bahamas, Cuba, Dominican Republic, Grenada) mentioned the introduction or increase in the use of interdisciplinary approaches to curriculum development, particularly relevant to the teaching of the themes of the seminar (see Box 8)

In line with contemporary trends, some reports indicated that their education systems are adopting an outcomes-based approach in curriculum development. This will clearly impact on assessment procedures. 'Outcomes based education seeks to link teaching and learning strategies more directly to student performance. Parents will also be able to monitor their children's progress more closely' (Report from Barbados, p. 3). Trinidad and Tobago have established six essential learning outcomes for all secondary students which should be attained by the end of their third year in secondary education and which should 'result in a solid foundation of knowledge, skills and attitudes which form a foundation of literacy for living in the Trinidad and Tobago society...' (Report from Trinidad and Tobago, p. 11). These cover aesthetic expression, citizenship, communication, personal development, problem-solving and technological competence. Regarding citizenship education, 'students will assess social, cultural, economic and environmental interdependencies in the local and global contexts' (Report from Trinidad and Tobago, p. 12).

Box 8: Interdisciplinary approaches to citizenship education

In the Dominican Republic, the seminar themes are also taught transversally in all subject areas with the aim of integrating different areas of knowledge and combining cognitive, affective and behavioural aspects of learning in an effort to develop reflective and critical attitudes in students. These transversal themes aim to 'facilitate the development of values, attitudes and norms which allow for humanistic development, which promote the building of a democratic society founded on principles of justice and equity.' Themes include: democracy and citizen participation. Dominican culture, identity and diversity, the social and natural environment, work as a means of personal development and the basis of social development.

Cuba similarly treats issues of citizenship, human rights, peace education, and related areas as transversal themes in the curriculum. Values education is taught as a cross-curricular subject (*cátedras de valores*) which includes extra-curricular activities and the involvement of members of the wider community. Values are also taught during the reflection and debate session (*turnos de reflexión y debate*) which take place weekly. During these sessions, students discuss and analyse specific issues (Reports of Cuba, Dominican Republic).

Assessment

In line with innovative teaching strategies, various reports referred to efforts to introduce new and more varied methods of assessment, some of which would be relevant to evaluating social and behavioural learning. Most existing assessment in Caribbean schools is cognitive using traditional pencil and paper tests. St. Vincent and the Grenadines proposed that assessment/measurement and evaluation be made an integral component of the teacher-training curriculum. This report also proposed alternative assessment procedures (journals, portfolios, check lists) and improved reporting procedures for parents and students. Barbados will be implementing authentic assessment strategies which should serve to improve the learning process, enable students to become active participants in their own learning, and also engage the participation of parents.

Other efforts

Countries referred to efforts which may help reduce the threat of marginalization or exclusion for some students. Cuba puts special emphasis on the educational diagnosis of students in order to provide them with an education suited to their specific needs. Remedial education using the concept of multiple intelligences to cater to the learning styles and abilities of all students is used in Jamaica and Grenada. Grenada has also introduced a pilot programme focusing on male underachievers, a major problem for Caribbean schools and the wider society in general. Jamaica, meanwhile, is putting emphasis on special education in an effort to make its system more equitable and cater to the needs of those who may be disabled or come from deprived backgrounds.

In another effort to reduce the chances of the school contributing to the problem of social exclusion, Jamaica has introduced the Programme for Alternative Student Support (PASS). This programme attempts to keep children in school through counselling and reform rather than expelling them for unacceptable behaviour, as was done in the past.

However, countries referred to the difficulties experienced in implementing changes into the reality of Caribbean classrooms where traditional methods have been autocratic and teacher centred, and where staff, resources and space are lacking for easy adoption of these approaches. Furthermore, training has not kept up with the new ideas and teachers are often not adequately prepared for these innovations, many of which would be truly revolutionary for Caribbean schools.

Teacher Education

Some reports referred to specific training efforts for teachers in the implementation of new curricular content and approaches. In St. Vincent and the Grenadines, a two-week training workshop in co-operative learning was organized for both primary and secondary school-teachers. Trinidad and Tobago undertook teacher training in a range of new approaches as part of their ongoing secondary education curriculum reform. In St. Lucia, thirty university trained teachers participating in an in-service programme are required to take a social issues course that focuses on human rights and the Rights of the Child. Belize conducted a summer course for teachers on issues of thematic planning, cross-curricular approaches, and teaching and assessment strategies. The Bahamas intends to train its teachers intensively in new curricular areas related to the themes of the seminar: HFLE, Social and Religious Studies, Modern Languages.

Problems/Challenges

Reports indicated that problems have been experienced at all stages of the curriculum development process, which threaten the successful realization of efforts to introduce or strengthen education for citizenship and social cohesion. Some of these problems constitute challenges to the broader curriculum reform process while others are specifically related to the sensitive and complex nature of the issues involved: educating for democratic citizenship, non-violence, and acceptance and appreciation of diversity.

Furthermore, fundamental limitations to access and equity in education challenge the very concepts of democratic citizenship and social cohesion in certain countries and sectors of society in the region.

Unequal educational opportunities

Limited access to schooling for children in some territories and unequal provision by schools in terms of educational quality contradict efforts to promote values of democracy and harmony in the society. Instead, the school as an institution may be promoting and fostering inequality and discriminative practices. This also applies to the differing treatment of students within the same institution, where some are discriminated against due to their socio-economic or cultural backgrounds. While there is free primary education provision for all children in the countries of the region, with the exception of Haiti, access to secondary education is limited in some territories, and there is considerable difference in the quality of education offered by various schools.

In some countries there appears to be no common curriculum for citizenship education. It may be only taught in some schools, with the result that some students do not benefit from this type of formal education.

Approaches to curriculum development

A number of countries referred to and acknowledged the need for more participatory approaches to curriculum development in which the key stakeholders have a significant input. Belize suggests that participatory approaches to curriculum development and implementation with a strong emphasis on parental involvement should lead to genuine sharing of values and appreciation of difference, while Grenada and Jamaica mention efforts to incorporate this process. Suriname refers to the interest of the community in curriculum development issues, and the key role they play in influencing curricular change.

However, attempts to make the curriculum development process more participatory have failed to be very successful in some cases, as was pointed out by St Lucia and St Vincent and the Grenadines. Neither the public nor the teachers are adequately involved despite expressed intentions to increase participation. In the case of teachers, it is felt that this results partly from their crowded schedules and the absence of substitute teachers, and partly from the fact that they are largely untrained for curriculum development.

Limited personnel resources

Many reports wrote of the inadequate numbers of personnel working in curriculum development departments or units, and the subsequent difficulties which this causes. Suriname referred to the fact that curriculum development only recently became a field of study at university level there, with subject teachers having to be employed at the curriculum development department and trained on the job. Rapid staff turnover leads to depletion of the trained personnel. This latter is a problem common to all countries of the region. Inadequate staffing means that curriculum reforms are not properly supervised and monitored, nor is there enough contact between curriculum specialists and teachers.

Teacher training

There appears to be a widespread problem of insufficient numbers of adequately trained teachers at both primary and secondary levels, with inadequate structures and programmes in place for quality and relevant teacher education. Areas such as Moral and Values Education require open sensitive attitudes, and specific skills, such as communication and negotiation, and teacher education programms need to be appropriately developed. Responses to the questionnaire indicated that the concepts to be taught may cause difficulty to teachers who may shy away from certain issues or fail to teach them well.

Attempts to introduce a number of innovations into teaching practice may face resistance or inadequate responses by teachers who are unwilling or professionally unprepared to implement the advocated changes in their style and methods. Some reports spoke of the persistence in the classroom of methods which are teacher-centred, with emphasis on transmission of content knowledge, with St. Lucia referring to the resistance of teachers to the use of more democratic classroom methods (see Box 9).

There was also the suggestion that teachers may not consider the issues in question to be priorities in their work and thus not accord them the necessary amount of time in their classroom teaching. This may be attributed to the attitude to teachers and their personal perspective on the issues at stake as indicated in this response from St. Kitts and Nevis: 'The personal values held by teachers are not always congruent with the values which one expects would be passed on to students, hence conflicts between the 'written/ formal' and the hidden curriculum and in some cases the suitability of teachers to teach certain content/values pose difficulties for implementation' (St. Kitts and Nevis, response to questionnaire).

Box 9: Obstacles to change in the classroom

The culture of teaching in St. Lucia constitutes a huge barrier to democratic initiative in the school and classrooms. While it is desirable for our children to learn and practice the skills associated with democracy, our schools continue to be models of undemocratic practice. Generally, there is no room for negotiation in the classroom. The teacher is often the sole determiner of what is taught, what is right and wrong, what is acceptable and unacceptable, what behaviours merit punishment and when, and even simple things such as when students talk. Related to this are the strategies employed in values education where teachers impose their own values as the right values and children often do not get opportunities for examining and questioning their own values and that of the teacher. Such rigid control is often sought by teachers who fear that relinquishing some degree of control and autonomy in learning to students will result in indiscipline and provide an unwanted challenge to the authority of the teacher. With respect to this, many teachers do not see the need to educate children about their rights as, in the view of those teachers, this can give children a basis for challenging authority and thus give rise to indiscipline and disorder (Report of St. Lucia, p. 13).

However, the failure of teachers to prioritize values and citizenship education may also be the fault of a school curriculum which does not adequately cater for the inclusion of the teaching of these concept. Reports spoke of overcrowded curricula which made addition/acceptance of new subjects a problem, especially where they are examined externally.

Curriculum overload

Overcrowded curricula prevent effective inclusion of new areas of learning or reinforcement of key issues. Trinidad and Tobago, for instance, referred to the challenge of effectively integrating three subjects (history, geography, sociology/social issues) into the social studies curriculum in a balanced and feasible manner. Areas such as values education are not considered to be priorities, especially if they are not on the syllabus for national or overseas examinations. Subjects offered at these examinations tend to dominate the curriculum at upper secondary school and areas not examined get marginalized: 'there is a tendency for teachers to take their cue regarding what and how to teach from the examination. As a result, much that is identified as desirable in education is ignored or given scanty treatment in the actual curriculum. Social action projects and the development of democratic behaviours are just two examples of what is deemed educationally desirable but is ignored' (Report of St. Lucia, p. 12). This problem is also likely to make it difficult to introduce new assessment methods.

Medium of instruction

Suriname and Belize referred to the variety of languages spoken in their societies and the fact that in school the official medium of instruction is the language of the former European colonial power. Although the reports speak of the practicality of having a common language, they recognize the difficulties this poses to children in school: 'Children at their early age are caught between the cultures of their home and the culture of the official English language' (Report of Belize, p. 9). The report informs that the language policy of Belize states that 'children should be given the right and encouragement to build on their home languages during the teaching/learning process as a means of easing the transition between home and school' but does not indicate how this is being done. Suriname refers to a similar tension between the local languages and Dutch, the official medium of instruction, which is a foreign language to most students. The country is multilingual with over a dozen languages spoken. Lack of resources means that no curricula have been prepared in other languages, putting students from the rural areas, in particular, at a serious disadvantage. However, preliminary studies into the possibilities of teaching in the native languages are being carried out.

This problem of the medium of instruction exists to a greater or lesser degree throughout the Caribbean where the first language of the majority of the population is Creole, while the teaching language is English, French, Spanish or Dutch.

Assessment

As mentioned earlier, traditional methods of assessment using product-based pencil and paper tests, which focus on cognitive development, prevail in the Caribbean, with the evaluation of social and emotional learning being neglected (see Box 10). A further problem identified by St. Vincent and the Grenadines is the regular failure of teachers to link instruction to assessment, with the result that students are not being evaluated properly on what they have been taught. This country is introducing diagnostic tests which should help to address this problem. For new assessment procedures to be successfully integrated in schools, curriculum developers and teachers and students have to be adequately prepared, and parents properly informed of the changes. Assessment is an integral part of curriculum development and must be seen as such.

Box 10: Challenges to implementing innovative assessment methodologies in the classroom

The dominance of standradized examinations in the society, in order to facilitate selection for scarce secondary places, affects learning/teaching methodologies and learning as a whole. Aspects of curricula (especially in the affective domain) which cannot be easily tested by standardized written tests are often omitted. As a result, many primary school graduates are ill-equipped with the knowledge and skills they need to comfortably survive post-primary education and life. Many secondary pupils also lack the requisite knowledge and skills for post-secondary education and the world of work (Report of St Vincent and the Grenadines, p. 11).

Teaching conditions

A number of reports referred to limited teaching resources as a deterrent to implementing curricular changes effectively. Countries suggested that greater capacities and resources for the preparation of suitable teaching learning materials were needed.

Another difficulty is the high student/teacher ratio in many Caribbean schools which makes effective teaching and learning a considerable challenge. Teachers are less likely to wish to experiment in such conditions, although some of the advocated teaching/learning approaches may in fact facilitate their task.

Community reactions

The Bahamas reported that there was some opposition from the community to teaching children about different religions in the religious studies programme, as well as some debate about how to teach issues of tolerance and non-violence. Education for values is a sensitive and often controversial topic which excites the interest of the public and which they should be closely involved in.

Conclusions

The numerous changes taking place in Caribbean societies are impacting on decision-making in education, reflecting the need for an adequate response to the challenges brought by diverse transformations in the traditional way of life. The reports show that Caribbean education systems as a whole have recognized the critical importance of education for democratic citizenship and social cohesion in the process of sustainable development. There similarly appears to be growing recognition of the need to celebrate the cultural diversity of Caribbean societies, building on the rich heritage and potential which this offers for development and well-being. Genuine efforts are being made to both introduce or improve content for the teaching of knowledge, values, attitudes and skills for living together. There is widespread awareness of, and increasing experimentation with, a range of new teaching/learning methods in classroom teaching. Similarly, the need for diverse and alternative methods of assessment is acknowledged with alternative strategies being introduced in some education systems. A few countries indicated that greater attention to assessment has led to improvement in overall teaching as teachers make the link between learning and assessment. In all of this, a child-centred approach which recognizes the existence of diverse learning styles and multiple intelligences is being increasingly acknowledged as the preferred way to teach. Jamaica suggests that a more positive image of the learner has emerged in the society as a result of these new trends.

All of these efforts require corresponding mechanisms for improved and ongoing training and support for teachers, as was acknowledged by most reports. Greater involvement of teachers in curriculum development processes can provide valuable practical experience. St. Kitts and Nevis reported that schools are now requesting more specific training in order to implement proposed new teaching methodologies. St. Lucia proposes 'onsite support for teachers in curriculum planning, and delivery'. Some reports spoke of the need for improved infrastructure for the monitoring of curriculum delivery and reform, this appearing to remain an area of considerable weakness.

Developing and implementing curricula to effectively deal with the complex issues involved requires skilled and committed education professionals who are prepared to work closely with other key stakeholders, particularly with the students themselves and their parents, and with other influential persons/institutions in the community (see Box 11). A number of reports indicated that education systems are increasingly aware and accepting of the vital role to be played by the wider community in curriculum development.

Box 11: Profile of the curriculum developer

A curriculum developer should:

- Be familiar with major areas of research on teaching and available resources;
- Have a clear understanding of the major concepts of the various subject areas and the realization that the subject matter is complex and ever changing;
- Be aware of the fact that children's physical, social, emotional, moral and emotional development influence learning;
- Be able to identify the different approaches to learning—different learning styles, multiple intelligences, etc.
- Have a good knowledge of a variety of instructional strategies which encourage development of critical thinking and problem-solving skills;
- Understand individual and group dynamics—how to help people work productively and co-operatively;
- Be able to use effective verbal and non-verbal communication techniques to promote collaboration and interaction;
- Be able to utilize learning theory, subject matter, and knowledge about student and curriculum development to plan instruction and meet curriculum goals;
- Be familiar with a range of formal and informal assessment strategies to ensure ongoing development;
- Be cognizant of cultural and community diversity which exists in the society;
- Be sensitive to the importance of establishing relationships with colleagues, parents and the wider community (Response to questionnaire—Bahamas).

Some reports revealed an increased awareness of the crucial role of parents, referring to the introduction of parent-education programmes. St. Vincent and the Grenadines has introduced such programmes in the curricular areas of reading and HFLE. Belize has begun remedial mathematics and language programmes for parents as part of the primary education curriculum reform and spoke of the involvement of parents in the planning of school activities.

Successful curriculum reform can only come about with a proper understanding of the change process, as recognized by Barbados. There need to be adequate mechanisms for monitoring curriculum delivery and, more specifically, of curriculum reform. Some reports referred to regional co-operation in aspects of curriculum development as a positive step. There remains considerable scope for expanding such co-operation in the field of values education in the Caribbean sub-region. The report from Jamaica observed that the teaching of values and attitudes is now seen as a key curricular issue and the content of the other reports similarly indicated that increasing efforts are being made to address these as fundamental elements of curriculum development and reform. However, as expressed in the report of St. Vincent and the Grenadines, considerably more needs to be done (see Box 12).

Box 12: Suggestions for curriculum reform for citizenship education in St. Vincent and the Grenadines

- Primary: redesign the Social Studies curriculum to include a substantial amount on citizenship education.
- Secondary: introduce modules from Forms 1-5 (Grades 7-9) to deal with citizenship education.
- An aggressive planned counselling programme should be introduced at all levels to support and reinforce what is taught in the subject areas. The peer counselling strategy which is used by a few schools can be extended to other institutions.
- At both the primary and secondary levels, teachers will have to be trained to teach all students these social values as a way of life and not as a subject to be examined in a traditional manner.
- There is a need for all types of curriculum materials/resources to support the implementation of the curriculum.
- [Deliberately widen] the scope of assessment to emphasize a holistic approach including social/behavioural and the desired properties of all assessment instruments and criteria for use (Report of St. Vincent and the Grenadines, pp. 10-11).

3

Quality Education for All: Living Together, Democracy and Social Cohesion

Simon A. Clarke

Introduction

It is my belief that all human beings are born with an inalienable capacity for excellence in at least one thing. The purpose of education in general and curriculum development, in particular, is to stimulate the development of inborn talents and to provide students, at all levels, with carefully planned programmes and experiences that will bring these talents to their fullest expression. In this regard, let us now examine the present context of the human situation that must be taken into consideration when developing the content, methods and structures of new curricula.

The phenomenal advance in science and technology, especially during the second half of the last century, has led to unprecedented achievement in almost every field of human endeavour: the development of land, sea, air and space travel; the rapid expansion of telecommunications; the invention of the computer and the impact of informatics; advances in medicine; the development of biotechnology, and recently the cloning of animals, the mapping of the human genome and the possibility to alter the genetic constitution of human beings as was recently reported in a case involving two young children. The latter achievement has serious moral and ethical implications for the future quality of human life and has created much debate in international scientific, political and religious circles. Whether the results of our research make us apprehensive of the future or not, the fact is that these achievements are the result of the discovery and application of new knowledge, which is itself a direct product of the process of education.

Despite these staggering accomplishments, this past century (the twentieth) is said to have been the most violent known in human history—the two World Wars, Korea, Viet Nam, the Cold War, ethnic and religious hostilities taking place in almost every part of the globe. The end of the Cold War brought little relief, for the alienation, polarization and conflict that had previously divided the world into ideological camps, now reared its ugly head in local communities. Indeed, several countries of the Latin American region are experiencing an escalation of political, ethnic and domestic violence. Violence against the most vulnerable of the society—women and children, the mentally ill, street people, the homeless—these elements are fast becoming part of a culture of alienation and exclusion, especially among young people. During this violent period of human history, the skills of living together, the practice of democracy and social cohesion, have come under threat, especially in developing countries. One Caribbean country now records a murder rate of approximately 1,000 per year.

This crisis of the human condition is further exacerbated by the inequities in production and consumption between rich and poor countries and between different groups of people living in the same country. Over the past fifty years, the industrialized countries of the world have become richer through their model of economic and physical development. During that same period, however, the majority of countries, classified as 'developing', have become poorer, with growing problems in the areas of illiteracy, malnutrition, poor health, and rapid population growth, stagnating agriculture, as well as the degradation of the environment, all increasing in alarming proportions. This has led to marginalization, alienation, exclusion, and the lack of integration not only between rich and poor countries but also between affluent and deprived communities within single nations.

Something was clearly wrong with the development model that widened the gap between the 'haves' and the 'have-nots', for there is far more to human development than this. Human development should contribute significantly to the elimination of alienation and exclusion and consequently to the eradication of conflict and violence. It implies the full realization of innate human potential at the individual as well as at the social level. It is also rooted in the values of freedom, justice and the respect for human rights, values that are necessary for social cohesion. It is this new approach to human development that provides an unprecedented opportunity for the provision of quality education for all.

The Role of Education in Development

For education to be relevant today to the challenges of human development, our main task must be to examine and interpret the present condition and context of human existence, to be better able to select and apply the appropriate content and methodologies and the appropriate experiences that are required for responding to the needs of people struggling for survival in an environment that, for the majority, is very hostile. Education must therefore break through the artificial world of the mere acquisition and dissemination of theoretical knowledge, to the real world of the application of this knowledge to the training in those personal, social and technical skills that will ensure not only survival, but which will guarantee the kind of human development that can be sustained.

The purpose of education, therefore, cannot be merely to provide intellectual stimulation or to prepare citizens for the world of work. Education must go further and must serve a wider human purpose. It must play the central role of establishing cohesion and harmony within the local as well as the global society. It must assist in breaking down ethnic, religious, economic, class and political barriers by bringing people together in creative co-operation and collaboration. It must also be responsive to the disintegration of human society through greed, selfishness, crime and violence. In the final analysis, it must serve to make people more human.

The Universal Declaration of Human Rights, adopted on 10 December 1948, encapsulates this ideal:

> ***Education shall be directed to the full development of the human personality and to the strengthening of respect for human rights and fundamental freedoms. It shall promote understanding, tolerance and friendship among all nations, racial or religious groups, and shall further the activities of the United Nations for the maintenance of peace.***

Throughout the history of the human race there have been three significant periods of human development or education. These periods of radical change were brought about by the acquisition and application of knowledge. In other words, these changes came about as a result of education. Before the first period of radical change, the agricultural age, mankind survived by hunting, fishing and gathering and was at the mercy of the elements of nature. Later, with increased knowledge of their surroundings, the hunters and gatherers learned to farm what was needed for survival.

The second period of societal transformation, the Industrial Revolution, was characterized by mass production, mass distribution and mass consumption. This transformation had personal as well as social consequences. It depleted rural populations, created urban masses, and stimulated the development of the mass media. The Industrial Age, dissolving the cohesion of families and rural communities, lead to the consequent isolation and alienation of various groups, and also contributed to the mass destruction of the First and Second World Wars.

Today, we are in the third period of transformation and the pace of change has accelerated to the extent that we are now passing from the industrial period to a new civilization, a new culture and a new way of life. This new way of life is driven by the discovery and application of new knowledge, which is said to now be doubling every four years. Of special importance to this age is the impact of science and of information and communication technologies. This knowledge/information/communication age has transformed mass production and mass employment and assembly line operations to the customer-sensitive production of goods and services and has created increasing opportunities for self-employment, and word-alone and work-at-home arrangements.

What makes the development agenda so complex is the fact that these periods of change do not exist in separate watertight compartments. In a society, especially in the developing world, different periods of human growth can exist side by side. In the Caribbean, we are struggling with the agricultural, the industrial and the information and communication ages all at once. In some parts of our larger region, in Central and South America, a few indigenous tribes still live under pre-agricultural conditions. This situation makes the task of education for human development a very complex one. How do you make education relevant to the development needs of a society where the cultures of the agricultural, industrial and information and communication age co-exist and often collide? It is the diversity of these cultures that often leads to alienation and exclusion and, ultimately, to crime and violence.

The United Nations Charter advocates the practice of tolerance and understanding so that people of different nations, races and cultures might live together in peace as good neighbours.

The Universal Declaration of Human Rights affirms that: 'All human beings are born free and equal in dignity and rights. They are endowed with reason and conscience and should act towards one another in a spirit of brotherhood' (Article I); and that, 'Everyone has the right to life, liberty and security of person' (Article III).

Despite these stated intentions and declarations to promote the development of people, the priority for development, following the two great wars, turned out to be physical reconstruction and economic development and expansion. Although education played a major role in this kind of development by discovering, transmitting and applying new knowledge, especially in the fields of science and of information and communications technology, the development of people was not the priority. Notwithstanding the theoretical ideals that were held about the purpose of education, in practice, its content, processes and even philosophy were not inconsistent with the materialistic world-view of development. The human resource was like any other physical resource. Its development was to serve a greater economic and sometimes political objective. It was a means to an end. The end was not human development. Knowledge was a means of attaining power and 'development' was the increase in the value of goods and services and their expansion over time at the least cost.

To respond to the inequities in development between the rich and the poor, the United Nations saw the need to redefine the concept of development and to place people, human beings and their conditions of living at the centre of their efforts to transform the world. This new concept of development went beyond the traditional or classical approaches to economics, concerned with the efficient allocation of scarce productive resources and with their sustained growth over time. Consideration was now to be given to the social and institutional mechanisms that were required for bringing about large-scale improvements in the living conditions of the large-masses of the illiterate, poverty-stricken peoples of the world. It was 'development with a human face'.

As a consequence, the development of human resources became the principal concern for the Fourth United Nations Development Decade. Human development was now defined as:

> *The process of enlarging the range of peoples' choices—increasing their opportunities for education, health care, income and employment, and covering the full range of human choices from a sound physical environment to economic and political freedoms [...] Human development is concerned both with developing human capabilities and with using them productively [....] Human development also means development for people, including the creating of economic opportunities for all. And it means development by the people, requiring participatory approaches (UNDP, Human development report, 1992).*

Human development is education in its broadest sense. It empowers the individual and the society, by developing innate potential to the fullest and by eliminating exclusion, alienation, inequities and violence. It also contributes to the prevention of hostilities and therefore favours social cohesion and the establishment and maintenance of a culture of peace. It is further enhanced when conducted within the context of a vast system of interdependencies, which encompasses the external as well as the internal ecosystem. Sensitivity towards the internal environment brings into consideration the importance of the emotional, spiritual and psychosocial dimensions of human feelings. This approach to education gives strength to the values of freedom, democracy, human rights and tolerance. It is 'transformative' education.

Education that consists purely of new information and new knowledge cannot by itself ensure that people will live together in harmony. It cannot guarantee the promotion of democracy and social cohesion. It must go beyond this. It must deal also with the fundamentals that affect the human spirit as it struggles with self-expression and survival in an environment that is often hostile. It must seek to transform in the individual sentiments of selfishness and hate to expressions of caring and love. This will eventually transform the nation into a society that shares and nurtures the survival of all.

The World Declaration on Education for All points out in Article I:

1. Every person—child, youth and adult—shall be able to benefit from educational opportunities designed to meet their basic learning needs. These needs comprise both essential learning tools (such as literacy, oral expression, numeracy, and problem solving) and the basic learning content (such as knowledge, skills, values, and attitudes) required by human beings to be able to survive, to develop their full capacities, to live and work in dignity, to participate fully in development, to improve the quality of their lives, to make informed decisions, and to continue learning. The scope of basic learning needs and how they should be met varies with individual countries and cultures and, inevitably, changes with the passage of time.
2. The satisfaction of these needs empowers individuals in any society and confers upon them a responsibility to respect and build upon their collective cultural, linguistic and spiritual heritage, to promote the education of

others, to further the cause of social justice, to achieve environmental protection, to be tolerant towards social, political and religious systems which differ from their own, ensuring that commonly accepted humanistic values and human rights are upheld, and to work for international peace and solidarity in an interdependent world.

3. Another and no less fundamental aim of educational development is the transmission and enrichment of common cultural and moral values. It is in these values that the individual and society find their identity and worth.
4. Basic education is more than an end in itself. It is the foundation for lifelong learning and human development on which countries may build, systematically, further levels and types of education and training.

Paradoxically, the same education that is liberating to some may be enslaving to others and may serve as a means of widening the gap between the affluent and the deprived. Equity should be guaranteed by ensuring that the same quality of education is made available to all.

Science and technology education is of special importance in ensuring equity in the human development agenda. The notion of science and technology education as separate disciplines must now be replaced by a holistically integrated set of experiences that should be seen on a continuum from the earliest years through to adult life. It is a fundamental component of the kind of education that is required for survival in the twenty-first century. It should begin at the pre-school stage, instilling in young children an attitude towards problem-solving that they will need as an important foundation for future learning.

Expanding access to science and technology education goes hand in hand with efforts to improve the quality and relevance of general education at all levels. To improve quality, one must draw on the whole range of resources affecting educational performance and efficiency: curriculum development, teaching materials, laboratory equipment, information systems, financing, management techniques, evaluation strategies, the design of buildings and school furniture and, most important of all, teacher-training.

Teacher education

Important as a relevant curriculum and adequate materials may be, we cannot improve the quality of education unless we improve the quality of those who facilitate its delivery. What stands out as the most important factor influencing 'quality' in the classroom is the quality of the teacher, who is performing not only the traditional pedagogic role as we have come to know it, but the role of the teacher as a caring human being.

The individual teacher must experience personal transformation as coach and role model for his/her students, before any real positive change will take place in the classroom. The teacher of today must move beyond the crippling confines of time-worn and irrelevant approaches, to the establishment of new ways of thinking and to the application of a new philosophy, new principles, and new methodologies. What is required is a new set of beliefs and a new set of values and attitudes governing the teacher's behaviour and practice. The role of the teacher is so crucial to ensuring quality education for all and for the attainment of democracy and social cohesion that I wish to propose that a massive global thrust in 'education for the transformation of teachers' be launched as a major strategy for carrying forward the Education for All agenda. It is also important to recognize that, the role of parents cannot be overlooked.

Educational innovation

Innovation designed to making the curriculum more relevant is essential. Best practices must be shared, especially in such areas as the development of new and relevant content, the development of new material and more effective teaching and learning methods, and the enlightened use of new technology. It is because of the importance of innovation to the improvement of the relevance and quality of education that the role of educational networks such as CARNEID becomes so significant. Every effort, therefore, should be made to strengthen, support and expand CARNEID's work in the Caribbean region.

The problem of violence

If what is done in the classroom is related to the context of how people live together in communities, then the problem of violence must be addressed, for it is the greatest deterrent to social harmony and social cohesion. The problem of violence and the need to establish a culture of peace have serious implications for the education of all. The problem itself created such a cause for concern throughout the world that the United Nations designated the year 2000 as the International Year for the Culture of Peace and Non-Violence. The year 2000 also launched the Decade for the Culture of Peace.

Violence is not caused by genetic factors nor is it characteristic of a particular ethnic group or social class. There is much support for the position that human violence, in the home, school or community, is a learned behaviour. Children learn to be aggressive by imitating their parents or teachers or other role models in the society. The perception and experience of violence engenders violence. Children who are over-exposed to violence in the media, especially through television or video games, have a greater tendency to use violence as a solution to conflict. Other factors that contribute to violence are:

- The disintegration of the family:
- The adherence to purely materialistic values that lead to a culture of accumulation, competition, possessiveness and selfishness;
- The personal, social and emotional underdevelopment of children and young people;
- The increased availability of illicit drugs and weapons to children of school age and young people;
- The lack of respect for the principles of human rights, justice and democracy;
- The authoritarian style of instruction and school management and poor communication between those who teach and those who learn;
- The absence of conflict resolution, mediation and family-life education programmes in schools;

- Discrimination with respect to race, class, economic status, gender, religion and political affiliation;
- Rapid social change and the impact of the economic recession and structural adjustment on the ability of parents and teachers to provide adequately for their children and students.

Violence is not only the exercise of physical force so as to inflict injury on or to cause damage to persons or property. Violence is sometimes due to the subtler, but no less devastating, economic, social and political structures that reinforce the conditions of inequity, alienation, exclusion and poverty.

Violence in the classroom

Violence is sometimes the dominant culture of the classroom. There are far too many situations today where students and their teachers break out into open conflict, or where students attack each other. Teachers who are disrespectful of their students and who are rude, sarcastic and unpleasant in their interactions with them are not likely to stimulate improvement in the quality of education and the consequent development of social cohesion and the establishment of a culture of peace. They are rather likely to stimulate resentment and hostility and even violence in their students.

Further, the principles of democracy cannot be effectively taught in a school administered by an autocratic dictator, however benevolent, and where the participation of all stakeholders is not encouraged.

Education for peace

The Culture of Peace Manifesto advocates six basic ingredients for ensuring social cohesion:

1. Respect all life;
2. Reject violence;
3. Listen to understand;
4. Share with others;
5. Protect the planet;
6. Rediscover solidarity.

However, the introduction of programmes to minimize and eradicate violence in schools and in the community is no guarantee for the establishment of peace, for peace is not just the settling of disagreements, the suspension of hostilities or the absence of overt conflict. The fundamental quality or essence of sustainable peace depends on the establishment and maintenance of harmonious relations. It demands not merely tolerance but understanding, dialogue, a basic respect for the rights of others and a sense of belonging to something worthwhile. It recognizes that each individual is an integral part of a wider ecosystem that embraces nature and all life. When people learn to live together within a democratic framework, social cohesion, a prerequisite for human development—stands a good chance of succeeding. In this regard, the work in support of peace education currently being conducted by the UNESCO Kingston Office is to be highly commended.

Peace, therefore, is not just a social or political phenomenon. It is a personal quality, which is reinforced by education for non-violence and for social transformation. The acquisition of those values, attitudes and behaviours that promote non-violence, the establishment of a culture of peace, demand that full involvement of parents, teachers, the police, community leaders, opinion-makers, managers, workers, political leaders and the media. The individual as well as the entire society need to find, through a process of learning, the roots of the values of human dignity. This process starts from a curriculum, an education, which stresses the moral and the ethical, for if violence is learned, establishing a culture of peace and non-violence can also be learned and therefore becomes central to education.

The report to UNESCO of the International Commission on Education for the Twenty-first Century puts it in a nutshell:

> The cohesion of any society is predicated on shared activities and purposes, but also on shared values, which represent different aspects of the desire to live together. In the course of time, these material and spiritual links enhance each other and become, in the individual and collective memory, a cultural heritage, in the broad sense of the term, on which the sense of belonging and the feeling of solidarity are based.

If human progress is to be achieved, quality Education for All must be available to all. It must create unity out of diversity, and social cohesion and a sense of community out of the chaos of contemporary isolation and exclusion. The International Commission on Education for the Twenty-first Century identified four pillars on which education should stand: learning to know, learning to do, learning to be and learning to live together. For these principles to be applied, those who teach, what they teach, how they teach and where they teach, must be radically transformed. These four pillars should form the foundation for the transformation of those who teach and those who learn. One thing we should never forget in our encounter with students in the classroom—nothing never happens, for whether we like it or not, something always does.

Section 2

Citizenship Education: Learning at School and in Society

4

Education for Democratic Citizenship: Cuba's System for the Protection of Minors

Pedro Jorge Pascual Betancourt

Introduction

We would like to provide a panoramic view of how in our country it is not simply a slogan when we say that education is an undertaking of everyone and for everyone; thus, I will familiarize you with a series of actions related to programmes which are being carried out in Cuba in an integrated manner.

You are certainly aware of the complex and adverse circumstances in which we pursue our efforts. However, since 1 January 1959, when the first laws and measures were approved to modify the overall political and social structure, our people have been able to speak with their own voice and set a destiny in which the majority have the opportunity to live first as human beings, and then, to exercise their rights as such for the first time in all their history.

The problem of literacy was not only a human and social imperative; it was, above all, the basis of the educational progress our island has now achieved, which is intimately linked to the transformations underway economically, politically and socially.

The responsibility for the shaping and development of a happy childhood and the proper insertion of children into society falls on the family as well as on the educational and formative role of the school and all the social elements surrounding a child.

Our National Hero José Martí, in his dedication to 'Ismaelillo' (a work written for his son) said: 'I have faith in human progress, in future life, in the usefulness of virtue and in you.' The human quality of future generations as expressed by this the most emblematic of Cubans has its basic framework of action in its acceptance by our citizenry of the responsibility for inculcating ethical and moral values in future generations based on the exemplary quality of the family that created it. This ensures the safety and well-being of the entire population and the protection of their rights as citizens.

Provision of Education and Care for Children in Cuba

The right to education is backed by a broad and free system of educational institutions that ensure that every child and youth, regardless of the economic conditions of his/her family, has the opportunity to study, with every citizen having the duty to acquire a general basic education.

Suffice it to say that to comply with these constitutional principles the number of schools has been increased from 7,664 prior to the Revolution (1958/59 school year) to 12,442 at present, and teaching personnel from 22,800 to 250,000, giving Cuba one of the lowest ratios of inhabitants per educator (42 inhabitants/educator) while the world average is 103 inhabitants per educator.

In Cuba, we not only have 100% of children in school, but the vast majority of education institutions provide a double session, that is six to seven hours of school time a day for 220 school days a year, one of the highest in the world. This enables us to set very high demands for this huge investment of resources to be used as a means of producing higher qualitative results every year. While we are aware that in any education system curricula design must maintain a level of quality, we recognize that the determining factor in educational performance will always be the teacher, for it is the human factor that will ensure achievement of our goals.

In addition to the protection provided by the social security system, programmes for children and youth are based on policies established by the State with legal and economic backing, such as:

- The Constitution of the Republic of Cuba;
- The Platform of the Communist Party of Cuba.
- Thesis on Educational, Scientific and General Cultural Policy (1976);
- Law 1289 (1975) implementing the family code;
- Code of Childhood and Youth established by Law 16 (1978);
- Decree Law 76 (1984) on adoption, minors' homes and foster homes;
- Law 95 (1986) that creates the Commissions of Prevention and Social Care;
- Convention on Children's Rights (1989) of which Cuba is a signatory;
- Decree Law 175 (1997) Penal Code and Law 87 (1999) concerning modifications of the Penal Code.

Among the overall objectives articulated for the care of children and youth are:

- The formation of fully developed personalities, capable of receiving and enjoying the achievements of national and universal culture and contributing to their development;.
- The promotion of the regular practice of physical education and sports, as well as broad participation in recreational activities, which constitutes a major component of overall education.

On the other hand, the society and state ratify and recognize the role of the family in the moral, physical and spiritual upbringing of its youngest members, with the obligation to society to guide the overall development of children and youth, enabling them to exercise both their rights and duties in the home.

Returning to the legal frame of reference, we must bear in mind why Cuba has no children out of school and an example of this is found in our Code on Children and Youth (Law 16/1978) which states:

> Children and youth are obliged to study and obtain the general, basic education defined by law, and parents or their wards are responsible for the schooling of minors under their custody.

Minors are legally immune until the age of 16, with corrective measures being seen as essentially an educational task, and the subsequent adoption of a wide variety of efforts ranging from the reinforcement of the educational role of parents and the community to internment in boarding schools designed for children with behavioural disorders. Thus, when a serious problem arises, the relevant authorities work in a context of specialized care with the minor, the family and the community, with priority given to avoiding interruption of schooling.

It is precisely this preventive approach underlying all programmes of social or community work concerning children in Cuba which has seen the implementation of such initiatives under the guidance of the Ministry of Education, as:

- Study plans and programmes of the national education system.
- National Action Programme to fulfil the agreements of the World Children's Summit.
- 'For Life'—a community education programme.
- 'Educate Your Child' programme for pre-school children not attending kindergarten.
- Comprehensive, preventive care programme for socially disadvantaged minors.
- Comprehensive medico-pedagogical programme for pre-school, school-aged and working youth in educational centres.
- Programme of promotion and education for health.
  - Personal and community hygiene;
  - Sex education;
  - Nutritional education and food hygiene;
  - Accident prevention and traffic education;
  - Traditional and natural medicine;
  - Anti-tobacco and anti-alcohol education.
- Programme on environmental pollution.

- Audiovisual programme:
  - An important tool for educators, which through language and images, contributes to the cultural and scientific training of students and the community as a whole. The programmes are broadcast on national television, hence the effort of the state to equip all educational institutions with a TV set and VCR for every 100 students in all subsystems. The programme promotes and disseminates educational materials and films where students express their opinions through reflections and debates.

Another important programme is the enhancement of aesthetic education, where the ultimate goal is to provide a holistic and humanist training for students, allowing culture to be expressed in its broadest sense, which translates into:

- The conversion of educational institutions into the most important cultural centres of the community;
- The promotion of the habit and taste for reading;
- The use of the mass media for instruction and education;
- The development of knowledge, motivation and interest through visual arts and musical programmes.

We would like to point out that these programmes involve a large number of beneficiaries and thus a large number of institutions, bodies, popular and social organizations, both state and non-governmental, through which the programmes are conveyed.

Development in the field of information technologies and communication and their application to different spheres of social development, particularly education, has made it necessary to undertake a new phase in the development of computer education. The Cuban state has acquired 19,790 state-of-the-art computers, which are used from pre-school age onwards for familiarization with the technology and the development of intellectual skills.

The state pays special attention to the development of special schools for children with physical or mental impairments or behavioural problems and in accordance with their individual aptitudes; helping them not only to become self-sufficient, but also to be integrated into the life of society. There is a broad system of scholarships that are awarded on the basis of economic and social factors.

Exceptional cases in our society, such as abandoned children who have no family, are sheltered by the state in regulated homes which are made as close to a real home environment as possible. Protection of children and youth is included in the ongoing process of legislative reform, increasing the severity of penalties for all individuals, who mistreat, induce or use minors in acts that are detrimental to their normal development.

Conclusion

Long before the implementation of the Convention on Children's Rights, our country had developed a complete legal and constitutional framework for caring for children and their families, which has resulted in the principle of the family, school and community linkage and has eliminated discriminatory or exclusionary situations. This is reflected in:

- Free education;
- Creation of a network of educational institutions in urban and rural areas;
- Compulsory education until the completion of basic general education;
- Guaranteed continuity of education for sixth, ninth and twelfth grades;
- A network of boarding and semi-boarding schools of primary and special education, as well as scholarships at the secondary and higher levels that include free board, lodging, clothing and footwear, educational materials, teachers, medical and nutritional care, and transportation;
- Leisure activities for children involving recreation, sports and culture;

- Assistance for disabled children or those with other special educational needs, both within the system of special education and through family assistance including teaching personnel and other types of needs.

These are the principles brought to life in the educational system of our country, making a reality of the standard set by José Martí, when he said:

> The true aim of education is to prepare man so that he may live in a dignified manner, without losing the graciousness and generosity of the spirit, and the dignity and power of the Homeland.

58A

Citizenship Education: Experiences from the Classroom

Erik Prinds

Introduction

The subject of this workshop is how to further citizenship education in school and in society. Considering the shot time available, I have chosen to focus on what is going on in schools and more particularly in the classroom, with my main focus on the implementation of reform. I have been a high school/upper secondary school-teacher in the fields of social science and ancient history since 1972.

I came with European experiences from a country, Denmark, where material resources are considerable. However, I think with Caribbean countries we share the same problems in schools and in many ways reflect upon the same solutions.

The Teaching/Learning Process

First I will examine the teaching and learning process in the classroom, because I think this is the most important way to influence citizenship among students in school. In UNESCO, the concept 'curriculum' is normally used to cover both the content of subjects, the way teaching is organized and the evaluation. In Europe, the term 'curriculum' only covers the content of subjects. In my opinion, the UNESCO use of the concept also tends to focus on content and forget the other aspects.

A couple of years ago, I asked a colleague to attend one of my lessons. The topic of the lesson was democracy in various forms. We had to go through a chapter in the basic reader. I asked my colleague to bring a tape recorder, a stop watch, and paper and pencil, in order to note down who talked and for how long, because I wanted to know how much the students said.

I thought the lesson went well. Some students raised their hands when they wanted to say something and others were asked to say something without their having raised their hands. I wrote a lot on the blackboard and the pupils carefully took notes.

After the lesson, the colleague and I listened to the tape. Fifteen out of twenty-five students had answered my questions. Some had given correct answers, others had given incorrect answers. Only one pupil's answer had been longer than fifteen seconds. It was due to the fact that she had to explain why she hadn't done her homework. But it turned out that I had been talking 70 per cent of the time. Only *one* pupil asked a question—about a word she didn't understand.

What did the pupils learn about democracy? How much did this lesson further citizenship, even though they had read about democracy in the basic reader and we had gone through the text together?

I tested the students a month later. All the students—with very few exceptions—had forgotten all about the topic.

Concepts of Citizenship

What do we mean by citizenship? It is a concept which varies historically and from country to country. Therefore, it may be best to take your starting point from the report to UNESCO of the International Commission on Education for the Twenty-first Century: *Learning: the treasure within.* According to this report 'citizenship' means learning to live together, which should be the basis of all education. This entails:

- Developing an understanding of other cultures—their history and values;
- Being able to participate in shaping the future and solve conflicts in a peaceful way.

This goal is also based on three other pillars:

- Learning to know—general knowledge and in-depth studies;
- Learning to do—to deal with a variety of situations and to work in teams;
- Learning to be—to develop greater independence and capacity for judgement with responsibility.

If this is the purpose of teaching, according to the report just referred to, the lesson I mentioned above did nothing to further citizenship:

- The students were passive;
- They didn't learn to live together; they didn't even learn to speak together;
- They didn't get an in-depth knowledge of the topic;
- They didn't learn to work in teams;
- They didn't practise how to be more independent in their learning;
- They did not learn to make judgements with responsibility.

Why must schools focus on citizenship? The following are some of the principal reasons:

- Society changes, as do the demands on young people;
- The knowledge society demands lifelong learning;
- Society and the business world need people who can solve problems, think creatively and work in teams;
- Values, such as tolerance in relation to other people, should be promoted;
- There is a need for active participation in democracy—locally and globally.

Citizenship in the Classroom

Since the previously mentioned lesson, I have tried to develop new teaching methods together with colleagues that give the students the possibility of developing citizenship *within* the school (see Box 1). Our idea is that school should involve and educate the students. We are far from reaching the goal, but we seem to be heading in the right direction.

Box 1: Concrete examples of teaching methods

1. The lesson can begin by letting the students ask questions about difficult material given for homework.
2. A fictitious or real problem can be formulated for the students to solve.
3. Group work is organized where the students discuss what they have prepared/read at home, or where they attempt to find solutions to problems.
4. Students are asked to determine their own attitude to questions when they have worked with a topic. These may be questions about causes or ethical problems.
5. Pair work is organized in language teaching where the students speak together.
6. The teacher asks the students what they think about the teaching or he/she makes them fill in an anonymous questionnaire.
7. We only give marks three times a year, but we speak with the students frequently about their problems.
8. We encourage the students to continue working even if they have not understood the material or if they give the wrong answer.

We try to let the students work more, to be more active, and assume responsibility. We think that the students learn better if they work with the subject themselves. How do we learn outside school? By looking and listening? No, rather by trying and acting. Only those who work actively learn. A Dutch study has shown that active students remember 80 per cent of the material worked with three years after, whereas passive students have forgotten 80 per cent three months after.

How do we work at my school?

- We see to it that there is a respectful relationship between teachers and students, so that students feel confident in class. They are not told off for giving wrong answers. We want them to speak openly and freely and to express themselves without having to fear for the consequences. All experience shows that students learn best when they feel safe. One of my friends recently said that the most important thing is that the students love their teacher. If they do, it is a sign that they feel/are respected.

- We train the students in forming attitudes about essential topics through discussion.
- We often have the students work in groups/teams. The tasks can be very different. Why do we do this? Only the student who works learns. Besides, they learn to work together. The Delors Report says that group/teamwork is not given sufficient priority in education.
- We encourage them write in order to learn.
- We let the children's natural curiosity play a prominent role in the lessons. They are encouraged to ask questions.
- We have them identify problems, analyse them and decide their own attitudes to the solution of problems.
- We have the students evaluate their own work and the work done in class.

Citizenship should be furthered in all aspects of the school. It is essential to establish a respectful relationship between teachers and students. In school there should be a students' council where the students have a right to make proposals to the principal and the teachers. Students should have the right to express their views in relation to fundamental decisions. Student democracy gives many possibilities of developing citizenship. Students grow more responsible if the teachers and the principal involve them in dialogue. However, I am aware that there are few countries where students have influence like they have in Denmark.

The ideas I have proposed here are not a guarantee of success. But on the basis of my own experiences they improve the students' involvement and learning. When the students work in the classroom the way I have described, they get better possibilities for developing citizenship and at the same time for achieving qualifications. You can use my ideas as you do when you shop. Take what you need and let the rest remain on the shelves.

Implementation: The Key Role of Teachers

When governments and administrations make reforms, for instance, in curriculum in the broad UNESCO sense, the main problem is not the decision-making for the reform but its implementation. The most difficult thing is to change the culture in the classroom. The longest distance in the world is the distance between the intentions of a civil servant and the mind of a pupil.

Teachers do not change easily. Why? They are educated as teachers in the traditional way. They may have been teaching the same way for twenty years. In order to change, teachers need time. For authorities, time is money and therefore a scarce resource.

One must ask: what is the incentive for a teacher to teach in another way than usual? Are the principals and the administration able and willing to support the process? Everybody involved in a reform and implementation process must acknowledge the principle of 'T.T.T.'—'Things Take Time.'

Teachers need to co-operate in order to help each other to develop new ideas and share experiences. In-service training ought to be integrated into the teaching process. In this regard, co-operation among teachers is especially necessary.

Conclusion

Finally, I will draw your attention to a global project instituted by the Organization for Economic Co-operation and Development (OECD) called PISA (Programme of International Student Assessment). The aim of this project is to identify a number of 'soft' competencies, which will prepare young people for life in modern society. The PISA project has also the objective to find methods to measure these competencies.

The first three competencies which the project has measured in OECD countries are reading, mathematical and scientific literacy. The results of tests on 200,000 15-year-old students will be published in December 2001. Later, PISA will examine competencies such as problem-solving, social competencies, learning to learn and so on. The process will continue for at least the next ten years. I mention this because I think the PISA project could be an inspiration for you, since learning these competencies is part of the process of becoming an active citizen. It goes without saying that the new competencies are taught as a part of the content and not separate from it. In the country report from Trinidad and Tobago this approach is very precisely expressed: 'skills in content and content in skills' (the objectives of social science).

To indicate the spirit of the PISA project I will quote the Director of the project, Andreas Schleicher. He once observed: 'To teach children how to learn and to teach them to co-operate is just as important as factual knowledge'. (www.oecd.org/els/pisa).

To conclude: Changing the content in, for instance, geography and history is a necessary but not sufficient change to further citizenship among our students. The way teachers teach or organize the learning process *in all subjects* is crucial to giving children and young people the conditions to develop the capacity to become citizens in their societies.

Report of Workshop 1

The workshop activities were organized by Mr. Erik Prinds (Denmark) and consisted of discussion in small groups, leading to a presentation of the main outcomes of this discussion. For linguistic purposes, the participants were divided into four groups, one Spanish-speaking and three English-speaking. Countries with more than one delegate had to split between two groups.

The themes discussed were:

1. What kinds of classroom practices are needed for promoting citizenship?
2. How can these reforms be implemented in the classroom?

Outcomes of the Workshop

The discussion of classroom practices raised issues about which pedagogical approaches and strategies to use, which skills to teach, how to assess, and how to help students to define their role and responsibilities as citizens.

1. The general pedagogical concept that emerged was that of a learner-centred, activity-based classroom with a co-operative, participatory learning strategy. The teacher should serve as a role model of good citizenship. Teachers should make an effort to improve the general climate in the classroom with the focus on strengthening the identity of the student. They should focus more on

the use of thematic approaches and problem solving. Group work was recommended as a way of helping students to learn to respect the opinions of others. Social action and civic projects were recommended for promoting citizenship values at school.

2. It was felt that the role of the teacher thus needs to be changed with the student being given more responsibility and opportunity for active participation in planning and carrying out classroom activities. Common standards of acceptable behaviour in the classroom and the school should be jointly established by teachers and students. Students should further be helped to define their roles and responsibilities as citizens in the society as a whole.
3. The following skills were identified as important: creative, critical and independent thinking, high-order thinking, problem-solving, capacity for co-operation and participation.
4. Varied and alternative assessment techniques and strategies were proposed for effective citizenship education including peer, self, portfolio, performance and continuous assessment.

Participants then discussed the ways of ensuring that proposed reforms were implemented in the classroom. These included the following:

1. Undertake an integrated diagnosis of the educational and broader socio-cultural context prior to designing the reform.
2. Involve all stakeholders (Ministries, local authorities, universities, teacher colleges, local community, principals, parents, students and teachers).
3. Prepare good publicity strategies for the reform, making particular efforts to 'sell' it to teachers.
4. Ensure adequate financial support.
5. Recognize the role of teachers as central to change.

For teachers to be effective implementers they require:

- continuous and professional training based on site-based transfer of knowledge, sensitization to key issues and accreditation. This should include appropriate training for principals. Teachers should also be encouraged to undertake action research.

- the establishment of professional networks, providing moral as well as technical support. Networking should enable sharing of information and resources. This should reduce the difficulties for teachers of accessing relevant research findings on the issues.
- proper and sustained supervision during the implementation of classroom reforms and commendation for their efforts.

6. Design adequate monitoring and evaluation procedures as an integral part of the reform process.

One of the main challenges identified was that of persuading teachers and principals to change their teaching and administrative methods. It was pointed out that, alone, a teacher cannot successfully bring about change; it must be a collaborative process. The teacher must undertake reform together with other teachers and bear in mind that changes take time to prepare and implement and also that the school has many other tasks to accomplish.

To conclude: changing the content in, for instance, geography and history is a necessary, but not sufficient change to further citizenship among our students. The way teachers teach or organize the learning process *in all subjects* is crucial to give children and young people the conditions to develop the capacity to become citizens in their society.

Section 3

Social Exclusion and Violence: Education for Social Cohesion

Education for the Promotion of Social Cohesion and a Culture of Non-violence

Winthrop Wiltshire

Introduction

Cohesion is the tendency to unite or stick together or the process or state of sticking together. Culture, in the sense of a *culture of non-violence,* means usual, or normative ways of being, doing and relating.

A cohesive society is one that is imbued with a great deal of internal harmony. In a few multi-ethnic Caribbean countries, competition between different ethnic groups for political and economic resources sometimes has the tendency to lead to social tension between the different groups in question. Such a situation recently arose in Guyana in the aftermath of the March 2001 general elections.

However, in many countries of the Caribbean the greatest threat to social cohesion appears to be the increasing levels of societal crime and violence. In a newspaper report in mid-April 2001, it was revealed that in one Caribbean country there had been as many as 233 killings since the beginning of the year. In such a scenario, one may extrapolate that there have been many more cases of physical injury that have not resulted in death.

In addition, frequent cases of rape and other forms of violence against women are affecting most of the countries in our region, and it is to be noted that young persons perpetrate much of this deviant antisocial behaviour. The use of illicit drugs throughout the region is a significant contributory cause of youth crime and violence. It seriously impacts on the cohesiveness of individual families and that of the wider society. In my view, the root cause of the drug problem is the low self-concept of so many young persons irrespective of social status.

The term 'white-collar crime' is a term often used to depict office-related illegal activity where there is no physical injury. I would point out that the absence of interpersonal physical injury does not in itself imply the absence of violence. Interpersonal violence can also be meted out by the use of the harsh word or the brutal invalidation which may be considered to be a kind of 'white collar violence', but which is violence nonetheless.

The Importance of Emotional Health

Social cohesion can be guaranteed only when the predominant reality in a society is that individuals feel comfortable with themselves as a result of inner emotional calm reflecting a high degree of emotional health. Many of the behavioural problems being manifested by the youth are indeed a manifestation of low self-concept and latent feelings of resentment, isolation and anger. Children have an inherent need for praise and approval and demonstrations of love. If instead they are subjected to systematic mistreatment in the form of disapproval, rejection and other put downs, whether this is their dominant reality in the home or the school environment, their psyche may suffer severe damage.

It is well known that a person's feelings can have a profound influence on behaviour. Unresolved negative feelings resulting from experiences of early emotional hurt can result in antisocial behaviour including violence. (See: W. Wiltshire, The critical role of love in educating for non-violence: the messenger is the message, *European journal of intercultural studies* (Abingdon, UK), vol. 9, no. 3, 1998, p. 261-68).

The education system in the region generally has been overly concerned with academic performance of students and has been paying very little attention to their emotional needs. It is true that parents have an important responsibility to raise emotionally healthy children. The reality, however, is that many parents, as a result of their own inadequate socialization, do not themselves have the skills to perform this critical role. Indeed, many of them as a result of this inadequacy inflict enormous emotional damage on their young charges.

The education system, therefore, has a key role to play in fostering emotionally healthy children. My thesis is that the focus can no longer be exclusively be on academic concerns. A holistic approach must be adopted in the education of young persons in the region if the system is to contribute to the promotion of social cohesion and the reduction of levels of societal violence.

A Redefined Role for the Teacher

A holistic approach to delivery of education implies that the role of the teacher has to be perceived very differently from what has been traditionally accepted. The essence of the role of a teacher in the Caribbean in the twenty-first century must be to assist in the moulding of well-adjusted young persons who:

- Are able to love themselves;
- Are emotionally secure;
- Are full of self confidence;
- Take full responsibility for their actions;
- Trust their own thinking;
- Respect self and others;
- Respect the views of others even when different from their own;
- Respect persons of different cultures;
- Respect and treat with dignity persons with physical and other disabilities;
- Acquire good writing, speaking, listening and numerate skills;
- Acquire competent information-seeking skills;
- Acquire sound problem-solving skills and good critical-thinking skills;

- Additionally, young persons need to be put in touch with their innate spirituality.

Commentary on desired personal attributes

This list of attributes cited is not meant to be exhaustive. The issue of responsible sexual behaviour, for example, not included here, is of paramount importance in today's world. However, the elements highlighted constitute an indispensable core for moulding the personalities of socially and emotionally well-adjusted young persons who, embodied with these characteristics, will be centres of inner calm and who will not only promote social cohesion, but will be predisposed to achieve personal success in whatever field of endeavour they choose to pursue.

Loving yourself implies accepting yourself as you are, warts included, while taking active measures to change those personal characteristics that you deem in need of being changed. One who does not love self is incapable of loving anyone else. Self-hate is the antithesis of self-love. It is intimately linked with personal insecurity and lack of self-confidence and is usually the cumulative result of systematic mistreatment in early childhood. Someone who is overwhelmed with self-hate is capable of doing an enormous amount of societal damage, including the perpetration of overt forms of violence.

Learning to disagree with someone else's point of view and yet respect it as valid is the basis for nurturing a culture of tolerance in society. This also provides a basis for respecting and accepting persons from different cultures.

Teaching young persons to trust their own thinking is a big challenge for parents and the educational authorities. It is so easy instead to teach them to trust the thinking of the authority figure. But this is a trap because it serves to erode self-reliance, making it easy for such persons to be led astray by strong personalities who indulge in anti-social behaviour.

A key point highlighted here is that the spark for the promotion of social cohesion has to be ignited by the individual through feeling at ease and comfortable with the self.

Powerlessness as a deterrent to social cohesion

When a person or group of persons feels powerless, it is sometimes in relation to a perception of others having power over them. When young people, particularly young males, feel a sense of powerlessness and alienation, they are likely to promote disharmony in society.

If what transpires in the classroom contributes to making the students feel a sense of powerlessness, this is likely be counterproductive to fostering social cohesion and a culture of non-violence. Conversely, if the classroom atmosphere is one of partnership between teacher and students, rather than a power relationship in which the teacher is seen as the authoritarian figure, this is likely to facilitate the development of self-confidence and social responsibility among the students.

It ought to be self-evident that the use of corporal punishment as a sanction in the school system is quite inappropriate, because it is simply impossible to promote a culture of non-violence through the use of violence. Trinidad and Tobago recently abolished corporal punishment as an option for disciplining students. It is noteworthy that a cross-section of teachers expressed their disappointment.

The teacher as counsellor in the classroom

In many countries of the region, guidance counsellors are attached to schools. One of the main aspects of their function is to interact with students who manifest behavioural problems. Their function is usually conducted outside of the normal classroom activities where the students interact with teachers teaching the various subject disciplines. It is my considered opinion that although the 'fire fighting' role of guidance counsellors is important, what is even more critical is that teachers function as counsellors in their normal classroom interaction with their students.

Functioning as counsellor in the classroom simply means that the teacher adopts as a norm a nurturing, pupil-enhancing posture where every child is treated with full respect, is listened to attentively and is perceived as valuable and capable of learning. It is such an environment that is most conducive to young students learning to love and respect themselves and others.

It is not necessarily easy for teachers to function in this nurturing mode where students are given constant attention and encouragement. Often their working reality is one of overcrowded classrooms, with children exhibiting all kinds of disruptive behaviour. Additionally, the teachers themselves, like all other normal adults, are saddled with their own emotional 'baggage', in the form of their unresolved emotional issues. It is this 'baggage' which will tend to manifest itself as inappropriate reactions to classroom situations.

It is quite a challenge for the teacher to see the student as separate and distinct from his/her disruptive behaviour.

Curriculum Implications

Traditionally, the curriculum has been perceived as the elements of the course content of the particular academic subject being taught. It appears, however, that increasingly, it is being recognized that everything that is relevant to classroom dynamics can be a legitimate concern for the curriculum. This development is fortunate because it is important that the elements or attributes cited for the moulding of socially and emotionally well-adjusted young persons be made explicit in school curricula irrespective of the academic subject matter being taught.

Values education should be made an important content component of curricula in primary and secondary schools. Activities such as the Peace and Love in Schools (PALS) programme, spearheaded in Jamaica, could be evaluated to identify what generic elements can be adopted in curricula throughout the region. In addition, an initiative such as the Health and Family Life Education programme that has been endorsed by Ministries of Education throughout the English-speaking Caribbean could be very useful in communicating important values to young persons.

If, however, we were to rely primarily on the course content of material to be imparted to students in primary and secondary schools throughout the region to promote social cohesion and a culture of non-violence among the youth, we would be missing the mark. What is of even greater importance in the socialization of these students during classroom hours is the quality of the teacher/student interaction, independent of subject matter being taught.

Whether they are teaching mathematics or social studies, teachers in primary and secondary schools of the region will find that, when they adopt an approach which aims to nurture and encourage students, not only will they contribute effectively to producing emotionally healthy young adults, but management of their classrooms will become considerably less problematic.

Changing the Culture of the Classroom

There are many conscientious and dedicated teachers throughout schools in the Caribbean, but their ability to create, on an ongoing basis in their classrooms, a nurturing, valuing environment will very much depend on their own early socialization and how successful they have been in releasing emotional hurts encountered in their early youth. It will be recalled that culture was defined simply as usual or normative ways of being, doing and relating. It is clear that, for the objectives being sought, the entire culture of the classroom has to be one in which students are encouraged to believe in and develop their abilities.

The Changing the Culture of the Classroom programme, which has been led by UNESCO/CARNEID, has been eloquently described by Colleen Winter-Brathwaite in *EFA in the Caribbean: assessment 2000* (Port-of-Spain, UNESCO, 1999). However, some additional remarks seem relevant in the current context.

In a Changing the Culture of Classroom training workshop that was conducted with teachers from a junior secondary school in Trinidad and Tobago, the teachers reacted with great surprise when I asserted that there are no problem students. One teacher interjected 'If there are no problem students, you have to be implying that there are problem teacher.' After repeating my assertion, I pointed out that there *are* students with problems but it is not only undesirable to label them as problem students, it is very damaging to them. The basic point that was being established is that the student must be seen as a distinct entity, not to be identified with his/her behaviour, however inappropriate that behaviour might be. When the student is seen by the teacher as separate from the behaviour it is then possible for the student to be helped by that teacher.

In these experiential training workshops, the teachers learn specific skills for classroom management. At the same time, they explore themes such as: early distress experiences and the natural recovery process; the essence of the role of the teacher; the concept of flexible intelligence; internalized oppression and its impact on behaviour; limited categories of new adult hurt, the concept of restimulation of early distress experiences; acknowledgement and appreciation of student efforts as a nurturing tool; appropriate and inappropriate sanctions; use and misuse of the syllabus; the undesirable use of fear as a control mechanism; the challenge of maintaining discipline in the classroom; empowerment of the teacher for optimum effectiveness.

Conclusion

Although the topic of this presentation has implications for young and old in every Caribbean society, the emphasis in this discussion has been on education in the regular school system, in particular at the primary and secondary levels. My thesis is that the education systems in the region, as well as individual teachers, have to redefine their role. This should essentially be seen as the moulding of socially and emotionally well-adjusted young persons who are equipped with both a well-defined set of personal attributes and a predetermined range of aptitudes and skills.

This reorientation of focus away from the short-sighted academic emphasis will more than likely lead in the medium term to societies which are more socially cohesive and in which there is much less violence because young people will emerge from the school system with a healthier self-concept.

This change of emphasis to a more holistic model of education has profound implications both for the development of school curricula, and for teacher orientation and retraining. As much emphasis has to be placed on 'how' things are done in the classroom as on 'what'. Thus, in the design of curricula as much attention needs to be placed on the strategies for implementing course content as on the course content itself.

8

Education for Social Cohesion

Juan Esteban Belderrain

In his work, Professor Winthrop Wiltshire looked at the chances of education offering solutions to the problem of 'social cohesion'. The author emphasizes the psychological aspects of education's potential contribution, focusing on the need to strengthen students' self-knowledge and self-esteem and paying special attention to the emotional aspects involved in educational processes. Based on the shared conviction that education for emotional health is a necessary condition for achieving greater social cohesion through education, this contribution considers other sociological, ethical and educational factors which are equally necessary for achieving this objective.

Education and its Contribution to Social Cohesion

We have to begin by specifying why social cohesion may be considered to be one of the objectives of education. This, in turn, leads us to identify different approaches to the subject. Some, descended from the functionalist sociological tradition and starting from a neutral stance towards values, postulate forms of social cohesion which are aimed at sustaining and reproducing a given social order and alleviating conflicts. Others, following a critical tradition with clear libertarian leanings, identify and analyse the forms of social cohesion that appear in a historically determined society and become morally committed to achieving forms of social cohesion that are more just and humane. In this case, it is not a matter of obtaining just any form of social cohesion, but one that produces the best results in terms of liberty, equality and solidarity among the members of society.

In the field of education, those theories exerted a powerful influence over the educational policies that were developed in the last century in the countries of the region. In a nutshell, it might be said that the former approach influenced the spiritualist and positivist belief that education systems should be part of the process of constituting and consolidating nation states. The second approach, on the other hand, was more related to critical education and so-called 'popular education' movements, and has been behind many of the educational reforms developed in recent decades. Although the effect of these reforms on general practices cannot yet be evaluated, it may be observed from their theoretical constructions that their strength resides in the critical aspects of social diagnosis.

On the other hand, that strength is not apparent in terms of a moral commitment, when it comes to proposing forms of social cohesion and effective ways of achieving it. In relation to the critical approach, the criticism of traditional teaching methods has invalidated many of the methods that have proved effective in traditional education. One example is the reluctance in such approaches to offer practical ethical education, on the assumption that it is enough for the latter to be implicit in scientific training and in educational practice, or their tendency to restrict specific ethical training to the formation of moral judgement. Another example, related to more practical teaching methods, is the negative attitude to storytelling. These resources of traditional education, which have proved useful in the past for building shared feelings and expressing emotions and values, have been depreciated on the grounds that they are subject to the risk of ideological abuse.

Because of these and other drawbacks, eclectic positions have emerged in most of the curriculum reforms in Latin America, with elements being taken from both approaches under different labels, such as humanist, systemic, holistic or integrationist.

Our own work has been part of this search for improvement, which led to the process of curriculum reform developed in Argentina between 1995 and 1999. An effort was made to recover social criticism and some of the tools of traditional education. The aim has been to direct educational processes towards the achievement of forms of social cohesion which maximize the potential of all the members of the educational community, with particular attention for the potential of the most underprivileged. In order to give a brief overview of this approach, we may look in turn at its main elements, namely learning contents, educational subjects and learning processes, in relation to traditional education.

Content

With regard to contents, traditional education never pretended to inquire into the nature and dynamic of social and political life; on the contrary, it presents the forms of life as something already given. Its analysis of such forms amounts to mere consideration of technical matters of organization. Value considerations remain external to the system concerned. For instance, learning about democracy or economic systems in this case means learning about how social life is organized through legislation. It does not matter whether that legislation complies with ethical principles or not. The knowledge acquired must merely ensure that actions correspond to the prescribed rules, without enquiring too much either into the underlying basis of the rules or into the way they are assumed. Thus, the sphere of practice is reduced to the technical problem of getting to know predetermined rules and abiding by them. As the rules do not need to be 'critically assumed', changes occurring in the legal framework will produce not reactions, but merely adjustments to resolve once again the technical problem of adaptation.

Approaches aimed at improvement, on the other hand, should emphasize the *ethical principles* which support democracy as a form of government and a lifestyle, namely liberty, justice and solidarity. It entails a critical approach to these principles, which begins in the early stages of education with the recognition that they are needed for social coexistence, moving gradually towards an assimilation of the principles as independently as possible in the higher levels of education. The effort of subjecting these principles to philosophical criticism of their foundation, scope and application in itself implies an opportunity to learn these contents. What does it mean to be free? How, when and in what circumstances is it possible to express solidarity?

In view of the concern for social cohesion in our countries, the principle of justice deserves special mention among contents that need to be learned. This is because social justice is one of the weightiest concerns of our societies. There can be no real social cohesion in unjust societies. Equal opportunities for accessing knowledge and participating in dialogue should therefore be recognized as *necessary conditions for social cohesion.* Once this is recognized, it will provide a basis for a feeling of solidarity with the most underprivileged and the starting point for a practice directed towards change. This objective therefore constitutes the keynote of our proposal and should become the focus of educational processes aimed at achieving greater social cohesion in the countries of the region.

Having a knowledge of social processes and organizations also means knowing them as *legal organizations* based on those ethical principles, i.e. standard setting entities socially and historically established to guarantee a certain social cohesion and to administer conflicts. The critical approach helps to understand the perfectibility of rules established in relation to given circumstances and subject to stated ethical principles. Right from the early stages of education, students can learn and understand the meaning and scope of such rules. Gradually they can learn to relate to them, by observing them, criticizing them and participating in their construction.

This is why it is also important to impart a sense of the *historic awareness of the circumstances* in which the rules used to organize social life are constructed and developed. In the present context, for instance, for any analysis of democracies, families or social working relations, it is essential to refer to institutional crises, the search for new models of representation and participation, the nation-state identity crises brought about by globalization, changing methods of production, etc. If students are able to find some beacons within the uncertainty of change, this will give them a better understanding of the dynamic quality of concepts such as 'democracy', 'family' and 'community'. Hence when learning the modes of organization of social life, it is important not to lose sight of the fact that these forms of organization are 'historically situated'.

Developing a learning community

With regard to those who are the subjects of education, the central notion that prevails in traditional education is the notion of the individual, through references to individual achievements, individual obligations, individual responsibilities and individual rights. On the other hand, educating for social cohesion makes it necessary to consider the learning subject as a *learning community*. Social cohesion implies coexistence; therefore the minimum subject cannot be the individual, as a being aware of standards/norms, but rather the 'cohabitants', i.e. the 'learning community'.

This working approach raises the need for educational contents which are relevant for dealing with the challenges facing the countries of our region, namely *a sense of belonging* and *solidarity*. The school, in its traditional socializing function, provides a scenario of coexistence that can bring together traditions and communities of different origins. In this scenario, students and teachers undergo the daily experience of building a collective identity that allows for their differences. The outcome of this experience will then to a great extent determine the future integration of the citizen in the public life of the local, regional or national community.

Preparedness for participation and public responsibility does not manifest itself spontaneously on departure from school. It requires a considerable effort of learning which begins when at the very outset of education the subject learns to appreciate the meaning of the word 'us'. It later culminates in the knowledge and appreciation that individual differences and conflicts resulting from those differences are not an obstacle, but are part of the process whereby this collective identity is constructed. These differences and conflicts can therefore offer opportunities to enrich the collective identity insofar as they are duly treated as a means of learning the ethical principles that are being pursued.

Hence, the importance of changing the way students are considered in our countries, which are faced with the challenges of redefining identities in the context of globalization and of the changing relationships between the state, society and the market. The socializing function of the school, which was often in the past suspected of complicity with the prevailing ruling systems, must now be recovered, in line with this perspective, as offering the possibility of rebuilding a public awareness in the face of the divisive and individualizing tendencies which prevail under the hegemony of the logic of the marketplace.

This also implies a change in the attitude of teachers, who can be active players in constructing this communal, transforming subjectivity, to the extent that they become aware that they too are cohabitants. Learning for social cohesion therefore requires a 'classroom atmosphere', where the ethical principles that constitute democratic life emerge as ideals governing concrete practices. It requires an *opening of the school to the community.* Converting the physical space of schools into an open centre for cultural activities in the community has proved to be an effective means of tackling problems that seriously affect social cohesion, such as juvenile violence and drug addiction.

Learning Processes

With regard to *learning processes,* traditional education was centred on a knowledge of the modes of organization of social life as laid down by the law, without much concern for the ways such laws were assumed. By contrast, the central notion underlying education for social cohesion is that of praxis, understood more in the sense of acting than as mere technical doing. Praxis is action charged with meaning and values. This also raises the need for a comprehensive consideration of actors. Traditional education was geared to focus only on the cognitive capacity of students. Today, affective and practical aspects must also be included. It is not a matter only of knowing how a particular community is ordered and what it values, but of knowing whether that order or that set of values can stand up to rational criticism, and of checking whether the reasons put forward to defend it are sufficiently convincing to want to act in accordance with those rules and values, and consequently to act.

For example, in our society we might consider that co-operation is an essential value for social cohesion and that, as such, it is something that our educational system should support. So ethical training should not only provide the necessary tools to learn that co-operation is socially valuable, but is should also provide an opportunity for the student to analyse critically the reasons why co-operation is said to be good, while at the same time undertaking to ensure that the student wants to and knows how to co-operate effectively. To put it in simple terms: *it is not a matter only of knowing that it is good, but also of knowing why it is good and in addition wanting to do good and knowing how to do it.*

In this way the school could provide a forum for reflection and action which could help detect and criticize existing values and moral standards. This in turn would enable students to adopt behaviours and habits consistent with those principles and standards. It would also allow students to develop capacities for judgement and action that conform to the ethical principles.

It is generally recognized that confronting problem situations is a very useful teaching tool for training moral judgement. When such situations involve the modes of organization and related practices, the tool becomes even more useful. Knowledge and dialogue are essential elements, which developed in suitable conditions combine to facilitate cautious decision-making. A knowledge of codes, procedures, processes and the institutions involved is needed to identify the best solution to problems. Rational dialogue, in which reasons are put forward and well-founded arguments are exchanged, provides the opportunity to arrive at agreements and to settle conflicts peacefully.

Whence the importance that both students and teachers should acquire basic abilities for dialogue and discussion (by learning to listen, by giving reasons, by respecting the rules of logic, etc.) and should prefer consensus as an ideal way of resolving conflicts. Among dialogue and communication strategies, special emphasis should be placed on those aimed at the non-violent resolution of conflicts. Persuasion, negotiation, mediation and arbitration are commonly used strategies in democratic societies which can and should be learned in schools. The search for forms of dialogue and discussion that facilitate free and open communication is not an externally or arbitrarily set objective, but is implicit in democratic praxis itself.

The practical approach which is proposed means changing the definition of students as *agents* in order to consider them as *actors*. Agents are people who represent and/or reproduce an external discourse. In the traditional approach, education trains agents to reproduce social, political and economic discourses which are alien to their own interests and realities. The critical approach proposes instead to train actors, that is, subjects who are able to choose and therefore able to construct their own courses of action and the social and political systems in which they participate. Such *actors*, while being part of political, legal and economic systems, are in no way predetermined by them, but thanks to their margin of liberty and to the extent of their possibilities, may become creative transformers of those systems.

Another trait to be developed in actors is a *strategic capacity for action*. This implies an ability to assess the effectiveness and efficiency of different resources or courses of action in order to attain specific targets. With regard to social cohesion in particular, it is best to be able to experiment with different forms of collaboration, co-operation and association in order to be able to appreciate the various possibilities and limitations of individual and collective actions.

School plays a fundamental role to the extent that it offers students considerable opportunities for internalizing the values and procedures of democratic life by exercising *institutional participation,* which includes knowing how to participate, to dialogue, to petition and to claim rights, to resolve conflicts, to elect and be elected, to be represented and to represent, to build standards and fulfil obligations, etc. This enables them to face the complexity of exercising democracy, to understand the dynamic of its processes better and to assess its scope and limitations as a form of social coexistence and political organization.

Actions of solidarity on the part of the school towards the community, stimulated and planned from within the school with a clear pedagogic purpose, have proved to be extremely effective educational strategies. Combined with the learning of the ethical principles underlying these practices, they can lead to a noticeable improvement in the motivation of students by helping them to understand the significance and relevance of other learning contents.

In the light of all the foregoing arguments, it may be concluded that no education for social cohesion is possible unless it is practised in schools, both in the classrooms and at the managerial and organizational level, and projected on the surrounding communities.

To enable students to participate in study leading to knowledge, in rational, free dialogue, in committed, supportive action and in decision-making is the key point of this proposal, which is intended as a significant contribution towards achieving more just forms of social cohesion in our countries.

Bibliography

Belderrain, J.E. La educación para la democracía en la transformación educative. Argentina. *Revista latinoamericana de innovaciones educativas* (Buenos Aires-OEA), vol. 8, 1997.

——. Educación para los derechos humanos. *En:* Gobierno de Salta. *Un alegato inconcluso, hablemos de derechos humanos.* Salta, Argentina, 1999.

Braslavsky, C. *Re-haciendo escuelas. Hacia un nuevo paradigma en la educación latinoamericana.* Buenos Aires, Santillana, 1999.

Carr, W.; Kemmis, S. *Teoría crítica de la enseñanza: la investigación acción en la formación del profesorado.* Barcelona, Martinez Roca, 1988.

Jares, X. El lugar del conflicto en la organización escolar. *Revista Iberoamericana de educación* (Madrid), no. 15, Diciembre 1997.

Tenti Fanfani, E. La escuela constructora de subjetividad. En: Filmus D. (comp.). *Las transformaciones educativas: democracía, desarrollo e integración.* Buenos Aires, Troquel/OEI, 1998.

Tenti Fanfani E. *Más allá de las amonestaciones.* Buenos Aires, UNICEF, 1999.

Report of Workshop 2

Dr. Winthrop Wiltshire (Trinidad and Tobago) and Prof. Juan Esteban Belderrain (Argentina) conducted this workshop, which had four different components. The first three were short exercises on listening to and acknowledging/approving others and the self. For the last exercise, the participants were divided into four groups. They were given a few minutes to reflect on strategies for incorporating into the curriculum ideas and concepts from the two thematic presentations that would promote social cohesion and non-violence.

The groups identified various strategies that touched different levels of intervention: the school, students, the curriculum, teachers, policy-makers and other stakeholders. These are outlined below:

- The curriculum could and should be better adapted to promote social cohesion and non-violence. It should emphasize the sanctity of the human person and the place of each person in the education system. Exercises such as the first three activities of the workshop, on listening and validating, can be very helpful for students and teachers.
- The curriculum of most Caribbean countries already includes values education, but these contents could be made more explicit and relevant. An integrated multi-disciplinary curriculum would help build and maintain meaning and connectedness between

subjects in the student's mind. The approach to curriculum planning should therefore also be interdisciplinary. Another strategy would be to harmonize health, family life, moral and human rights education into one subject, thus giving it more importance within the curriculum.

- Student involvement is central to successful implementation. Metacognitive strategies can be useful in giving students opportunities to reflect on, evaluate and modify their attitudes, values and behaviours. Using this strategy will offset the overly academic focus in the curriculum. It also puts the student in the driving seat, making for more reflective decision-making and a student-friendly, caring and non-threatening classroom. By learning skills such as mediation and negotiation, students can apply them to real school experiences to solve conflict situations.
- Teacher education is also regarded as a major issue for fostering social cohesion. Training should integrate major concepts across the curriculum, both in terms of content and behaviour. Teachers should be trained to include in decision-making their own knowledge of specific values and skills needing priority attention. They must be encouraged to be critical, not simply accepting 'expert opinion', and to value their own experience. Provision of on-site coaching for teachers who are using and teaching strategies, skills and concepts that promote social cohesion was proposed.
- The emotional 'baggage' of teachers often determines the climate in the classroom as well as the successful implementation of the curriculum. The teacher's emotional health needs to be addressed by helping him/her to build a strong sense of personal and social identity and awareness of his/her values. In this way, he/she can teach the pupils to do the same. Teacher training strategies must therefore include practices to increase emotional and affective skills.

- **The curriculum into which these concepts/strategies for social cohesion must be incorporated can be represented as shown in Figure 1.**

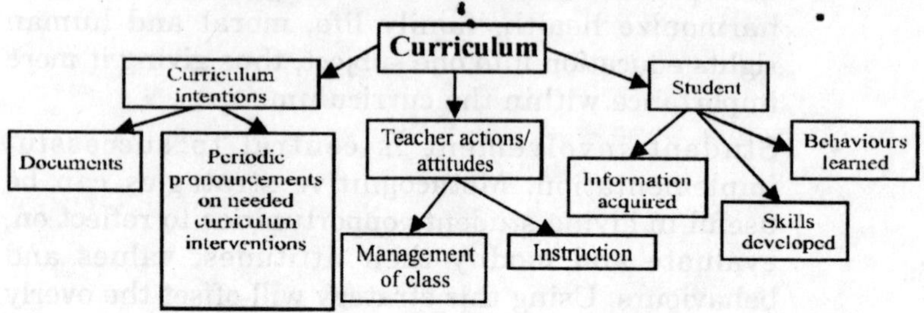

Figure 1. A curriculum for social cohesion

- **The characteristics of each school (context/ background) and the surrounding community should be taken into account when implementing any curriculum. Challenges at the school and community levels as well as other factors that contribute to social exclusion and/or violence need to be identified.**

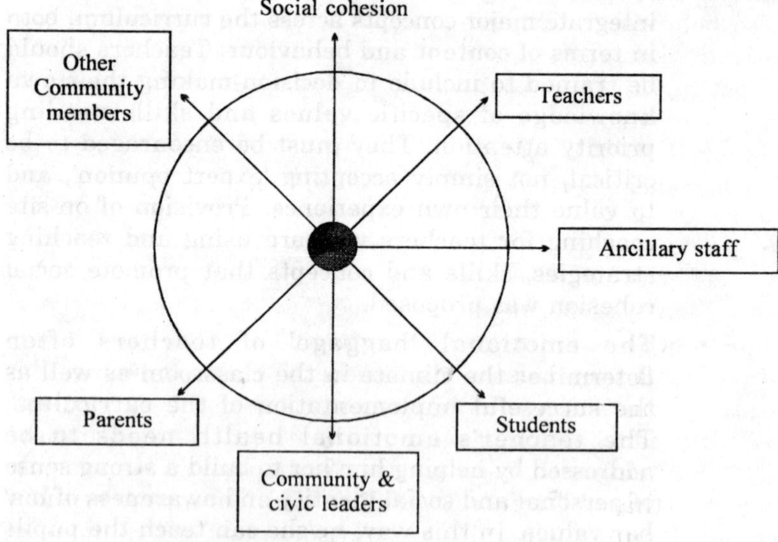

Figure 2. Involving all stakeholders in curriculum implementation

- Support of policy-makers is fundamental to effective curriculum implementation. This includes support for teacher training (pre- and in-service) and for professional supervision of curriculum implementation in the classroom. For the realization of a student-centred, rights-based approach in schools and the recognition of concepts such as the diversity of learning styles, multiple intelligences, and critical thinking, policy must focus on appropriate teacher development.
- Involvement of all stakeholders is also a prerequisite for successful implementation and sustainability (see Figure 2).

The debate which followed the presentation of the outcomes of the workshop, concentrated mainly on the issues of assessment and corporal punishment.

Assessment

If education for social cohesion is to be integral to the curriculum assessment must evaluate not only content but also behaviour. Teachers tend to be driven by examination results and ignore other aspects of learning. It is therefore important to provide the opportunity for them to facilitate holistic development of their students. However, participants referred to the difficulties of assessing non-academic performance.

Violence

It was reported that in many cases, in Caribbean education systems, efforts have been made to reduce corporal punishment and other forms of violence by teachers towards students. It was stressed that teachers need to be shown that with the necessary effort and goodwill a classroom without violence can become a reality. They need the appropriate training, research results, real examples and materials showing that children can produce and learn more without corporal punishment. Participants requested examples of effective non-violent disciplinary action by teachers that could be used in teacher education courses.

Concerning the issue of good practices for non-violence in schools, it was pointed out that practices recommended from other contexts are not always easily transferable to other cultures and countries. Context-specific strategies therefore need to be developed. Curriculum developers and teachers should be aware of and use as basic texts in curriculum design, relevant international instruments such as the Universal Declaration on Human Rights and the International Convention on the Rights of the Child, etc. Many elements can be included in the curriculum from kindergarten onwards.

It was recognized that violence towards students can take many forms and that there are many types of violence affecting the school: within it, towards it, around it. Students and teachers may be victims or perpetrators of violence in their homes, schools or wider society. One participant noted that students from less-privileged backgrounds are far more likely to be the targets of discipline and punishment from teachers. Tackling the phenomenon of violence in schools has to be considered the responsibility of the entire society, with parents, in particular, being targeted.

Section 4

Shared Values and Cultural Diversity: What to Learn and How

Charting a New Course for Education in Anguilla: The Teacher Gloria Omololu Institute

Oluwakemi M. Linda Banks

Introduction

In 1998 I was invited to Atlanta, Georgia, by a relative to attend a personal development workshop. The workshop was focused on helping participants to see 'life as possibility', the view being that we have many limiting beliefs about who we are and who we could be. These beliefs prevent us from exploring the possibilities in our life and, as a result, we become less than we could be. Consequently, as one of the final activities of that workshop each participant had to declare herself or himself as a possibility:

> *I am the possibility of universal transformation through spiritual leadership in a world manifesting the beauty and the glory of the Creator!*

It was this assurance of universal transformation, although not verbalized until I formulated my vision statement in 1998, that had unconsciously infused me with the determination to chart a new course for education in Anguilla and develop the Teacher Gloria Omololu Institute some four years earlier. This philosophy also kept me motivated to persevere in the face of the many challenges and hardships and the skepticism of many who fear anything new. There were, at that time, no other private primary schools in Anguilla. I was convinced that a more child-centred approach to education, which was based on psychological principles, could make a difference in the lives of the children of Anguilla and, by extension, in the lives of the people of the nation and the world.

My training, my experience, and all the research findings I had access to, had led to my firm belief that when children develop a strong positive sense of themselves, their entire outlook on the world, on others in their world and on their potential for success, is positively affected. I further believe that these children will exert positive influences on others, including the adults in their lives. Thus, changing the world in which they live in essence, they transform their world.

This conviction has been substantiated by the extraordinary success of the institute after just seven years. The children of the institute are creative, expressive, inquisitive, highly motivated, self-confident and affectionate. They excel, not only academically, but in many other areas of their lives. I see the Teacher Gloria Omololu Institute as the epitome of all my human resource endeavours.

The institute was established on 3 September 1994 as a private-assisted government school, to provide an alternative to the government's primary school system. It was introduced at a time when several challenges in the education system were made evident by an escalation of behavioural and emotional problems in the school as well as in the wider society. Children were exhibiting signs of alienation and lack of identity. As the founder, I sought to provide an alternative system based on the empowerment and valuing of children which would enhance their self-esteem and lead to higher levels of academic achievement and social adjustment. As a consequence they would become more productive citizens of Anguilla in particular, and of the world at large. In essence, they would be educated for life.

The Omololu Educational Institute Incorporated, a non-profit organization with a board of ten directors, operates the Teacher Gloria Omololu Institute. The institute has been named after my sister, Gloria Cassandra Banks Harrigan, who epitomized the characteristics of a model teacher. Teacher Gloria's life on earth came to an end through a tragic accident in 1987.

Omololu is a Yoruba name from West Africa which means 'children are the summit of achievement'. The word 'institute' has been used to embrace the total concept of education for life, as the school plans to ultimately provide educational opportunities to people at all stages of development.

The institute, which commenced its operations with two pre-school classes and one primary class and an enrolment of forty-five students, is now into its seventh year with an enrolment of just over 150 students. An additional class was added each year until, in September 2000, the institute achieved the landmark status of a full primary school with seven primary classes. In September 2001, the first primary school graduates will be ready for secondary school. Parents are lobbying for the introduction of the institute's own secondary school. If this is not viable, students will attend the island's only secondary school.

The curriculum of the institute is directed towards the holistic development of the child through a sound core curriculum, multicultural education (including our cultural history as African Caribbean people), foreign languages, and the creative and performing arts, all in a safe, nurturing and stimulating environment. Parental and community involvement are critical components of the institute's operations at all levels.

Objective of the Institute (Phase One)

To provide the residents of Anguilla with an alternative form of primary and pre-school education for their children and to help them accept ownership of the system through parental involvement.

Aims

1. To provide pupils with instruction that is designed to meet their individual developmental needs and provide them with a sound education foundation.

2. To provide opportunities for pupils to achieve multilingual competence (i.e. Spanish, French) by exposure to these languages from early in their school careers.
3. To provide students with information on; (a) their heritage—to help foster a sense of identity and; (b) other cultures—to foster the development of greater tolerance and understanding of the uniqueness and worth of each human being.
4. To provide for the development of expressive and creative skills and for involvement in the performing arts and other non-traditional forms of education.
5. To involve parents and the wider community in the educational process.
6. To develop gender sensitivity at an early age, thereby promoting better interpersonal relationships between the genders.
7. To foster an appreciation of and caring for the environment.
8. To provide an alternative system of private primary education that is affordable and therefore inclusive rather than elitist.
9. To educate children in an atmosphere that is safe, nurturing and stimulating.
10. To ensure that qualified, committed personnel are recruited to implement the philosophy of the institute.
11. To provide a holistic approach to education.
12. To help children develop healthy self-concepts and positive attitudes so that they can commit to excellence and maximize their potential.

Critical Components of the Programme

Solid core curriculum

The basic curriculum has been drawn from existing models with additions and modifications. A thematic approach, which integrates the various subject areas, is used. The Anguilla primary school curriculum forms the core of the institute's educational programme. However, this has been supplemented by many critical components as identified earlier. The result is a holistic curriculum which teaches children to strive for excellence as they live together harmoniously with themselves, with others, and with the environment. This outcome is achieved through a variety of innovative techniques, focused interventions and the infusion of psychological principles into the regular classroom activities.

Multilingual competence

As international borders collapse and nations become more dependent on each other for survival, communication between people becomes more essential. Language barriers stultify communication and understanding. In preparing our children for meaningful involvement in the twenty-first century, multilingual competence is therefore vital.

As the Anguillan society continues to grow and change, we find that the development of a Spanish-speaking population has become a part of our reality. This population, which is largely comprised of descendants of Anguillans living in Santo Domingo, is here to stay and will only grow in the future with the inevitable return of Anguillans of Cuban descent. The realization of this situation led to the start of a Saturday morning Spanish educational programme in 1992, open to all children. A community French education programme began in 1997. Headstart classes for students entering secondary school have also been held during the summer.

Research on the acquisition of a second language has shown that mastery is more easily achieved when children are exposed to the foreign language at an early age. However, presently foreign languages are taught only at the secondary school level in Anguilla. At the Teacher Gloria Omololu Institute, the Spanish language is introduced at the preschool level (three-year-olds) and the French language is started by grade four.

Multicultural education

Children and teachers at the institute also come from many different cultures. Educational institutions around the world have acknowledged the critical importance of multicultural education in a holistic educational programme.

At the Teacher Gloria Omololu Institute, this education is infused throughout the regular curriculum and special themes related to multicultural awareness are also developed. In fostering a greater sense of identity and positive self-esteem, our history, as Caribbean peoples predominantly of African descent, is revisited and the more positive elements of those cultures are emphasized.

For peaceful coexistence on this planet, a knowledge and appreciation of other cultures is important. Children learn prejudices from the world around them. Ongoing exposure to other cultures can help to increase tolerance and goodwill as children learn to acknowledge and appreciate the differences in people that create our interesting world. This also enriches the educational experience.

The multicultural programme at the institute involves parents, teachers, children and the wider community sharing their cultures, often using art displays, pictures, artifacts, visits (e.g. art galleries with exhibits or artists demonstrating their work from other countries, visit to the island's mosque), songs, dances, drama and discussions. Children share in and/or learn about many cross-cultural and notional celebrations—e.g. Canada Day, Jamaica Independence Day, African Liberation Day, Guyana Independence Day, Black History month, Martin Luther King's birthday, Anguilla Day, Kwanzaa celebrations, etc.

A programme twinning each class with a different country around the world is about to be launched. This programme involves exchange visits, latter writing and cultural exchanges. Classes will spend an entire year being totally immersed in another culture.

Creative and expressive skill development

Children enter the school system with a natural curiosity, a live imagination and an eager and expressive mind. However, by the time they leave our schools, they seem to have lost these characteristics. Another speaker at this seminar, Erik Prinds, said that they 'enter as question marks and leave as semi colons'. I have heard a similar quotation that affirms that they leave as full stops. Our education systems are stifling the very qualities that we recognize as integral to true education. At the Teacher Gloria Omololu Institute there is a systematic programme for the development of the child's creative and expressive skills. This programme includes providing opportunities for children to create and express themselves through art, dance, music, drama, storytelling, poetry, writing and the use of their imagination through other non-traditional, cultural forms.

Although uniforms are used to minimize the visible signs of the different socio-economic levels of students, these have been made in different colors and designs to support individual expression. Children can wear any colour on any day, so on every day our classrooms and playgrounds are beautiful gardens of flowers. Children can express their creativity and individuality as they choose the colour and combination for each day. The mountain motif reminds children to always reach for their own mountains tops.

Parental and community involvement

Parental involvement is very important to the success of education. It the child is aware that the home and the school are working together on his/her behalf, then he/she is motivated to do his or her best.

During admission interviews, parents are advised that their application can only be considered if they made a verbal and written commitment to being totally involved in their child's education. This includes attending parent/teacher (PTA) meetings, monitoring their child's progress, assisting with homework, and sharing their skills, expertise and knowledge with the institute. A record is kept of attendance at PTA meetings, and of general parent participation in the institute. A parent assessment category is included in children's report cards.

The institute aims at providing opportunities for parental development through workshops for parents and the community. Foreign-language classes have also been conducted for them.

Parents have been willing to share their expertise. Assistance so far has been in many areas, including art lessons, Spanish classes, storytelling, drama, painting of school furniture, cleaning and setting up the playground, swimming lessons, physical education, substitute teaching, supplies, fund-raising and other general assistance. Parents have also been involved in the multicultural education programme.

Community interest in the institute has resulted in donations of money, equipment, tuition assistance, time, and other forms of general support. The institute continues to solicit this type of support.

Positive gender relations

There is heightened awareness today of the need to foster better relations between the genders. Unfortunately, much of the material (nursery rhymes, stories, books, videos) prepared for children, reinforces negative attitudes in this regard. There is also a noticeable absence of males in early childhood education classrooms. The institute endeavours to promote healthy gender relations, positive role models of both genders, respect for all, and also aims at minimizing the impact of stereotyping.

Environmental awareness

The importance of caring for our environment should be emphasized from an early age. Children at the institute are provided with opportunities to discuss, learn about and care for their environment. This information is infused through the general curriculum and is covered through related themes. As example of the infusion is through discussion of the natural fibres (cotton) and the natural dyes used in the production of the uniforms worn by the children. The historical link with cotton is also demonstrated as cotton was actually cultivated on Anguilla up to the late 1960s. The institute has also been used for a pilot programme by the Anguilla National Trust. Children are involved in ongoing ecological activities.

An affordable and inclusive system

The Teacher Gloria Omololu Institute is open to all residents of Anguilla who have a genuine interest in this alternative to the regular education system. Parents' interest and involvement do not necessarily coincide with their economic status. Consequently, tuition is being kept at an affordable rate. The institute has also been successful in soliciting tuition assistance from the local commercial sector for parents experiencing financial problems. As a result of this inclusive policy, the student population represents a wide cross-section of the Anguillian community, unlike that normally found in private schools.

A safe, nurturing and stimulating environment

Children learn best in an atmosphere in which they feel cared for and valued. A bright stimulating environment is another important factor in the education process. Children are supervised from the time they enter school until they leave. This includes early morning supervision, playground supervision, lunch-hour supervision and after-school supervision. Some parents volunteer to assist.

The school provides a nutritious cooked meal for students whose parents wish them to partake of it. Children are provided with opportunities to learn acceptable table manners—derived from discussions with them. A programme of rotating lunch servers (waiters/waitresses) allows all children to learn how to appreciate and give good service.

Many children live in homes where they do not receive positive nurturing and acceptance. It is a well-documented fact that a positive self-concept can only be developed when a child feels accepted, approved of and appreciated. This positive sense of self is associated with healthy adjustment, positive interpersonal relations and success in life. The Teacher Gloria Omololu Institute is committed to providing the type of environment in which children will realize their maximum potential.

Qualified committed teaching staff

One looks with appreciation to the brilliant teachers, but with gratitude to those who touched our human feelings. The curriculum is so much necessary new material, but the warmth is the vital element for the growing child and for the soul of the child—Carl Jung.

The quality and commitment of teachers in the education system is a major determinant of its success. Teachers at the

Teacher Gloria Omololu Institute are carefully screened and recruited. It is imperative that they believe in the philosophy of the institute and are committed to working as a team to ensure that students receive the best educational opportunities. Our teachers are sensitive, caring, love children and must be willing to go 'the extra mile'. These include teachers voluntarily holding after-school classes and Saturday morning classes and even assisting with the preparation of the lunch programme when they perceive a need.

Teachers' academic and professional qualifications, as well as their experience, are carefully assessed. They all bring a variety of specialist skills which they use for the benefit of the institute. They also receive intentional nurturing during staff development sessions and staff meetings and spontaneous nurturing from both the children and other staff.

The recruitment of male teachers is a present day challenge for early childhood education. The institute has been successful in recruiting one male teacher, who actually holds a Master's degree. Male volunteers, usually parents, also offer assistance in physical education and other programmes.

Dr Clarke's (see List of participants) admonition that nothing never happens reminds me of an old Chinese proverb which affirms that: A childs life is like a piece of paper on which every passerby leaves a mark. It is important that those who are poised to make several marks on our childrens' papers are themselves well-adjusted. Dr Wiltshire (see List of participants) has reminded us that it is only when people have positive feelings about themselves that they can project positive feelings to others.

Holistic approach

The educational programme of the Teacher Gloria Omololu Institute fosters holistic development on several different levels—moral, spiritual, physical, intellectual, emotional, and psychosocial. This should prepare children to face the challenges ahead with the confidence of their ability to succeed, which is fueled by a positive sense of self. Our children are marvels of God's creation and we must always be reminded of this. Bernie Siegel reminds us: *Please continue*

to look at your children as your valuable treasures. Honour them and yourself.

Positive self-esteem and commitment to success

The theoretical underpinnings of the school's philosophy are that an individual must be intrinsically motivated to succeed. Maslow's hierarchy of needs sheds some insight on the internal forces that hinder or enhance that process. According to Maslow, the satisfaction of the individual's needs for love and belonging allows him/her to move on to satisfy other needs.

At the Teacher Gloria Omololu Institute, an atmosphere is created which enables the child to feel accepted and appreciated. The intrinsic value, worth and dignity of every human being is emphasized, and behaviours, rather than individuals, are labeled. In fact, a literal interpretation of *omololu* is 'children of God'. Children at the institute are therefore nurtured as miracles of God's creation and supreme gifts to humankind. They are constantly reminded, by word and action, that they are special and unique, and positive reinforcers are used for acceptable behaviour. Children are also encouraged to mentor each other informally and through a programme of volunteer peer helpers. The Omololu Super Child of the Week programme provides opportunities for each child to receive positive acknowledgement and appreciation from his/her classmates every week. The Omololu Super Child is applauded by the entire school during the weekly Omololu Time programme. The 'super child' also receives a certificate listing the attributes about which her/his classmates are commending her/him, after they have read them to the entire school.

Omololu Time

Omololu Time is a special weekly programme during which the school is brought together (pre-school and kindergarten form one group, and Grades 1 through 6 form the other group) for a highly interactive session. Many themes related to values, love and respect for self, for others and for our world are discussed. This session is facilitated in a manner that allows for full participation and respectful sharing of experiences and insights from students and teachers. The aim is to help children internalize the values, morals and attitudes which would contribute to their healthy adjustment as citizens of Anguilla and the wider world community. Different classes usually conduct the assembly time which immediately precedes Omololu Time. They use many creative expressions including song, dance, poetry readings and plays to highlight an important value, concept or message that they want to share with the school.

Discussions during Omololu Time might focus on:

- Principles of living together harmoniously, e.g. children might be asked to recount (or teachers asked to suggest) if they are facing relationship challenges. The other children will then propose ways in which they will try to help them. Reports of improvement will be made in subsequent sessions;
- Multi-cultural exchanges;
- Environmental issues, e.g. global warming and our responsibility to care for the world;
- Ways of helping others who are upset (e.g. children who are grieving);
- New students are welcomed, school rules shared and children propose ways in which they will help to make the new children feel welcome;
- Acknowledgement and celebration of our successes—children, teachers and parents are applauded for successes and ways in which they have helped others;
- 'Attitude of Gratitude' programme—saying thanks to others.

Omololu Time is designed to be a period when childrens' self-esteems are enhanced, and they are encouraged to be their best and strive for excellence as they pursue their goals. They are reminded of the motto 'Omololu', and to reach for their summit.

The school's logo, which is a mountain with the sun rising behind, it is the motif pattern on the school's uniform.

This is meant to be a constant reminder that with each new day we can continue our ascent to the summit of our achievement.

Conflict resolution

Children are taught constructive ways of resolving conflicts which result in 'win-win' situations. They are invited to talk about the challenge, how they have dealt with it, and how they could have dealt with it differently so that it would not have escalated. Apologies are exchanged, as well as commitments to do things differently. They are then asked to talk about things they appreciate about each other. This is easier or more difficult depending on the emotions involved, but usually children are able to walk away after having embraced each other, feeling better about the relationship. The resolution sometimes involves negotiation, compromise, or further individual, class or family consultations. We have noted remarkable changes in the behaviour of children who had been taught to 'defend' themselves, either in the home or at school.

Conclusion

If you treat an individual [...] as if he were what he ought to be and could be, he will become what he ought to be and could be—Goethe

Testimonials from countless students through the ages have acknowledged the impact of a particular teacher or teachers on the lives of children. I can still hear the echo of the words 'Linda Banks, you can do it' from my English teacher when I was uncertain about my ability to perform a certain task. In fact, I went back to her several years later when I was in graduate school and told her of the lasting impact of those five words. When one teacher questioned his student about his tremendous success one year following a year in which he had failed miserably, the student simply said 'I like myself when I am with you'. I can still remember how honoured I felt when a friend from Trinidad came to the phone to receive my call and said that her daughter, who could not remember my name, described me as 'the lady who makes me feel good about myself'.

The children of the Teacher Gloria Omololu Institute have demonstrated to me beyond the shadow of a doubt the truth behind Goethe's statement cited above. They surprise their teachers with parties, gifts and other demonstrations of appreciation, and show empathy when others are hurting. During Omololu Time they might spontaneously invite the school to applaud a teacher, another child, or a parent. They have written inviting parents to send their children to our school. In these they have demonstrated their understanding for the principles of the school and have shown their appreciation.

Children have been involved in individual fund-raising efforts for the school using their own initiative. One of the most significant efforts is the group of three 10-year-olds who planned a dance concert. They selected and choreographed most of their own dances, used the computer to prepare their tickets and flyers, and to solicit support for their costumes from business places and they regularly and patiently practised for the programme with the help of teachers whom they selected.

In short, the Teacher Gloria Omololu Institute has demonstrated that for these children 'Education is not the filling of a vessel but the kindling of a fire' (Plutarch). But to light those fires we must have the match. That match is our own, our own enthusiasm, our own desire to make a difference. We must be on fire ourselves. We all represent the possibility of universal transformation!

11

Curricular Content and Skill Development for Learning to Live Together

Betty A. Reardon

Cultural Difference: Essential Curricular Content for Learning to Live Together

My comments relate mainly to curricular content and skill development at the secondary level. I must begin by noting that the development of these skills and the presentation of the proposed content would not be possible without an elementary education that nurtures the positive learning communities, belief in self and respect for others exemplified by the Omololu Institute, its purposes and programmes as outlined by Dr Banks. I make these comments from the perspective of a peace educator who sees the goal of learning to live together as the overarching purpose of all education.

My presentation assumes that, although they may be contended, there are, indeed, shared values that can serve to derive and sustain a community among culturally diverse groups. It also intends to argue that such diversity, when organized within the ethical principles that can be derived from the shared values, serves as a source of communal strength and resilience. Thus, the task of education in facilitating learning to live together lies largely in developing the capacities, not only to live with and among cultural differences, but the skills to devise and practise positive arrangements of difference and ways to mediate points of contention that work for the benefit of all.

The substantive content for such education should pervade all grade levels and infuse all subjects. It also should be included in school programmes in explicit curricula designed to achieve the learning objectives identified as essential to the development of these capacities. The core of this content, to illuminate the shared values, should be the international standards for the protection of human rights, with particular emphasis on the principles articulated in *the* Universal Declaration of Human Rights (UDHR). The curriculum should make possible the actual study of the UDHR, the principles from which it is derived and the meaning it holds for persons and communities seeking to live in peace with justice. Learning to live together, achieving a culture of peace, will require particular skills for a culturally diverse world in which we can learn to share values and work together for common social purposes. The UDHR was devised as an instrument for developing and maintaining such a world.

Curricular substance, complemented by an intentional pedagogy, should also provide the basis for understanding culture itself, how it develops and the functions it serves in the formation of human identities, the articulation of social aspirations and the evolution of the institutions that mediate meaning (including education) and provide governance. A pedagogy for appreciation of cultural differences would be one in which the varieties of historical experience and physical environments are revealed as sources of the cultural difference which broaden and enrich the store of human knowledge and offer depth and variety to the possibilities for confronting common human challenges and solving mutual problems—such as the social violence we have lamented at this meeting. So, instruction in history and environmental issues (among other subjects) can provide opportunities for the study of cultural diversity, and how history and environment are both formative influences on culture and are, in turn, profoundly affected by culture.

We should be teaching for deeper understanding of *the* culture and cultural differences required for respect for difference and appreciation of diversity. We should also be working to develop the skills of applying the resources of cultural diversity to common social goals and problems. Perhaps, most of all, appreciation of cultural diversity calls us to nurture the wondering capacity, to ask along with students, how is it that one single species experiences their humanity in so many wonderfully different ways?

Cultural Contention and Conflict Resolution

The focus on common values should not exclude the role of cultural differences in conflict formation. Cultural contentions and those political conflicts arising from or clothed as cultural clashes, whether of the present or of the past colonial history in which culture was distorted into categories of power and unequal human worth, can be explored as mutual problems, presenting obstacles to the well-being and aspirations of all involved. Developing the skills to mediate such contention and resolve conflicts between parties of different cultures are fundamental to learning to live together. Reframing conflicts to reveal the mutual problematic, and finding within cultural differences multiple perspectives from which to view and better understand the problematic, as well as alternative approaches to resolution, can lead toward mutually acceptable solutions. Thus, cultural contention like cultural diversity can become the source of transforming destructive conflict into a process of positive change. Learners can come to understand that the chief obstacle to communal harmony is not conflict as such, but rather conducting conflict in violent and harmful ways. Both the philosophy and the strategies of non-violence are elements that should be at the core of a curriculum that teaches positive relations among the culturally different.

For educators, the major challenge now is to move beyond the formal statements of intention and principle that have long acknowledged the need for, and advocated, a revised and reformed education for a culturally diverse, peaceful and just world society. We must now undertake the development of curricula and the preparation of teachers for an educational practice that is: imbued with the principles and norms of the shared values; applies a pedagogy consistent with appreciation of diversity; is based on a curricular content that teaches both the substance of the shared values together with the nature, origins and positive possibilities of cultural differences; and, finally and specifically, develops explicit skills to transform conflict from a violent drive to overcome and eliminate differences to a process of mediating and constructively arranging diversity, be it cultural, ideological or political.

A Pedagogy of Valuing

While we would never seek a common curriculum or identical pedagogy, we can elaborate approaches to enable us to work in our different ways toward a common purpose and varied but complementary pedagogies. The proposed approach is a pedagogy of valuing that emphasizes active realization of values, moving beyond the recommended basic instruction in value principles, to preparation for the application and fulfilment of these principles, such as those that underlie the international human rights standards.

Clearly, the pedagogy of the Omololu School that starts with the valuing of the child, enabling him/her to undertake the many value challenges that will continue to face all our communities, is an example of the pedagogy of valuing. Some of the challenges to be faced threaten not only the well-being of particular nations, groups or persons but the very survival of the wonderful and varied human species.

A pedagogy of valuing should look beneath *shared* values to *common values*. It needs to address *contended* values and deal directly with *conflicting* values. Each of these value categories, the common, shared, contended, and conflicting, requires the development of a different skill and the development of each skill rests upon a fundamental learning formation such as provided in the Omololu Institute. A pedagogy of valuing requires a safe learning environment in which learners will be able to risk being changed, and it requires also teachers willing to risk changing themselves.

Defining value categories

Each of the value categories defined here is integral to major goals of the Omololu Institute: appreciation of other cultures; creative expression; positive gender relations; mentoring and peer support. Each can be illuminated by a process of inquiry directed toward teaching skills of value realization. As Table 1 shows, the value categories are in a continuum: common; shared; contended; and conflicting.

- *Common values* are those widely recognized as universal human values, aspirations articulated in varied and diverse cultural forms. Among a range of such values are dignity, intimacy, meaning and belonging. Around these values we humans have developed, in Dr Wiltshire's words, 'multiple ways of being, doing and relating'. These values are largely unexpressed, taken for granted. They need to be brought to awareness. One way to do so is through an interpretation of the meaning of the principles expressed in the UDHR. Curricula could address the concerns which produced the statement of the particular rights, the cultural and political contentions through which they were mediated, the continued differences in interpretation and the cross-cultural movements for their realization.
- *Shared values* derive partly from common human values, but they are 'shared' because there has been a conscious articulation and negotiation of the values. Such an articulation is exemplified in the Convention on the Rights of the Child (CRC), an internationally negotiated values statement derived from the common value principles set forth in the UDHR. Sharing is the active process of explicating, assessing and allowing for value differences; and creatively applying the principles in different cultural contexts.
- *Contended values* may be shared values, but the manner of their actualization is distinct, and in some communities and on some issues, they are a source of public controversy. If the community is to survive, the controversy must be moved to consensus through clarification. The Convention on the Elimination of all Forms of Discrimination

against Women (CEDAW) is a standard from which considerable contention of cultural values still arises related to gender roles and relations. These contentions offer significant possibilities for clarifying value differences with the goal of seeking culturally appropriate accommodation to the core principles of this international standard.

- *Conflicting values* appear to be in opposition, the realization of one antithetical to the realization of the other. Again, the health and survival of the community requires that the conflict be resolved and the parties reconciled. Some areas in which accommodation through sharing has been reached in principle remain contended, even conflicting in the application of specific points. CEDAW and CRC both contain such points in specific articles of their respective texts. (Examples are noted in Table 1)

Designating skills and devising an inquiry

For each category I propose some suggested pedagogies of skill development, essential both to 'learning to live together' and to the implementation of the 1994 UNESCO Integrated Framework of Action on Education for Peace, Democracy and Human Rights, which argues for the holistic citizenship education we have advocated here. The matrix (*see* Table 1) illustrates these skills development pedagogies in relation to the goals of the Omololu Institute, a suggested line of inquiry into some cultural values issues raised by the UDHR, CEDAW and CRC as core curriculum content for learning to live together. As with the human rights standards, the framework of this matrix can be adapted and its substance accommodated to different cultural contexts and educational needs. Alternative value content and inquiries could be used to teach the same skills and work toward similar goals. Human rights are suggested here because they are fundamental to peace and are central to the purposes embraced in UNESCO's Integrated Framework for Action. I want to emphasize that the foundation of an education such as that offered by Omololu makes the development of these complex valuing skills possible. Children must experience

Table 1: Matrix for a pedagogy of valuing

Values continuum	Goals of the Omololu Institute	Skills/pedagogy	Process of inquiry into culture	Human rights examples
Common	Appreciation of other Cultures	Interpretation (making meaning)	• What does it mean? • How is it manifest in my culture and other cultures?	*Universal Declaration of Human Rights* (Article 16.3) • '...family natural and fundamental Group unit of society'
Shared	Creative expression	Negotiation (reflective/interactive communication)	• Would that be good in this culture? • Is it good in other cultures?	*Convention on the Rights of the Child* (Article 3) 'In all actions concerning children, the best interest of the child shall be a major consideration.'
Contended	Positive gender relations	Clarification (see as the other sees)	• What changes are required in this culture? • Are these changes reasonable, sustainable?	*Convention on the Elimination of All Forms of Discrimination Against Women* (Article 3) Guarantees basic human rights and fundamental freedoms to women on an equal basis with men
Conflicting	Mentoring and peer support	Resolution (multiple problem-solving skills)	• How can we frame the conflict as a common problem, mutual to the parties and cultures involved?	*Convention on the Rights of the Child* (Article 17) 'A child shall have access to information from a diversity of sources [...] guidelines to protect children from harmful material encouraged.'

valuing to learn the valuing skills that will enable them to become active and constructive citizens of the kind of world community envisioned by the drafters of the UDHR. I also wish to note that cultural adaptation is not synonymous with cultural relativism, for the principles of human rights and human dignity are inviolable and absolutely essential to living together in peace.

Conclusion

I conclude then with this argument that human rights and peace issues, as addressed by the Integrated Framework for Action should be the core content of an education for shared values and cultural diversity, assuring you that there are now curricula and teacher-training designs for these purposes, such as the units displayed here from Guyana, and the UNESCO guides for teaching toward tolerance at the elementary, secondary and teacher education levels. There are also manuals and guides available from the Hague Appeal for Peace Global Campaign for Peace Education.

I should also like to argue that introducing these issues into the school curricula will require a massive effort, involving teachers, training institutions, curriculum development specialists, ministries and civil society. All these sectors are now working together on the Global Campaign for Peace Education. Many supporting the Campaign meet at the annual International Institutes on Peace Education, a joint project of the Campaign, the Teachers College Peace Education Center and the host institution in a different country each year. In 2002, the Institute will be hosted by the Peace Education Center of Miriam College in the Philippines. One year we hope to have it in the Caribbean. It is an intensive residential experience in learning to live together such as we have had at this most productive sub-regional meeting.

Report of Workshop 3

The participants, divided into five groups, were asked to reflect on ways in which multicultural education can be included in the curriculum.

One group began by defining the concept of multicultural education, concluding that it should have at least four components:

- Awareness of various peoples/cultures that make up a nation;
- Awareness of various peoples/cultures that make up the world (concepts of national identity and universality);
- Acknowledgement of various cultures (concepts of respect and tolerance);
- Meeting the needs of various cultural groups (concepts of human rights education, justice, peace, concepts of relevance of curriculum).

The Content of Multicultural Education

The participants reflected on the need for multicultural education with reference to the composition of their populations. They expressed the need for a more multicultural type of education, based on values of tolerance and understanding of different population groups. The region has a high rate of migration amongst islands. The cultural influences related to the very rich colonial history of most of the countries have created a broad spectrum of values and behaviours.

In formal education, the subjects that foster shared cultural values include natural sciences, social studies, language arts, literature, religious studies, peace and human rights education, and the arts. Amongst the non-formal activities mentioned were music, dancing, cultural celebrations and exhibitions, inter-school competitions and fairs, traditional handicrafts, cuisine and games.

In most countries of the region, multicultural education starts at the pre-school level and develops all through basic education. In general, it consists of understanding geographical, cultural, economic, social and political influences and inter-relations in one's society and the wider world. The main objective of multicultural education may be to develop national identity whilst fostering respect for cultural and racial diversity. The values, attitudes and behaviours that it seeks to promote therefore mainly concentrate around these themes.

To promote national identity, schools teach awareness of, and sensitivity towards, national symbols and traditions. Studying the social context in which one lives also contributes to developing a sense of identity, while sharing national, Caribbean, and world-wide historical experiences and cultural practices helps students to develop a better understanding of both self and others.

Multicultural education should celebrate diversity as an asset, and recognize equality and differences. The best defence against discrimination is therefore understanding and tolerance. Most countries have integrated into their curriculum elements of human rights education, which focus on respecting cultures and religious values, and promoting equality and non-discrimination.

Implementation in the Curriculum

Again it was agreed that one way of guaranteeing successful curricular implementation is to involve all stakeholders—principals, teachers, parents, experts, religious institutions—in the creation and development of the curriculum.

Once again, the role of the teacher was regarded as central to the success of multicultural learning, including the provision of teacher education in this field. Together, teachers should reflect on how to include more subjects that integrate multicultural elements across the curriculum. Emphasis was thus again put on co-operation and networking amongst teachers for sharing ideas and materials. Exchange visits between schools and exploitation of the new information and communication technologies were recommended. Other suggestions for sharing experiences were: (a) documenting multicultural 'best practices', dance, music, drama and videos; and (b) holding workshops or seminars to address multicultural education. Additional research studies and exchange of results on the similarities and differences are required.

Participants referred to the many cultural events organized in the region. Events involving not only the students, but the whole community, can be excellent venues for promoting different cultures. It was agreed that there is a need to integrate multicultural education into the curriculum in a more practical rather than purely academic way. Dance, music and other performing arts representing the diverse groups in the society should be incorporated into the school programme.

The main challenge raised concerning the inclusion of multicultural education in school programmes was that of constructing a curriculum which focuses more on local and regional contexts. Furthermore, present curricula often do not address the needs of the various ethnic groups of each country. Changing the ethnocentrism in the curriculum requires including more local, national and regional elements in the curriculum of individual countries with adequate reference to the various ethnic groups within the countries in question.

Section 5

Final Outcomes and Proposals for Action

13 Conclusions of the Workshops and Debates

The inter-relatedness of the three sub-themes of the seminar meant that a number of similar issues emerged from the outcomes of the workshops and the discussions that followed them. On the last day of the seminar, a final discussion took place as a means of summarizing the proceedings. Following is a summary of the main conclusions and proposals which were put forward.

The curriculum of most of the countries of the Caribbean already includes elements of education for citizenship, social cohesion and cultural diversity. It was generally agreed that the promotion in schools of the values discussed in the seminar depends as much on changing classroom practice to reflect democratic and humane principles, as on the inclusion of new content in the curriculum. Furthermore, the learning of skills and attitudes is as important to the teaching of values as is academic content.

Additionally, it was noted that there is a need for more sharing of information and good practices among educational professionals of the region.

Targets

- Effective curriculum development for citizenship education should involve all stakeholders, including students, parents and various community members. To effectively participate in the curriculum development process, stakeholders need to be properly sensitized to the key concepts and issues. Education for citizenship should thus extend beyond the school into the wider community, and be based on active participation of the latter.

- Citizenship education should be conceived not merely as content but as a holistic process, which permeates all aspects of classroom practice, informs the teacher/student relationships and is central to the whole curriculum based on an inter-disciplinary and cross-curricular approach. Education for democratic citizenship must therefore be infused throughout the curriculum, becoming a way of thinking about and practising education.
- Social and emotional learning should be considered central to curricular goals, with a nurturing environment being created in the classroom.
- The role of the teacher is key to changing the culture of the classroom. The teacher often needs first to change his/her attitudes and values, with adequate training, supervision, networking and support being essential.
- The active involvement of students in classroom processes is essential to effective citizenship education.
- The emotional health of both teachers and students should be ensured.
- Education for social cohesion should seek to promote both liberty and solidarity.

Methods

- Citizenship education (and education more generally) should be learner-centred with students actively involved in classroom processes and prepared for critical reflection on society. Participation should be central to the creation of rules and norms, and students should begin to practise this in school.

- Training in listening skills should become an essential part of both student and teacher education.
- Assessment practices consequently need to be reviewed and reformed to take social and behavioural learning into proper account, and to allow for effective implementation of the proposed innovations in teaching/learning methods.
- Teaching/learning methodologies and teacher education for citizenship should be based on the principles of ethics, morals and human rights, with international instruments such as the Universal Declaration of Human Rights and the International Convention on the Rights of the Child being central to the design and implementation of such curricula. In addition, the Integrated Framework of Action on Education for Peace, Human Rights and Democracy and the 1997 CARICOM Declaration of the Ideal Caribbean Person should be used as guidelines for designing and renewing such curricula.
- Education for cultural diversity should include the teaching of modern languages and the study of culture. This latter should comprise aspects such as multiculturalism, inter-culturalism, uniqueness of cultures, trans-culturality, wider identities—human identity. The study of culture will assist in identity formation, as well as promoting international understanding. Ongoing co-operative meetings and cross-cultural exchanges for both teacher and pupils will facilitate such learning.
- Teacher preparation must be seen as key to effective citizenship education. The teacher education curriculum should include a component on emotional/affective learning (from both the teacher's and the student's perspective), with teachers also trained in methods for mediation. The most effective teacher education is felt to be in-service and on-site (school-based). Teachers must be trained how to adopt an interdisciplinary approach to values education.

- Examples of appropriate curricula already designed, such as the Guyana human rights education curriculum and Haiti's curriculum for citizenship education, should be adapted for schools and teacher training colleges in the other Caribbean countries and piloted on a regional basis. It was proposed that CARNEID and the IBE assist in such a project.

Proposals for Furthering the Seminar Initiative

- It was recommended that countries that had already developed explicit curricular programmes related to the issues discussed, should develop these further and establish actions which enable their implementation. Countries that have not yet developed such programmes were urged to include these values in an interdisciplinary manner across the entire curriculum. It was suggested that the IBE and CARNEID develop/disseminate to the participant countries sample curricula related to the themes of the seminar.
- Participants committed themselves to urging their Ministers of Education to give support to these proposals and to incorporate them into on-going education policy. They would attempt to garner support from Ministers of Education for renovation of the curriculum to encompass values for citizenship education based on the 1997 Declaration of the Ideal Caribbean Person.
- Participants should consolidate professional links through on-going regional meetings/seminars and networking to share experiences and develop joint projects. Attempts should be made build and strengthen networking based on contacts made at the seminar and those already existing. IBE and CARNEID should be focal points in such a process. This would allow for the exchange of information on good practice, and for sharing of other resources for staff and programme development. It was also proposed to make greater use of the new

technologies to obtain and share information. Networking should also be developed/strengthened with other institutions, such as the University of the West Indies School of Education, teachers unions and principals' associations.

- Countries proposed to report to the IBE, on an annual basis, progress made nationally and regionally in education for citizenship.
- It was agreed that, as part of the follow-up to the seminar, participants will serve as the contact persons for the IBE and CARNEID with regard to national curricular activities in citizenship education and related themes.

Annex: Educational Diagnosis

Margarita Silvestre Oramas

Introduction

The quality of education is revealed not only in the rates of enrolment and continuation of students in schooling, but also in the quality of the teaching of institutions, in rates of promotion and the marks attained by students, in indicators of repetition and dropout and is associated with school failure. This latter is in turn linked to educational problems on the one hand, and socio-economic problems on the other.

While these problems are at the forefront of the agenda today and exist in all countries, they are manifested quite differently from country to country. A look at these indicators reveals some interesting data, as in Table 1.

Differences can be seen first of all in magnitude: in some areas they are quite sharp and cover large populations, whereas in others the population affected is a minority. But in all cases they tend to be associated with limitations in the level of development attained by the group of countries, or country, of the population group or the family in question.

A study conducted by INEI (Peru) shows a favourable progression of schooling rates from 1949 to 1993, particularly in the age group 6-14, which reaches 86 per cent. In the age of 15 to 19, it rose from 17 per cent in 1940 to 56 per cent in 1981 and then falls to 52 per cent in 1993. Growth in the 6-14 age group shows that roughly 15 per cent of the group dropped out of school or did not attend. Nevertheless, during the second half of the twentieth century substantial progress was made in the schooling of the 6-14 age group.

Table 1. Estimation of net rates of matriculation and children of primary school age and out-of-school children in 1995.

	Coverage		Net rates of Matriculation	Schooling rates/thousands	Apparent rate of survival until 5th grade	Estimation of repeaters at 1995
	No. of Countries	School-age population %	Total %	Total	% (no. of countries)	As % of matriculated Students of all Grades
World total	126	82	87,1	84,331		
More developed region	21	95	99.5	275	99(17)	
Latin America/ Caribbean	26	99	90,4	7,112	67(17)	13

Source: *Oportunidades perdidas: cuando la escuela no cumple su misión y la repetición en la enseñanza primaria,* Part II, pages 11, 13, 17. París, UNESCO, 1998. (Educatión para todos, situación y tendencias, vol. 4.)

Similar indicators can be seen in this age group in other countries of the region. However, they are considerably lower in underprivileged areas, such as the rural sector and in schools for indigenous populations. In these areas the underprivileged may leave school without knowing how to read or write, and their children in turn, to a certain extent, go down the same path.

In analysing the issue of academic success, it can be seen that school drop-out rates are still very high between first and second grade, and in many countries between first and fourth grade, though degrees of repetition vary among countries and within the same country. Most Latin American and Caribbean countries conform to this type of behaviour.

Studies conducted on the effect of repetition reveal a diversity of problems. Shepard and Lee-Smith reach the following conclusion: 'Contrary to popular beliefs, repeating a grade does not help students gain ground academically and has a negative impact on social adjustment and self-esteem.'[1] An infinite amount of evidence could be cited concerning this problem. In one way or another, and although teachers would like to convince students and parents that it is a process that favours students in the long term, the negative effect of repetition is quite evident.

The relationship between repetition and drop-out rates has been studied extensively. 'A report by the Carnegie Council on Adolescent Development estimated that a single grade retention increases the likelihood of drop out between 40% and 50%. A second one raises the risk to 90%.'[2] The problem of repetition is purely educational; it is decided in the school and is resolved or not resolved there.

The problem is more acute and is manifested in a high percentage of *non repeaters,* whose problem did not appear to be serious: they move on automatically to the next course without having mastered the basics, such as fourth graders who are still unable to read syllables and cannot write. What grade are they in? What indicators can reveal this sort of problem? Is the problem the quality of the school? This educational problem has a major effect on the learning process and is associated with different factors.

A study by researchers in thirteen European Union countries, directed by the University of Barcelona, reveals that: 'In Europe, school failure is a problem that has persisted in spite of many years of improvement. It has fallen, but the 15 per cent of students that suffer from it face a worse situation than they used to. A higher proportion of children from ethnic minorities or families with a low level of education are affected by failure.'[3]

Different studies have revealed the relationship between the education of parents and the learning results of children. A study of Cuban children shows the significant influence which the degree of schooling attained by the mother has on their learning, particularly at the age of 7 and after the age of 11.[4] Also, children of working mothers obtain better results than those of unemployed mothers. In an analysis of the factors that influence educational quality, Schmelkes links the extent of the mother's education with school failure. 'Children of fathers, and above all mothers, with more education advance with more regularity in the system and show more regular attendance records. It has been said that the mother's schooling has an immunological effect on scholl failure.'[5]

Other studies disclose the role of different factors in learning achievement. For example, the First Meeting of Mercedarian Schools of Spain, in 1999, analysed school failure and pointed to the magnitude of the phenomenon in concluding that 'one-third of the students of ESO fail or drop out without obtaining a basic school diploma' and also stressed that 'the term failure is inappropriate, for in addition to the students themselves, responsibility lies with the government, professionals, such as ourselves, counsellors and parents.'[6]

The problem leads to the following question: 'Whey do students with normal learning potential fail in school?' In an analysis of causal factors, Salicioni draws attention to the issue of time which she analyses from different angles, emphasizing that 'there are ever more students who show an incapacity to learn at least one of the areas set by the curriculum in the time prescribed [...] On the whole they are students labelled by the time/rhythm variable of learning.'[7]

Studies conducted by LLECE[8] on these factors reveal the powerful effect of pedagogical factors including the belief on the part of teachers regarding the origin of students' problems, and other factors such as the family situation. The learning environment factor is highlighted as having the greatest effect.

In a study conducted by the ICCP, Cuba, on the progress of students through primary school,[9] it was shown that most underachieving children were mature in their behaviour and their capacity for work was above their school performance. Their teachers, however, were unsuccessful in identifying the more dynamic from the more static students, their analysis was insufficient, their teaching was ineffective, as was their control over the progress of learning. It was also shown that 75 per cent of students' problems originated between the first and fourth grades, and half between first and second grades. Moreover, when analysing in depth the learning of first-grade children, the influence of preparation for school entry[10] became evident in their educational results in primary school and particularly in the first grade.

PAREIB's Diagnostic Study for Improving the Quality of Education[11] revealed the tendency of teachers to explain students' learning problems by referring to causes external to the teacher, the teachers' inability to predict students probable results in tests of knowledge and their inability to foresee possible transformations in their work or in students' results.

The actions undertaken by PAREIB in San Luis Potosí, Mexico, to raise the quality of basic education from the first to the fourth grades showed the effects of teachers' work in rural areas, in a situation where an in-depth diagnosis of the students and related factors and in-service professional development had taken place, with a focus on a methodological approach to problems in the learning of mathematics and Spanish.

The data presented shows the need to guide the learning process in terms of knowledge of the factors that govern its effectiveness, on the basis of a comprehensive diagnosis of the diverse factors which influence the learning process, and in particular a comprehensive diagnosis of students with a specific focus on an in-depth diagnosis of learning.

Brief Considerations on Pedagogical Diagnosis

Studies on pedagogical practice and its enhancement and the effect of factors related to educational quality confirm that pedagogical diagnosis is an indispensable requisite for improving education in the classroom, the school and in an area, region or country. In this sense, several levels could be taken into account:

- Diagnosis of a student;
- Diagnosis of the educational institution—micro-diagnosis;
- Diagnosis of the area, school region, municipality, state—macro-diagnosis.

The diagnosis must be comprehensive, both in dealing with the diverse factors that are key to the success of education, and in assessing the student, with regard to the totality of his/her personality; and it must also identify relations between success and these factors.

Diagnosis of the Student

Pedagogical approaches must be based on what the student knows and is able to do, what the nature of his/her intellectual development is, how he/she thinks, acts, his/her interests, aspirations, emotional problems, so that teaching can be aimed at the instruction, development and education of the student, taking into account the interaction of different aspects of his/her personality, whose effect must be seen holistically.

Obtaining in-depth knowledge of what a student thinks of school, of his/her family, of social values, of school subjects, of relations with other students, teachers, family members are all elements that can yield important information to the teacher (Figure 1).

Assessing the student becomes a need, given the close links and interdependence between cognitive, emotional, motivational and volitional factors. In students' learning the following must be taken into account:

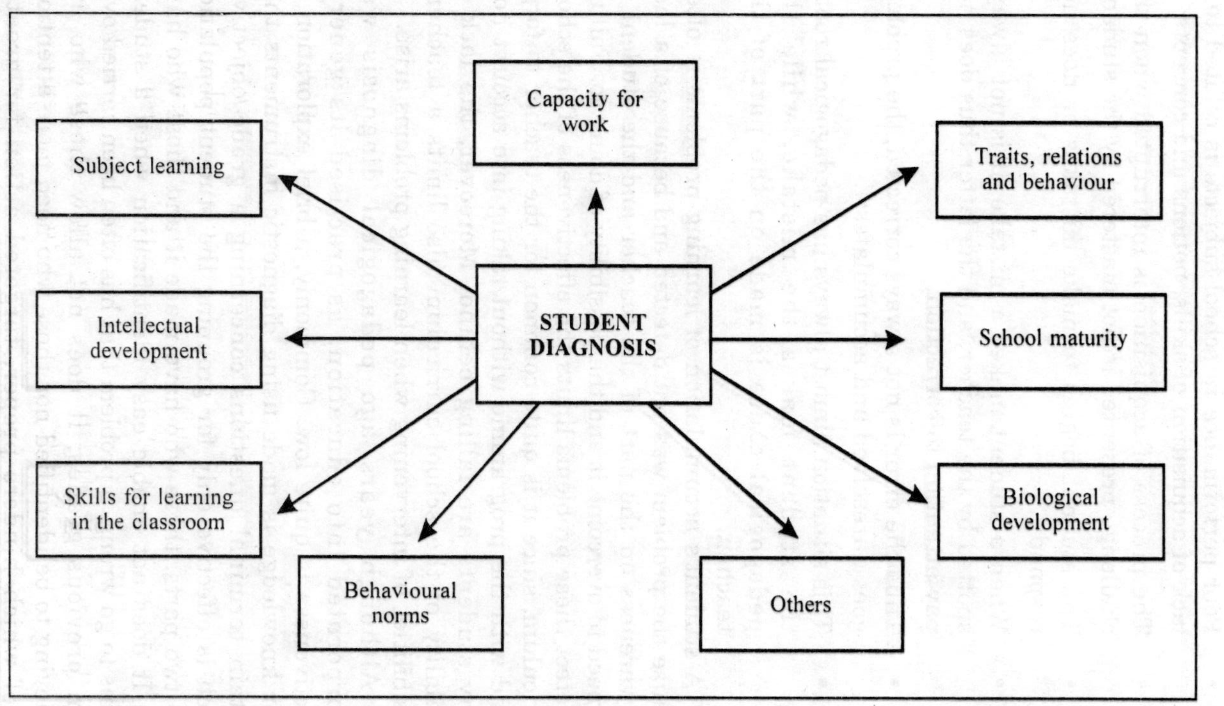

Figure 1. Diagnosis of the student

- Poor performance in school subjects is related to a lack of acquisition of skills, notions and concepts;
- The process of acquisition is interrupted when the challenge presented is not mastered by the student;
- The student begins to make mistakes or does not respond;
- When a student makes a mistake, it is not always spotted by the teacher, and the latter thus does not pay attention to correction;
- Thus the error is not always corrected, the problem goes unresolved and accumulates;
- This situation almost always has pedagogical roots: the student makes the mistake, while the pedagogical cause is made on the part of the teacher.

A student's accumulation of learning problems is often because the problem was not detected and because of a lack of awareness on the part of the teacher and the student of the need to overcome it and the possibility of doing so. Failure to detect these problems limits the effectiveness of the school curriculum, since it is quite common for the teacher to forge ahead with the programme without taking into account how many students are falling behind. Moreover, the lack of flexibility of the school curriculum also limits a teacher's possibilities of intervening when learning problems arise.

Although years ago pedagogical diagnosis was incorporated into education, as practised its general effectiveness is quite low. Commonly, a brief exploration of prior knowledge is made using diagnostic instruments that contain terminal questions concerning a grade objective, which is effective only for grouping the student population into two parts: those who have made it and those who have not. It does not enable easy identification when a student begins to go wrong, a problem that has often been carried over from previous grades; it does not allow those who are achieving to be identified nor those who need more attention, all of which hinders proper, targeted action for greater success.

Work cannot be conducted blindly, with insufficient information on the students' preparation and behaviour. A fine-tuned analysis is called for, which in the search for successful teaching/learning strategies, enables identification of what a student can do on his/her own, and where he/she begins to make mistakes in the acquisition of basic knowledge, particularly in mathematics and Spanish. This knowledge is needed to prevent any accumulation of difficulties.

In a learning diagnosis, the technique of analysis testing by elements of knowledge is used which through analysing the difficulty which the student is presently experiencing, enables the student's level of learning in the specific area of knowledge to be determined, identifying where the learning difficulty began, even if mastering this area of learning had been an objective of earlier grades. The diagnosis seeks to reveal difficulties and potentialities upon which to outline strategies that respond to the needs identified.

In the process of formation of knowledge or acquisition of a skill, a gradual movement occurs from the simplest level to more complex ones. Attempting to enter this process without knowing the level achieved by the student would be a mistake: for example, without the background required, the student will be unable to absorb knowledge structured at higher levels of difficulty, or make use of a supposedly acquired skill, for the performance of a task or the acquisition of another skill.[12]

However, limited knowledge of the real level of achievement of each student affects not only the immediate work concerning the individual differences between students, but it also limits the possibilities of achieving a more homogenous group in terms of their prior knowledge, which is a necessary condition for enhancing the teacher's possibilities of success with the group and guiding its development towards more demanding levels.

Let us take the opposite case, i.e. a group of students in a classroom among whom there are substantial differences of achievement in the acquisition of basic knowledge in a subject area: how many complications can arise?

The search begins by trying to establish a group's initial homogeneity in relation to a basic common level, a minimum for the broad majority, in terms of the grade they are in. This might be considered as a necessary condition for raising the level of achievement in learning and strengthening diversity, a balance between homogeneity and heterogeneity of the group, or a levelling of the group. Attaining this will enable planning the most immediate goals for each student, offering the right help at the right time, favouring success, raising motivation, reducing low grades, decreasing the number of failing students and drop-out rates, and will move the group towards higher challenges.

Levelling the group in this way in relation to its background requires a fine-tuned diagnosis that enables determining the point at which the student has arrived in his/her learning, what difficulties have begun to emerge, and where. For example, if the aim is to acquire a procedure, it must be determined at up to which point the student can progress alone in the task, and of where problems begin.

There exists a relationship between different levels of demand, which a student cannot skip, there being a linkage between one piece of knowledge and another. When new levels of learning with respect to earlier knowledge are in question, it is impossible to break this link in the learning process. Thus, for example, if a student has not acquired *A*, he is not ready to absorb *C*, and even less so *N*. This is the reason why it is very important to establish the real level of the student in order to create the bases of efficient learning.

In preparing a diagnosis, the aim is to present the gradient of difficulties in decreasing order, so as to identify the point the student has reached on his own and where errors begin to arise. The recommendation is to use more than one exercise for the same difficulty so as to reduce the chances for occasional error owing to inattention, error due to lack of knowledge, or if the student is in a stage of acquisition where he answers correctly at times and incorrectly at other times.

Analysis testing by knowledge elements is a type of instrument that enables identification of those knowledge elements upon which a student gets blocked and cannot advance, where it is indispensable to offer the right help in acquiring the skills and concepts and to bring the teacher closer to exploring the student's areas of potential development. It is not uncommon for a class to have major differences in terms of mastery and use of knowledge, skills and the formation of set habits for the same contents taught by the same teacher and studied in the same textbooks.

Deficiencies in students' degree of readiness to begin a subject in a specific course, which are not responded to with proper methodological approaches, might explain poor results in the school year. The need to homogenize students in relation to a basic common starting point becomes a crucial condition for achieving the objectives of the subject in the given grade.

The ability of the educator to fully understand the learning problems of a group on the basis of a fine-tuned diagnosis facilitates decision-making regarding necessary curriculum adjustments and provides a way to achieve curriculum flexibility according to the students' real needs and possibilities in order to bring about effective learning.

The analysis of learning results, by means of analysis tests by knowledge elements, enables different levels of information to be obtained based on identification of the type of difficulty the student failed to overcome. The results of test analysis are supplemented by observation of classes and the review of notebooks. As an example, Figure 2 gives four levels of processing of information obtained, from the most general to the specific.

Tables 2, 3 and 4 give comparative results in two zones in first grade Spanish, showing the levels of analysis referred to above.

Table 5 shows that the achievements and difficulties of *each student* were perceived, by *elements of knowledge,* which enables identification of the type of problems of each and outlining of strategies for specialized attention and work with the group.

To the learning diagnosis, other elements are added related to how the student thinks about him/herself, his/her school, family, community, country, different social problems, his/her motivations and interests, aspirations, relationships with classmates, among others. In like manner, it is at times

Table 2. General results for subject

General evaluation of student in first-grade Spanish	High	Average	Low	Critical
Zone X	26 (22.6%)	16 (13.9%)	17 (14.8%)	56 (48.7%)
Zone Y	3 (3.8%)	15 (19.2%)	10 (12.8%)	50 (64.1%)
Zone ...				
Total	71	69	48	354
Total percentage	13.1%	12.7%	8.9%	65.3%

Table 3. Results for individual components of subject

Percentage of correct elements of knowledge of Spanish	Writing	Reading	Speaking	Total Spanish	General evaluation
School Zone X	30.4%	41.0%	74.0%	48.5%	Low
School Zone Y	11.5%	30.8%	47.0%	29.7%	Critical
School Zone...					

Table 4. Breakdown of one component: reading

Specific insufficiencies	Silent reading	Clarity and relevance to subject
Zone X	66.7% (one-third considered word-by-word readers)	50.1% (roughly two-fifths did not express ideas clearly and one-fourth did not adjust to situation)
Zone Y	59.5% (nearly one-third considered word-by-word readers)	73.3% (roughly three-fourths did not express ideas clearly, nor adjustment to the situation)

necessary to go into depth concerning developmental aspects, such as school maturity, work capacity, level of development of thinking, among others.

Instruments have been designed for this, and simple methods that can be used by the teacher to obtain part of the basic information that will assist in designing strategies

Table 5. A chart to plot the achievements and difficulties of each student by knowledge elements

Student				Elements of correct reading						
Code	Name	Age	Sex	Changes	Omissions	Accentuation	Inversions	Repetitions	Reverses	Additions
1	Bernadina	10	F							
2	Leocadio	11	M							
3	Benjamin	11	M							
4	Etc.									

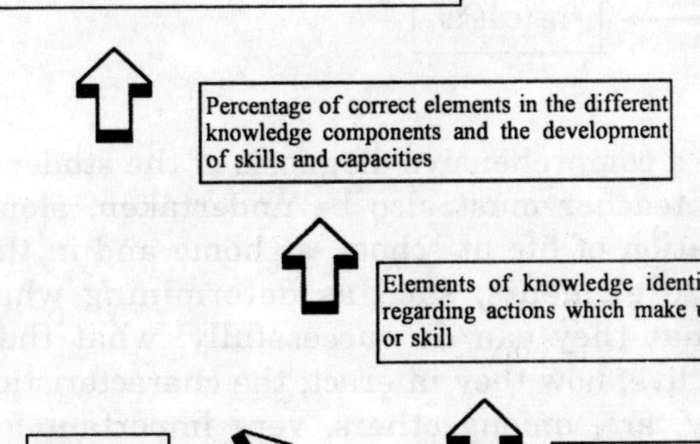

Figure 2. Four levels of information.

for pedagogical work for specialized attention in accordance with students' needs. Systematic observation, exchange of viewpoints, analysis of dilemmas are ways of achieving better understanding of students.

Diagnosis of Educational Institutions

A comprehensive diagnosis of educational institutions includes teachers. students as well as the family and community, thus enabling an integrated understanding of the main phenomena that are involved in the educational process.

In comprehensive diagnostic studies aimed at improving a school, the student is considered the centre of the problem to be investigated, and other variables are explored in relationship to him/her.

Figure 3. The student at the centre of the problem being investigated.

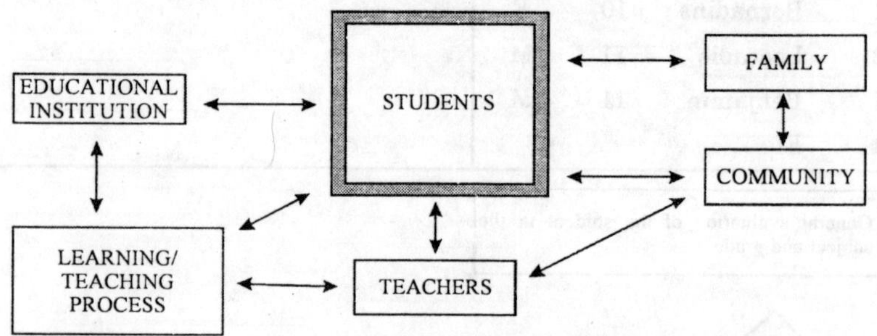

Together with a comprehensive diagnosis of the student, a diagnosis of the teacher must also be undertaken, along with a characterization of life at school, at home and in the community. Diverse elements, such as determining what students know, what they can do successfully, what they aspire to, how they live, how they interact, the characteristics of their community, are, among others, very important for properly guiding the learning/teaching process, the life of the school, relationships and attention to the family and orientation for supporting potentialities in the community, as well as orienting efforts to counter the negative effects of the surroundings in which the school is located and where students live.

The search for the teacher's role in the origin of learning problems and their solution, identifying the real level of student's achievement, the specific needs of each and the true potentialities of the family, the climate and learning style, the climate of the institution, in terms of the relationship between its components and the style of leadership, are, among others, decisive factors that a diagnosis must identify; they constitute

the indispensable starting point of strategies for transformation. Figure 4 depicts these ideas in a graphic form and includes the relationship between the institutional

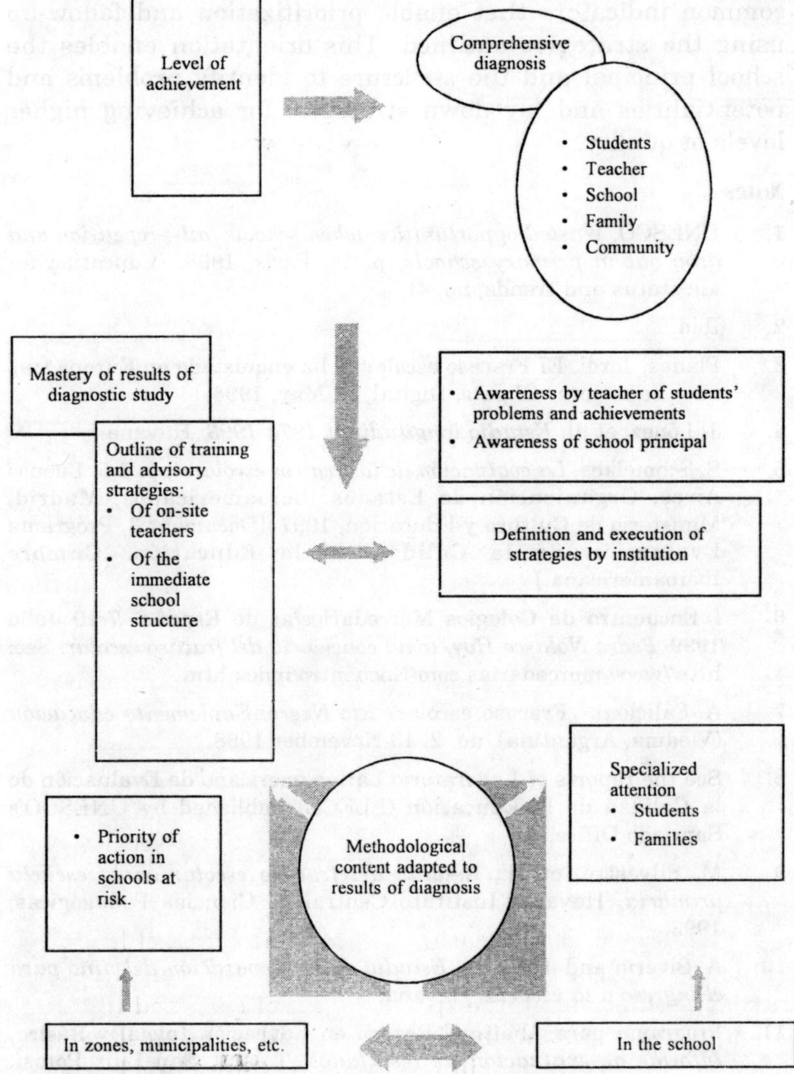

Figure 4. The relationship of different factors in the origin of learning problems.

diagnosis and the eventual integration of the diagnosis within a zone or municipality.

Note should be taken of the identification of 'at risk' schools as a result of the diagnosis made, on the basis of common indicators that enable prioritization and follow-up using the strategies outlined. This orientation enables the school principal and the structure to identify problems and potentialities and lay down strategies for achieving higher levels of quality.

Notes

1. UNESCO. *Wasted opportunities: when schools fail—repetition and drop out in primary schools,* p. 16. Paris, 1998. (Education for all: status and trends, no. 4)
2. Ibid.
3. Planas, Jordi. EI Fracaso escolar se ha enquistado en Europa tras años de mejora. *El país*. Digital, 12 May, 1998.
4. J. López, et al. *Estudio longitudinal 1973-1993.* Havana.
5. S. Schmelkes, *La evaluación de los centros escolares,* p. 4-5, Buenos Aires, Organización de Estados Iberoamericanos; Madrid, Ministerio de Cultura y Educación, 1997. [Document 3, Programa Evaluación de la Calidad de la Educación. Cumbre Iberoamericana.]
6. I Encuentro de Colegios Mercedarios/as de España, 7-10 Julio 1999. *Pedro Nolasco-Hoy, toma conciencia del fracaso escolar.* See: http//www.mercedarias.com/Encuentro/index.htm
7. A. Salicioni, ¿Fracaso escolar? *Rio Negro: Suplemento educación* (Viedma, Argentina), no. 2, 13 November 1998.
8. See the reports of Laboratorio Latinoamericano de Evaluación de la Calidad de la Educación (LLECE) published by UNESCO's Santiago Office.
9. M. Silvestre, et al., *Estudio del fracaso escolar en la escuela primaria,* Havana, Instituto Central de Ciencias Pedagógicas, 1993.
10. A. Siverio and J. López, *Estudio de la preparación del niño para el ingreso a la escuela,* Havana,
11. Programa para Abatir el Rezago en Educación Inicial y Básica, *Informe de evaluación de resultados,* Toluca, San Luis Potosí, Mexico, 2000.
12. M. Silvestre y R. Rico. *Proceso de enseñanza aprendizaje.* Havana.

Annex: Quality and Equity in Education: Present Challenges and Perspectives in Modern Societies

Héctor Valdés Veloz

Introduction

In the 1990s major reforms in education were carried out in most Latin American countries. Efforts at educational development did not centre only on achieving greater access to schooling on the part of an increasing school-age population—though even in quantity success has not been total—but the concern for quality has also assumed greater importance year after year. The goal now is higher quality education with equity.

However, we must analyse the world context in which our society has set itself such lofty and desirable aims. Throughout the world there are both old and new problems that constitute veritable social catastrophes. Drug addiction, violence, poverty and AIDS, to name a few, are some of these plagues.

Then, we must wonder: can these problems be solved without the human race fully developing its capacity for thought?

If we consider thought to be the creation of information by means of cognitive processes, i.e. the generation of information on the basis of available information through the use of mental action, then there is no doubt that in order to find solutions to the social evils mentioned, we need an education that ensures the full development of the thinking capacities of our children, adolescents and youth.

At the same time, we must educate new generations to aim for the most noble and desirable sentiments, based on the assimilation of our most deeply held moral values. Hence the need for education of greater quality and equity.

Quality of Education

If we try to specify what we mean by quality, we encounter the following definition:

> *The quality of something refers to one or more properties of that thing that enable its perception as equal, better or worse than other examples of the same type. As an essentially evaluative, concept, determining the quality of something demands familiarity with its nature, and an expression of it in such a manner so as to render it capable of comparison.*[1]

A detailed analysis of the literature available in Cuba and in ten other countries on the treatment given to the concept 'quality in education', where we have found more than fifty attempts to define it, leads us to the conclusion that there are three clearly distinct general tendencies: *one seeks to discuss and define it in a constituent or conceptual form, i.e. seeks to define it theoretically; the second seeks to define it operationally; and the third avoids defining it.* Obviously, these tendencies are determined by the diverse philosophical, pedagogical, psychological and sociological ideas of the authors studied.

What follows is a brief analysis of each of these tendencies grounded in concrete examples.

First Tendency: Discussion and definition in a constitutive or conceptual form.

The Argentine author Pedro Lafourcade claims that:

> *An education of quality can mean one that enables mastery of a neutral knowledge which translates into the acquisition of scientific or literary culture, one which develops the greatest capacity for generating wealth or converts someone into the best possible human resource for contributing to the production process; or one that encourages a sufficiently critical spirit and strengthens the commitment to transform a social reality that is alienated by a power structure benefitting only a few.*[2]

The author attempts to provide a theoretical definition of quality in education. Yet in our view, he commits the error of trying to give an adjectival character to quality when he speaks of 'a quality education', assuming the existence of another education 'of no quality'. This is a grave philosophical error, for the quality of an object, in this case education, is intertwined with the entire object, completely encompassing it, and is inseparable from it. The concept of quality is linked to the very being of the object, which, being the same, cannot lose its quality.

Therefore, all education has a certain quality; although this may be higher or lower to the extent that its characteristics fulfil (or otherwise) the philosophical, pedagogical, psychological and sociological paradigms that predominate in a given society.

Moreover, for our society, the formation of a useful 'human resource' is not the essential purpose of education; but rather that each man and woman fully develops in accordance with his/her own potentialities, being able and prepared to place him/herself at the service of society on the basis of the universal and national values which he/she believes in. Furthermore, education must not only provide mastery of 'knowledge' but also of a 'know-how' and of a 'knowing-how-to-be. This last element is determined by a set of personality qualities that cannot be reduced to simply having a certain critical spirit.

Within this first tendency, we would note the existence of several sub-tendencies, the main one including 'process-centred definitions versus product-centred ones'.

Most of the theoretical definitions we have seen link quality to results. Education understood as a simple revision of final products results in a loss of vision of the school as an ecosystem that enables explanation and meaning to be given to the overall operations and processes by which learning occurs.

We would *prefer to understand quality of education as a tendency, a journey, as a process of continuous construction and improvement of products.*

Each of the above tendencies sheds light on essential aspects of the work of educators and the vital elements in the education system, such as the school and the curriculum.

Second Tendency: Defining quality operationally

The Mexican author Sylvia Schmelkes claims that in countries, such as those of Latin America where universal education is not yet a reality, it is important to point out that quality in this sense is understood to be a complex concept that includes at least the following components:

- *Relevance:* To be of quality, an education system must be able to satisfy present and future demand with learning that is relevant to the present and future lives of those being educated, as well as the present and future needs of the society in which the educated live. The relevance of objectives and educational achievement become the essential component of this way of understanding quality in education, chiefly because it is closely related to the capacity to ensure coverage and continuation of students in the education system.
- *Effectiveness:* This should be understood as the capacity of the basic education system to meet its objectives—presupposing that they are relevant—for all students who theoretically should pass through a specific level, in a projected time frame. The closer an education system comes to reaching this aim, the more effective it will be. The concept includes coverage, continuous enrolment, promotion and real learning.
- *Equity:* A basic education system—until completion of the level understood as compulsory for the entire population at a certain age—is of quality if it recognizes that different types of students come into the system from different starting points. It therefore offers differential support to ensure that educational objectives are met—in an equitable manner—for all. Equity means giving more attention and support to those who need it, and is reflected in effectiveness.
- *Efficiency:* A system is of greater quality to the extent that, in comparison with others, it achieves

results that are similar, though with fewer resources.[3]

This author commits the same error as the previous one commented upon regarding the use of the expression 'education of quality'. In our opinion, this definition is not philosophically appropriate. Moreover, on the basis of an operational concept of quality in education, without it being grounded in a theoretical definition, we lose the link between theory and practice, leaving many essential questions unanswered. For example, when can way say that a given learning process, objective or achievement is relevant?

Third Tendency: Avoiding a definition

In their book *Claves para una educación de calidad* [Keys to quality education], the Chilean authors Juan Casassus and Violeta Arencibia claim that: 'Quality in education is one of those concepts that is significant, that mobilizes and is charged with emotional force that is broadly employed in society. Its power lies in its very ambiguity'.[4]

From a general philosophical and logical point of view, we consider this position to be inadequate to the task of finding the essence of this complex object, i.e. quality in education (QE). Defining, describing, exemplifying, dividing, limiting and making known a concept are logical operations that must be performed in order to gain in-depth knowledge of it, and it is unquestionable that without sufficient clarity concerning the essence of this concept, little can be done to design a proper system for evaluating it.

What position do we take then, in which tendency do we include ourselves?

Without a doubt, all efforts to determine what QE is are valid, for they help in pinpointing its essence. Nevertheless, we begin from the principle that, whereas the paths towards knowing an object are infinite, certain paths aid in this task and others obstruct it.

As we are unsatisfied by the theoretical definitions found in the literature consulted, we have articulated our own, which is as follows:

> Quality of education refers to the characteristics of the process and the results of the formation of the human being, where this

> process and results are socially and historically conditioned; they assume a concrete meaning through the purposes and objectives of education, established for a specific society and which is measured by the distance between these objectives and the results actually achieved.

This definition requires a clear knowledge of the ongoing developmental objectives for students in accordance with the relevant grades and levels of learning, which means that their formulation must encompass the cognitive, behavioural and emotional spheres of the learners' personality development.

Equity in Education

Regarding the important subject of equity in education, we believe that two essential ideas must be emphasized as a point of departure, namely:

- Differences that arise in how individuals make use of their learning efforts are more acceptable than if conditions of identity (gender, race, religion, nationality, region of birth, etc.) were to determine the course and destiny of any social group.
- The legitimacy of democracy rests on the equality of opportunities for all people.

Genuine equality of educational opportunities is a necessary condition for Latin American societies to achieve the democratic goal of equality of social opportunities. The struggle to achieve greater equality of opportunities in our region has gone through the following phases:

First (1960s-70s): Equality of opportunities as expansion in access to educational services.

Lost decade (1980s): Obsession with management and financing. Insufficient attention paid to increasing educational equity.

Second phase (beginning of 1990s): Emergence of compensatory policies and rhetoric of positive discrimination.

Current phase: Struggle to implement affirmative action and positive discrimination.

But the fact remains that today there are still substantial signs of inequity in the educational services provided. The following should suffice as examples:

- *Inequity in access:* The utopia of quantity or universal coverage is not yet a reality: at present there are 42 million illiterate people in Latin America.
- *Inequity in services provided by existing educational institutions:* We need only note that considerable gaps exist, as reported by countries' quality measurement systems, in terms of such comparisons as urban-rural, private/public, boy/girl, etc.

Present State of Quality and Equity in Education in Latin America

For the past five years, UNESCO has been working to assess the quality of education in Latin American countries. Hence, on 10 November 1994, in Mexico City, the Latin American Laboratory of Assessing Quality in Education (LLECE) was founded, with the participation of ten Latin American countries and the co-ordination of the Regional Office of UNESCO for Latin America and the Caribbean (OREALC).

In 1995, another four countries joined, among them Cuba, and the remaining countries in the region have requested entry. Today, the following countries belong to LLECE: Argentina, Bolivia, Brazil, Chile, Colombia, Costa Rica, Cuba, Dominican Republic, Guatemala, Honduras, Mexico, Paraguay, Peru and Venezuela.

The Laboratory was set up in a regional framework of co-ordination between Latin American countries in the field of educational evaluation and as a technical backup in human resources and databases for member countries. It also functions as a forum of technical/political discussion on learning and the variables that affect it, and as a source of information.

The objectives of the Laboratory consist of creating regional standards, establishing a system for gathering and disseminating information about these standards, organizing a research programme on the variables related to the quality of basic education and reinforcing the technical expertise of ministries of education in the field of evaluating educational quality. It also plans to undertake comparative studies on the quality of education in Spanish and mathematics, and to carry out international studies on special areas such as evaluation linked to transversal, multi-cultural and social competence objectives.

Between September 1995 and May 1996, the organization, supported by specialists in each country, designed its First International Comparative Study, and conceptualized and validated the instruments to be used in it.

From May to December 1997, tests were conducted in mathematics and Spanish in third and fourth grades to an approximate sample of 4,000 students in 100 randomly selected schools in each of the participating countries. At the same time, questionnaires were given to students' parents or guardians, to school principals and teachers.

A stratified sample was made for the study based on two criteria, one main and another special. The first or main criterion was determined by the number of inhabitants of the town where the school was located, and the second or special one, by the type of management or dependence of the school. Implementation of these criteria produced the following result: main strata (metropolitan cities, urban and rural areas), and special strata (public and private).

To place in context the theoretical-conceptual and methodological framework used to conduct the study, the five fundamental questions that underpinned it must be asked. These questions, which deal with the quality and educational level of students in the region's countries, and the influence of factors related to school performance, are as follows:

1. What do students learn?
2. At what level did students learn Spanish and mathematics?
3. What skills have they developed in relation to what they have learned?
4. When does learning take place?
5. Under what conditions does learning take place?

An effort was made to identify the specific learning areas that third- and fourth-grade students are taught in primary school in Spanish and mathematics. In the case of Spanish, an assessment was made of learning attained in: reading comprehension, meta-linguistic practice and text composition. In mathematics these were numeration, working with common numbers, common fractions, geometry and measuring. All these goals aimed at skill development.

Results in Spanish and mathematics were identified according to previously defined scales of performance in the two subjects.

A central interest of the study was factors that directly or indirectly influence the learning process. The fact is that students learn according to the opportunities they are provided with. These opportunities to gain access to learning, in turn, are conditioned by a combination of factors that belong to different areas (institutional management, the family's commitment to education, school management, school curriculum, pedagogical management and student commitment, among others).

The answer to the fifth question permitted the level of explanation to be arrived at. Thus, not only is a description of the student's learning process available, but substantial explanations were also obtained, thereby enabling a definition of the most suitable spheres for targeting new educational policies in the countries of the region.

To gain answers to the questions listed above, a hypothetical framework was prepared, which was both the result of the Laboratory's Initial Conceptual Model and of empirical data revealed by research in countries in Latin America and other parts of the world.

Below are the main findings of the study.

Results by Performance Levels

Spanish

Analysis of the test yielded three performance levels in Spanish, namely:

- *Performance level 1: Literal reading—primary level*

  Literal reading—primary level is understood as the semiotic reconstruction of a text superficially.

Questions at this level deal mainly with recognition of immediate explicit structures. Thus, questions require the reader to identify the characters in a story, identify key segments in events, find explicitly stated relationships between sentences, etc.

- *Performance level 2: Literal reading as paraphrase*

  This level involves a greater degree of complexity, as the point is not to identify explicit fragments of the text but to achieve a semantic understanding of the literal meaning of it. The idea, then, is to 'say' the text in other words, without as yet making an in-depth interpretation of it.

- *Performance level 3: Inferential reading*

  At this level, the reader fills in the blank spaces in the text, identifying the premises upon which it is structured, linking together micro- and macro-textual propositions, and identifying the different forms of involvement, events, timing, space, inclusion and exclusion that comprise it.

We now present the results in terms of students' percentages at each performance level. The percentages considered acceptable for each are: Level 1, 90%; Level 2, 75% and Level 3, 50%. Differences are significant whenever they reach 6% or more.

It would be ideal for a student to be able to give perfect answers to every question, which means a 100% score at every level. As this, in fact, will not be the case and more realistic goals are needed, 60% was set as the score for a satisfactory performance. That is, a student is required to answer correctly 60% of the questions or more to be considered to have successfully completed a level.

Mathematics

- *Performance level 1: Recognition and use of basic mathematical elements and relationships*

  This level includes students who are able to deal with exercises that require knowing how to read and write numbers and identify ordinal relationships in

Table 1. Results in Spanish in region as a whole.

Level	% of students per strata				
	Public	Private	Metropolis	Urban	Rural
1	90.47	93.96	93.15	90.83	82.48
2	64.91	75.06	75.84	64.45	48.93
3	44.52	54.56	54.16	44.63	31.81
What should be expected?					
1	90% of students				
2	75% of students				
3	50% of students				

the decimal system, recognize plain figures and use some common algorithms. That is, this level addresses those contents and skills that serve as the basis for mathematical comprehension.

- *Performance level 2: Recognition and use of simple mathematical structures*

  This level represents the first step in the development of skills in applying mathematical structures as tools for solving problems. Students here are capable of recognizing patterns, seeing regularities and performing operations in non-conventional situations. That is, they can handle simple mathematical structures that underlie everyday situations solvable by mathematics

- *Performance level 3: Recognition and use of complex mathematical structures*

  Here students are able to recognize complex mathematical structures that underlie mathematical situations or everyday situations solvable by mathematics. This enables them to deal with common classroom exercises, situations that underlie simple and complex addition and multiplication structures that demand both common and uncommon algorithms to be solved. Moreover, this recognition of complex structures enables them to deal with problems that involve recognition of the structure of the decimal system and handling of positional value to establish equivalencies.

Furthermore, problems that can be dealt with by students at this level do not necessarily involve the use of strategies, procedures and usual algorithms but instead enable the use of non-routine strategies, reasoning and plans that call on the student to bring to bear his/her mathematical knowledge and skill to find a solution.

Table 2 shows the results in mathematics by performance levels at a regional level.

Table 2. Results in mathematics in the region as a whole.

Level	% of students by strata				
	Public	Private	Metropolis	Urban	Rural
1	91.07	93.70	92.57	91.59	85.16
2	48.2	56.14	54.12	49.11	39.82
3	14.94	15.01	18.19	13.40	11.92
What should be expected?					
1	90% of students				
2	75% of students				
3	50% of students				

The results show that a long road lies ahead before we are able to realize our most cherished democratic dreams. In coming years, the achievement of this noble and necessary aim must be the focus of all our energy and talent.

Notes

1. P. Lafourcade, *Calidad de la educación,* p. 1, Buenos Aires, Dirección Nacional de Información, Ministerio de Educación y Justicia, 1988. [Difusión estadística y tecnología educativa.]
2. P. Lafourcade, op cit., p. 2.
3. S. Schmelkes, *La evaluación de los centros escolares,* p. 4-5, Buenos Aires, Organización de Estados Iberomericanos; Madrid, Ministerio de Cultura y Educación, 1997. [Document 3, Programa Evaluación de la Calidad de la Educación. Cumbre Iberoamericana.]

4. J. Casassus and V. Arencibia, *Claves para una educación de calidad,* p. 9, Buenos Aires, Kapelusz, 1997.

Bibliography

Casassus, J., et al. *Primer Estudio Internacional Comparativo sobre lenguaje, matemática y factores asociados en tercero y cuarto grados.* Santiago de Chile, OREALC/LLECE, 1998.

Casassus, J., et al. *Primer Estudio Internacional Comparativo sobre lenguaje, matemática y factores asociados para alumnos del tercer y cuarto grado de la educación básica, segundo informe.* Santiago de Chile, OREALC, 2000.

Valdés, H. *Concepciones teóricas acerca de un sistema para evaluar la calidad de la educación en la enseñanza primaria.* Thesis submitted for Masters Programme in Educational Research, Havana, 1995.

Annex: List of Participants

- **Anguilla**
  Rosena Brooks
  Education Officer (Curriculum)
  Teacher's Resource Center
  Department of Education
  The Valley

- **Antigua and Barbuda**

  Vincent Lewis
  Principal
  Glanville's School
  Sea Glans Community
  St Johns

  Ekua Richards
  Curriculum Development Officer
  Curriculum Development Office
  Ministry of Education, Culture and Technology
  Church Street
  St Johns

- **Aruba**

  Richardina Gricelda Garcia-Dijkhof
  Co-ordinator Curriculum Development
  Wayaca 33-A

- **Barbados**

  Wendy Griffith-Watson
  Chief Education Officer
  Ministry of Education
  Elsie Payne Complex
  Constitution Road
  St. Michael

- **Bahamas**
  Leanora Archer
  Deputy Director of Education
  P.O. Box N 3913
  Nassau, N.P.

- **Belize**

  David Eck
  # 5/15 U Street
  Belize City

- **British Virgin Islands**

  Quincy Lettsome
  Deputy Chief Education Officer/
  Curriculum Officer/Specialist
  Department of Education and Culture
  Central Administration Complex
  Road Town
  Tortola

  Prudence Mathavious
  Education Officer—Language
  Department of Education and Culture
  P.O. Box 72
  Road Town
  Tortola

- **Cuba**

  Paulina Blanco Caballería
  Jefe del Departamento de Ciencias Sociales
  Ministerio de Educación
  Calle 17 y O, Vedado
  La Habana

Lesbia Cánovas Fabelo
Directora del Instituto Central de Ciencias Pedagógicas
Ministerio de Educación
Calle 17, No. 1, Vedado
La Habana

- **Dominica**

Edward Lawrence
Education Officer/Curriculum Officer
Ministry of Education, Science and Technology
Curriculum Development and Materials Production Unit
Cornwall Street
Roseau

- **Dominican Republic**

Nurys Del Carmen González
Directora de Currículo
Secretaria de Estado de Educación
Ave. Maximo Gomez
Santo Domingo, D.N.

- **Grenada**

Jean Brizan
Curriculum Development Officer
Ministry of Education
Young Street
St. Georges

- **Guyana**

Merle Mendonca
Human Rights Education Co-ordinator
HRE Joint Programme
C/o Guyana Human Rights Centre
56B Hadfield Street + Austin Place
P.O. Box 10653
Georgetown

- **Haiti**

Pierre-Michel Laguerre
Assistant Chief Education Officer
Curriculum and Quality
Ministry of National Education, Youth and Sports
5, rue Dr. Audain
Port-au-Prince

- **Jamaica**

Phyllis Reynolds
Assistant Chief Education Officer
Core Curriculum Unit
Canewood Centre
Ministry of Education, Youth and Culture
37 Arnold Road
Kingston 5

- **Netherlands Antilles**

Muriël Canderlaria Meyer
Teacher of Pedagogy and Psychology
Co-ordinator of Practical Training
Akademia Pedagógico Kórsou
Scharlooweg z/n
Curacao

- **St Christopher and Nevis**

Eveth Bloice
Edgar T. Morris Primary School
Carty's Pasture
Tabernacle, St Kitts

Gweneth Hanley
Director, Curriculum Development Unit
Ministry of Education
P.O. Box 333, Lockart Street
Basseterre, St Kitts

- **St Lucia**

June Sifflet
Curriculum Specialist/Social Studies
Camdu
Ministry of Education
Castries

- **St Vincent and the Grenadines**

Sylvia Jack
Senior Education Officer (Curriculum)
Curriculum Development Unit
Ministry of Education

Tyrone Errol Burke
Principal
Park Hill Village
Part Hill P.O.

- **Suriname**

Anita Breeveld-Linger
Head, Department for Curriculum Development
Ministry of Education
Commewijnstraat 31
Paramaribo

- **Trinidad and Tobago**

Ival Melville-Myers
Curriculum Co-ordinator
Rudranath Capildeo Learning Resource Centre
Mc Bean, Couva

Ceronne Prevatt-Wiltshire
Curriculum Supervisor
Rudranath Capildeo Learning Resource Centre
Mc Bean, Couva

- **Resource Persons**

Linda Banks
Principal/Executive Director
Human Resource Development Consultant
Teacher Gloria Omololu Institute
P.O. Box 85
The Valley
Anguilla

Juan Esteban Belderrain
Coordinador Programa de Educación Media para Sectores Desfavorecidos
Calle 39 No 1056 e/18 y 19
Villa Elisa
C.P. 1894
Argentina

Pedro Jorge Pascual Betancourt
Especialista en Educación Especial
Ministerio de Educación
Calle 17 y O, Vedado
La Habana
Cuba

Simon Clarke
Special Advisor on Youth and Culture
Ministry of Education
P.O. Box 3007
Kingston 8
Jamaica

Erik Prinds
Viborg Amtsgymnasium
Skaldehøjvej 12
8800 Viborg
Denmark

Betty Reardon
Director, Peace Education Center
Teachers College # 171
Columbia University,
New York, NY 10027,
United States of America

Margarita Silvestre Oramas
Vice-Director
Central Institute of Pedagogical Sciences
Head of Scientific Area
Ministerio de Educación
Calle 17 esq. O, Vedado
Plaza de la Revolución
La Havana
Cuba

Héctor Valdés Veloz
Investigador
Instituto Central de Ciencias Pedagógicas
Ministerio de Educación
Calle 17 y O, Vedado
La Habana
Cuba

Winthrop Wiltshire
C2#4 La Reine Court,
Flagstaff, St James
Port of Spain
Trinidad and Tobago

- **Government of Cuba**

Calos Alfaro Alfaro
Director de Cooperación y Relaciones Internacionales
Ministerio de Educación
Calle 17 y O, Vedado
La Habana

Victoria Arencibia Sosa
Profesora Titular del Departamento de Matemática/Computación

Vice-rectora de Investigaciones y Posgrado
Universidad Pedagógica "Enrique José Varara"
Ministerio de Educación
Calle 17 y O, Vedado
La Habana

Julio Carranza Valdés
Oficial de Programa UNESCO
Oficina Regional de Cultura para América Latina y el Caribe (OREALC)
Calzada No. 551, Esq. A D, Vedado
La Havana

José Luis Hernández Baez
Investigador Titular
Instituto Central de Ciencias Pedagógicas
Ministerio de Educación
Calle 17, No. 1, Vedado
La Habana

Madelaine Masses Balvidares
Especialista Principal de Organismos Internacionales
Ministerio de Educación
Calle 17 y O, Vedado
La Habana

- **Unesco-International Bureau of Education**

Cecillia Braslavsky
Director
International Bureau of Education—UNESCO
P.O. Box 199
1211 Geneva 20
Switzerland

Isabel Byron
Assistant Programme Specialist
International Bureau of Education—UNESCO
P.O. Box 199
1211 Geneva 20
Switzerland

Claudia Harvey
Head, UNESCO Kingston Office
The Towers
25 Dominica Drive
Kingston 5
Saskia Rozemeijer
Associate Expert
International Bureau of Education—UNESCO
P.O. Box 199
1211 Geneva 20
Switzerland

Colleen Winter-Brathwaite
Co-ordinator Unesco Carneid
1st Floor, Coles Building
Lr Bay Street
Bridgetown
Barbados

Part 2

Management of Curriculum Change and Adaptation

* The Final Report of the Seminar held on the Management of Curriculum Change and Adaptation in the Gulf Region held in Musat, Oman. (c) International Bureau of Education

Introduction

The Seminar on the Management of Curriculum Change and Adaptation in the Gulf Region, organized by the International Bureau of Education (IBE) and the Omani National Commission for UNESCO, took place in Muscat from 17 to 21 February 2001. It was one of the series of seminars/workshops that the IBE has organized during 1998-2001 in different regions of the world in order to exchange views and experiences with the responsible experts and authorities in the field of curriculum development and educational contents.[1] The aim has been to draw attention to the necessity of a fundamental reform in school curricula to make them more adapted to the momentous and diversified challenges of the twenty-first century and, at the same time, to seek in a collaborative manner what type of response should be made to that necessity through concrete actions. Another objective was the intellectual preparation of the countries concerned for constructive participation in the forty-sixth session of the International Conference on Education, to be held in Geneva in September 2001.

As is indicated in this publication, five countries of the region participated in the seminar, in addition to the Arab Bureau of Education for the Gulf States and the UNESCO Bureau of Education in Qatar. A great number of specialists from these countries and several international experts contributed their valuable experience, which ensured the success of the seminar.

As the reader will appreciate, this publication contains not only a synthesis of all national reports, giving a clear picture of what is going on in each country of the region in terms of curriculum adaptation and change, but also reproduces the papers presented by the international experts from within and outside the IBE. The publication, therefore, should not be considered as geographically limited in scope, since it presents many observations about the trends taking place at the global level in the field of curriculum reform and its management.

The IBE grateful to all participants who accepted to take part in the seminar and to those whose contributions have made it possible to prepare this publication in time for the forty-sixth session of the International Conference on Education

Notes

1. The outcomes of these meetings have already been published and several IBE publications were presented at this seminar:
    - Aglo, J., ed. *Réforme des systèmes éducatifs et réformes curriculaires, 23-28 Octobre 2000, Libreville.* Genève, Suisse, BIE.
    - André, Y., Mouzoune, A., eds. *Rapport find du colloque sur le thème: apprendre à vivre ensemble grâce à l'ensignment de l'histoire et de la géographie, 12 juin 1998.* Genève, Suisse, BIE.
    - Braslavsky, C. *Secondary education curriculum in Latin America: new tendencies and changes—find report of the seminar organized by the IBE, 2-3 September 1999, Buenos Aries, Argentina.* Geneva, Switzerland, IBE.
    - *Final report of the pilot intensive sub-regional course on curriculum development. The Mediterranean Region, 11-18 September 1998.* Geneva, Switzerland, IBE.
    - Hallak, J.; Poisson, M., eds. *Globalization and living together: the challenge for education content in Asia: final report of sub-regional course on curriculum development, 9-17 March 1999, New Delhi, India.* Geneva, Switzerland, IBE.
    - Poisson, M., ed., *Science education for contemporary society: problems, issues and dilemmas—final report of the international workshop on the reform in the teaching of science education, Beijing, 27-31 March 2000.* Geneva, Switzerland, IBE.

15

The Dynamics of Educational Change for the Twenty-first Century—the Emergence of the Networking Paradigm

Cecilia Braslavsky

The twin paradigms consisting of management and educational policy are the dualities on which today's schools and national education systems have developed. The first of these was the 'community' paradigm and the second was the 'state-control' paradigm. Both were widespread throughout the West, sometimes coming into open conflict and at other times interacting with varying degrees of success.

The 'community' paradigm was predominant in the Anglo-Saxon world. In England and the Netherlands, for example, parish churches instituted schools that were in communion with the local population. As soon as they became commonplace, local authorities in the more prosperous cities of northern Europe, northern Italy, and even in sixteenth-century France launched lay establishments that competed with church schools. This paradigm was even more applicable to the way education began and prospered in the United States. In the present day jargon, it might be referred to as a 'bottom-up' model.

The 'state-control' paradigm, on the other hand, began to dominate from the eighteenth century onwards in the large nations—initially they were feudal in character and subsequently used the state to further the interests of modern industrial capitalism, as in the absolutist states of Spain and France and the French republics from the eighteenth to the twentieth centuries. Again, in terms of professional jargon, this might be seen as being a 'top-down' model.

The 'community' paradigm was governed by a decision-making approach close to what is considered nowadays as 'micro-policy'. The schools themselves took a considerable number of decisions regarding what and how to teach. For instance, they decided study plans and programmes with very little interference either from the state or from highly placed public authorities. Even the local authorities interfered very little with the decisions of individual schools. In the light of the considerable influence wielded by the schools, the interactions between its actors were—and are still—extremely relevant. It might almost be said that they exercised a certain sway over the higher echelons of society.

Practically all the elites who founded the Latin American education systems tried to create foundational models that combined all that was perceived as comprising the positive aspects of the two models. They aimed for strong dynamism by central governments, while allowing for local bodies that could bond individual schools with their surrounding communities. However, the effect of relations between central governments, that were relatively stronger and more dynamic than societies and markets, was to establish the clear predominance of a pyramid structure of decision-making and day-to-day administration in the education system. In that structure, the state gave orders; the schools complied (or did not) and the principals and teachers executed.

In the progressive and culturally speaking relatively more homogeneous countries, this model came to be associated with noteworthy achievements in terms of the speed and spread of education. They also facilitated the transition through a deserving phase of social construction and national integration. But it appeared to exhaust its potential in the 1960s, when some of the tendencies that would eventually lead to the civilizing revolution at the turn of the century were already firming up and when for a variety of reasons it attracted criticism from all sides. The neo-liberals thought it was too inefficient, and the libertarians found it too authoritarian. For lack of a more suitable alternative, it was mooted that the primary requisite was a form of self-management that permitted the key players to participate in administering the system, and thereby secure a more sizeable space for school autonomy. Both of these proposals in one way or another drew their inspiration from the 'community' model, which was the only recognized alternative. Both had a limited impact, however, or were quite simply rejected.

The time has perhaps come to elude the trap of debating the merits of 'top-down' or 'bottom-up' models. The technical means of building a networking model, utilizing the opportunities presented by modern technologies, are feasible today. Its advantage would involve creating a healthier interaction between the different levels of management and to redefine them as co-operators (instead of some giving orders to others at the receiving end) in a processes where all existing institutions can experience a shared sense of a common, co-coordinated and productive mission. The question then arises regarding the nature and quality of skills that are required to create the new model, as to whether the present players possess these in adequate measure, and if not, how to generate these and empower them to cope with the demands of the new millennium.

Section 1

Curriculum Development in the Twenty-first Century—New Challenges

The Challenges Facing Education in the Twenty-first Century: Contributions of the IBE

Cecilia Braslavsky

The objective of this statement is twofold: it is aimed at presenting to you a lucid picture of the UNESCO International Bureau of Education (IBE) in its contemporary phase of evolution, as well as sharing with you our vision and thinking on the forthcoming UNCESCO International Conference on Education, that is being organized by the IBE. Ministers of Education from all over the world will be participating in the forty-sixth International Conference to be held in Geneva in September 2001. As the sheer magnitude of the numbers suggest, the conference has its traditional moorings and is rooted in history. It will focus on the challenges on the horizon of a new millennium that threaten to nullify our undertaking to provide education for all. We will also explore ways and means to optimize our contributions in an effort to lend quality to the experience of living together.

We believe that the wealth of ideas and experiences in the custody of professional teams specializing in specific topics and areas of expertise, such as those on offer in this seminar, provide the basis for our preparations for ministerial conferences. The International Bureau of Education is privileged to function at once in three different areas:

organizing a platform for discussing and monitoring what goes into education; facilitating political dialogue; and establishing network to champion curriculum change. The quantum of the progress made is directly dependent on the extent of synergy generated by the seamless convergence of these three streams of our activities.

This being the case, allow me to posit three fundamental factors that warrant our attention:

- firstly, the trends that characterize our world at the beginning of this century need to be identified;
- thereafter, the challenges arising from a specific tend need to be dealt with specifically so that each one of them receives our unreserved attention;
- finally, we need to make holistic efforts to eliminate the collective threats posed by these trends.

Against this backdrop, the International Bureau of Education proposes to help find responses so that you, over the coming days, can decide in the light of your own experiences, interests and intended contributions, how best we can organize our energies and direct our efforts.

The Identification of Seven Main Trends

There are at least seven main trends that pose fresh challenges to education. The first—I shall just go through them, in no particular order—is that different educational profiles are needed for a working environment that is in a state of permanent and dizzying flux. The amount of work that remains to be done to empower people to meet their basic physical requirements for survival is mounting by the day. Worldwide, though not necessarily in every country, there are likely to be ever-fewer chances of landing a rewarding job. It is worth bearing in mind that the jobs that do exist are becoming increasingly varied. It is most likely that by the time the children now in school reach adulthood, in 2020-2030 or thereabouts, they will have sizeable opportunities.

The second trend is the shift from a pyramid-to an inverted-pyramid-shaped society, with the associated risks of disintegration. Many of us in our generation are used to talking in terms of the social pyramid or the job pyramid. The underlying assumption is that there are people at the bottom, people in the middle and people at the top. Within the next ten to fifteen years, we are likely to find ourselves with not one pyramid but two circles. One will comprise the people doing complex, creative jobs, who will find themselves at a certain point in time occupying a certain space in the circle, and at a different point in time a different space: somewhere work-related, say today, somewhere study-related tomorrow. The other circle, needless to say the bigger one, will be all the people left out, some of them living off public welfare, some off charity, some off crime. In this scenario, the two circles will only drift further apart, with the mobile elites in the smaller circle spiraling away and upward.

Of course, there is no law in nature that decrees that this is the shape of things to come. Such turns of events can be averted. IF we wish to live together in peace and harmony, such twists must perforce be averted, in every society. And one way, or need I say the only way, of constructing alternatives to this prospect of a society comprising mutually exclusive circles is to provide an education that will bring one and all into that first circle so that the larger circle loses its *raison d'être*. Policies and practices to provide such an education must enlighten educational structures, curricula and assessment.

The third determining characteristic of the first decade of the twenty-first century is growing inequality, and the manner in which inequality can become deprivation. In the pyramid-shaped society, the people at the bottom were still within the pyramid, still part of society. In a two-track society, the way the fruits of the overall output of goods and services are shared may be so attractive to some, and so infuriating to others, that the risks of violence will multiply explosively. Violence may be unleashed by those in the favoured circle, to ensure their dominance and continuous enjoyment of the benefits of growth and development. Violence by those outside, to seize such crumbs as may be had, is but to be expected.

The fourth major trend is for diversity to become accepted as an asset, something that must be kept distinct from deprivation and inequality. Modern society both accepts and demands that indigenous languages should be fostered, and that the differences between communities, religions and individuals should be accorded their due recognition. That being so, we need to find new ways of fostering diversity, with tolerance as the starting point, along with a quest for harmony, for alternately, everyone will be fighting to be diverse in his or her own precise way to the detriment of everyone else's distinctive features.

The fifth trend is the drive to find fresh, more intense, more creative ways of global integration that respects tradition and does not suppress or supplant it with dubious arrangements arrived at in compromising circumstances.

The sixth is an awareness that the contours of knowledge are changing rapidly—that it is far more variables then we are habituated to imagining, and the changes are both quantitative as well as qualitative. Education systems all over the world used to be accustomed to the thought that geography was geography as a given; we built up our knowledge of geography at the university and we taught 'geography' at secondary schools as a subject we imagined would be valid for twenty-five or thirty years. Nowadays we know that things are not what they seemed to be. Knowledge assumes different guises. But schools still cling on to knowledge in its fossilized forms, and what we are teaching today may not hold still or true in two or twenty years. Efforts are belatedly being made to identify basic skills and abilities that extend beyond the numbing rapidity of these change in learning and ways of imparting wisdom, knowledge and information, that are, if not eternal, at least contemporary.

The seventh trend is the power that today's population enjoys in broadening its horizon if it so chooses. New-fangled issues are awaiting resolution. The ethics of using genetic engineering to manipulate the gender of an unborn child is a case in point. If people can—as a matter of technical nicety—they may even begin to choose what kind of a child they will have, with all its hazardous implications. The generation that will inherit the future and the Earth, and everything that goes along with these will need to be equipped with a more finely honed value system and a keener sense of judgment.

II. The challenges ahead

Everybody here is aware that the various developments I have mentioned demand careful consideration with regard to teaching content and methods in the twenty-first century. What needs to be taught, and how? Can we still maintain, with Emile Durkheim, the father of the entire school of modern educational psychology, that the purpose of education systems is to transmit to younger generations the cultural heritage of the adult population? Is it not probable that education systems will end up totally obsolete and abandoned as institutions of the past, given the increasingly rapid developments in the evolution of knowledge and a younger generation with its own culture, means of self-expression and music that it wishes to see respected?

The answer is clear: education system and schools will be left far behind unless they adapt. They can, on the other hand, play a central role if they adapt and rise to the challenges of the twenty-first century. If they manage to adapt, to become more dynamic and flexible while retaining their ability to impart vital human values so that humanity is able to live together—values that will foster life, the quest for truth and solidarity—then perhaps their future role will prove to become more elemental to society than is the case today. All the more so as our society is riddled with dynamic pulls and pressures, anxiety and uncertainty. It is to be borne in mind that another recurring problem is that people want continuity in which to practice living together so that these value can be applied and be built upon.

In a number of formerly prosperous cities that have been caught up in the sweeping economic changes of the present day, the only institution left to foster exchange, dialogue, joint effort and the construction of self-help networks is the school. Factories are closing down, community institutions no longer work or have become ineffective; the schools, amidst all this, are just about menaging to remain. Many people work out of homes, others drift from one job to another; the strongest single factor that gives children and teenagers stability and a sense of belonging is the fact that they carry on going to school. But people are also beginning to realize that they do not want the inflexible schools of the past, where subjects were taught from A to Z and information was to be imparted so that children could repeat it even if they did not understand it. They want schools to remain in existence but they want them to be responsive to the changing realties—because they are all aware of the changes I referred to before. To change, and to do so very quickly, is imperative.

How do things stand in your respective countries? That is what, among other things, we are here to explore.

The Contribution of the IBE

Let me now turn to my third and final point: the role that a modest little institution like the International Bureau of Education in Geneva should be playing in all this, striving to create value-addition, changing what needs to be changed while retaining what is still desirable in teaching content, working methods and organizational arrangements. I am carefully not using the world 'classroom' because no one knows whether the institution to be rebuilt out of what exists today will include classrooms, as we know them.

We want the new institutions to have content. There is the danger of believing that, since conceptual and informational content change so quickly, we could have an educational institution bereft of significant content to teach children. When active teaching methods were at their most popular—the 1970s in the West, for instance—active teaching was sometimes confused with content-less teaching, as though personalities could be shaped without concentrating hard on content. Content, it is to be emphasized, is more than just facts to memorize: it is procedures to follow, values to apply, information to update and refresh. To know whether you can gather, analyse and communicate information you have to work with information, while recognizing that it will lose its value and need to be updated; what you retain is not so much the information itself, which is still there, albeit diminished in value, as the ability to work with it.

A curriculum, as you all know, is primarily a means of marking territory, of defining the rules of the game. It is the law, not in a judicial but in a sociological sense. It sets out what has to be done and how to go about it—not rigidly, with no regard for the individual, but as a set of reference points allowing the individual to belong to one or several different communities at once—so that people can sense that they are at one and the same time citizens of their nations, of the world at large, as well as of their local communities, and have their own identities to retain and nourish.

Facilitation and training facilities are becoming evermore important. The IBE is working to strengthen capacity for lasting change in education by supporting training activities backed by an international educational quality-promotion network based chiefly on curricula. The mission of the IBE is to become a content and methodology centre for education in the art of living together, encouraging political dialogue and discussion on the new educational challenges posed by worldwide trends at the opening of the twenty-first century, gathering and analysing information on curricula, other rules and regulations and key innovations, fostering capacity-building and supporting meetings such as today's. The Bureau knows very little about certain parts of the world, and both needs and wants to know more about them, It hopes it will pick up some ideas and experiences here, learning what there is to be learnt and doing what it can to encourage you to continue exchanges amongst yourselves.

We have invited colleagues from other countries to join our network of experts: from Australia, given its long academic tradition in this area; from India, given its sizeable and varied recent moves towards innovation; and from Malta, given its efforts on a scale similar to those of many of the countries represented here. It is our earnest hope that this will become a keen process of joint learning. The IBE wishes to think the Omani National Commission and Ministry of Education for the considerable trouble they have taken in arranging this seminar.

17

The Challenges Facing Education and Curriculum Development at the Beginning of the Twenty-first Century

Shapour Rassekh

Introduction

Confronting us today are three types of challenges to education and curriculum development that need to be closely scrutinized;

1. global challenges which are external to the world of education;
2. internal challenges of the education systems themselves;
3. challenges specific to the Gulf Region.

With regard to the global challenges, we may refer to the eight critical processes to which the curriculum planners should respond. These are:

1. the process of globalization and the corresponding interdependence of all nations;[1]
2. accelerated pace of scientific and technological progress particularly in the area of communication and information as well as in the field of biology;
3. radical transformation in the field of work and employment.
4. increasing social inequalities;
5. progress of democracy and human rights and the aspiration of civil society to take part in the arena of political decision-making;

6. multi-culturalism and greater contacts among various cultures;
7. prevalence of rapid changes and the consequent uncertainties in the social life. The feeling of insecurity that sometimes provoke depression and other times violence;
8. moral decline and the felt need to revitalize moral and ethical values.

It seems to me that in a number of countries, if not in all, the education systems experience great difficulties in coping with these complex challenges. Even if reforms are planned, they are not always implemented or managed properly. And the reforms in structures, curricula, programmes, contents and methods, which are being executed, very often meet with a great deal of resistance—from parents, teachers' unions and sometimes even from pupils or learners themselves.

It is not my intention to declare that education everywhere is in deep crisis, but I do believe that it is faced with a number of barriers and hurdles as it struggles to find the right way out of the present state of flux. Curriculum reform is no doubt inexorable, but it would not suffice if it is not being monitored from the very beginning, evaluated with regularity, continuously updated and improved. In addition to these global challenges, countries in the Gulf Region seem to face some specific challenges, which may be summarized as follows:

1. the challenge of universal literacy;[2]
2. the challenge of a shortage of highly skilled human resources, including in the field of education;
3. the challenge of reconciling traditional orientation of education with the aspiration for modernity;
4. the challenge of privatization of schools in some countries;
5. the challenge of diversification of the economy to become less dependant on oil revenue and the consequent increase in the need for competence training and management development in other sectors of the economy;
6. the need to invest more in research in various priority areas, including education;

7. the need to derive optimal benefit from the complementary nature of the Gulf Region economies through enhanced co-operation.

It appears that countries in the Gulf Region are very much committed to the objective of education for all, endorsed by Jomtien Conference. However, we continue to find that many children sill leave school without completing their education. We are aware that some of these countries such as Kuwait and the United Arab Emirates have applied in the past a generous system of social welfare (free schooling, free healthcare, etc.). They had to unfortunately withdraw these schemes due to the fluctuation in the prices of oil and consequent economic instability.

This may turn out to be an additional obstacle to fulfilling the ideal of implementing education for all. Although the international community has recommended life-long education for some decades now, the Gulf Region countries do not seem to have made any noteworthy progress in this area. While the continuing evolution of science and technology and the changing requirements of the labour market necessitate quality education, attention should also be paid to the democratic exigencies and the compulsions to provide equal opportunities for all.

Some Responses Adopted by Education Systems

We had earlier referred to eight types of global challenges. We could perhaps now make a short presentation of the responses that educational planners and curricula designers have adopted in facing up to these challenges.

Response to globalization

Some of the responses to this process at the level of school curriculum are:

1. greater emphasis on the learning of an international language;
2. better knowledge of geography and history of the world and of world civilizations;
3. better appreciation of the role of major international institutions (such as the United Nations) and other major players in the international scene;

4. knowledge of computerization and access to the Internet;
5. acquiring the art of living with others in peace and respecting cultural diversities;
6. better acquaintance with the major problems confronting the world that necessitate the co-operation of all concerned to attain sustainable solutions.

As *Learning: the treasure within* (Delors et al., 1996, p. 51) affirms:

> *We must be guided by the Utopian aim of steering the world towards greater mutual understanding, and greater sense of responsibility and greater solidarity, through acceptance of our spiritual and cultural differences. Education, by providing access to knowledge for all, has precisely this universal task of helping people to understand the world and to understand others.*

To this list, Hallak and Poisson add 'promoting consensus on a common core of values'. Globalization is not limited to capital movement and trade. It also includes the cultural dimension. And the Universal Declaration of Human Rights could become the axis for that common core of values, provided it is supplemented by the endowment of human responsibilities (Poisson, 2001, p. 17).

Some years back, UNESCO was insistent on the necessity of discussing major world problems at higher levels of education. The concept of 'globalization' covers not only these universal problems but also some significant advances that humanity is accomplishing in this exceptional era.

Response to scientific and technological progress

The accelerated pace of scientific and technological advancements necessitates regular revision and updating of science curriculum as well as the organization of refresher courses for science teachers.

In the Beijing international workshop (Poisson, 2001), Albert Pilot summarized the general trends in science education in one of the developed regions of the world (Europe) as follows:

1. from teaching towards learning;
2. from individual learning towards co-operative learning;
3. from subject knowledge towards intellectual competencies:

4. from separate subjects towards integration of subjects:
5. integration of information and communication technology in all areas;
6. and finally, the professional development of teachers.

The first point refers to a drastic change in modern education where the student, and not the teacher, becomes the centre of attention. More emphasis is laid on experimental work of the learners, their library, CD-ROM or Internet research, or any other type of student activities. The second concerns teamwork among learners instead of the individual paper or laboratory work. With regard to the third, the author believes that: 'the development of competencies to learn independently using books, articles and papers (instead of learning from teacher presentation) and the development of skill to solve problems in a systematic method, to work in team and communicate are seen as more important than before'. While dealing with the third trend, we should remember one of the key aspects of science education today—the adoption of a multidisciplinary approach. Today we talk more about a cluster of interrelated subjects rather than a long list of individual subjects.

'New curricula have more learning activities aimed at integration of knowledge and skills of competence-based learning, problem-based learning or project-oriented courses' (Poisson, 2001, p. 109). We have already referred to the fifth issue and as for that concerning the sixth, the tendency to undermine the professional aspect of the teaching job is to be avoided and the necessity of professional development of teachers needs to be emphasized. The intensive sub-regional course on curriculum development (International Bureau of Education, 2000, pp. 30-31) refers to ten types of competencies that have to be developed in the teachers. Pedagogical skills are very important but have to be supplemented by several other competencies, one of which is the adaptation to the requirements of new curricula.

Response to transformation within the world of work and employment

A number of changes are occurring in the world of work, some of which are referred to in Braslavsky's report on Latin America (Braslavsky, 2000, pp. 6-7):

1. A reduction in the employment opportunities caused, among other things, by great technological progress and robotization of some painful and dangerous tasks.
2. The availability of jobs in a greater number in the service sector (tertiary) because of the expansion of information technology, the development of scientific research and also the expansion of social security, health, education and leisure activities, etc.
3. Growth of informal, compared with formal, employment, because among their factors we need to bear in mind the employment opportunities for the coloured population and new Third Word migrants, as well as the development of a 'self-service economy'.
4. Rapid changes taking place in job profiles, particularly with regard to specific skills (such as communication and problem-solving skills).
5. The changing scale on which the work lives of individuals are conducted in practice, because of the internationalization of the labour market and greater facility of movement.

The following should also be added to the above-mentioned developments:

6. The importance of team-work in business companies.
7. The tendency in many advanced societies to privatize public services because of the dominant liberal ideology (that of faith in regulation my market forces).
8. The tendency for workers and employed persons tc change jobs frequently (therefore the necessity of more flexibility in response to increasing mobility).
9. The search for highest return on capital investment leads not only to the merging of various enterprises (companies, societies, banks, etc.), but also to the 'possibility of locating the units of production of goods and services almost anywhere in the world' (IBE, 2000, p. 10). The quest for maximizing profits results in the disbanding of some departments in a company and the assignment of the same work to external enterprises.

These changes invite curriculum planners to consider drastic revisions in the school programmes. The new jobs created both in the secondary and tertiary sectors require in most cases not only a higher level of knowledge and a better training compared to the past, but also some new skills such as the capacity to adjust to new circumstances, problem-solving skills, creativity and so on (Rassekh & Vaideanu, 1987, pp. 50-57; Bertrand, 1994, p. 157-93). We have already indicated the importance of exposure to practical experience, during the time of study or thereafter (pre-employment training). In addition to the integration of productive work or learning by doing in the school programme, the planners advocate 'more frequent alternation of study periods and work in an education process henceforth considered as spanning a whole lifetime' (Rassekh & Vaideanu, 1987, p. 56).

Some other trends in curriculum adaptation in response to the changes in the world of work and employment are:

1. The importance of developing the right attitudes and behaviours in the students because in the autonomous environment prevalent in employment situations, a sense of responsibility and communication skills in relation to colleagues and customers are pre-requisites (Bertrand, 1994, p. 166);
2. A tendency to increase the number of students in vocational courses, and their continuation beyond the secondary level, particularly in order to train an increasing number of technical specialists.
3. A search for flexibility and a greater capacity for response on the part of the training system. This may be sought by reducing the degree of specialization and broadening the scope of training to make it more transferable and less specifically oriented towards a particular job. It may also concern the courses taken by students (breaking down barriers between courses) and be reflected in a trend towards decentralization.
4. a 'marriage' between school and business institutions, by increasing the participation of employers' representatives in deciding on options, the development of partnerships, and the contribution of firms to the training itself.
5. A considerable increase in continuing training, which relieves the basic education system of the burden of supplying 'finished products ready for employment' (ibid., p. 174).

To these, we have to add the arrangement made by many countries, very often with the help of employers, to provide fresh training to unemployed youth in order to enable them to meet the needs of some sectors of the economy.

Response to increasing social inequalities

One of the features of the present time is the widening gap between and within countries in terms of wealth, income and access to various social services, etc. The annual human development reports of the United Nations Development Programme present a daunting picture of these growing disparities. One aspect of the problem is the uneven distribution of knowledge between developed and developing nations as Jacques Delors et al. (1996, p. 72-74) indicate. The other is the monopoly of quality education possessed by the children of rich families. Various solutions have been considered and applied to reduce this gap within countries.

George S. Papadopoulos (Papadopoulos, 1998, pp. 39-43) and others suggest the following solutions:

- taking some moderate measures of 'positive discrimination' in favour of gifted children of poor families;
- continuing the fight against gender inequalities, particularly in the prestigious disciplines of science, technology and in research;
- fighting against school failure and school drop-out of poor children, among other things through the introduction of some remedial teaching:
- opening some outlet toward vocational and professional education for less academically inclined pupils and at the same time raising the status of that type of education (for example, the Germanic dual systems);
- recognizing the convergence between general and vocational education and translating it into curriculum and instructional designs.

As our subject is curriculum development rather than other educational activities, we draw attention to this last solution. In this respect, we should indicate that many authors are in favour of some sort of vocationalization of school curriculum, at least through the inclusion of practical activities useful to both school and community. We endorse also the suggestion of Mishra in the sub-regional IBE course held in New Delhi (9-17 March 1999) that 'all vocational education programmes and activities should stress the concept of sustainable development with a focus on fostering awareness of key environmental concerns and the rights of all to a decent standard of living' (International Bureau of Education, 2000, p. 34). One of the characteristics of economic development in the Third World during the last few years has been that the growth has not reduced poverty in many countries. The new jobs created (very often in relation to the world economy) have disproportionately favoured those with higher level of education—levels that are not always accessible to the youth coming from poorer families (Reimers, 1999, pp. 482-83). The solution to this unequal access to 'high-productivity employment' has to be sought at the level of educational institutions.

In a particular issue of the UNESCO review *Prospects* (December, 1999) about education, poverty and inequality, many lessons can be learned from various countries in respect to ways of dealing with the persistent problem of inequality in school: affirmative action, remedial action and preventive measures are only some examples of what is being done in the United States. In respect to prevention, it seems to us that in schools or communities where a high proportion of people are poor, the curriculum should put a particular emphasis on the value of effort and qualities such as courage in order to inspire the learners to overcome resigning themselves to what is considered as fate. The concept of 'education for liberation' applies in this case.

We do not enter into the discussion of some preventive measures working outside the system of curriculum such as free tuition, free food and transportation, the struggle against child labour, refuge centres for street children, appropriate pre-school education for the poor, 'second chance' schools to attract high school drop-outs, etc. However, as sometimes the poor children belong to cultural minorities using languages different from the national language, production of literacy materials in those languages is particularly recommended.

We have to admit that if the issue of equity and equality was the main concern during the 1950s and the 1960s, today's primary preoccupation is with quality, relevance and competitiveness at least for many governments around the world (Reimers, 1999). Nevertheless, certainly the problem of equality of access and success cannot be entirely bypassed because of the potential resources that exist within the poor children, not to mention service the cause of justice and equal opportunities for all.

Response to the progress of democracy and human rights

No doubt that the democratization of political systems has been a highly significant feature of the last decade. This process, which will no doubt continue through this century, has also been reflected at the level of schools, changing gradually the relation between the pupils and the teaching staff, and placing greater emphasis on the necessity of producing active and responsible citizens.

Education in tolerance and respect for other people is a prerequisite for democracy according to Jacques Delors and his colleagues (1996, p. 60). It should be regarded as a general and ongoing enterprise. Democratic dialogue and peaceful resolution of conflicts should be taught early in the school life.

As multi-culturalism becomes the rule in most societies, 'the single notion of tolerance must therefore be transcended in favour of an education for pluralism based on respect for and appreciation of other cultures' (ibid., p. 60).

Some trends in the education sectors, in response to the democratization process, are:

1. Utilizing schools to make the learners familiar with their rights and duties and with what is expected from them in their different social roles as consumers, as voters, as partners in the family, as members of various associations, etc.
2. In addition to civic instruction, including familiarity with civil and political institutions, laws, etc., providing students with practical experiences in a democratic atmosphere (e.g. setting up pupil parliaments, role playing to stimulate the functioning of democratic institutions, school newspapers, exercises in con-violent

conflict resolution, service to local community, etc.) (ibid., p. 62).

3. Involving family, local community and associations in the education for citizenship and democracy.
4. Considering civic instruction not restricted to the transmission of a set of well-established rules, but as an occasion to develop the sense of judgment in the learners, who sooner or later have to participate in real public life.
5. Paying particular attention to the type of education suited to different minority groups in order to enable them to 'take control of their own future' and bring their enriching contribution to society.
6. Preparing students for life in the new information society by mastering technology and at the same time 'displaying a critical spirit in sorting and ordering information'.
7. Using history, geography and social science courses to promote the concept of living together and co-operating (André & Mouzoune, 1999).
8. Putting particular emphasis on human rights education while benefiting from the enormous experience accumulated in this field by UNESCO and some other United Nations Agencies.[3] The concepts of human dignity, human rights and freedom should not be restricted to specific subjects and particular courses but form an integral aspect of most school disciplines (philosophy and humanities, history, geography, civic instructions, history of sciences, etc.).[4]

6. *Responses to the need for cultural dialogue and interaction*

One aspect of the present process of globalization is precisely what can be considered as the beginning of cultural globalization. Politically and economically dominant societies of the West are considerably influencing the mode of thinking and behaviour of the people of the South and the East. At the same time, we are observing zealous reactions to this process, people defending their traditional values and ways of conduct. 'Peoples everywhere want to find their roots beyond the vicissitudes of recent history and recreate a solid link with their past' (UNESCO, 1985). In fact, the world is enriched not by the homogenization of various cultures but the appreciation of their original diversity, and the possibility offered to them to interact constructively and learn from each other.

The school curriculum can play an important role in promoting creative cultural dialogue and interaction, not only through history and the history of civilizations, devoid of chauvinistic and ethnocentric contents, but also by injecting the intercultural approach in other disciplines (e.g. in teaching mathematics, one can say that the Western world has a debt to the Indian and Islamic civilizations). Extra-curricular activities should also provide ample occasions for such positive intercultural education (Delors et al., 1996). As Delors and his colleagues have stated 'Knowledge of other cultures leads to an awareness of the uniqueness of one's own culture but also an awareness of a heritage common to all humanity' (ibid., p. 50).

Curriculum designers should pay special attention to the following:

- including in the school programme guided visits to the interesting cultural sites of their own countries and elsewhere in the context of different study areas (such as history, geography and languages);
- making young people aware of the need to protect the world's cultural and natural heritage;[5]
- excluding from textbooks the strong nationalistic approach which creates a false sense of superiority and leads to the rejection of other people's achievements and merit;
- fostering the sense of shared values and a common destiny, as basic for international co-operation and solidarity;
- giving the linguistic minority groups the possibility of starting the acquisitions of literacy (reading and writing) through their own language or dialect and then move to the learning of national and international languages for further studies;
- providing through aesthetic and artistic education the occasion for students to become familiarized with the outstanding works of art in different cultures.

Responses to the need for revitalization of moral values

The need to revitalize moral values is felt in many aspects of life. Ethics have once again become a point of reference in politics, business, biological and medical fields, journalism, etc. Curriculum designers have therefore to give appropriate place to value education in school programmes (Rassekh & Vaideanu, 1987, pp. 155-62; Delors et al., 1996, pp. 276-310). Other partners of education (parents, local community, church, media, etc.) should also support this trend or at least avoid contradicting it.

The teaching of the Universal Declaration of Human Rights has its place in many schools such as those associated with UNESCO. This has to be supplemented by the presentation of human responsibilities not only toward other human beings and neighbours, but also toward nature, the past and future generations and even toward history (where are we and where do we want to go?).

One of the negative features of the present world is the prevalence of violence in society, in the family, in school and elsewhere. The need is great to include in the school curriculum lessons on peaceful resolution of conflicts. Aggressiveness and violence are not basic natural characteristics of human beings as several scholars in various fields (psychology, biology, anthropology) have demonstrated (UNESCO, 1980); therefore they can be controlled and even eradicated. Children have to be taught dialogue, consultation and co-operation early in their lives. School should continue their teaching and practical training in this direction.

Referring to the globalization movement and certain other significant evolution of the present world, Küng comes to the conclusion that we need a set of global ethical values that respond to the current challenges (Küng, 1995).

Most of these values (such as respect for human dignity, respect for life and altruism moderation, etc.) have formed the basic tenets of the great universal religions. The time has come to revitalize them and reflect them in the teaching/ learning programmes as well as in our daily practices.

Many writers have referred to humanistic values, such as respect for others, concern for a better understanding of other cultures in their diversity, desire and will to understand things objectively. UNESCO has promoted in the last few years what has been called the 'culture of peace'. After the Rio de Janeiro conference on environment and development (1992), reference is often made to the importance of an ethics of environment.

These 'new values' have to be added to the traditional ones in order to reinforce the model education of the present generation. Some trends in the field of value education according to a UNESCO regional workshop in Tokey (NIER, 1994) are as follows:

1. There is a great need to promote and emphasize in the curriculum the culture of peace, tolerance and democratic attitudes, openness to international understanding and co-operation and a new attitude towards the environment.
2. With the requirements of the changing situations in the world, some of the values have to be modified or adapted (e.g. the concept of world citizenship has entered into educationist consideration, thanks to the International Labour Organization initiative at the Copenhagen Social Summit of 1995).
3. Curriculum designers should try to link the new values to the traditional norms existing in the country to make the new ones better understood and accepted; if there exists contradictions between them (for example, between traditional nationalistic attitude and the new sense of world citizenship), the justification of the new values should be elaborated.
4. Teachers have to be convinced that the world of the twenty-first century needs new values such as gender equality.[6] Teacher training or retraining programmes should include such issues.
5. Evaluation of pupils and students should not be limited to their cognitive performance in school but also take into account their attitudes and behaviour toward other persons and toward the establishment; respect and love for other people, spirit of service, and readiness to co-operate are among the qualities that need to be particularly evaluated.

6. As Roberto Carneiro said (1996, p. 201-04): 'love is not enough'. As he has indicated 'education for justice' should be considered as the core of moral education: And this means 'the acquisition of a sense of abstract justice (equity, equality of opportunity, responsible freedom, respect for others, protection of the weak, and awareness of differences) [but at the same time] that attitude predisposing people towards taking practical steps to promote social justice and defend democratic values'.

Educating for the time of uncertainty

As Hughes has rightly indicated 'in the period leading to a new century and a new millennium, the global society is in a period of reappraisal and self-doubt, with few clear and convincing visions of future' (Hughes, 1998, p. 47). He adds that 'without such visions, social aims [including those of education] tend to be limited or confused, lacking a coherent and comprehensive set of purposes'. No doubt, we live in such times of uncertainty. Technological and social changes are so rapid that the educational efforts have great difficulty to shape and direct them.

One can find uncertainty plaguing all aspects of life. Young people are anxious about the employment options ahead of them on completion of their studies. There is a feeling of uncertainty about the quality of food, the condition of the environment (as an example, we may refer to water pollution or atmospheric warming, security in large cities, the fluctuation in the stock market, the use of nuclear weapons in the case of any international conflict, etc. What can education do in anticipation of such situations?

To our knowledge, little attention has been paid by education specialists to these crucial questions.[7] We have some studies about education in times of tension and crisis. Violence in school became a subject of study and publication in the last few years (violence is not always caused by anxiety or feelings of uncertainty as shown by Ohsako[8]). But how are we expected to cope with these uncertainties in school and particularly through curriculum changes and reforms?

We find references in a number of books to the necessity of equipping pupils with the capacity to adapt to change, with the ability to create, with the power of task-taking and other entrepreneurial qualities. In an older document (Gullberg-Hansen, 1991, p. 199), the reference is made to the development of skills such as precision in carrying out one's work, a methodological approach to work, meticulousness, the ability to adapt to new kinds of work and the ability to co-operate. The translation of these goals into learning materials and methods will not be easy.

Many believe that future studies should form an integral part of the curriculum at least at the higher level of education. The study of the future and the analysis of the major problems confronting the world can go hand-in-hand (Rassekh & Vaideanu, 1987). The objective should be to give confidence to the young learners that humankind can favourably influence their future, if the right decisions are taken and acted upon today.

One aspect of the changes ahead of us relates to the world of employment and work. As Hughes has rightly said on the basis of a 1993 study (Hughes, 1998, p. 57), expectations of students contrast adversely with those of teachers. While the latter give priority to personal and social development of the learners, students are particularly interested in vocational and academic development. This means that young people are looking much more to their own professional future to the exclusion of other vital issues. Therefore, secondary and tertiary level students should become familiar not only through reading materials (in addition to the textbooks) but through other means as well (vocational guidance, debates on television, information on the Internet) about the changing needs and requirements of the labour market.[9] Textbooks may refer to a forthcoming new knowledge-based economy and its likely impact on various aspects of human life. Concepts such as post-industrial society or post-economic society may form part of the discussion.

Some other suggestions concerning the preparation of youth for the time of uncertainty are:

- extending and reinforcing compulsory general education to further consolidate its foundation for subsequent specialized lines of study (Hughes & Skilbeck, 1994, p. 27);

- specific preparation of the pupils (by information, guidance, and a crescendo of self-reliance) for increasingly varied and autonomous learning and training at post-compulsory levels of education (King, 1979, p. 238). The capacity to learn and keep learning is more crucial than specific skills learnt in school;
- greater emphasis on development of qualities necessary to adapt better to the changing conditions that characterize our world today (these qualities have been already referred to); practical experiences should be introduced to strengthen qualities such as problem-solving, the ability to search for innovative solutions, consultation and co-operation, courage to face the unexpected. Closer bonds between community life and school are required to make the pupils agents of change and development in their own social environment;
- to reduce uncertainty, at least as far as the world of work is concerned, the dialogue between business and industry sectors and the education sector is crucial if a better understanding of each other's positions is to be achieved. This will be crucial from yet another point of view: 'Increasingly, much vocational education will occur on working sites' (OECD, 1994, p. 34).

Internal Challenges Facing the Education System

It is important to remember that challenges to the education system do not emerge only from the outside world but at times arise from within the system itself. With developments in psychology and educational sciences, more and more schools have become learner-centered, using active and participate methods. They encourage students to explore, investigate and learn by themselves, promote new technologies like computers, stimulate openness and interaction with the surrounding world (local community, enterprises, media, natural environment, etc), facilitate co-operation and co-operative learning, create occasions of experimenting democratic life within school. This process transforms the role of teacher from that of a reservoir of knowledge to one of an animator, guide, moderator, etc., who helps to develop in students skills and qualities which are indispensable to live a happy, balanced and successful life.

Curriculum designers can no longer be left alone to their own devices. They have to be assisted by all the stakeholders in the education system (parents, church, economic enterprises, experienced teachers and supervisors, representatives of educational authorities, etc.) through joint committees in order to reach a consensus on the type of programme contents that effectively cope with the diverse challenges. The curriculum development or change will then become a technical subject for the specialists to deal with.

Several concepts have attracted the attention of the educational planners during last decades, such as:

1. orientation toward a variety of goals (learning to know, learning to be, learning to do and learning to live together);
2. universalization of education (basic education for all);
3. considerations to ensure equal opportunities for all (of access and success);
4. quality as a priority concern;
5. efficiency of education (particular care for the economy of education);
6. relevance of education (particularly to the needs of labour market);
7. the continuity of education (lifelong education).

We may say that these seven concepts, even if they have always preoccupied the decision-makers, have received varying emphasis in different times and places. Curriculum designers in various continents and countries pay greater or lesser attention to every one of them. To give an example, in the case of Latin America today we refer to Braslavsky (2000) who considers that the following trends exist at the level of secondary education:

1. combining richness or quality of learning and flexibility in the curriculum (flexibility in the sense of admitting variations according to the characteristics of the individual establishment in which the curriculum is being implemented);

2. going from a fragmented curriculum to a more unified one; replacing the concept of subjects by the concept of curriculum space or area;
3. exposing pupils to practical learning experiences (projects, workshops and activities);
4. when subjects are maintained, offering the possibility of opting between subjects within the same field of knowledge;
5. making timetable prescriptions more flexible;
6. moving from limited and pre-distributed time to extended and free time (this free time being left to the decision of schools for appropriate utilization); and
7. directing efforts toward changing radically the learning methods (more active and participatory approaches, development of research and active projects in the local community).

Talking about the challenges to education emanating from within, one cannot avoid discussing the enrichment of the curriculum, because of the necessity of including therein a number of new contents (Rassekh & Vaideanu, 1987) such as environment, population, democracy, human rights, intercultural relations, disarmament, peace, etc. There are number of reasons which justify the inclusion of these new subjects, the most important being the necessity of preparing the new generation to face the requirements of a new epoch.

In order to avoid excessive burdening of the programme, a number of measures have been adopted. Some of them are: the infusional approach (integrating new contents in those courses which are already taught such as history, geography, biology, civic education and the like), interdisciplinary approach (as applicable to the study of environment), out-of-school or extra-curricular activities which cannot only be the entry point for new contents but also help to break down compartmentalization of subjects; use of some educational aids such as the Internet, websites designed for educational purposes, and yet others.

Notes

1. Which means also globalization of problems such as environment pollution, poverty and exclusion, drug trafficking and consumption, etc.

2. According to UNESCO *(Statistical yearbook 1999),* the rate of illiteracy is as follows: UAE 20.8%; Kuwait 21.4%; Oman 28.1%; Qatar 22.9%; Saudi Arabia 29.2%; and Bahrain 17.7%.
3. See the documents of the International Congress on education for Human Rights and Democracy, Montreal, 8-11, March 1993 (UNESCO and the United Nations Centre for Human Rights). See also the pertinent chapter in Rassekh, 1996.
4. The 1993 Montreal World Plan of Action for Human Rights and Democracy includes also education for human rights in a non-formal setting (media, workplace, professional associations, cultural organizations, etc.).
5. Which are seriously threatened by pollution, population pressure, wars, poverty and sometimes by illicit trafficking of cultural property.
6. On this important issue, refer to one of the twelve recommendations (strategic objectives and actions) of the Fourth World Conference on Women (Beijing, September 1995) including women training and education, and human rights for women.
7. We may still refer to some old books about education and change such as *Education for uncertainty* by Edmund King (1979).
8. See T. Ohsako, *Violence at school,* IBE, 1997; S. Tawil, *La destruction et la reconstruction de l' éducation dans les sociétés perturbées,* IBE, 1998.
9. See among the other documents Suzanne Berger, *Globalization and the future of work in debates on issues of our common future,* edited by Wilhelm Krull, Germany, 2000, p. 75-85.

References

André, Y.; Mouzoune, A., eds. 1999. *Apprendre à vivre ensemble grâce à l' enseignement de l' histoire et de la géographie.* Geneva, International Bureau of Education.

Bertrand, O. 1994. *Education and work. Education for the twenty-first century,* pp. 157-93. Paris, UNESCO.

Braslvsky, C. 2000. *The secondary education curriculum in Latin America: new trends and changes.* Geneva, Switzerland, International Bureau of Education.

Carneiro, R. 1996. Revitalizing the community spirit; a glimpse of the socializing role of the school in the next century. *In:* Delors, J., et al. *Learning: the treasure within,* pp. 201-04. Paris, UNESCO.

Gullberg-Hansen, N. 1979. A curriculum for uncertainty. *In:* King. E. *Education for uncertainty.* Thousand Oaks, CA, Sage.

Delors, J., et al. 1996. *Learning: the treasure within.* Paris, UNESCO.

Hughes, P. 1998. Goals and expectations and realities for the young people. *In:* UNESCO. *Education for the twenty-first century: issues and prospects,* pp. 47-60. Paris, UNESCO. (Contributions to the work of the International Commission on Educaiton for the Twenty-first Century, chaired by Jacques Delors.)

Hughes, P.; Skilbeck, M. 1994. Curriculum reform: recent trends and issues. *In:* OECD. *The curriculum redefined: schooling for the twenty-first century,* pp. 20-28. Paris, OECD.

International Bureau of Education. 2000. *Globalization and living together: the challenges for educational content in Asia.* Geneva, Switzerland. IBE.

King, E. 1979. *Education for uncertainty.* Thousand Oaks, CA, Sage.

Küng, H.; Kuschel, K.J. 1995. *A global ethic: the Declaration of the Parliament of the World's Religions.* New York, NY, Continuum.

National Institute for Educational Research. 1994. *Enhancing humanistic, ethical, cultural and international dimensions of education in Asia and Pacific: final report of a workshop.* Tokyo, NIER.

OECD. 1994. *The curriculum redefined: schooling for the twenty-first century.* Paris, OECD.

Papadopoulos, G.S. 1998. Learning for the twenty-first century. *In:* UNESCO. *Education for the twenty-first century,* pp. 39-43. Paris, UNESCO.

Poisson, M., ed. 2001. *Science education for contemporary society: problems, issues and dilemmas.* Geneva, Switzerland, International Bureau of Education.

Rassekh, S. 1996. *Education et culture de la paix: selectiv bibliographique mondiale.* Paris, UNESCO.

Rassekh, S.; Vaideanu, G. 1987. *The contents of education: a worldwide view.* Paris, UNESCO.

Reimers, F. 1999. Educational chances of the poor at the end of the twentieth century. *Prospects* (Paris, UNESCO), vol. 29, no. 2, pp. 481-91.

UNESCO. 1980. *Violence and its causes.* Paris, UNESCO.

——. 1985. *Culture and the future.* Paris, UNESCO.

——. 1998. *Education for the twenty-first century; issues and prospects.* Paris, UNESCO. (Contributions to the work of the International Commission on Education for the Twenty-first Century, chaired by Jacques Delors.)

Selected Bibliography

A. *Theoretical approaches, context and trends*

Anderson, L.W., ed. 1995. *International encyclopaedia of teaching and teacher education,* 2nd ed. Oxford, UK, Elsevier Science Ltd. (Section VII: Teaching for specific objectives, p. 437-93.)

Balsara, M. 1999. *Principles of curriculum reconstruction.* New Delhi, Kanishka Publishers.

Black, P. 1998. An international overview of curricular approaches and models in technology education. *Journal of technology studies* (Bowling Green, OH), Winter-Spring 1998. (http://scholar.lib.vt.edu/ejournals/JTS/Winter-Spring-1998/black.html.)

Bähr, K., et al. 1999. *Curriculum-making: structures, expectations, perspectives. Implementation report. National Research Programme 33.* Aarau, Switzerland, Fasler Druck AG.

Henderson, J.G.; Kesson, K.R., eds. 1999. *Understanding democratic curriculum leadership.* New York, NY, Teachers College Press.

Hughes, P.; Skilbeck, M. 1994. Curriculum reform: recent trends and issues. *In:* OECD. *The curriculum redefined: schooling for the twenty-first century,* pp. 20-28. Paris, OECD.

National Institute for Educational Research. 1999. *An international comparative study of school curriculum.* Tokyo, NIER. (Sections B-E, pp. 21-58.)

O'Donnell, S. 2000. *International review of curriculum and assessment frameworks: comparative tables and factual summaries.* Qualifications and Curriculum Authority/National Foundation for Educational Research, UK (Available at: http://www.inca.org.uk.)

Rosenmund, M. 2000. Approaches to international comparative research on curricula and curriculum-making processes. *Journal of curriculum studies* (Champaign, IL), vol. 32, no. 5, pp. 599-606.

Ross, A. 2000. *Curriculum construction and critique.* London, Falmer Press. (Chapter one: curriculum gardening, pp. 1-17.)

Skilbeck, M. 1998. School-based curriculum development. *In:* Hargreaves A., et al., eds. *International handbook of educational change,* pp. 121-44. Dordrecht/London, Kluver Academic Publishers. (Kluver international handbooks of education, vol. 5.)

B. Case studies

Braslavsky, C. 1998. El proceso contemporáneo de transformación curricular en la República Argentina [The process of curriculum development in present-day Argentina]. *In:* Filmus, *D., ed. Democracia, desarrollo e integración* [Democracy, development and integration], pp. 365-402. Buenos Aires, Ed. Troquel.

Carless, D.R. 1997. Managing systemic curriculum change: a critical analysis of Hong Kong's target-oriented curriculum initiative. *International review of education* (Hamburg, Germany), vol. 43, no. 4, pp. 349-66.

Curriculum 2005 Review Committee. 2000. *A South African curriculum for the twenty-first century. Report of the Review Committee on Curriculum 2005.* (Under the co-ordination of Linda Chisholm). Pretoria. May 2000. (Available at: http://education.pwv.gov.za/Policies_Reports/Reports_2000/Chisholm_2005.htm.)

Künzli, R. 1999. *Curriculum policy in Switzerland.* (Paper presented at the International Symposium 'Curriculum-making processes and curriculum research', Zurich, 2-4 December 1999.) (http://www.lehrplan.ch/symposium/Kuenzlie/htm)

Kyriakides, L. 1999. The management of curriculum improvement in Cyprus: a critique of a 'centre-periphery' model in a centralised system. *In:* Townsend, T.; Clarke, P.; Ainscow, M., eds, *Third millennium schools: a world of difference in effectiveness and improvement,* pp. 107-24. Lisse, The Netherlands, Swets & Zeitlinger Publishers.

Lowe, J. 1997. Curriculum reform in Poland: putting new needs into an old system. *Education* (electronic journal, Budapest, Winter 1997. (Available at: http://www.neumann-haz.hu/english/contents.html)

Ohlhaver, F. 1997. *Syllabus work between 1990 and 1995 in Germany and Switzerland: a cross-national comparison.* (Paper presented at the European Conference on Educational Research Symposium 'Curriculum research in cross-national, comparative perspective', Frankfurt am Main, September 1997, http//www.helrplan.ch/d/research/conferences/ecer/ohlhaver.pdf.)

Philips, D. 2000. Curriculum and assessment policy in New Zealand: ten years of reform. *Educational review* (Abingdon, UK), vol. 52, no. 2, pp. 143-53.

Rinne, R. 2000. The globalization of education: Finnish education on the doorstep of the new EU millennium. *Educational review* (Abingdon, UK), vol. 52, no. 2, pp. 131-42.

Strajn, D. 2000. *Comprehensive school reform in Slovenia: a brief account.* (Paper presented at the 'Intensive training workshop on curriculum development in Kosovo', Geneva, 1-10 December, 2000.)

Task Force on Curriculum Reform. 1997. *Reaffirming the mission of our schools.* Report of the Task Force. Ministry of Education of Quebec, Canada. (Available at: http://www.meq.gouv.qc.ca/REFORME/curricu/anglais/school.pdf)

Yamagiwa, T. 1994. Curriculum reform and its implementation: new trends in the revised curricula in Japan. *In:* OECD. *The curriculum redefined: schooling for the twenty-first century,* pp. 70-88. Paris, OECD.

C. *Reference documents*

Amadio, M. 2000. *World data on education: a guide to the structure of national education systems.* Paris-Geneva, UNESCO:IBE. (Including the third edition of the CD-ROM *World data on education.)*

Carnoy, M. 1999. *Globalization and educational reform: what planners need to know.* Paris, UNESCO:IIEP. (Fundamentals of educational planning, no. 63.)

International Bureau of Education; Central Board of Secondary Education, India. 2000. *Globalization and living together: the challenges for educational content in Asia.* Final report of the sub-regional course on curriculum development, New Delhi, India, 9-17 March 1999.

Morin, E. 1999. *Seven complex lessons in education for the future.* Paris, UNESCO.

Tedesco, J.C. 1997. *The new educational pact: education, competitiveness and citizenship in modern society.* Paris, UNESCO.

Section 2

The Management of Curriculum Adaptation for Curriculum Specialists from the Gulf Countries—A Round-Table on Curriculum Change

18

Planning Curriculum Reforms: Some Reflections

Shapour Rassekh

The transmission and acquisition of reliable knowledge has been the primary goal of curriculum development for several decades. In 1970s however, educationists such as P.H. Hirst (1974) believed that the curriculum should be built around several logically distinct forms of knowledge such as various fields of science, art, philosophy, etc. 'From the early 1970s onward, philosophers of curriculum turned increasingly toward an exploration of defensible general aims and attendant ethical values', observed J. White in the *International encyclopedia of education* (1994, p. 1326). Ideas such as the contribution of curriculum to personal autonomy, personal well-being, to general happiness, or to civic and economic ends soon entered the discourse.

In the 1990s, ethics rather than epistemology seem to have received greater emphasis in the curriculum. The International Commission on Education for the Twenty-first Century (UNESCO) believed that acquiring the necessary qualities as human beings, as citizens (learning to be), and learning to live with other people in peace, harmony and friendly co-operation should constitute a vital aspect of education.

The dominant model of curriculum planning which serves as a reference point is the Tyler rationale (Tyler, 1969) that has been summarized by G. Posner as follows:

> When planning a curriculum, four questions need to be answered. *First,* planners need to decide what educational purposes the school should seek to attain. Specialists should derive these 'objectives' from systematic studies of the learners, from studies of contemporary life in society, and from analyses of the subject matter. These three sources of objectives are then 'screened' through the school philosophy and through the knowledge available about the psychology of learning. *Second,* planners need to determine what educational experiences can be provided that are likely to attain these purposes. Possible experiences are checked for consistency with objectives and for economy. *Third,* the planner must find ways that these educational experiences can be effectively organized. *Fourth,* the planner needs to determine whether the educational purposes are being attained. Objective evaluation instruments (e.g., tests, work samples, questionnaires, and records) are developed to check the effectiveness of the curriculum *(International encyclopedia of education,* 1994, p. 1329).

We have to remember that curriculum planning is never a purely technical matter as Tyler or Taba (ibid., p. 1328-34) assume. In most cases, even in the democratic countries, there is an intervention of political authorities in that process. The extent of reform in the curriculum is often decided by the political leaders because of the differences in political perspectives amongst different political groupings. The harmonious growth of personality or learning in the sense of the acquisition of knowledge and know how, are no longer the only purposes of the education system. Greater emphasis is being laid on the development of specific attitudes such as devotion to national goals or developing desirable characteristics in the learners. Governments are particularly interested in such approaches. Even in the context of developing qualified human resources to meet the growing needs of the economy, the issue of quality, attitude and behaviour of the individuals to be trained are never overlooked.

The technical production perspective in curriculum planning, represented by Tyler, Taba and others is the predominant mode of thought prevalent in the United States. As opposed to this, we have the critical perspective of thinkers such as P. Freire for whom 'curriculum planning is not viewed as a technical matter, but instead as a political and ideological one... the end product is not a learning outcome, but critical reflection and action upon reality'.[1]

We believe that there are aspects of truth in both technical and critical perspectives and one does not necessarily contradict the other. There are many cases where the political decision-makers define goals of the education system and its curriculum, but the precise educational objectives and means to reach them efficiently are left to curriculum specialists. More deliberations involving all the partners of the education process are being organized. Objectives and means are not being viewed as two separate entities but as J.J. Schwab suggested (Schwab, 1970) they are being seen as part of a 'flexible, varied and interactive planning process'.

Returning to the concept of *objective setting* as the first step of curriculum planning, Maitreya Balsara in a recent publication (Balsara, 1999) proposes the following criteria for choosing the right objectives;

- the educational objectives must be conceived in terms of the demands of the social circumstances (for example, the conditions prevalent in a society where science and technology have the highest position, or a society faced with the challenge of globalization process, etc.);
- education should lead toward the fulfillment of basic needs (such as access to a job, acquisition of communications skill, etc.);
- be consistent with democratic ideals (such as producing responsible citizenship);
- be either consistent or non-contradictory in their relationships with one another;
- be capable of reduction to behaviouristic terms (for example, with critical thinking means in terms of behaviour at different levels of study).

According to the same author, the process of curriculum change involves four stages:

1. recognition of need;
2. planning and formulation of a solution;

3. initiation and implementation of the plan;
4. institutionalization of the change.

In the opinion of the author, a plan is formulated to satisfy the need identified at the first stage.[2] The participation of all stakeholders such as experts, students, administrators, the public, even the media in the formulation of educational policy and plan is recommended.

Having decided upon the changes to the curriculum, its implementation needs additional efforts such as communication and publicity, leadership from administrators, generating broad-based support, awards, resources and finally appropriate forms of innovative management and organization (ibid., p. 33).

The paper by Macelli in the present publication proposes a systematic model in the form of a practical operational manual of a certain approach to the initial responsibilities of a curriculum planning team. In Balsara's terms these would be: recognition of need; planning and formulation of a solution.

How are the multiple objectives, some socio-economic and others related to the development of the individual, expected to be derived and managed in the context of their interrelationship? How are the multiple stakeholders to be consulted beneficially and their interests judged in terms of their relationship to one another? The complexities of such requirements make a systematic approach to curriculum revision inevitable. Outside the field of education, there are tools that managers and planners use to cope with such complexities. Macelli in his paper develops an approach that customizes one such set of tools from the field of project management and adapts it to meet the challenges facing curriculum reforms.

The emphasis of his paper is on the first step, that is, the diagnosis of needs and formulation of objectives. In respect of both these curriculum development responsibilities, his approach involves dealing with the education system in its entirety. As a result, the derived objectives inevitably represent two inter-linked planning agendas: one for the change of the curriculum itself and one for the reform of the education delivery systems involved. The challenge then is seen to be 'curriculum review and related education system reform'.

In an attempt to take the reader and potential user through the proposed method, the paper presents the adapted tools in systematic format that provides examples so that the outcome of each step can be visualized. This is done for example in connection with building a 'problem-tree', or a tree comprising hierarchical unfulfilled educational and social needs. An 'objectives-tree' for the revised curriculum and for the education delivery systems is then derived from this.

Notes

1. H. Taba, *Curriculum development, theory and practice,* New York, Harcourt & Brace World, 1962, Taba proposes seven steps (a linear model) in curriculum planning:
   - diagnosis of the needs;
   - formulation of objectives;
   - selection of content;
   - organization of content;
   - selection of learning experiences;
   - organization of learning experiences;
   - determination of what to evaluate and of ways and means of evaluating.

   Tyler and Taba belong both to the school called 'technical production perspective'. For them, schooling is a process whose main purpose is to promote or produce learning. Objectives are conceived in terms of desirable learning and the planner should develop scientifically the means necessary to produce the desired learning outcomes.
2. We refer readers to other chapter of the book including principles of subject matter selection, use of instructional time, curricula aids, etc.

References

Balsara, M. 1999. *Principles of curriculum reconstruction.* New Delhi, Kanishika Publishers.

Hirst, P.H. 1974. *Knowledge and the curriculum.* London, Routledge.

Postlethwaite, T.N.; Husén, T., eds. 1994. *International encyclopaedia of education,* 2nd ed. New York, Pergamon Press.

Schwab, J.J. 1970. *The practical: a language for curriculum.* Washington, DC, National Education Association, Center for the Study of Instruction.

Tyler, R.W. 1969. *Basic principles of curriculum and instruction.* Chicago, University of Chicago Press.

19

Planning for Curriculum Review and Related Education System Reform

Tony Macelli

Introduction

Educational content, educational methods and aims, and educational delivery systems—as the parents and midwife in the birth of new generations—all face contemporary challenges, such as the changing world economy, globalization, regional integration, the Internet and so on. They also often face the challenges that consist of their own failings in the past.

To reformers at country level, education district level or autonomous school level, there are two phases or major aspects to the process of achieving educational and societal change through curriculum revision. The first is the process of bringing about change in the curriculum; and the second is the process of bringing about the institutional and operational changes that are required for the proper implementation of the new curriculum. Quite different activities may characterize the two phases. Also, there might be delays and political difficulties in the interim period between the curriculum revision phase and the education reform phase.

There is a case to be made, however, for some kind of integration of these two phases at the planning stage, and also with related major activities, such as public communication strategies or political-content changes. This may render benefits, such as more built-in foresight, better consultations and a wider sense of ownership of the whole process. If these benefits do occur, they bring a greater chance of success. Here, therefore, we shall consider the two processes as two phases in a single overall process of curriculum revision and educational reform.

What makes these processes challenging to manage is the diversity of attitudinal, political, educational, institutional and cultural changes necessarily involved, and the number of diverse interests of various stakeholders: parents, teachers, teacher trainers, educational experts, school administrations, district and regional education systems, and national and other politicians. There are, however, proven methods and approaches for managing such complex multi-faceted processes of change. One of them in widespread international use is the 'objectives-oriented project planning' (OOPP) or 'logical framework method'.

The logical framework method[1] was developed for the United States Agency for International Development and later transformed by the German International Development Agency (GTZ)[2] into a participatory and client-centred holistic tool for a process of planned change.

Such methods, if applied to the field of curriculum revision and related education system reform, may be expected, based on the experiences of their use in various other contexts, to have a number of strongly desirable features, including:

- rationalizing and focusing the whole enterprise;
- formally processing conflicting and other stakeholders' interests;
- providing a framework for seamless creative collaboration and synergy of various teams;
- properly and usefully recording outcomes of planning work for later re-use;
- making provision at early stages for monitoring and evaluation;

- reducing arbitrariness and using logically interrelated elements in a plan;
- providing persuasive justifications for all major innovative elements;
- providing an institutional memory that enhances similar future waves of reform.

The purpose of this paper is to enable change agents—such as educational administrators charged by the political sector with the task of reform—to visualize the application of the OOPP method of the process of curriculum revision and related education system reform in schools. It is assumed here that many or all of the school subjects at compulsory education levels are involved, and that new outlooks, methods and approaches are being introduced, but the tools used in the present paper should be useful for single-subject curriculum revision and for non-schools post-secondary educational contexts.

The intention here is not to present a watertight model that can be used independently of national and regional conditions, independently of different starting points and different political systems, or independently of the broad directions of desired change. It would be simplistic to imagine that this could be done. The intention is rather to stimulate educational change agents to develop the tools and processes that are required for their own region and country. The process described here is idealized and rationalized. It is acknowledged that, in real scenarios, planning and the implementation of plans are often non-linear, non-sequential, iterative, unexpectedly complex and even chaotic. Nevertheless, the map has to be smaller and simpler than the terrain, and in that, hopefully, lies its usefulness.

Unless stated in a footnote to be fictitious, all the illustrations in the present paper of material generated at various point of the idealized process are taken of faithfully adapted from real processes of curricular reform that have actually occurred. However, it has been difficult to find cases where the OOPP framework has been used in the context of curriculum-development and related educational reform.

Table 1. OOPP for curriculum review and education system reform.

Step	Description	Curric Revision	Education System Reform	Document produced as a result
	(I) ANALYSIS AND CURRICULUM FORMULATION PHASE of curriculum review and education systems reform			
S1	Conduct stakeholder analysis (CR, ESR)	Yes	Yes	A stakeholder analysis chart or report in relation to curriculum change and education system change
S2	Conduct problem analysis (CR, ESR)	Yes	Yes	A problem-tree spanning problems in learning and problems in delivery systems.
S3	Conduct analysis of student learning objectives (CR); alongside institutional change objectives (ESR)	Yes	Yes	An objective tree spanning problems in learning and objectives and institutional reform objectives.
S4	Draft, publicize and revise a new curriculum document with stakeholder participation (CR)	Yes	No	A curriculum document, revised or new and authoritative (e.g. a new minimum curriculum), a revised set of curriculum standards, new guidelines, etc.

Table 1. (Contd...)

	(II) PLANNING PHASE of education system reform			
S5	Define intervention logic for ESR	No	Yes	A LogFrame planning chart for curriculum implementation and education system reform. It is a 4x4 or 5x4 matrix. The *narrative first column* in filled.
S6	Specify assumptions and risks for ESR	No	Yes	The *assumptions and risks columns* of the LogFrame chart is filled, and the first column revised if necessary.
S7	Identify indicators and means of checking them for ESR	No	Yes	The *indicators and measures columns* of the LogFrame chart are filled, and the first column revised if necessary. Monitoring and evaluation plan
S8	Prepare activity schedule for ESR	No	Yes	The *activities and outputs rows* of the LogFrame chart A list of activities with responsibilities assigned to (individual, corporate or collective) agents. A set of targets/milestones/deliverables/ outcomes/outputs. Training programme items are derived from other targets and activities, and added to them. PERT flowchart plan if required.
S9	Prepare cost schedule for ESR	No	Yes	Cost analysis of the activities. The *inputs row* of the LogFrame (if 5x4 cell format used). Calendar charts of inputs and activities.

Thus, these illustrations have had to be taken from other approaches and graften onto the OOPP approach to help us visualize the use of this method for our context.

The literature put out by various authors and consulting firms is not always identical as regards the steps of the OOPP method. Even the LogFrame, or 'logical framework' chart—a fundamental part of the approach—is not always exactly the same. Sometimes OOPP and Logical Framework Method (LFM), are used interchangeably. This should hopefully not cause too much confusion, and we shall here present a representative list of steps of OOPP and later an acceptable version of the LogFrame chart. The sequential parts of the OOPP approach are presented in Appendix I of the present paper.

A Customized Approach

The 'project' in our case[3] would take root as a result of locally felt need in a specified area, such as a country or a sub-national region or school district, depending on the nature and location of the felt need and the amount of educational and political autonomy available in the region concerned. The project would be given a specific title such as 'Curriculum Revision and Related Education System Reform', possibly with a more specific subtitle specifying the type of reform the geographical scope, and other detail. This prevents confusion of different broad expectations in the early parts of the process; but the focus will become progressively sharper and more clear as the first steps proceed. We assume also that policy mandate, authorization or clearance has been given by an appropriate source, e.g. an electoral programme, a ministry policy paper, a departmental business plan, or other document.

Who undertakes or co-ordinates the planning activities in steps such as those shown above? In a relatively contained scenario, there may be a single planning team to do all the work. But if the context of the project is geographically wide or educationally complex, there may be a progression of actors, each taking charge of a group of steps, ideally with a single body overseeing general progress. Thus the work of curriculum revision or design may be assigned to a suitable design team including a core of educational experts, while the planning of subsequent curriculum-implementation, for example, at the national level, may be assigned to a quite different team of persons. More detailed planning at the level of school districts or more local level could be the responsibility of yet another set of teams, one for each local area. At various stages, the several categories of stakeholders themselves would have to be involved, in the interests of graining ownership and increasing the chances of success. These various scenarios notwithstanding, we shall refer to 'the project team' for convenience.

What scenario can be assumed for the purposes of the present paper? We assume a scenario in which holistic 'curriculum revision' (CR) *as well as* significant 'education system reform' (ESR) are required, the latter being necessary to support, enable and complement the changed curriculum. The use of the term 'curriculum revision' here, rather than 'curriculum development', is deliberate. It is meant to suggest that in the assumed scenario there is a strongly felt need for fairly radical changes in the content and methods of the curriculum. It suggests that that normal incremental methods of revising the official curriculum for schools are either nonexistent or too slow to cope with the pace of change within the country or within the global context. Similarly, it is assumed that fairly radical reform is required in the education delivery systems. This refers, for example, to the modernization of procedures and information flows, the upgrading of skills, the introduction of new styles of teaching, the recognition of diverse styles of learning, the utilization of new classroom technologies, and so on.

For such a scenario, the present paper proposes a modified OOPP-type method of planning, which is summarized in Table 1.

This method, which we may refer to as the CR-ESR or 'curriculum review—education systems reform' model, intertwines these two processes of change to account for their interrelationship. The first 'steps' are devoted to them both, and then a 'step' is devoted mainly to curriculum review, followed by several steps devoted to the planning of education systems reform. There are two successive phases, called firstly the 'Analysis and Curriculum Formulation Phase', and then the 'Planning Phase for Education Systems Reform'.[4]

The Analysis Phase, represented by the first three steps in Figure 1, must focus on both the CR and the ESR challenges. The results of these three steps need to be crystallized by the project team with the aid of stakeholders into a consistent and publishable new 'curriculum document' in the fourth step. The starting point would be the detection of two types of problems: learning problems *versus* institutional problems. Institutional problems here refer to deficiencies in education service delivery and difficulties related to education felt by other societal institutions, for example employers not finding the right job skills in school-leavers. The learning problems and institutional problems as conceptually distinct, but have to be recognized in their strong interrelationship and formulated correspondingly.

Thus, for example, in step S1 a certain *problem* in children's learning may be found to exist, to a significant extent, because of a certain education service delivery problem (or problems). For example, low levels of numeracy or literacy (a curriculum achievement problem) may be maintained by a defect in teacher training or class organization that does not take into account different learning styles of different students (this being an institutional problem). This interrelationship is the justification for our proposal to have a joint problem analysis for the CR and the ESR areas. In the spirit of the OOPP approach, the analysis in Step S1 makes use of various sources for identifying the problems and their linkages, and results in a hierarchical problem tree.

Then, when in step S2 *objectives* are derived to solve these problems, these objectives similarly have to be conceded together, even though they may be objectives in distinct domains. These objectives, in the same example, may be: (a) a learning objective, with is to be used in curriculum design; and (b) and institutional objective, which is to be used in the reform of education systems. The need for identifying simultaneously the CR-related and ESR-related problems (with their relatedness), and similarly also the corresponding objectives, is the reason for the double scope (CR and ESR) assigned in the proposed approach to the first two steps. The subsequent fourth step, S4, where the 'curriculum document' is generated, revised and published, does not really correspond to any one of the standard OOPP steps.

The remaining steps after this are standard OOPP-type steps for designing and planning a complex project. Here they are used to design the intervention required in the education service delivery system. They aim to discover what activities and achievements are necessary so that the institutional change objectives and all the learning objectives are sustainably met.

We shall now present each step (as described in Table 1) of this CR-ESR approach to planning, indicating what work is required by the various actors at the planning and giving examples of the results that may be obtained. Phase One—Analysis and Curriculum Document Formulation—comprises steps S1, S2 and S3 to be carried out by the planners' team, and step S4 to be carried out by the curriculum drafting team.[5]

Step S1: Stakeholder Analysis for CR and ESR

This step (SI) aims to obtain a lost of stakeholders and their interests in relation to the envisaged process of curriculum change and in education delivery systems. In this step, the planning team aims to involve, and where possible to bring together, representatives of as many of these stakeholders as possible.

The importance of this step is that it ensures that all persons with a stake in the result will be involved, if possible, in the process leading to that result. It has been found in many politically and developmentally diverse countries that a sense of ownership in curriculum change processes is critical to the success of the reforms. Ownership is obtained by involving the persons concerned appropriately in the process, be they teachers, teachers' unions, political decision-makers in the educational and related sector, opposition politicians, school heads, departmental director and staff, local educational experts and teacher trainers, the general public, parents, school students, employers, non-state school boards, local government councils, school councils made up of teachers and parents, and others.

There may be reasons for which no co-operation is forthcoming from one or more of these persons, groups, institutions or categories of persons. The teachers' union may be insisting on holding the crucial parts of the process to ransom unless their demands regarding conditions of work are met. Opposition politicians may not wish to collaborate publicly because of the political dynamics of the day, perhaps determined by non-educational issues. Administrative personnel may be reluctant to take on more work. Some parents may be against innovation and may be afraid of a decline in recognition of school-leaving certification by employers. It may or may not be possible to resolve such obstacles to universal support for the important societal change processes of curricular and educational system reform. However, even in the case of non-co-operation, it is important that planners are aware of the real interests of the various dissenting or co-operating groups. In the case of dissenting groups, it may be possible to incorporate some, if not all, of their concerns and interests as the planning proceeds; if they will not take part in the initial meetings, then somebody else may have to formulate their presumed interest or 'stake' on their behalf.

Thus, one of the purposes of the present step is the identification of the diverse societal interests involved, in the interests of harmony—or at least of a rational strategy in the process of change. In a slightly wider sense, the purpose of this step is to have as many diverse perspectives as possible for clarifying the politics of the change. Politics is a field of resource distribution, of distributions of power, of interests and conflicts of interests. What is at stake includes such valued items as tradition, money, authority, power, prestige, public credit and acknowledgement of one's contribution—and such negatively valued items as the loss of the above values, including shame or loss of face.

In the present context, questions to be answered during this step are therefore similar to the following ones: What are the important aspects of the situation comprising learning, teaching, service delivery and so on? Who is involved; who is going to be involved; who has a right to be involved? Who has the expectation of becoming involved? Who decides what; who implements what; and who is going to be affected? Who will benefit, who will pay, who will take the risky decisions? Who will bear the consequences of failures? Who will feel threatened? Which persons, in broad terms (such as the authors of out-of-date textbooks), will be actually worse off after the changes being contemplated?[6]

OOPP approaches suggest a number of preliminary meetings for this step, possibly using brainstorming techniques on the topic of 'problems and opportunities faced by the stakeholders', as well as other forms of research, such as analysis of past documents, interviews with key persons, questionnaires and so on. They may generate material for the next two steps, but their key purposes lie in the areas of: (a) involving stakeholders in the reform process where possible; (b) harmonizing the process to their interests where possible; and (c) mapping the landscape of diverse interests.

One method that has been suggested for the creation material for the stakeholders analysis is to generate for each major corporate stakeholder the replies to the questions: What are the organization's strengths, weakness, opportunities and threats or problems faced? This so-called 'SWOT analysis' can generate information about stakeholder interests used in the present step, and also about the problems and objectives used later in step S2 and S3. The replies to these four questions can be generated by the representatives of many corporate stakeholders at a meeting organized by the planning team. The political context, for course, may make such a meeting inadvisable, but conversely such a meeting, where everybody understands the other stakeholders' interests, aims and constraints, may actually reduce some types of conflicts.

At the end of this step, the planning team would create, not necessarily for publication, a document called a

FIGURE 2. Stakeholder analysis chart for a CR-ESR process—a partial example

Stakeholders in CR-ESR	What is their interest or 'stake'? +=potential benefit -=potential negative effect	Requirements for their continued support for the project	Appropriate participation mechanism
Teachers	+More professional job responsibilities +High quality in service training –More work for profiling and farmative assesment of students	Consultation on own problems; consultation before curriculum change in their subject	Questionnaires; school-level and district level teacher' diagnostic and problem-solving meetings; contributions recorded and given to planners Postal contributions invited on drafts of new curriculum and on experts' implementation plans
Primary school students (from middle-class neighbourhoods and families; girls and boys)	+Wholesome, creative personality development, building on preferred learning style; joy, wonder, curiosity; fulfilling relationships; academic tools; whole future life; entitlement for education		Sample pre- and post-reform interviews of pupils by expert educational psychologist to determine environmental and pedagogic strengths and weaknesses of school, curriculum, teaching styles etc.
Teachers' unions (etc.)	+/- Opportunity for winning better conditions of work by temporarily blocking a reform desired by government +More professionalization of their members	Early negotiations with government; special strategy needed by government in case of non-cooperation	Negotiations behind closed doors with agreed confidentiality and provision for arbitration

stakeholder analysis. Like other planning documents, this may be revised whenever better insights appear later in the planning process. It should be deposited within the records of the planning institution, and possibly elsewhere, for the sake of long-term institutional memory. However, it will be directly useful again in the present planning process, especially during those later stages where objectives are set (S3) and where assumptions and risks are being identified (S6). A realistic partial example is included as Table 2. An actual list of stakeholders appears as Appendix III.

Decisions may now be made—based on such a chart, based on previous experience and based on current political situations—about who to invite to the subsequent series of planning meetings. Even those who are not participating should have their interests considered at the time when the problems and objectives are being identified, in the next steps.

Step S2: Problem Analysis for CR and ESR

An overview of the undesirable aspects of the present situation should now be undertaken. The existence of these undesirable elements in the curriculum and in the education delivery system is the justification for carrying out curriculum review and education system reform. Problems may include difficulties faced by stakeholders, unfulfilled potentials and unfulfilled opportunities—all, of course, related either to the teaching and learning process or to the education delivery systems.

The persons to be actively involved at this stage should be chosen by the planners for a strategic reason: they should probably include the major stakeholders. The exercise of carrying out this step may have a beneficial effect on certain types of minor conflict. Because it enables problems to be faced dispassionately and some-what scientifically—that is, with at least an intuitive analysis of cause and effect—the participants tend to retreat from adversarial positions and perspectives, if possible. The planning team may therefore use this step, and the next one, not only for the sake of its theoretical results but also for the results in terms of interpersonal and inter-group relationships, and some measure of conflict resolution. If the correct informal and good-humoured atmosphere can be achieved, this step and the next one are highly enjoyable and highly tought-provoking sessions. In order to obtain a perceptive and comprehensive result, the informality and freedom from fear of criticism are important factors, and so this should be explained and built into the expectations of the meeting or meetings.

In both modern and traditional, religious or secular cultures, serious consideration should be given to surveying and soliciting public opinion, and the opinions of various types of bodies. There is no enterprise that is as far-reaching and multi-faceted as the education of a generation of new citizens. There is no enterprise that affects an entire population as much as the education of its children and futures families. The legitimacy of educational reforms derives not only from what educational experts think, but equally from what the citizens are noticing, feeling, wanting and saying. In steps S2, S3 and S4 therefore, questionnaires, meetings and appeals in the media for public contributions should be included among the means of getting information and opinions. In the present step S2, these public opinions can complement, enrich and reality-check the experts' and planners' answers to questions such as: What are the problems in the present curriculum and syllabuses? What are the problems in the manner that educational services are delivered?

OOPP-type methods require at this stage that the problems are identified and placed hierarchically in the form of a branching tree of items, known as a 'problem-tree'. The 'technology' for doing this in a group requires small cards on which participants can write one problem per card. The cards are then stuck on a larger sheet or sheets of paper, such as wrapping paper, wallpaper or flip-chart paper, that has been fixed onto a wall with a detachable glue for the participants to examine. Markers or pens should be available to make the background paper, if necessary with hierarchy lines and loops around large clusters of items. The chart thus formed may take up the best part of a wall of a room or hall. Participants should be free to walk around the chart as it is being created, and severall persons can share the tasks of collecting and placing the cards in a hierarchical order.

What determines the hierarchy? More focal, more basic problems are to appear high up on the chart, but even further above them may be some of the anticipated problems, or 'effect' problems. If there is an existing problem *X* on a card on the chart, and another problem *Y* is being examined, then if Y contributes to *X,* it is called a 'cause' and is placed below *X.* If Y is created or affected by *X,* then it is called an 'effect' and is placed above *X.* If *Y* is neither a cause nor an effect, then it is placed to the side, neither directly above nor below *X.* Some pairs of problems are mutually influencing, and this can be indicated by arrows drawn on the paper. Arrows may also link problems that are not near each other. `Regions' or clusters of problems for the chart may emerge naturally. In such a case, each cluster would consist of inter-connected problems, but is weakly linked to other clusters. Each cluster may have a top .or focal problem. The cluster may be delineated with a marker pen, and may be given a name. If necessary, a section may be given to a sub-group or an external group for more careful or more expert elaboration.

At least one company has produced software for following an objectives-oriented project planning approach, including the creation of problem-trees. However, as already stated, beneficial experience can be gained from the hands-on method using several interacting participants, cards and glue, and so if the software is available it probably should not be used as a substitute.

In our CR-ESR method, colour-coding of the cards is required to distinguish between two types of problems. One type of problem is classifiable as curriculum content (or omission). The other type consists of those that are classifiable as institutional or education system problems. There is some overlap, as in the area of teaching methods, but this is of no great concern in this step. It is in the next step, where objectives are to be derived from these problem-cards, where it is important that the twofold classification be made. This is because *curricular* objectives will be used to create a new curriculum or a new curriculum document (authoritative standards or guidelines, etc.) while the *institutional* objectives will be used to create a plan for the implementation of the curriculum and for reforming the necessary aspects of the educational delivery systems.

What does a problem-tree look like in the context of the CR-ESR model? An illustration of a small part of such a tree is given as Figure 1. Discussion about the problem-tree may later need to identify one or more core problems. Often in OOPP-type methods, only one core problem is identified per project team, as this leads to focused solutions and effective problem-solving. However, in the case of complexities of holistic curriculum and education systems review, it is doubtful whether the luxury of identifying only a single core problem is available or useful. Figure 2 clarified the position of two core problems identified from the problem-tree in Figure 1—one institutional, the other curricular.

Step S3—Linked objectives analyses for CR and ESR

Converting problems into objectives

The aim in this step is to develop a vision that would solve the problems indicated in the problems analysis just undertaken. To be more exact, what we need to develop at this point is two visions: one for what the future completed curriculum document should look like; and secondly, a view of what the education delivery systems should look like. We need to be able to visualize our destinations and, to some extent, our paths as well.

Fortunately, the OOPP-type procedures break this daunting task into steps that often can be easily carried out by the planning team, possibly together with the main stakeholders. The type of meetings required is similar to those of the previous step. The problem tree derived in the previous step is *converted into* an 'objectives tree'. This conversion is not a mechanical process, but nevertheless consists of manageable actions that do not present a major challenge. Moreover, there is the opportunity for inspired insight when

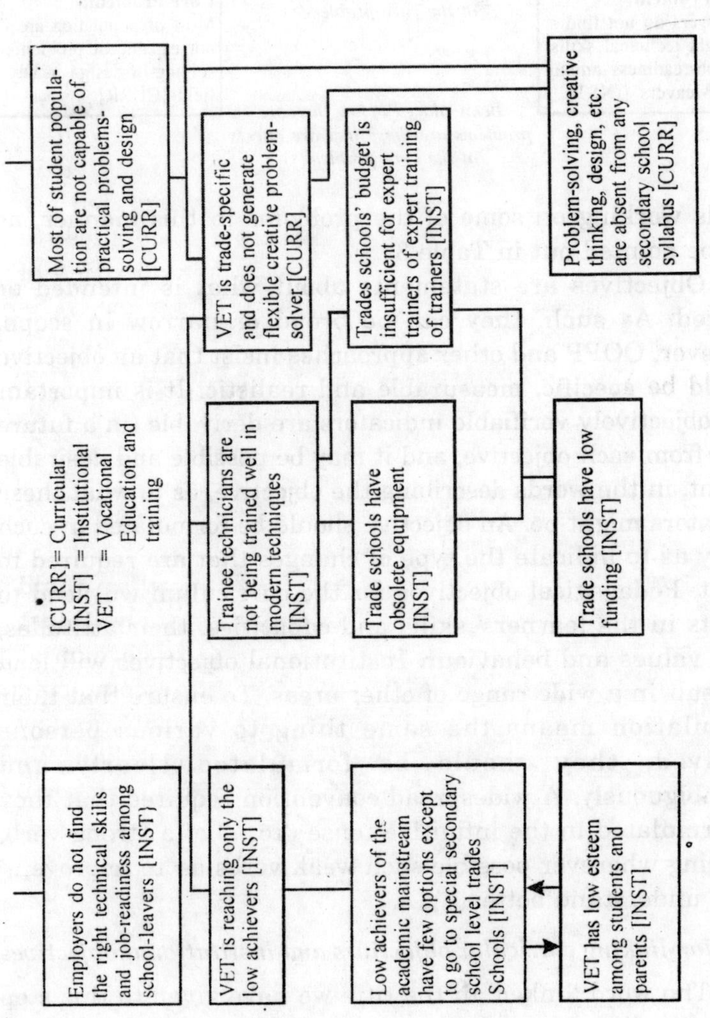

Figure 1. Part of a problem-tree showing related curricular and institutional problems

Figure 2. Identification of two core problems is the problem-tree of Figure 1.

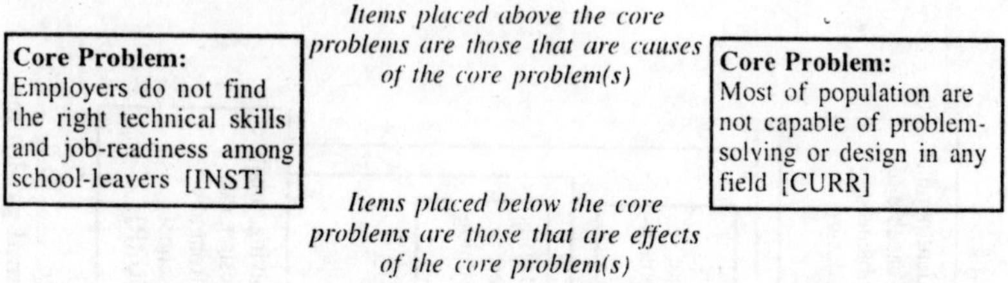

Core Problem: Employers do not find the right technical skills and job-readiness among school-leavers [INST]	*Items placed above the core problems are those that are causes of the core problem(s)* *Items placed below the core problems are those that are effects of the core problem(s)*	Core Problem: Most of population are not capable of problem-solving or design in any field [CURR]

one is working on some of the problems in this manner, as will be pointed out in Table 3.

Objectives are statements about what is intended or desired. As such, they can be broad or narrow in scope. However, OOPP and other approaches insist that an objective should be specific, measurable and realistic. It is important that objectively verifiable indicators are derivable (in a future step) from each objective, and it may be possible and desirable to hint, in the words describing the objective, as to what these indicators might be. An objective should be formulated in such a way as to indicate the type of changes that are required to result. Pedagogical objectives for the curriculum will lead to results in the learners' skills and capacities, their attitudes, their values and behaviour. Institutional objectives will lead to result in a wide range of other areas. To ensure that their formulation means the same thing to various persons involved, they should be formulated clearly and unambiguously. A widespread convention required that they be formulated in the infinitive tense ('to...') of a strong verb, avoiding wherever possible such weak verbs as 'to improve...' or 'to understand better...'.

A vision linking curricular objectives and institutional objectives

The word 'linked' in the title we have given to this step indicates that there are two generally different, but linked, types of objectives that will appear; they correspond to the two branches of the CR-ESR model—on the one hand improving the curriculum and on the other hand improving

Table 3. Deriving a set of objectives from a set of problems—vocational education and training (VET)

From this problem...	...was derived this objective(s)	Comments—how and why.
Employers do not find the right technical skills and job-readiness among school-leavers [INST].	To develop a job-market oriented workforce with modern skills and international-level qualification [INST/CURR].	*Straightforward conversion; note that an institutional problem has required an objective that is partly curriculum related.*
	To achieve attitudes and skills of retrainability and lifelong learning among most school-leavers and in adult education [CURR].	*This additional objective was intended to tackle the indicated problem more radically and with a more holistic perspective.*
VET is reaching only the low achievers [INST].	To ensure that VET successfully reaches and motivates many persons of all abilities including high achievers [INST/CURR].	*Straightforward conversion; note that an institutional problem has required an objective that is partly curriculum related.*
VET is trade specific and does not generate flexible creative problem-solvers [CURR].	To develop practical problem-solving and design skills in most students [CURR].	*This objective is of wider scope than the problem was (i.e. it relates to all forms of schooling, not just* VET). *This is deliberate and was chosen in view of other problems recorded elsewhere.*
VET has low esteem among students and parents [INST].	To raise the esteem of vocational and technical education by enabling most students to familiarize themselves early with technical subjects.	*Straightforward conversion, plus a specific approach visualized ('most students...etc'.).*

(Contd...)

From this problem...	...was derived this objective(s)	Comments—how and why.
Most of student population are not made capable of practical problem-solving and design [CURR].	To include practical technology education in all primary and secondary schools [CURR].	*A creative insight gave rise to this additional objective as a way of resolving the stated problem (low VET esteem) and several others Related to skills*
Problem-solving, creative thinking, design, etc., are absent from any secondary school syllabus [CURR].	To include problem-solving, creative thinking, design and autonomous learning skills in all primary and secondary school curriculum [CURR].	*Straightforward conversion.*
Trainee technicians are not being trained well in modern techniques [INST].	See below.	*This problem suggests to the planners that something is seriously wrong with the whole institutional model that is being used to supply VET, perhaps an automatic carryover from a different past.*
Trades schools have obsolete equipment [INST]. Trades schools' budget is insufficient for expert trainers or expert training of trainers [INST] Trades schools have low funding [INST].	See below	*These three problems could have been translated in a straightforward manner into their converse objectives ('to upgrade equipment for trades schools' and 'to allocate more public funds to trades schools') but this was not done because it was felt that something is wrong with the current institutional delivery model and throwing money at it would not resolve the problems.*

From this problem...	...was derived this objective(s)	Comments—how. and why.
Low achievers of the academic mainstream have few options except to go to special secondary-level trades schools [INST].	To terminate secondary-level trades schools and set up instead a higher level but wide-access path to industry-useful vocational and technical qualifications [INST].	*The planners hare have a creative insight for the reform of service delivery; this is not a straightforward translation of the problem into an objective, but as soon as the insight appears, a strategy is conceived, and the institutional reform part of the project begins to seriously take shape, as also does the curriculum review part of the project.*
	To offer post-secondary VET qualifications to certified international standards [CURR] To ensure access to post-secondary technical college courses by all ages above 16 years including employed and unemployed persons [INST] To set up a post-secondary College of Arts, Science and Technology with a wide spectrum of institutes and courses, international experts and expert twinned international partner institutes [INST].	*These three objective were developed by thinking about the college-related reform-insight (above) in their context. Their context consists of all the other problems in the problem tree.* *Note that the college is conceived as the* ***means*** *to a higher* ***end*** *already identified: 'to set up...a higher-level but wide-access path to industry-useful vocational and technical qualifications'.*

the institutions, such as schools and departments that implement it. In our CR-ESR model, colour coding or the codes CURR and INST will be used on the cards on which the objectives are written. Some cards will be marked 'CURR' (see Figure 3) to indicate that they contain *pedagogical and other curriculum objectives,* that are to be fulfilled by developing the text of the new curriculum policy document containing a new curriculum or curriculum guidelines or standards. These CURR objectives will thus be fulfilled by educational experts, curriculum experts and subject experts. They may change the included subjects, the teaching approaches, the overall guidelines, and so on.

By contrast, some of the objectives cards will be marked 'INST' to indicated that they contain *institutional objectives* that are to be fulfilled by the curriculum implementation activities and by the innovations and reforms required in the education service delivery systems. Unlike the CURR objectives, which will be fulfilled by the formulation of a curriculum document, the INST objectives will be fulfilled by institutional changes of various kinds. Some of the changes will be curriculum implementation strategies of a system-maintenance type, while others will involve strategies of a system-changing type, such as the creation or termination of a college, the setting up of monitoring and evaluation systems where they have been absent, and so on. Unlike the curriculum objectives, these institutional change will be carried out, not necessarily by curricular experts but possibly by administrators, managers, directors and politicians.

There are bound to be some objectives that need to be marked as belonging to both categories, i.e. CURR/INST. Such objectives are to be treated as if they occur twice, once in each category. If colour-coded cards are used to build the objectives-tree, each such objective can be written on two cards, one of each colour.

The result, initially prepared in the form of cards on a wall as in the previous step, will look similar: near the top are more fundamental or ultimate objectives, and near the bottom are more instrumental objectives for reaching them.

Thus, vertically upward is the means-to-end direction, but it can also indicate lower objectives being encompassed by higher ones.

An example of a partial objectives-tree is shown in Figure 3. This was derived from the partial example of a problem-tree in Figure 1. To create this objective tree, the problems were reviewed and, where useful, a corresponding objective was generated, as is shown in Table 3.

Special objectives?

At this stage in the present model, the planning team should consider whether, besides the objectives derived directly from the problem-tree, it is also necessary to include a number of *special objectives,* as in the examples given below.

One category of special objectives that will almost certainly be required, whether or not it corresponds directly to anything in the problem-tree, is a set of *sustainability* objectives. How are the various innovations, curricular standards and so on to be sustained?

A second category of special objectives that will be required, to the extent that they are not already provided for elsewhere, is a set of objectives related to *monitoring, evaluation, curricular revision, and institutional corrective action.* The last two of these are responses to monitoring and evaluation exercises and processes. The education system, from child to minister of education, from teachers' groups to high-level committees, must generate information about its functioning, and especially about the functioning of the new or changed processes now being planned. Monitoring obtains this information. Evaluation processes examine this information and compare it to stated aims, and they inform the appropriate units, departments or persons about the result, and ensure that timely corrective action is taken.[7] The curriculum now being revised will need to be revised again eventually, perhaps after four or five years—or sooner. At that future time, the decision-makers and planners will appreciate it if, from the earliest possible time, information about monitoring and evaluation has been placed accessibly in some form of institutional memory, and that it will continue to be accessible and meaningful even when individual persons have moved, changed responsibilities or retired.

As in standard OOPP methods, certain provisions for monitoring and evaluation are built into the approach, as we shall see later. Those provisions, however, are part of the logical framework of the project design, and so they relate directly to the changes being planned within the 'project' that is currently being defined and designed. Systems that are automatically regularly monitored, evaluated and corrected are generally more 'intelligent' and robust or non-failing systems. Thus, in the interests of basing the present reforms within robust education delivery systems, the present step would be a good time to examine the delivery systems as a whole to see whether essential work is covered by successfully functioning systems of monitoring, evaluation and corrective change. If it is not, then it is likely that some special objectives to ensure the creation and use of such mechanisms may need to be added.

A third category of special objectives that may be required at this stage is related to *decentralization.* From the perspective of system vitality, the *principle of subsidiarity* should be seriously considered: no function is retained at an organizationally higher level if it can be carried out appropriately at a lower level, such as at the school or class level. For many countries, progress towards such as scenario would probably represent a considerable measure of decentralization. Decentralization generates ownership and motivation, and therefore increases effectiveness and efficiency in educational service delivery and in reform of delivery systems. There are, of course, intermediate functions of responsive support, monitoring and communications that must be carried out to sustain a healthy decentralization. A great deal of local creativity and commitment is purchased at low cost by an emphasis on centrally supported decentralization. The present step would be a good time to check out to what extent decentralization-related special objectives are necessary in the curriculum and in the institutional reform process.

The results of the creative problems-to-objectives conversion process are placed into and objectives tree, as shown in Figure 3. It should be noted that, as they are formulated and reformulated, the objectives will probably, as in our example, fall naturally into relationships with each other that are quite different from the relationships among the corresponding problems of the problem-tree. The structure of the objectives-tree is not the same as the structure of the problem-tree

Selecting project strategies from closely linked clusters in the objectives-tree

As regards the *curricular objectives*—those marked CURR in Figure 3—these are to be used to create a new curriculum document in the subsequent step (S4) of the present model. Here, we assume that there is a special team of experts who will be commissioned to convert these objectives into a new curriculum document. The curriculum expert team will need to know the context of these curricular objectives, so the entire problem-tee and the entire objectives-tree is reproduced and given to them along with their briefing. Their terms of reference would directly cover only the *curricular* objectives and the drafting of the document. They can be told to assume that some or all of the institutional objectives may be met by the time the curriculum document comes into effect or becomes law. The curriculum drafting team should, however, keep in touch regularly with the overall planning team, because such assumptions may have to be modified as the institutional planning and implementation work proceeds. Also, the planning team will be developing, among other things, a curriculum implementation plan and so they have to liase with the curriculum-drafting expert team. That being said, we may now assume that the curriculum drafting work can proceed to some extent in parallel with the work on the institutional objectives.

Let us now consider just the institutional objectives, those marked INST in Figure 3. The planning team can now identify clusters for the objectives-tree. A cluster is a group of objectives with many connections to each other in the objectives-tree. Using the word 'strategy' only slightly differently from its use in ordinary language, we may permit the OOPP tradition to define a 'strategy' as one or more clusters choses from the objectives-tree—preferably with a top-level or 'strategic' objective for each cluster.

The decision about how many of these strategies to identify and take up depends on the magnitude of the task and the resources available. How to proceed from here depends upon the complexity of the issues being addressed and the size, available time and expertise of the planning team and their groups of colleagues and, of course, on the gravity of the problems and the magnitude of the funding and human resource allocation for the planning and implementation stages. Thus, one or more strategies may be taken up as the nucleus of a project to be designed and implemented. One or more clusters may become a project. Alternatively, more than one project may be necessary from this point onwards, and different teams can be made responsible for different projects. A strategy can be given a name for identification purposes. For each project the next steps require the formulation of the intervention logic or Log-Frame plan. For simplicity, we shall now assume that, as regards the institutional objectives, there is one project with one strategy.

Step S4—The new curriculum document

The purpose of this step

What is a curriculum document? Here we use this phrase to refer to the various kinds of document that formally guide the manner in which education and training is to proceed. The document may be a complete set of objectives or guidelines, with some indications of the outcomes desired in the students. Or, it may be a formal list of educational outcome standards,[8] the standards being written in such a manner as to facilitate legal enforcement and to permit straightforward monitoring and evaluation of progress to be achieved. The document may be complete in itself, or it may consist of additions to, or revisions of, an existing curriculum. The purpose of the present step S4 of the CR-ESR approach is to create the curriculum document required in the given situation. The requirements for a curriculum are embodied in two groups of objectives:

(a) *Challenge-related objectives.* Objectives for meeting contemporary challenges—these would have appeared in the objectives-tree; they occur at various levels, some being instrumental to others or contained in others, whether they are grouped into strategy(ies) or not;

(b) *Comprehensiveness objectives.* All other objectives required for completing a curriculum as comprehensively as the situation requires. These may be compiled from various sources[9]—educational experts, public surveys, previous curricula, other countries' curricula, and international documents and conventions, such as those on human rights or the rights of the child. Here again, there will be various levels of objectives, some more instrumental for achieving others, and some will be more comprehensive than other ones that may focus on some tiny detail.

At the beginning of this step, the curriculum drafting team will have information from the previous steps, especially the strategies consisting of branches from the objectives-tree. From these, a curriculum document is to be created in the current step. There are, no doubt, many alternative approaches to the successful organization of such work.

Also numerous are the possible situations or scenarios that will have made the new curriculum document necessary. Questions such as the following will determine the scope of the activities required to create this document: Do a few aspects of the existing curriculum need to be changed, or is a radical re-writing or replacement of the current curriculum required? At what hierarchical level is the document required to be used? Is there are two or more hierarchical levels from centre to school, what level of decentralization/local autonomy is appropriate? Is the curriculum limited to one or a few specific school subjects (e.g. information and communications technology or ICTs) or considerations (e.g. gender equity), or rather is it supposed to cover holistically the entire educational activity of schools at one or more levels? Depending on the replies to these questions, the need and sources of additional objectives will become clear.

Who and how?

This step is carried out by curriculum-related educational experts, with the internal and external collaboration of stakeholders, experts and the users of important subjects being introduced or approached in a new way, such as ICTs in the classroom, or technology education. In a democratic environment, decisions about the content of a school's curriculum, such as the various levels of objectives embodied in the document, derive their legitimacy from the citizens and residents of the area, as much as from the experts. Thus, wide public consultation through postal enquiries and open public meetings is recommended. Clearly, there will not be total agreement among all stakeholders as to what is desirable at all levels. The following two considerations may be useful in this respect.

Firstly, the inclusion of a large number of actors or at least 'talkers' in the consultation process takes time and invites disagreements, but it is undertaken not so much for the cost-effectiveness of obtaining ideas in this way, but rather for different reasons. Ownership and commitment generated by such consultation has been shown time and time again to increase the success of such ventures. A person or institution that has been consulted may cease unnecessary opposition upon simply being consulted and listened to—that is, acknowledged. In many cases, especially perhaps where there is a history of insensitive or unresponsive bureaucracy or autocratic government, the real need of social actors may be to be acknowledged as participants and potential contributors, rather than to insist on their own opinions being accepted. Thoughtful persons are likely to realize that an entire set of conflicting opinions sometimes has to be consolidated in just one position. The acknowledgement comes

Figure 3. Example of a partial objectives-tree derived from the problem-tree example

[CURR] = curriculum reviews objectives; [INST] = institutional reform objectives

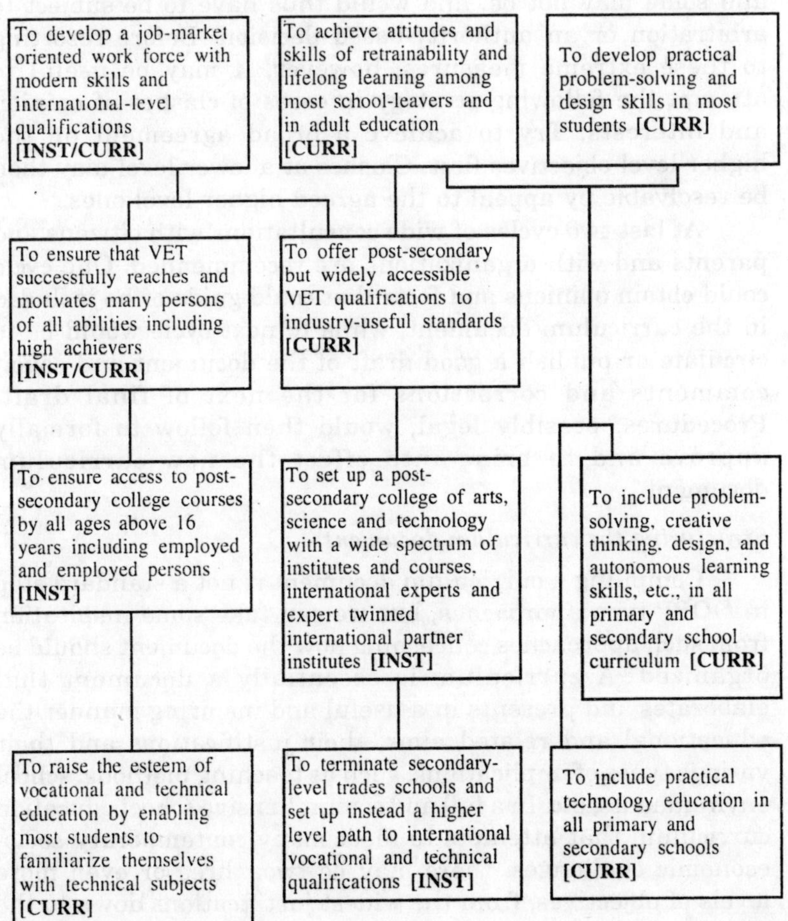

from being consulted, from getting feedback after a postal contribution, from being permitted to write a minority report, and so on.

Nevertheless, of course, we may expect divergences that arise from a real clash of interests. The stakeholder analysis will have anticipated many such clashes, and a strategy such as clash-focused early consultations or thinking about novel solutions that transcend the polarization may have been adopted to minimize such incidents. Still, real clashes of interest or of strong opinion will remain. Some are resolvable, and some may not be, and would thus have to be subject to arbitration or an authority-based decision. Before resorting to these extreme measures, however, it may be useful to attempt the following strategy in cases of clashes of opinion and interests: Try to achieve a broad agreement on the higher-level objectives first. Clashes at a lower level may then be resolvable by appeal to the agreed higher-level ones.

At last two cycles of wide consultations with citizens and parents and with organizations are recommended. One cycle could obtain opinions and facts that could guide or be included in the curriculum document, while to next cycle would be to circulate or publish a good draft of the document and solicit comments and corrections for the next of final draft. Procedures, possibly legal, would then follow to formally approve and to bring into effect the new curriculum document.

Structuring the curriculum document

Compiling a curriculum document is not a standard step in OOPP-type approaches, but we can take some inspiration from such approaches concerning how the document should be organized. A curriculum is essentially a document that elaborates and presents in a useful and inspiring manner the educational and related aims, their justifications and their various types of implications, such as teaching methods, school environments, etc. In a full and comprehensive school education curriculum that attempts to meet many contemporary socio-economic challenges, there may be two, three or even more levels of objectives, from the widest justifications down to the instrumental aims and desired teaching methods. An illustration of this seen in Appendix IV to this text entitled 'Examining the structure of a revised curriculum document', where the entirely new national minimum curriculum of a small country is shown to have principles and objectives of several levels and types.

We turn now to the two groups of objectives mentioned earlier. The challenge-related objectives, derived from the problem tree, would be important in a scenario where they have to be integrated into an already comprehensive curriculum or set of curricular standard. Both the challenge-related objectives and the comprehensiveness objectives, of course, would have to be included if the situation demands a comprehensive new curriculum document.

In the spirit (if not the letter) of the OOPP paradigm, it is proposed here that the objectives be organized into a single hierarchical list of types. The more comprehensive types would be those that themselves constitute their own justification and thus do not have to be justified by other objectives. The next-lower objectives are justified by those of the former type. Such justification of specific objectives in terms of specific higher ones may or may not appear in the text of the document, but it certainly should be attempted by the drafting team to avoid the tendency for flowery language and obscure implicit justifications. Similarly, the next-lower objectives are identified and linked with those above them, and so on.

A set of principles or values, either general (social, philosophical, religious) or curricular may be necessary to clarify the desirability of the highest objectives, as well as the others. These should probably be limited only to the ones necessary to justify any non-self-evident items among the higher-level objectives. If possible, any other items here should be converted from values or principles to carefully-formulated objectives. This is because, in that way, future evaluations can actually determine the extent to which they have been reached. Also, an objective requires the identification of instrumental aims, or means or measures that are to be used to achieve it, while a value or a principle does not. The inclusion of principles and values outside these parameters may be misleading because readers may be misled into thinking that the curriculum will significantly contribute to progress towards the principles and values, without in fact having any instrumental aims or means to do so.

One should use the OOPP-derived insight that the only acceptable objectives are those that have explicit higher-level justifications, and explicit lower-level instruments for achieving them. This suggests a clear, 'mapped' hierarchy of objectives. It is 'mapped' in the sense of that word as used in mathematics: there is an assigned explicit one-to-one or one-to-many correspondence between items at one level and items at the more instrumental level immediately below them. This achieves as far as possible a reduction of arbitrariness and a completeness of the logic, which may be shown by a hierarchical numbering system.[10]

The organization of the document might therefore look something like Figure 4:

1. **Values and principles,** general and curricular—a minimal set, as explained above.
2. **Highest-level objectives**—self-evident or derived expertly from developmental psychology and the potentials inherent in the child and adult; from the desired nature of human life and of this society; and from values such as creativity, equity, justice, compassion, spirituality. Some of these objectives will derive from special contemporary challenges identified in the earlier steps of the CR-ESR approach.
3. **Next level** (more specific) **objectives,** *if necessary;* each justified as explicitly as possible by the specific highest-level objectives above. Some of these objectives will derive from special contemporary challenges identified in the earlier steps. It may be necessary to subdivide these for different levels or types of schooling, if various such levels or types are included in the scope of the exercise.
4. **Next** (most specific) **level objectives** each justified as explicitly as possible by the specific highest level objectives above. It may be necessary to subdivide these for different levels or types of schooling, if various such levels or types are included in the scope of the exercise.
5. **Expected results** (formulated as specifically as is appropriate in the context) or outcomes or *outcome 'standards'* expected in students. Each objective or set of objectives in the level above should here correspond to sets of expected changes respectively in *Wisdom, knowledge, skills and attitudes.*
6. **Indicators of achievement of results**—for each result, a number of factors are provided that indicate whether these results are being achieved. These factors

Figure 4. A possible structure of a curriculum document.

1. **Values and principles.** (minimal)

2. **Highest-level objectives**
(Arrows show item-to-item vertical correspondence)

3. **Next (more specific) level objectives**

4. **Next (more specific level objectives**

5. **Expected results,** separately such as:
   a. wisdom;
   b. knowledge;
   c. skills or capabilities;
   d. attitudes.

6. **Indicators of achievement of results**

7. **Means of:**
   a. reaching expected results;
   b. monitoring;
   c. evaluating achievement of objectives.

8. **Syllabuses** (if appropriate)

9. **Institutional implications,** preferably *institutional objectives.*

are such that they can realistically be monitored. Indicators are also recommended for showing future achievement of the objectives, though it will not be easy to indicate achievement of higher-level objectives.

7. **Means**—approaches, strategies, methods, activities and tools for achieving the results expected above, and for reaching the objectives. Approaches, strategies, methods, activities and tools for monitoring the indicators and for evaluating: (a) the achievement of the objectives; and, in future, (b) the continued applicability of those objectives.
8. **Syllabuses** detailing the content of the courses. Note that a certain level of decentralization, use of the 'subsidiarity principle' or devolution of authority makes it possible and desirable for schools to develop their own syllabuses, within the wide parameters of a national minimum curriculum. In such cases there may not be any such thing as a national syllabus.[11]
9. **Institutional implications,** preferably in the form of *institutional objectives* for the education delivery systems concerned. These items may or may not be published with the curriculum document, but they are necessary because they represent imperatives or assumptions necessary for the proper fulfilment of the curriculum document. These implications should be reformulated with the planning team and passed to the planning team so that these can revise their institutional planning.

Phase Two

The remaining steps of the proposed process are not covered here for reasons of space.

- CR-ESR Phase Two—Planning of education systems reform;
- Step S5—Logical framework analysis for ESR;[12]
- Step S6—Specify assumptions and risks for ESR;
- Step S7—Indicators and measures for ESR;
- Step S8—Plan results and required activities for ESR;
- Step S9—Cost analysis.

APPENDICES

APPENDIX I—STEPS OF A STANDARD OOPP APPROACH

The TEMPUS Manual[13] of the European Commission indicates the following major steps of a project planning team in following an OOPP approach.

Analysis phase of OOPP

- Step OOPP A: CONDUCT STAKEHOLDER ANALYSIS: identify groups, people and institutions which are likely to be affected by the project, and identify the key problems, constraints and opportunities they face.
- Step OOPP B: CONDUCT PROBLEM ANALYSIS: formulate problems; determine *cause and effect* relationships and develop a problem-tree.
- Step OOPP C: CONDUCT ANALYSIS OF OBJECTIVES: develop objectives from the identified problems; identify *means to end* relationships; identify clusters of objectives and determine the project strategy.

Planning phase of OOPP

- Step OOPP D: DEFINE INTERVENTION LOGIC: define the project elements, test its internal logic, and formulate objectives in measurable terms (the LogFrame chart is built or rebuilt during this step).
- Step OOPP E: SPECIFY ASSUMPTIONS AND RISKS: identify the conditions which are likely to affect the project's implementation but which are outside the project management control.
- Step OOPP F: IDENTIFY INDICATORS: identify ways to measure that progress has been achieved, formulate indicators, define means of measurement.
- Step OOPP G: PREPARE ACTIVITY SCHEDULE: determine the sequence and dependency of activities, estimate duration, set milestones and assign responsibility.

- Step OOPP H: PREPARE COST SCHEDULE: specify inputs required, develop cost schedule, prepare detailed budget.

APPENDIX II—Three variants of the LogFrame chart

We show on the following page, for the purposes of steps S5 to S9 of the present paper, three variants of the LogFrame chart, the tool that helps planners to make a logical framework analysis of a project being planned, or of an existing project. Essentially the same logic is involved. Some large donor agencies have adopted one or another of these and require it to be used by the applicant in all applications for funding. Variant A is the most elegant, complete and easy to remember. Variants B and C appear to be attempts to use a smaller number of cells. The basic idea is the same in all three variants.

APPENDIX III—Example of a list of stakeholders

This is an actual list of stakeholder related to the curriculum review and education system reform process in a small country.

The processes of curriculum review, and of educational reform based on it, necessarily involve a diversity of attitudinal, political, educational, institutional and cultural changes. It therefore involves also a number of stakeholders, that is, individuals, groups, institutions and categories of persons that have interests in the project. These interests are based on how they will be affected by the processes involved.

The following is a list of some of the main stakeholders in the case of changes to curriculum and delivery systems at compulsory education levels. Note that various specific themes and school-subjects emphasized in the new curriculum—for example gender equity, inclusion, use of information and communication technologies, and many others—bring into the picture a number of related interests and stakeholders. These are identifiable within the public (e.g. women), government, commerce and industry, nongovernmental organizations and religious groups. Such stakeholders related to specific subjects have been omitted from the list below or subsumed under wider categories.

A. ***Categories of individual stakeholders***

- Assistant heads of schools;
- Education officers;
- Educators of teachers;
- Employers;
- Facilitators for children with special needs;
- General public;*
- Heads of schools;
- Minister of Education
- Overseas experts (advisers, trainers);
- Parents of children who are not doing well at school;
- Parents;*
- Students in faculties of education;
- Students who are not doing well at school;
- Students (early and primary school);
- Students (secondary school);
- Suppliers of services and equipment newly de-emphasized by the National Minimum Curriculum (NMC);
- Suppliers of services and equipment newly emphasized by NMC;
- Teachers of subjects de-emphasized in NMC;
- Teachers;*
- Unemployed teachers.

*= *Various classifications are relevant in different subjects and contexts within the process of curriculum review and education system reform.*

B. ***Corporate stakeholders***

- Association of school councils;
- The Cabinet;
- Church schools: secretariat for religious education;
- Department of Curriculum Management;

Variant A – the 5x4 format

Source: Possibly GTZ, German International Development Agency

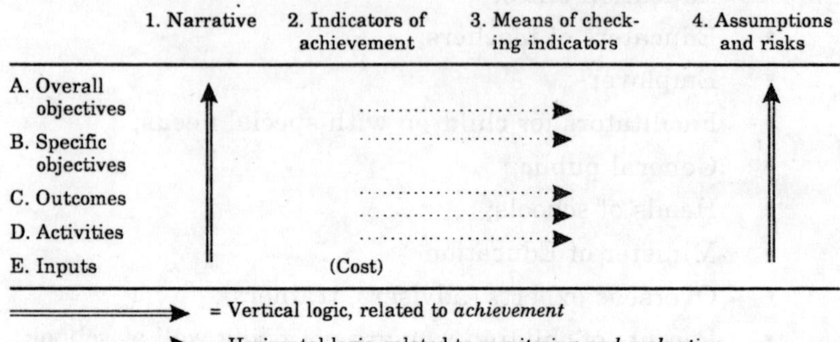

Variant B – the 4x4 format

Source: TEMPUS (European Commission, 1966)[13]

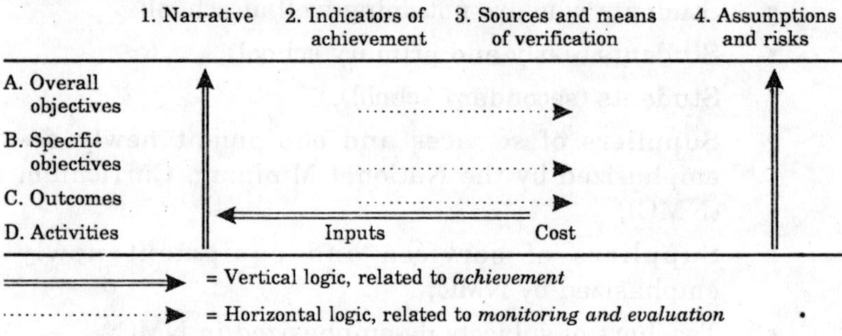

Variant C - the 4x4 format modified

Source: European Commission, 2001

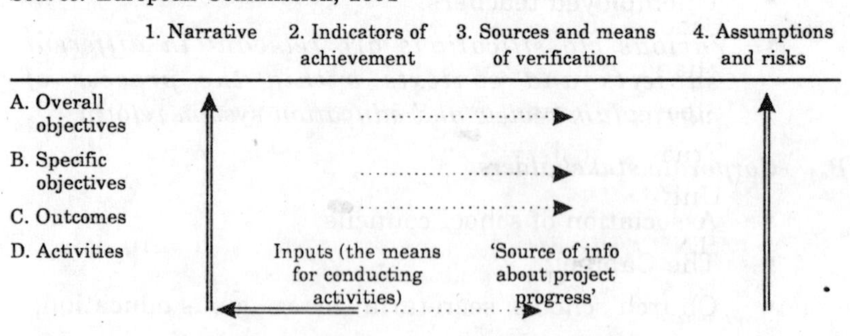

- Department of Student Services;
- Education Division;
- Educational experts;
- Employment and Training Corporation;
- Faculty of Education;
- Government ministries (Social Policy, Public Works, etc.);
- Government party
- Independent schools;
- Local councils;
- Teachers' union;
- Matriculation and Secondary School-leaving Certification Board;
- Colleges of arts, science and technology;
- Members of eighteen specialized groups;
- Ministry of Education;
- Ministry of Finance;
- National Minimum Curriculum, Drafting Committee;
- Opposition party;
- Parent/teachers associations;
- Parliamentary Social Affairs Committee;
- School administrations;
- School councils;
- Shadow Minister of Education;
- Steering Committee on the Implementation of NMC;
- Trade schools;
- University.

APPENDIX IV—Examining the Structure of a Revised Curriculum Document

Here we examine the structure of an actual curriculum document. In this case, the curriculum document is in the form of a holistic national curriculum for all schools teaching students of compulsory education age (ages 5 to 18). The document is the successor of a previous document that had been in force for a number of years. However, the present document has been constructed from scratch, rather than by reviewing parts of the older one. The document is not being proposed here as a model, although it was very well received when it was published in its country of origin. It is being examined simply to clarify the broad manner in which its content is organized, and especially to clarify how a hierarchy of objectives is managed in it. This review is being carried out for the purposes of step S4 of the present paper.

The curriculum document being examined is the or National Minimum Curriculum (NMC) of Malta. It is a legally authorized and endorsed national document, obligatory for all state and non-state schools. Malta is a two-party parliamentary democratic republic of just over 1.3 million people spread over only 120 square miles. Between the central structures and the school level there are no regional educational administration institutions, such as school district authorities or departments. The NMC text may be accessed on a web site at http://curric.magnet.doc. For present purposes, the numbering system of the text has been altered.

The NMC is not the type of curriculum that includes the detailed content of courses and classes. The document expects that, in the spirit of the educational aims and guidelines that it proposes, such course syllabuses be created at the school or other level. This expectation is part of a deliberate attempt at decentralizing, or at least diversifying, the choice of lessons, books and resources, and course design, which had previously always been designed centrally for state schools.

The initial pages of the published document present messages from the Minister of Education, the Director-General of Education, the Director of the Department of Curriculum Management, the President of the Malta Union of Teachers, and the President of the Association of School Councils, as well as a preamble.

Part I of NMC—Background to the review process

This section of the published curriculum document (see Box 1) given the legal background and justification for the creation of a new curriculum document. The purpose of such a text may be to emphasize the document's formal authority to readers, such as parents and teachers, other than those many teachers and parents who have contributed to it in some way. There is also a historical summary of how the curriculum review and re-creation took place (Box 2). The purpose of this summary may be to emphasize the moral authority that the document derives from the participatory methods and wide postal and other consultations that were used to create it.

Box 1. The Legal Framework of the Maltese National Minimum Curriculum—NMC

- Entitlement to education;
- State duties;
- Right of the State to regulate education;
- Minister's right to establish the curriculum; and
- The power to make regulations.

Box 2. The process of curriculum review

The initial stages:

- Establishment of working committees;
- Consultations;
- Analysis and discussion;
- Publication of the draft document;
- Immediate reactions.

Formulation of the final document.

Part II of NMC—Contemporary challenge and educational response

Recognizing the challenges: This section of the curriculum document identifies the social, economic and cultural challenges that face the country today, and from them derive some broad guidelines for education.

The educational reponse to the cultural, social and economic challenges: This section sharpens the broad guidelines of the previous section into 'responses', remedies or solutions for the education of citizens whose living and working environment will be characterized by the challenges mentioned in that section. The prescriptions appear to be a mixture of the following types of items: overall objectives for learning, overall objectives for change in the education service delivery systems; outcomes expected to result in the students. The text here says:

'The validity of the curricular experience can be judged from the extent to which the educational system succeeds in responding to the realities and challenges that have merged in Maltese society, in a world that is becoming ever more complex, global and interdependent. It appears, from the process of consultation, that there is agreement among the educational community regarding what should be the parameters of an educational system that prepares students to live and work in a world that is changing rapidly. The educational community generally agrees that a dynamic curriculum should provide an educational experience (1) promotes fundamental values among students; (2) facilitates their holistic development; (3) motivates and prepares them to be lifelong learners; (4) enables them to live a full and productive life in a shrinking global village; (5) prepares them for the world of work, where change is a fact of life.'

There are five sub-sections (see Box 3) to correspond to these five responses. These overall prescribed 'responses' for education are each discussed in more detail with some of their implications also listed in point from within each of the sub-sections.

Box 3. Sections of a dynamic curriculum

1. Values and socialization;
2. Holistic development;
3. Lifelong education;
4. Global perspective;
5. The world of work.

Part III of NMC—The curricular principles

A number of 'principles' are proposed in this major part of the document (Box 4). They are stated to be principles on which the curriculum document as a whole is based, but they are also proposed as tools for educators. Where did they come from? The curriculum drafters were very concerned about social justice and equity, especially the child's right to quality education, gender equity, and other aspects of justice and entitlement. The text here says, 'The principles that shape this document are inspired by the belief in social justice. Each of the principles described are indispensable for the implementation of this socio-educational project [of education].' It seems, therefore, that the drafting team: (a) took into consideration the then current educational practices and results, as well as complaints of parents and other who were consulted; (b) adapted a critical social-justice perspective on certain parts of the education services delivery system; and (c) crystallized their responses to the anomalies in the form of 'principles'. Each of these principles are presented and discussed in the text and possible misunderstandings are disposed of. The overall implications of each principle are presented as guidelines for interpreting the present curriculum, for teaching and for school organization.

Box 4. Curricular principles

Principle 1:	Quality education for all;
Principle 2:	Respect for diversity;
Principle 3:	Stimulation of analytical, critical and creative thinkings skills;
Principle 4:	Education relevant for life;
Principle 5:	Stable learning environment;
Principle 6:	Nurturing commitment;
Principle 7:	Holistic education;
Principle 8:	An inclusive education;
Principle 9:	A more formative assessment;
Principle 10:	The strengthening of bilingualism in schools;
Principle 11:	Gender equality;
Principle 12:	Vocation and competence;
Principle 13:	The importance of learning environment;
Principle 14:	Increasing participation in curriculum development.

Part IV of NMC—Educational objectives

A number of objectives are presented in the text, and a section devoted to each. Each of the following sections is divided into subsections of more detailed aims as follows:

- expected outcomes in terms of *knowledge/ information;*
- expected outcomes in terms of *skills;*
- expected outcomes in terms of *attitudes.*

Part V of NMC—Special aims and expected results for the different levels of the education system

Besides the widely applicable objectives given in the previous section, special aims are required for each of the bands or levels of education: early childhood, primary and secondary (Box 6). These age-related and level-related educational aims tend to be more specific than the ones in the previous sections, although no schema of mapping has been attempted that links each of the objectives numbered in the previous section to the more specific aims given in the present section.

Box 5. Education objectives.

Objective 1:	Self-awareness and the development of a system of ethical and moral values
Objective 2:	The development of citizens and a democratic environment
Objective 3:	Developing a sense of identity through creative expression
Objective 4:	Religious education
Objective 5:	Strengthening of gender equality
Objective 6:	Education on human sexuality
Objective 7:	Preparing educated consumers
Objective 8:	Media education
Objective 9:	Effective and productive participation in the world of work
Objective 10:	Education for leisure
Objective 11:	Wise choices in the field of health
Objective 12:	Greater awareness of the role of science and technology in everyday life
Objective 13:	Competence in communication
Objective 14:	Preparation for change

Box 6. Aims and expected results of education specific to the level: early childhood, primary and secondary.

1. Early childhood education

a. Intellectual development

b. Socio-emotional development

c. Physical development

d. Moral development

e. Development of a sense of aesthetics and creativity

f. Religious development (for those who believe)

g. Effective tools that facilitate the holistic development of children

2. Primary education

a. Learning a repertoire of skills

b. Strengthening of personal and social education

c. Development of enhanced skills, knowledge and attitudes linked to the basic subjects

d. Fulfilling principle of education for diversity

e. Linking summative and formative forms of assessment

f. Implementing a policy of bilingualism

g. The teaching of religion

h. Parent education programmes

3. Secondary education

a. Strengthening and refinement of the skills developed at primary level

b. Strengthening of personal and social education

c. Implementation of the broad aims within the curriculum content

d. Implementing a policy for language teaching

e. Adopting summative and formative forms of assessment

f. The development of projects revolving around themes

g. The teaching of religion

h. Strengthening of emotional development

i. Strengthening parent participation

Part VI of NMC—Part schools and the interpretation of the curriculum

This section encourages decentralization to the school level by challenging the 'educational community' within each school to interpret the curriculum and develop school-level curricula and course syllabuses based on it, using and boosting consensus and democratic processes in education. Heads are told their various special responsibilities in facilitating and supporting this process of school-level curriculum interpretation and development among teachers and heads.

Part VII of NMC—Conclusion

The conclusion indicates some institutional objectives.

APPENDIX V—CASE DESCRIPTION, STEP BY STEP.

The following events were recorded by the Policy Unit of the Ministry of Education in Malta, to give a picture of the steps followed in the creation of the NMC of that country and later an implementation plan for the NMC. The process was not smoothly progressive: it took several years and experienced two elections, both of which changed the party in power and ushered in a new Minister of Education. It is not being proposed here as a model. The process did not use the CR-ESR approach being proposed in this paper. It is included here as a non-idealized illustration from reality.

The first national curriculum was published through Legal Notices 73 and 76 of 1989 and 103 of 1990 in accordance with article 45 of the Education Act of 1988. The Education Act states that the mission of a national curriculum is 'to provide for the full development of the person, including the ability of every person to work'. The process of reviewing Malta's first national curriculum was started in the summer of 1994. Included on the following pages are the major milestones between 1994 and 2001, when the implementation process, approved by Cabinet, became operational.

A. ***Measures directed by the Minister of Education and Human Resources, Dr Michael Falzon, between 1994 and 1996***

1994

19/8 Minister appoints a *Consultative Committee on Education (CCE).*

22/9 Minister and Permanent Secretary meet CCE members and decide period for completion of CCE terms of reference.

1995

April CCE submits its report *Tomorrow's schools: developing effective learning cultures.*

19/4 Ministry disseminates the CCE report.

29/4 Ministry organizes a national colloquium on the CCE report.

May to Dec. - Written submissions from stakeholders trickle in.
- CCE members continue holding discussions with senior officials from the Division of Education regarding the report *Tomorrow's schools.*

1996

Jan. Minister writes to CCE members to thank them.

13/3 Permanent Secretary requests Director-General to direct the Department of Curriculum Management to plan and monitor formulation process of a draft curriculum for the Minister's consideration by the 31 March 1998.

27/3 Director-General communicates his mandate to the Director of Curriculum Management.

27/3 Director-General requests Director Curriculum Management to proceed with review exercise.

16/6 Director Curriculum Management forms a Strategy Building Team from among members of the Curriculum Department.

June Last written submission on *Tomorrow's schools: developing effective learning cultures* is received.

June to Aug. The Strategy Building Team:
- presents a proposed strategy for the curriculum review exercise to Director-General;
- proposes and sets up a Steering Committee made up of fifteen resource persons; and
- undertakes a consultation exercise with stakeholders.

B. Measures directed by the Minister of Education and National Culture, Mr Evaristo Bartolo, between September 1996 and August 1998

1997

14/2 Steering Committee for Curriculum Review holds its first meeting and decides to:

continue consultations with stakeholders and task groups;

analyse feedback received;

- Determine nature of required document; and
- Present first document to Minister by March 1998.

The Committee is made up of fourteen members representing the Ministry's Division of Education, the Faculty of Education at the University, the Malta Union of Teachers (MUT), the Association of School Councils, State and private schools, and the National Youth Council.

1997 Stakeholder feedback:

- 330 written invitations to participate were mailed;
- Written feedback received included 70 state primary and 20 secondary schools, 15 from non-state schools, 23 from education officials, 13 from members of faculty of education, 2 from other education sections, 5 from private organizations and 21 from individuals.

1998

March Document entitled 'Draft New National Curriculum for Education in Malta for students between the ages of 3 and 16 years' was presented to Minister.

March 8,000 copies of the draft national curriculum were printed and disseminated for the purpose of further consultations.

May Minister tables draft curriculum document in parliament.

Minister in press conference declares November as the deadline for ending the stakeholder consultations.

August Using a questionnaire, the Division of Education carried out a survey of parents' perceptions of the curriculum at the annual Malta International Trade Fair; thousands of parents filled in the questionnaire. A report was drawn up and presented to the Minister.

August The Ministry publishes a leaflet which is widely distributed at the Malta International Trade Fair. Through this leaflet, the Minister made a number of statements regarding the practice of streaming and about the junior lyceum entrance examination.

C. Measures directed and undertaken by the Ministry of Education, DR Louis Galea, between September 1998 and February 2001

1998

11/11 Minister meets senior Education Division officials to set in motion the continuation of the curriculum review process that had stalled after the March 1998 publication of the draft National Minimum Curriculum.

5/12 Dialogue session in Lija with a group of stakeholders from a range of sectors. Among the forty-four invitees present were:
from Ministry: Personal Assistant, Private Secretary, Permanent Secretary, Hon J. Mugliett (Parliamentary Secretary) and his PA, Mr Sciberras from Gozo Ministry, Prof P. Serracino Inglott;
from Education Division: Mr Charles Mizzi, Director General of Education; Ms Mary Vella (Director Curriculum), Ms Carmelina Debono (Director Operations) Ms Joyce Pullicino (Director Further Studies & Adult Education, Mr Joe Sammut (Director Planning and Development);
from Faculty of Education: Dr Ronald Sultana, Dr Paul Pace (Head Dept. Maths, Science and Technical Educ.), Dr Antoinette Camilleri (Head, Dept. Arts and Lang. In Educ), Dr Joseph Mifsud, Dr Mark Borg, Prof Saviour Chircop;
from Drafting Committee: fourteen members;
from Opposition: Mr Evarist Bartolo; and
others: 2 from MUT, 3 from Association of School Councils; 1 from Archbishop's Curia, 1 from St Aloysius College, 1 from Chiswick School, 1 from the National Commission of Persons with a Disability.

11/12 Seminar at the Mediterranean Conference Centre with heads and assistant heads of state and private schools.

15/12 Focus Group meeting at the Palace regarding the language policy. Present were Permanent Secreatry,

Director-General of Education, Director Curriculum Management, university lecturers, education officers, heads of state and private schools.

16/12 Focus Group meeting at the Palace with representatives of independent and Church schools on impact of curriculum on school management.

1999

12/1 Minister consults a large group of teachers about their views of different aspects of the curriculum.

20/1 Minister meets the shadow minister of education and the MUT Council.

21/1 Meeting with thirty representatives of constituted bodies at the Grosvenor Hotel. Among those present were Mr Evarist Bartolo, members of the Steering Committee for Curriculum Review and representatives of: CMTU, FOI, MUT, UHM, WPDC, SCOOPS, FHRD, ETC, Employers' Association, Chamber of Commerce, Young Enterprise.

27/2 Minister invited to a National Conference on the Curriculum organized by the Association of School Councils, at which the shadow minister of education was also present. Over 200 persons were present. The aim of the Conference was to discuss the contents of a parent-friendly version of the Draft Curriculum published in March 1998 and to formulate a memorandum for subsequent presentation to the Minister.

20/3 A second dialogue meeting with members of the Association of School Councils at which the shadow minister of education was also present. Members of the association presented the Minister with a memorandum.

March Conclusion of second phase of consultation with educational partners and stakeholders.

June Commencement of formulation of final document.

Sept. Finalization of formulation of National Minimum Curriculum. Minister and Policy Co-ordinator (Education) edited final version. Director

(Curriculum Management) prepared detailed index and chose illustrations.

Sept. Cabinet approves the National Minimum Curriculum.

23/9 Minister delivers address *Positive schools—capable pupils* at keynote conference for all secondary school teachers, held in Republic Hall, Mediterranean Conference Centre.

Oct. Final Draft of the National Minimum Curriculum and its abstract published for the purpose of deliberations by the Parliamentary Social Affairs Committee.

6/10 Ministers delivers a Parliamentary Statement on the NMC and recommends that the Final Draft National Curriculum be discussed by the Parliamentary Social Affairs Committee. He tables copies.

Oct. Parliamentary Social Affairs Committee invited a number of stakeholders to discuss the final draft. Sittings and deliberations were held on the following dates: October 18-20, October 25-26, November 2 (2 sessions) and 3 (2 sessions).

Oct. Minister addresses teachers on National Teachers' Day and focuses on curricular reforms and ministry vision and priorities.

11/11 Minister delivers an address entitled 'School and curriculum management: the Maltese perspective' during a Senior Staff Development Seminar for all heads of schools, education officers, assistant directors and directors of education. Seminar organized by the Planning and Development Department of the Education Division at Boffa Hall, Mediterranean Conference Centre.

29/11 Minister publishes a 3,000-word article entitled 'Malta prepares the next generations' in *The management journal*, a bi-monthly publication of the Malta Institute of Management. This important article is aimed at stimulating appreciation of the NMC and related ministry policies by intellectuals.

22/11 Minister delivers a speech on curriculum development entitled 'Landmarks' at the Euro-

Mediterranean Conference on the Establishment of a Mediterranean Network on Curriculum Management, organized by the International Bureau on Education of UNESCO in Malta on the 22-26 November 1999.

Dec. Curriculum printed in two language various: *Maltese version:* Inwelldu I-Gejjieni Flimkien; *English version:* Creating the future together, Around 20,000 copies printed.

2000

Jan. Minister writes letter to all teachers and sends them and the Division of Education personnel a complementary copy of the curriculum. Copies on sale for the public through The Department of Information bookshop in Valletta.

26/1 Minister appoints a National Steering Committee on the Implementation of the National Curriculum entrusting its twelve members with the task of preparing a national strategy and plan.

26/1 Minister appoints a Training Strategy Formulation Team to complement the work of the National Steering Committee.

1. Prof. Kenneth Wain, Faculty of Education, University of Malta—Chair of Steering Committee;
2. Dr Carmel Borg, Faculty of Education, University of Malta;
3. Mr Frans Borg, President, Association of School Councils;
4. Mr John Bencini, President, Malta Union of Teachers (MUT);
5. Dr Christopher Bezzina, Faculty of Education, University of Malta;
6. Ms Carmelina Debono, Director (Operations), Education Division;
7. Mr Evan Debrincat, Head, San Andrea School, I-Imselliet;
8. Bro. Saviour Gatt, Secretariat for Catholic Education, Archbishop's Curia;

9. Dr Tony Macelli, Adviser, Ministry of Education—Ministry Rep., & Exec. Sec of Committee;
10. Mr Charles Mizzi, Director General, Education Division;
11. Dr Ronald Sultana, Faculty of Education, University of Malta; and
12. Ms Mary Vella, Director (Curriculum), Education Division.

Dept of Curriculum places NMC on website: http://curric.magnet.mt

Feb. National Steering Committee appoints eighteen specialized working groups to formulate a theme-specific plan by May.

Feb. to June The Ministry, in collaboration with the Department Curriculum Management and the Association of School Councils, organizes community-based short courses and one-off sessions for parents to familiarize them: (a) with the nature, scope and content of the curriculum; and with (b) their role in the development of a school-based curriculum.

A number of series of radio and TV programmes are planned and broadcast.

The Ministry produces a brochure in Maltese highlighting the principles and educational objectives as enshrined in the National Curriculum for distribution among parents.

April Ministry prepares and prints a booklet in Maltese highlighting salient points from the National Curriculum of special interest to parents (50,000 copies).

May All eighteen specialized working groups, made up of 148 stakeholders, submit their written plans to the Executive Secretary of the Steering Committee at the end of May.

Aug. Minister establishes an Institute for Child and Parent Learning Support (ICPLS) and mandates it, through Legal Notice 135 of 2000, to develop effective strategies to combat the problems of school failure, illiteracy and habitual absenteeism.

9-11/6 A National Conference, *Curriculum on its way: a Conference on the Implementation of the National Curriculum,* is organized by the National Steering Committee on the Implementation of the National Curriculum in collaboration with the Division of Education, the Faculty of Education and the Socrates Office. Over 800 professionals and parents participated.

25/7 In exercise of the powers conferred on the Minister of Education by section 47 of the Education Act (CAP.327), Legal Notice 132 of 2000, *National Curriculum Regulations. 2000* is published in the Government Gazette.

Aug. Editing of Proceedings of National Conference starts.

1/10 On 1 October 2000, the National Minimum Curriculum took effect by law in virtue of Legal Notice LN132 of 2000 related to the Education Act (Cap. 327) entitled National Curriculum Regulations.

27/10 The Malta Union of Teachers declares industrial action and directs 'all teaching grades... not to attend any meetings connected with any matter related to the National Minimum Curriculum and not to implement any proposals contained in the NMC'.

29/12 Steering Committee submits to the Minister its National Strategy and Plan for the Implementation of the National Curriculum.

2001

5/2 Publication (3,000 copies) of the Proceedings of the National Conference *Curriculum on its way: a Conference on the Implementation of the National Curriculum,* held in June 2000. All papers and action plan proposals of the specialized working groups were included in the publication, as well as workshop reports and a reprint of the national Minimum Curriculam.

7/2 Minister concludes agreement with the Malta Union of Teachers, thus bringing to an end the industrial action declared by MUT that halted a number of NMC implementation measures.

Feb. Ministry produces an abridged version of the National Strategy and Plan of future publication.

12/2

19/2 Minister presents to Government for approval the National Strategy, Plan and Budget for the 2001-2005 implementation of the National curriculum.

The country is now ready to use a strategic plan for the integral implementation of the NMC

The following is text originating in the Ministry, showing the situation in February 2001: a Strategic Plan has just been prepared for schools, departments, and others to implement the national minimum curriculum.

The National Minimum Curriculum (NMC) comes at a time when school-levers and adults of all ages are required to be equipped: with skills in the learning and manipulating of information; with capacities to think, to use technology and solve problems; with the ability to relate well to oneself and others; with the transferable skills for taking up employment and taking up jobs; and of retraining and shifting jobs when the jobs become obsolete.

A 'National Steering Committee on the Implementation of the NMC' was created by the Ministry of Education early in the year 2000, with appropriate specific terms of reference, in order to create a Strategic Plan for the implementation of the NMC.

As a means to create the Strategic Plan for Implementation of the NMC, the committee has continued the participatory process that had given birth to the NMC itself. There are many stakeholders in curriculum change and educational system change, and many of them have a right to participate. The composition of the committee reflected the involvement of major stakeholders: Division of Education, Ministry of Education, teachers, educational experts from the Faculty of Education, church schools, independent schools, Association of School Councils. The committee worked in such a manner as to reinforce and develop the participatory processes that had led to the creation of the National Curriculum itself, and to use those processes to generate the required components of the Strategic Plan.

The main features of this participation-generating work have been: the publication of the NMC, meetings and courses for parents and for teachers and for heads, questionnaires to state and non-state schools, a special questionnaire for church schools, meetings for parents, many public media programmes and articles, 120 experts and practitioners in eighteen specialized working groups proposing action plans, a national conference of 800 persons discussing and augmenting those action plans, a compilation of questions and troubling issues as perceived by teachers and heads of schools, and various work contributed through the Education Division. During this work, the following stakeholders were themselves engaged as the active facilitators of participation among yet other stakeholders: The Steering Committee itself the Education Division, the Association of School Councils, the Secretariat for Catholic Education, and members of the Faculty of Education.

Less than a year after the setting up of the Steering Committee, at the end of 2000, the committee completed its work on time and submitted their consensual report. As a result of the participatory methods mentioned above, we now have a comprehensive strategy, in the form of a Strategic Plan for Implementation of the NMC, with several strategic goals and with 140 Targets for schools and other bodies to reach within five years. But, equally importantly, we now also have a certain readiness and a considerable sense of ownership among teachers, parents, and others. Common sense, local experience, and wide international experience has shown that such participation and sense of ownership of the process are quite essential components of successful curricular review and corresponding education system reform.

And now the time has come for a comprehensive and holistic implementation of all aspects of the National Minimum Curriculum, through the use of the strategic implementation plan. This will complete the process of making sure everyone has the basic skills for taking part in the world of today: literacy, numeracy, computer education, curiosity, learning skills and problem-solving skills, and skills of how to relate to oneself and others. What the country now needs is the human energies, the school-based school development plans, the implementation structures, and the monitoring and evaluation mechanisms that bring about such basic results, and other results of higher standards that bring us to par with several European countries.

There is much to be done, and much co-ordination is required. Much creativity needs to be stimulated at school level and other levels, and much expertise is still required. We have seen that it is quite necessary to have a steering body, a tailor-made institution that carries out the central functions required for this implementation process. Thus a new central institution was found necessary to oversee and manage activity in schools and other contexts according to the Strategic Plan. Such an institution was designed and proposed by the committee in their report in the form of a National Curriculum.

A number of expert and experienced focus groups need to be set up in association with the NCC, each based on a school subject or a NMC theme, to deliver expertise in those areas to the NCC, and to deliver customized needs-based support services to schools, including training, assistance with planning, school-level policy drafting and so on. The focus groups will, each group in relation to its special subject, keep themselves informed; develop new knowledge; support schools; help schools in networking and in managing research and project bids; and help integrate the different focus groups' efforts work and results so that a holistic approach is maintained in curriculum-based change. The focus groups will be accountable to the National Curriculum Council.

The many obligatory targets to be reached by schools and others are phased flexibly over the period from February 2001 to June 2005 depending on the special needs and emphases desired in each school. A number of priority requirements for the level of Ministry of Education have also been identified in the report, and my Ministry has taken note of them.

The Strategic Plan is not a substitute for the National Minimum Curriculum, nor is it a substitute for the creativity and autonomy of schools. Schools should follow the National

Minimum Curriculum in other ways besides reaching the targets listed in this plan. The targets allow and encourage a great deal of initiative and policy-making at school-level. For work outside these targets, the strategic goals outlined in the present plan, as well as the NMC itself. Will provide the required guidance.

Notes

1. The following historical summary appears in http://www.logframe.com/lf.htm, the web site of Team Technologies, Inc. 'The Logical Framework is a project planning approach designed by Practical Concept Incorporated (PCI) for the United States Agency for International Development. In late 1969 its president, Leon Rosenberg, created the original 16-box matrix in response to the Agency's need for improved monitoring and evaluation of its project portfolio. The initial intention of the LogFrame was to monitor and evaluate projects. However, users quickly discovered its added value for project design and implementation planning. The matrix was essentially a results-oriented approach to project design that began with a cause and effect model of the project's interventions and their intended impact on customers and clients. By the late 1970s, the Matrix was used widely by international technical co-operation agencies, however, it was not until the introduction at the German Technical Co-operation Agency (GTZ) in 1981 that the real power of the method was discovered. R. Moses Thompson, Claire Wheatly and Larry Posner of PCI worked with Lutz Zils and Ulrich Winkler of the GTZ to transform the LFA into a collaborative, client-centred methodology they called ZOPP (objectives oriented project planning) and then installed it globally for the agency. Thompson created a ZOPP Moderator (trainer/consultant) training program that produced a cadre of professional moderators in more than 100 countries. R. Moses Thompson went on to establish TEAM Technologies, Inc. to help further

develop PCM-based [project-cycle management] methods and help organizations install them on a sustainable basis.'

2. GTZ stands for Deutsche Gesellschaft fur Technische Zusammenarbeit.
3. The wide scope of our present scenario at a large-country level may probably be better served by a designing, not a 'project' but a 'programme', in the sense of a group of 'projects' each implementing one of more of the aims of the wider programme. Such a situation is also susceptible to OOPP planning methods, and the wider aims of each such project would be the specific aims of the wider programme. However, such considerations are being omitted from the present paper in the interests of simplicity.
4. In certain scenarios the two phases may overlap to the extent that step S3 may be found to take a long time and, before being fully completed, may nevertheless permit the second phase to start with step S4.
5. Phase Two, the planning phase of education systems reform is to be covered in a separate paper, Part II (forthcoming)
6. In the future step S3, the public input should be on questions such as: What should be the aims of education? In Step S4, opinions can be invited on non-final drafts of a curriculum document.
7. *A tool for tracking system-wide evaluations is proposed in Tony Macelli, The evaluations map: a framework for examining educational evaluation mechanisms, detecting systemic problems, and supporting educational reforms; Oct. 2000, an unpublished document for the International Bureau of Education, Geneva. It was prepared for IBE / BIE-MED Thematic Group 9: 'Implementing evaluation systems of educational reforms which help support changes' of the Mediterranean programme of International Bureau of Education, UNESCO.*
8. Such standards-based curriculum design is common in the United States.

9. To derive these from a comprehensive problem-tree and objectives-tree would probably require a map of 'the human condition'! In utilizing objectives from among those already formulated elsewhere, the drafting team acknowledges that they are not in the business of reinventing wheels, except where necessary.
10. For example, for a downward one-to-many mapping, as shown in the diagram, Level One: 1,2,3,...; Level Two: 1.1, 1.2,... 2.1, 2.2, ...; Level Three 1.1.1, 1.1.2, etc. Sometimes however, there will be the need for a downward correspondence of the many-to-one or even many-to-many type, something that is difficult to achieve with a numbering system!
11. School-leaving certificate syllabuses, if they need to be uniform for recognition of the certificate, may constitute constraints that restrict the creativity of the schools to create their own school curriculum and syllabuses. There is not necessarily an easy solution to this dilemma; it may be partly seen as the conflict of the student's own interests with those of employers and the world of work. University-entrance examinations may similarly pose a constraint on what teaching and learning may take place in late secondary school years, and this may be resolvable to some extent if universities are involved in the setting of curricular objectives for the late secondary school years.
12. Please see Appendix II entitled: 'Three variants of the LogFrame chart' for the framework to be used here.
13. This manual is obtainable free of charge from http://www.etf.it. Technical assistance to the European Commission for the implementation of Tempus is provided by the European Training Foundation, *Villa Gualino* Viale Settimio Severo, 65 I-10133 Torino Tel: (39) 11 630 22 22; Fax: (39) 11 630 22 00; e-mail:tempus@etf.it; www.etf.it The manual indicates that 'Tempus (the Trans European co-operation scheme for higher education) was adopted by the Council of Ministers of the European Union on 7 May 1990 and was since twice extended, with [an] extension lasting until

the year 2000. Tempus is a European Union (EU) programme designed to stimulate co-operation with the Partner Countries in Central and Eastern Europe and the New Independent States and Mongolia in order to support the reform of their higher education systems. Tempus forms part of the overall EU initiatives to support economic and social restructuring of central and Eastern Europe (Phare programme) and to foster the development of harmonious and prosperous economic and political links between the European Union and the New Independent States and Mongolia (Tacis Programme). In 1997 a total of 26 Partner Countries took part in Tempus. Funding is provided through Action Programmes, the individual amounts per country being the result of negotiations between the European Commission and the Partner Countries.'

'Tempus is a 'bottom-up' programme responsive to the specific needs of individual institutions and Partner Countries. Projects are formulated by universities in the Partner Countries in cooperation with their partners from the European Union, where the EU universities supply their know-how and experience. Tempus supports high quality projects aiming to restructure and develop curricula and teaching materials, upgrade teaching facilities, and/or improve university administration in higher education institutions in the Partner Countries. Tempus does this by providing financial grants for co-operation projects between higher education establishments in the EU and the Partner Countries in priority areas which are defined by the respective Partner Countries and the European Commission and which are in line with the overall socioeconomic reform process of these countries.'

20

The Management of Curriculum Change

Ashok Ganguly

Introduction

The process of curriculum mapping and its territorial adjudication is a matter of debate and concern to all stakeholders. The content and process of curriculum transactions and its implementation have always been impacted by the social, cultural, economic, technological and other contemporary concerns of a society and a nation. As all these factors have never been static in a vibrant and a progressive society, and as civilization has always ushered itself consequent to crosscurrents of the thought processes of the people who formed the society, the educational processes to have been vibrant and dynamic at all points of time. Little wonder, therefore, that curricular changes have been a matter of periodic concern to countries all over the world.

There are at least three different types of curriculum: the formal curriculum, the informal curriculum and the hidden curriculum. There are three other curricula as well: the written curriculum, the taught curriculum and the tested curriculum. Thus, there is a 3 × 3 curriculum matrix at work in schools. Most school administrators only consider the formal written, taught and tested curricula in their work. There is a need to integrate all these versions and manifestations of curriculum.

Curriculum development, curriculum implementation and curriculum evaluation are critical elements of curriculum policy. If development of curriculum is an important process then the implementation of curriculum is no less important.

Determine Curricular Goals

Curriculum is but an embodiment of the aspirations of the nation for its citizens. It is a vision endeavoured to be realized through educational processes. The national aspirations, in turn, are an accumulation of the dreams in different facets of the environment. They are comprehensive in nature. It is from the national aspirations that educational goals have to be derived—for education to be functional, relevant and realistic. In such an exercise of the derivation of educational targets, the following key considerations have to be taken into account.

Firstly, these targets should, in fact, be concrete and specific, enabling a pinpointed development and realization of the curriculum, and not be projected in vague and nebulous terms.

Secondary, because these targets are being listed for relization by the students, they should be stated in terms of learner behaviour. This needs to be specifically mantioned because normally what are set forth as educational targets are goals that are to be realized by the teachers, though it becomes incumbent on the student to accomplish them.

Thirdly, with regard to the *competencies* to be developed and evaluated, it ought to be emphasized that without an orientation to abilities, the mere listing of the themes of *content* remains meaningless and motivates only memorization. The inclusion of evaluation practices and procedures to be adopted enables us to spare a thought to the fact that what is being attempted to be developed can also be judged for its effectiveness in accomplishing the set goals.

Fourthly, targets are often raised to such unrealistic levels that it is practically impossible for the students to attain them with the available inputs at their disposal in the course of their pursuit of the curriculum. This makes everybody grope in the dark without being clear about what they have to accomplish.

Fifthly, targets are frequently enumerated in such global terms that it becomes almost impossible to precisely comprehend what is being conveyed as well as how it is meant to practically translate itself in specific contexts.

The design of curriculum has never been a simple process and has always necessitated entertaining all emerging issues at all intervals of time. The total review and modification of a curriculum, hence, needs a reasonable hiatus as it may change its direction substantially over even a short period. Such changes call for a grass-root level reorientation of functionaries implying phenomenal expenditure. In a fast-changing social fabric, long durations for curriculum modifications have not been seen as desirable—even more so given the influx of information in a globalized world and its facile access by the consumer. There is an urgent need for curriculum updating even while it is being implemented and the curriculum managers face the uphill task of managing curricular change during its implementation.

Any process of curricular revision during the life span of a curriculum should ensure that the major objectives and goals are not altered. Changing horses in mid-stream does not help. A revision's sole aim should be to enliven the existing structure and fabric to make it more vibrant. This exercise should be comprehensive, focused and relevant. While it should be user-friendly, one should not adopt a piecemeal approach, but the entire exercise should instead be based on a holistic approach that sensitively ensures that the interest of all the stakeholders are taken care of.

The basics of any such exercise on curriculum revision during implementation should take cognizance of its impact on the formal, informal and hidden curricula. It is, therefore necessary that the inputs should percolate to all levels of the curricular edifice homogeneously, laterally and vertically. The changes effected should have symmetry, correlation and should identify with the existing curriculum so that it does not end up being only an exercise in window-dressing on the part of the curriculum manager to please a particular interest group.

Current Trends

The following developments are likely to be influential in the first decade of the twenty-first century:

Increased importance of national and state norms

Norms will ensure that the citizens have shared knowledge. They will result in greater efficiency. Additionally, norms will encourage state and local boards to raise their standards, improve the quality of schooling, and ensure a large measure of educational equity.

Movement towards decentralized, school-based curriculum development

While there is increased interest in setting curriculum standards at both the national, the state levels, there is a simultaneously growing interest in having some flexibility in school-based curriculum development.

Increased interest in constructivist curriculum

It has its strongest impact on science and mathematics curriculum. Learning strategies should be taught in the context of solving problems.

Development of new approaches in vocational education

Emphasis on generic skills. These general, transferable skills can be used in many situations. The object is to equip the students with skills that will enable them to function in a changing economy and new situations.

Emphasis on integrating academic and career education. Greater integration of the two is required in order to reduce the dysfunctional barriers between academic and career curricula.

Development of integrated curricula

It is used to denote curriculum units that combine content from two or more disciplines. Though research generally supports the use of integrated curricula, some problems are associated with their use.

Institutionalization of technology

The use of the computer to mange the curriculum and to facilitate student learning is now widely accepted. Use of sophisticated technology will continue to increase.

The Four Curriculum Levels

1. State-level functions

1. Develop curriculum frameworks;
2. Develop and use test and other measures of evaluating performance;
3. Provide the local districts with the resources necessary to develop and implement quality curricula;
4. Periodically review state frameworks.

2. *District-level functions*

1. Develop a vision of quality curriculum based on the goals of the state.
2. Identify a common programme of studies and curriculum requirements for each level of schooling.
3. Develop the documents for the core curriculum related to each subject.
4. Select instructional materials.
5. Provide fiscal and other resources needed at the school level, including technical assistance.
6. Evaluate the curriculum.

3. School-level functions

1. Develop a vision of quality curriculum for every school that is harmonious with the vision of the districts.
2. Develop in-house programmes of curriculum transactions.
3. Determine the nature and extent of curriculum integration.
4. Assist in the implementation and monitoring of the curriculum.

4. Classroom-level functions

1. Develop yearly plans.
2. Develop units of study.
3. Enrich the curriculum and remedial teaching.
4. Evaluate the curriculum.

In introducing and managing changes, the curriculum manager has to keep in mind the following points:

- the need for a change;
- selection of the content;

- organization of the content;
- selection of learning experiences;
- organization of the learning experiences;
- methods and means of evaluating the learner.

He should address the following questions:

- Are the changes desirable or inevitable?
- Do these changes reflect the latest trends in a global context?
- Does the content provide just additional enrichment or newer dimensions in learning?
- Do the contents reflect contemporary developments and thinking?
- Do the learning experiences provide an insight into the learning areas?
- Are learning resources available to provide the required learning experiences?
- What steps are to be taken to ensure the effective and meaningful acquisition of these learning experiences by the learner?

The curricular inputs so incorporated should provide a smooth interface with the existing social, cultural, economic and technological aspects of the curriculum. Its modernity should not be in conflict with its ethnicity; its cultural creativity should not undermine the traditional sensitivity. The curriculum should provide flexibility, openness and creativity to justify its intervention into the normal life cycle of the existing curriculum.

Managing the Curriculum

Curriculum implementation depends largely on the classroom teaching strategies, which in turn depend on the teacher's commitment, competence and training.

The comprehensive management of curricular change demands undertaking various activities that may run concurrently. The basic components of successful curriculum implementation are as follows:

- spelling out curricular contents;
- training and re-training of teachers;

- curriculum delivery and transaction;
- providing learning materials, both for teachers and students;
- measuring learning outcomes; and
- use of ICTs.

It is therefore a question of overlapping layers of activities. The focus should be on ensuring minimum levels of learning at each stage, and that subjects are taught in a way that promotes understanding and thinking rather than recall and memorization.

There are several approaches to curricular interventions. However, care should be taken to ensure that these interventions are finely tuned to the existing structures. The interventions could be selective, partial or spread over the length and breadth of the territory covered by the curriculum. It could focus on lateral knowledge or on vertical thinking. What is important is the quantum and quality of management and planning that facilitates in smoothy synergizing the changes with the present spectrum of operations. A few approaches may be as follows.

The frontline approach

In this method of curricular intervention, emphasis is laid on introducing the latest information to an extent of say 10 per cent of the existing quantum of the content. The selection of content is central as this should be able to provide the learner opportunities for imbibing the current knowledge. The purpose is that the learner is familiar with the life processes and the thought patterns of the present society, its scientific and technological achievements, economic activities, challenges, threats and opportunities. Such interventions could be done selectively, subject-wise and in a phased manner.

The constructivist approach

The foundations of the curriculum could be reviewed for reinforcement of such inputs, which are contextual and need to be incorporated so that the learning process is more effective. The content, the learning materials have to be carefully scrutinized so that the interventional inputs construct a sound edifice and the learner experiences continuity and coherence. However, it is important to ensure that such reviews do not distort the established and defined aims and objectives of the curriculum. The content material should be objective and free from any bias lest it cause aberrations in the learning contexts and experiences. It must also be ensured that such inputs are not excessive.

The social context

The explosion of information technology

The movement from an agricultural economy to an industrial one brought about a change from classical vartical thinking to that of analytical thinking. This warranted a change in the learning processes of the people of the industrial society and the curriculum had to respond to these changes. A similar situation arose with the ushering in of the information technology-based economy to the industrial economy. However, the changes that occurred this time were faster and more extensive, and the curriculum had to respond at an equitable pace. The thought process of the people has now shifted to lateral thinking, exploring unlimited opportunities for discovery and innovation. The curriculum has little option but to meaningfully respond to this call. The amount of information being extensive and the life span of the information being so short, the curricular response and intervention has to be almost instantaneous—this is only possible during the normal life cycle of the existent curriculum.

Knowledge society

The emerging dimension is one of a knowledge society. The key player in this area is artificial intelligence. The human response to creating a base for effective organization and manipulation of the tools of artificial intelligence needs critical study and review. The emphasis is not merely on assimilation and retrieval of knowledge but in knowledge synthesis and knowledge economy. The entire focus of curriculum and the *modus operandi* of its implementation have to be carefully designed.

Consumerist tendency

The consumerist tendencies affecting the market dynamics do not spare the educational scenario either. In trying to make interventions at short intervals, care has to be taken that we do not succumb to these pressures. The broad objectives of the curriculum in strengthening human excellence have to be nurtured and nourished. Electronic media impact the minds of youngsters and seem to breed psychological violence. It is necessary to offset the consequent mental turbulence by appropriate inputs of emotional intelligence.

The role of the teacher is changing from that of a moderator and facilitator to that of a co-learner. The thrust will be on self-learning and hence the modules of learning have to be appropriately designed.

External influences on the curriculum

Even while the educational agency is not addressing itself to a curricular review, it must be admitted that the learning situations and learning experiences are being continually modified on their own by the impact of global information flow, thanks to the explosion of information technology. New software materials to enrich the educational content and the pedagogy available in the market and accessible to any learner provide not only additional inputs, but also additional experiences affecting the thought process of the learner. The learner would like to translate those experiences into the classroom and into the curricular framework, whether or not he is called upon to do so. Such experiences may have relevance to all the three domains: cognitive, affective and psychomotor. The teacher needs to be sensitized to handle these situations with a sense of confidence and conviction. Management of curricular interventions of such kind is a major challenge to curriculum managers.

It must also be admitted that the ascent of the technological interface with education has had a direct and a powerful impact on teaching methods. The methods of classroom teaching and the tools applied for effective learning too will have to change. The use of print media alone will not suffice and even the treatment of the content through the print media might attract changes.

A decline in rote learning and an emphasis on understanding and application will be a dire necessity. Concepts of lateral thinking the critical thinking skills need to be integrated in developing and implementing the curriculum. Ability to communicate effectively and meaningfully will be required and hence the language skills in classrooms have to be enlightened to a communicative approach. The decreasing importance of literature, poetry, arts, etc., will be a matter of serious concern to the educational agencies and administrators and appropriate strategies have to be developed to cope with the situation.

Education being a broad-based concept, it has to take care of the holistic development of the learner. The emotional balance of the learner will be critical in a progressive and dynamic society where there will be increasing problems of communication. It is in this context that the educators will be called upon to give a greater thrust to areas related to emotional intelligence. All curricular interventions have to take care of the affective domain and strengthen the same.

In order to achieve a balanced emotional and cognitive base in the curriculum, focus will be on interdisciplinary approaches to learning. To ensure that curriculum does not get heavily loaded, conceptual aspects relating to population education, adolescent education, value education, peace education and cultural education, etc., may be integrated suitably within the existing scheme of studies.

Following the implantation

Periodic monitoring of growth

The success of a curriculum can be determined by taking stock of the realization of the set objectives. Such monitoring has to be periodic, so that it is possible to provide some timely inputs in case shortcomings are noticed. Such monitoring should be so designed as to cover the *quantum* of growth among children realized through the curriculum. The *degree* of realization in respect of each identified aspect in previously mentioned quantum also deserves to be assessed. This, in fact, will be an important indicator of quality. It addition, it is also worthwhile to monitor the *pace of growth* of the students. This will vary from student to student. The significant outcome of such a process of monitoring will be the diagnostic inferences obtained for purposes of providing *remedial programmes* for greater equity (i.e. strengthening the weak) and *enrichment programmes* for bright students.

Infrastructure for curriculum change

A permanent infrastructure for shouldering the responsibility of managing the curriculum change is essential. Besides the generalists, it will also be necessary to have subject specialists for smoother and satisfactory implementation. The principals will need to work in close collaboration with the district leadership.

While policy decisions indicating the broad paradigms can be taken at the national/state level, it will be necessary to take a number of other decisions at the regional/district and the local levels to ensure that the curriculum is kept relevant to the felt needs at the grass roots. This will naturally necessitate the establishment of small teams operating at the regional and the local levels. To carry out the curriculum-related tasks, a curriculum task force may be appointed. The teams functioning in this area while working at the different levels are effective only if they function as a hierarchy with interdependence amongst themselves.

The role of supportive institutions in successful management of curriculum change is very critical. There must be such supportive institutions at the school cluster, district, state and national levels.

Curriculum revision must be undertaken based on feedback received during the implementation phase. The critical information received from different sources should strengthen development of curricular policies. Periodic reviews are also necessary to identify gaps and missing links for necessary correction.

Upgrading the skills of curriculum teams

To be able to work progressively and scientifically, it is

imperative that the people engaged in the task of curriculum review and renewal continuously upgrade their skills and catch up with the latest developments instead of just depending upon their experience as their sole professional equipment. Towards this end, in-service education programmes will be called for. For the senior level personnel, such training could even take the form of inter-country courses. This top-level team, after getting abreast of the developments in other countries, may design courses aligned to the national needs for the training of second- and third-level functionaries. Such training programmes will need to be built into the total schedule of activities with the provision of both time and money.

In addition to such formal training programmes, it would be highly beneficial if periodic meetings for exchange of experiences are also planned and conducted on a regular basis. These are likely to be very useful as the parallel teams working on the same programmes at different locations will be able to learn and gain from the experiences of their counterparts on how they have attempted to face and solve the problems that come their way.

Looking Ahead

Futurism in education is a topic of concern to all educators. There are numerous models available about what schools should and could be like in the future. What is needed in the future is an education system that serves individuals in successfully coping with the changing demands on them.

To conclude, some of the thrust areas of the future are:

- providing all learners with common skills;
- assisting individuals in becoming adaptive;
- guaranteeing learning by whatever means needed;
- recognizing the emergence of web-centric curricula;
- offering professional support to develop text books and other reading materials;
- calling for more synergies in the classroom environment rather than mere individual participation;

- emerging societies will be anticipatory in nature, hence the need for the component of future studies to be integrated in the curriculum;
- moving from knowledge testing to competency certification;
- curbing the tendency of one-shot learning and evaluation by commercial enterprises;
- using schools to engineer social development;
- shifting from an ad hoc to a systematized approach to manage curricular change, which will lead to institutionalization of a framework for this purpose; and
- training in various aspects of classroom transactions, including team teaching.

The Monitoring and Evaluation of Curriculum Reforms

Phillip Hughes

The Context

Curriculum evaluation needs to be considered together with the nature of curriculum reform, as evaluation is central to the reform process. Curriculum reform is universal. Every country is involved, sometimes with similar aims, sometimes with different aims. In China, the extension of compulsory education from seven to nine years provides the basis for curriculum reform and is now accompanied by a Joint Innovative Programme with UNESCO to improve the quality of teaching. In Cambodia, a major project underway is to improve the quality of public examinations. Weaknesses in the administration of the examinations had brought them into disrepute so that the results were no longer trusted. The project seeks to establish publicly accountable methods of examining and administration. In the United Kingdom, twelve years after the introduction of the National Curriculum a substantial effort is being made to increase the capacity of schools to evaluate their programmes and to establish procedures to help those that do not perform well. In Japan, a re-emphasis on moral education aims to impart values contributing to social harmony. In Oman, there is a need for the education system to produce more knowledgeable and skilled indigenous employees. In the United States of America, the new president announced an increased emphasis on evaluation and testing as a way to improve student achievement. The patterns may differ from place to place but the involvement with reform is universal. Given the specific purposes behind curriculum reform, it is vital that there are processes to evaluate their effectiveness and efficiency. In other words, it is essential to know that works and what does not.

The motivation for reform does not come from within but from the impact of external circumstances. Almost every dimension of life has changed fundamentally in the past fifty years. World population has grown from 2.5 to 6.1 billion, an increase which is partly linked to the increase in life expectancy from 47 to 64 years. While this is an uneven improvement, it still provides a glimpse of what can possibly be expected from programmes in health and health education. From a period when 300 million were in school and 250 million outside it, there are now 1.2 billion in school although still 100 million children are missing out. This massive effort by countries to increase participation, while being a significant success, also highlights the need to increase the effectiveness of education for those who do attend. Together with the improvement in school attendance there is a parallel improvement in adult literacy rates from 46 per cent to 79 per cent. Given the increase in population this means that there are still 875 million illiterate adults. These and other changes are indicators of the benefits that education bestows on enhancing life's potential and prospects. They also show the desperate need not only for an increased quantity so to speak, but also for quality education, if countries are to be able to manage their problems and strengthen the fabric of their societies. To invest heavily in curriculum reform lends weight to the methods of assessing its effectiveness and on deciding the nature of changes that need to be undertaken in the future.

Many of the changes that are underway make a particular impact on education and schooling.

- Technology and communication: the widespread access to information of all kinds via computer has moved from the 1950s, where there was a handful of computers worldwide, to a stage where there are millions, of greater potential and more available for individual access.

- The world economy: trade and production now flow across national boundaries in an increasingly interdependent global village.
- Ecology: the massive scale of development and correspondingly the excessive exploitation of resources and the resulting pollution that has endangered the health of our planet.
- Peace and security: in an interactive and interdependent global society laden with weapons of mass destruction, harmonious patterns of living together are indispensable, within countries and between them.
- The nature of work: increasingly, work involves a set of skilled tasks, each requiring specialized knowledge and thus the need for teams of people with different skills able to work together towards a common purpose.
- New knowledge on learning: human ability is one of the last areas of untapped resources and is far more rich and diverse than in our past conceptions. Varied and innovative approaches, new emphasis and the latest technologies can all contribute to significant advances in further developing this potential.

What responses are common in curriculum reform?

- Basic education is an essential prerequisite for all people. Basic education is the provision of a sufficient foundation for individuals to make effective choices on membership of society, on successful access to productive work and on personal well-being. Those people who do not receive an effective basic education are consigned to the margins of society and will be an economic burden and, often, a source of social tension.
- An extended concept of 'basic education', extended both in range and achievement. The breadth of this

concept of an enabling education, a choice-giving education, was enunciated most strongly through the Jomtien meeting in 1990, the World Conference on Education for All. The Jomtien Declaration saw basic education as the essential means of defining a broad social purpose, namely the capacity of each person to contribute effectively to society. The statement outlines the need for a much more diverse and demanding set of learning.

Every person—child, youth and adult—shall be able to benefit from educational opportunities designed to meet their basic learning needs. Those needs comprise both essential learning tools (such as literacy, oral expression, numeracy and problem solving) and the basic learning content (such as knowledge, skills, values and attitudes) required by human beings to be able to survive, to develop their full capacities, to live and work in dignity, to participate fully in development, to improve the quality of their lives, to make informed decisions, and to continue learning. The scope of basic learning needs and how they will be met varies with individual countries and cultures, and, inevitably, changes with the passages of time (Jomtien, 1990).

- Lifelong learning is a necessity. The spiralling growth of knowledge necessitates continuing study if we are to utilize it effectively. Education is no longer a stage to pass through but an activity that is a concurrent aspect of living. Periods of formal learning will need to be undertaken throughout life along with learning associated with activities such as work.
- Values as a central issue. In current curriculum reform the centrality of values is acknowledged as an essential ingredient of any curriculum change. Information is available to an unprecedented extent. In delivering information and the ways to use it, education enhances our capacities in the workplace, in production and trade, in developing the

> environment and in affecting the lives and health of people around us. If education does not also deal with values then it delivers these unprecedented powers to people who have no guidelines as to their use. It is akin to setting sail without a compass. Education cannot be value-free. It is inescapably a builder of values. The nature of the values it conveys is important not only to us as individuals, but to the type of society we wish to build. Victoria Camps emphasizes the danger of imparting education that is non-inclusive of the issue of values.
>
> Two points are vital: (a) that education must be the guiding light of democratic culture; and (b) that education is not possible unless it conveys moral values. At a time when modern societies are tending to subordinate all development to the dictates of the prevailing economic orthodoxy, we need to find a way of overturning this monopoly that has the effect of eroding political participation and citizenship (Camps, 1997).

The emphases in the Japanese reforms to be more specific about the values that are central to curriculum reform are echoed in many countries. The emphasis on the outcomes of value-based curriculum makes fresh demands on evaluation.

- Continuing development from evaluation. Curriculum reform is of little use without evaluation processes to assess the degree to which the purposes of the reform are met and to set the guidelines for future action.

How Can Curriculum Evaluation Help?

Definitions

Curriculum evaluation is an integral part of the curriculum. The curriculum is the totality of what happens in the education process as a result of intentions—purposes, learning activities, learning outcomes, resources—human and material, evaluation processes, means for change and development, school practices and culture.

Curriculum evaluation is the means by which the value of this total process is assessed. It involves gathering evidence to judge the degree of realization of aims and to enable decisions to be made on future progress. As a guide to decision-making, it needs to be transparent, fully informing the many groups involved in these decisions. Curriculum evaluation has a number of important functions.

- It guides and guards the quality of the education processes and benchmarks the outcomes.
- For public accountability purposes, it provides evidence that public money is being agreeably spent.
- It promotes and improves high quality processes and outcomes at individual institutions and provides a basis to disseminate sound practice, leading to overall system improvement.
- It informs student choice, so that they may make sense of a variety of offerings based on their quality and usefulness.
- It informs parents on the progress of their children and on how to assist their future decisions and work.
- It provides teachers with comparative data on the effects and efficacy of their teaching.
- It is the major effective means of curriculum improvement as it provides information on what works well and what is unproductive or even harmful.

Comparisons in evaluation

Curriculum evaluation is essentially carried out through comparisons. The traditional comparisons were between goals and outcomes and this retains its primacy.

- Goals and outcomes. How do intentions and outcomes match? What is the degree of achievement of stated purposes? Traditional methods include examinations at the end of a course and tests administered during it. Some of the long-term outcomes, both desirable and undesirable, are not identified in the course purposes and this is one reason for the necessary extension. However, many decades of experience and study have revealed the need for other comparisons.

- Implicit and explicit goals. In addition to the stated goals, there are often implicit or hidden purposes. These are indicated by outcomes not directly related to the explicit goals. A school may show in its actions a high valuation on sporting achievement yet not include such an emphasis in its stated goals. In evaluation, it is necessary to look at the whole range of activities and emphases of an educational institution.
- Intended and unintended outcomes. It is important to identify all outcomes, intended and unintended. Both of these groups of outcomes will have desirable and undesirable aspects that need to be identified. A major recent reform in New Zealand gave much greater freedom to schools in their budgets, allowing them to admit students from any source and publishing the results of tests for the schools. For many schools this meant a major boost as they attracted new students and the consequent government finance.

This was an intended result, to provide more choice and to reward good performance. For some schools the process was very harmful as they lost their best students, and with them the finance, and were left with the weaker students and less money for resources to assist them. This was the unintended result. A common example is where a rigorous course may produce effective levels of achievement but also creates a dislike for the subject. Such a finding is common in subjects such as mathematics where there is a high pressure for achievement. Tests and examinations are built around the course goals and are thus unlikely to reveal hidden or implicit goals or unexpected outcomes. Some evaluators recommend 'goal-free evaluation' for this purpose, i.e. a descriptive approach to evaluation, not built on the stated purposes but seeking to identify the full range of outcomes (Stufflebeam et al., 1971). A full range will include long-term outcomes.

A major benefit of most learning should be an increased capacity and interest in pursuing further learning. To what extent do those who have studied mathematics use mathematics in their lives or continue with the study? To what extent do those students who study literature continue to extend their reading in later life? Do courses in civics that provide greater knowledge of citizens' responsibilities also increase the possibilities of the students becoming pro-active citizens? These long-term aims are often stated purposes of a course but are seldom evaluated because of technical difficulties. The long-term outcomes of teaching are often the most important, even if difficult to assess. The teacher who arouses an early interest in some aspect of learning bestows an invaluable gift. Many students rediscover value from earlier learning much later in life, recalling with appreciation learning and teaching that were not liked or not recognized as valuable at the time. Short-term appreciation by students is of limited use if it does not grow into something more lasting. Motivation for continued learning is a necessity of the same order as having worthwhile courses and experiences from which to learn. If schools are to be part of the continuum of lifelong learning, they must be as concerned in cultivating the will to continue to learn, as they are concerned with ensuring higher achievement in learning. Michael Barber, formerly of the Institute of Education in London and currently principle adviser to Tony Blair on education, comments on this dual need, noting that we have a unique opportunity to achieve these aims:

> Perhaps for the first time in educational history, it is possible to arrive at a curriculum that satisfies this dual need magnificently. The economy and democratic society demand increasing levels of educational achievement from everyone, while the multiple threats to the continued existence of the planet give that drive the ultimate justification. The agenda for education, therefore, could hardly be more motivating. Meanwhile, information technology will provide new and exciting ways of teaching and learning. Moreover, we have, at last, a theoretical understanding of children and young people that will assist teachers in their task (Barber, 1996).

Processes and outcomes. What impact does the teaching and learning process within the course have on the outcome?

This comparison relates to our earlier question as to long-term outcomes. The easiest mode of teaching, the didactic approach, with a highly directive style based on information-giving, may yield good results in standardized tests which themselves emphasize information retention, but may have quite different long-term effects. It may fail to engage students and to motivate them for further study. Again, a careful analysis of short- and long-term effects is needed.

- Outcomes for different groups involved in the evaluation. This will include different groups of students, the key people in the process. Many students with strong and supportive home backgrounds find learning easy and customarily make good progress under a variety of conditions. The extension of basic education to all students brings into learning situations many who lack the background skills and the continuing home support. In all countries, such students have poor results and often leave education without any tangible benefits. The means of reaching such students are not easy but the need is great. They suffer a great handicap in life if they gain little from their basic education. The outcomes for teachers and parents as well as administrators are equally important. If teachers are not supportive of curriculum reform, the chances for success are low. This applies also to parents who can play an important role in helping their student children through difficult periods.

Reliability and validity

In making judgments as to the best forms of evaluation, the key properties are reliability and validity. *The reliability of an evaluation* refers to its accuracy, the extent to which the same result will be obtained in a repetition. Thus, for example, the measurement of length is highly reliable, given care and a good ruler. *The validity of an evaluation* is its meaning or significance. In practice, this means the capacity of a measure to predict some other criterion. Thus, a selection test or a selection interview can produce rankings of candidates. The degree to which the ranking agrees with subsequent performance, in a job or in a university course, is the test of its validity. There is always some trade-off between the two qualities. A simple short-answer test can give highly reliable measures of attitude, for example. However, the results on the test may show little relation to the practice of that attitude in everyday life. The validity of the test is low. To obtain better predictions may require more subtle methods, such as observation of behaviour over a set period. Validity is the essential property of an evaluation and the valuation has the complex task of choosing the most reliable of the valid approaches.

The Programme for Evaluation: Curriculum Monitoring

Curriculum monitoring is the process that can provide information to enable evaluation to be carried out as a regular part of curriculum. This is an essential aspect if curriculum evaluation is to be a reality and not remain in the realm of the notional. Curriculum evaluation must establish a process that is comprehensive but practicable. That is, it must cover the issues raised above but also be workable in schools, colleges and universities. These work places operate under high pressure with their regular programmes and those who have to implement any new system must be convinced that the monitoring will be both practicable and of value to them. The key people are the teachers. Any programme of curriculum monitoring will fail if it does not have teacher support. As discussed below, the support of other people will also be helpful. Monitoring becomes possible and easy to manage where there is a carefully planned system of data collection, carried out on a regular basis as part of the continuing teaching programme.

Tools for curriculum evaluation

Curriculum evaluation has changed greatly in recent decades because of studying the experience of the process over that period. A listing of the tools for curriculum evaluation shows the progressive change from simple numerical information to include more descriptive and more revealing forms.

- *Test:* this set of uniform tasks to assess knowledge or ability is the most common form of information provided. It is convenient and easy to control, occurring at a particular time and place and perceived as an evaluation. It provides information in a concise summarized form. Its great strength is its high reliability, given proper design and conditions of implementation. Its major weakness can be a limited validity. Tests may vary from simple and short lists of questions requiring single word answers or a choice among alternatives, to a much longer and more elaborate set of tasks in a standardized form. The process of designing and checking on the reliability and validity of such tests is now highly specialized. Examples are the tests produced for international studies such as the Third International Mathematics and Science Study (TIMSS), and the tests used for graduate entry at universities. Plomp, in a recent paper, asks the question: What can be learned from the international comparison of education results? The work done by the International Association of Evaluation of Educational Achievement (IEA) over thirty years has produced valuable insights. The latest example is TIMSS. Many countries such as England and Australia produce national tests of literacy and numeracy to be able to assess the progress of groups of students and to enable individuals to assess their progress relevant to particular groups. Effective monitoring of student progress requires both regular teacher-set tests and periodic standardized tests for whole groups. The former reveals individual problems in learning of value to the teacher. The latter enables teachers, students and parents to assess individual progress against group norms.
- *Examination:* this is usually a long and formal test given under standardized conditions. It has greater flexibility than a test, as long answers are possible, giving more information to the examiner. Short

answer tests do not require the student to organize and express complex information. For this reason, validity can be greater but at the cost of reliability. Essays are difficult to mark with reliability, yet they reveal aspects that are not available from the more reliable short-answer tests.

- *Questionnaire:* a formal list of questions designed for a particular inquiry. This is very similar to a test and with the same advantages and disadvantages and is often used in a mail-out, thus broadening the set of people contacted. This broadening is, of course, at the cost of being able to control the conditions. A test is administered under set and supervised conditions. With a mail questionnaire, such control is not possible.
- *Survey:* a description of a particular topic or institution in a comprehensive way. This might be an examination of the effectiveness of rural schools, both in terms of participation and performance. This may be done through sending out and analysing questionnaires or, more elaborately, through visits, interviews and telephone contacts. The Internet provides new modes of contact. In the United Kingdom recently, the Ministry established Education Action Zones (EAZ) to combat underachievement in the most deprived urban areas. An EAZ consists of a secondary school and its feeder primary schools and the project provided special support to raise achievement levels. After a year of activity, a survey revealed the following positive results.

  English, maths and science results for 11-year-olds in the first 25 EAZ's improved at level four or above by 11, 16 or 20% respectively in 1998. This compares with 10, 13, and 15% nationally. Truancy has been reduced and the schools report extremely positive benefits from improved partnerships with local business (DfEE, 2001).

  Of interest in this case is the improvement in truancy. This was not part of the original purpose of the change, to improve student performance. These unintended outcomes were, in this case, desirable. This shows the value of such surveys covering a wider area of results than those in the key purposes.

- *Case study:* a detailed study and analysis of a particular instance to provide insights into characteristics and reasons for them. This is an intensive look at a particular situation to penetrate beneath the surface of test results, for example, and seek to determine reasons. Case studies of both success and failure may provide beneficial information and insights to use in other situations. The case study can be of the work of an individual student or of an entire school. The choice of this approach is made where it is useful to explain the causes of results rather than just to describe them. It may well use all the tools described here.
- *Interview:* a face-to-face discussion on a particular topic. This approach is frequently used as data for a survey or for selection purposes for a task or job. Reliability is not high for this tool unless the interview is carefully planned and executed. Low reliability means low validity, also.
- *Portfolio:* a collection of work from an individual or group sometimes produced for a particular purpose. Traditionally this is the means by which artists exhibit their productions, e.g. paintings or sculptures. The proponents of 'authentic evaluation', such as Darling-Hammond (1993) and McDonald (1996) see it as a means of access to a representative collection of an individual's work, revealing development over time and the capacity to complete long or difficult tasks. Examinations with their tight time limits can never reveal these characteristics.
- *Authentic task:* an evaluation task that is close to a real-life situation. As mentioned, the portfolio is one of many forms of authentic evaluation. More traditionally, so is the practical examination

although this is limited in its reality because the time is usually set and so is the task for completion. An authentic task is a serious attempt to see if the student has the capacity to perform a task of long-term relevance or value. A student parliament can be one example or an assignment in the community. International Baccalaureate Organization schools throughout the world ask their students to complete a community service assignment as part of their graduation requirements. The task must be useful to others and students are required to submit a written report that, in part, requires them to reflect on their own learning experience.

- *Document analysis:* a study of all the documents produced or used in a given programme.
- *Longitudinal study:* a study of a situation, institution or group repeated over a number of years. This is of great value in determining long-term trends but is difficult to maintain over the period needed. While it can never be a universal approach, careful planning and maintenance of records can make it possible and the results will always be valuable.
- *Exhibition:* an assessment in which students exhibit for some public audience the results of a project they have undertaken or the understandings they have gained from a set of experiences. This is one of the approaches introduced in the Coalition of Essential Schools (Sizer, 1991). The emphasis in the Sizer approach was to ensure that students have the opportunity to undertake a substantial task and to present a comprehensive report or production.
- *Role-play:* an exercise in which people take on defined roles in a play, impromptu or planned. In teaching it is used for students to develop their understanding of diverse viewpoints or new situations. In evaluation, it may be used to test a student's capacity to react to hypothetical but realistic situations, for example, a medical diagnosis.

- *Practical test:* a realistic situation such as an experiment or practical task performed under test conditions. This differs from authentic evaluation in that test situations apply, including a set period.
- *Education indicators:* this involves the collection of information on a regular basis to give an appreciation of the system as a whole or some part of it. Such figures may be straightforward such as enrolments, attendance and progress through the grades. In recent years, OECD with co-operation from UNESCO has taken the lead in devising a set of indicators that will give a more complete description of a system including qualitative as well as quantitative measures (OECD, 1996). This project, still under active development, aims to devise and use education indicators as a means of providing significant, coherent information and to assist in assessing education systems. There are now indicators covering: the context of education; costs; resources and school processes; participation; staff and results of education. From a list of over fifty indicators, the aim is to reduce to a list of twenty for greater economy and ease of understanding.

The list of evaluation tools above shows the gradual change of emphasis in evaluation to methods that reveal more about the student, the programme and the education system than a set of numbers describing performance at a particular time. After a long period from the 1950s when psychometric methods predominated, using standardized tests, examinations and other methods directed to produce numerical scores, there was a swing towards more broadly based forms of evaluation. These included 'illuminative evaluation' (Parlett & Hamilton 1976) and 'responsive evaluation' (Stake, 1967), both of which considered the context of the evaluation more carefully and used case studies, interviews and document analysis extensively to provide a fuller description of the programmes under consideration. They also provided a more complete statement about students' learning but at the cost of more time and greater complexity.

More recent approaches such as those identified by Darling-Hammond (1993) and McDonald (1996) are inclusive of both strands, numerical measures to assess progress in particular areas and also the more descriptive tools which consider the context and seek to give a more inclusive picture. Prominent among these approaches are case studies, portfolios, exhibitions and authentic tasks.

In a recent analysis of the state of curriculum evaluation, Gipps(1998) points out the inadequacy of relying only on traditional tests and examinations. She makes the point that for current students the capacity to continue learning and to be able to apply learning in new situations will be of great value and these are not identified by earlier approaches to evaluation. Thus, while a national system of tests and examinations may help to monitor student progress, it must be supplemented by the approaches described under authentic evaluation.

Summary of necessary aspects of curriculum evaluation

A broad description of the pattern of evaluation to provide the basis for monitoring will need to include the following aspects.

- *Purposes.* There needs to be a continuous monitoring of the purposes of evaluation to ensure that they remain relevant and that new emphases may be included.
- *Participants and roles.* Many groups have an interest in modes of evaluation and may need to be included in planning in appropriate ways. Legitimate stakeholders include parents, students, employers and teachers as well as governments. Too often curriculum reforms and evaluation proceed without involving teachers actively in the process. No matter how well the initiatives are conceived they cannot be implemented without the support of teachers who will also need appropriate preparation. Similarly, other stakeholders need appropriate consideration.
- *Audiences.* Curriculum evaluations need to be reported in appropriate ways to the different

stakeholders. This needs to be kept in mind in the original design so that appropriate information is collected and forms of reporting devised.

- *Collection of information.* The original design must identify all forms of information that will be required for the purposes of the evaluation and the different evaluation audiences. In the example of the English EAZs the information on truancy was important to the judgment on the worth of the new approach. Unless this information had been included in the survey, a valuable outcome would have been unknown.
- *Develop a continuing, self-correcting process.* Any evaluation system will include an ongoing collection of information on a regular basis, through tests, surveys, etc. It will also involve special approaches at particular times to supplement the regular patterns. Many countries now, for example, co-operate in TIMSS and obtain measures of performance in those areas that are internationally comparable. Many others co-operate in the OECD indicators project.
- *Recognize the long-term nature of educational change.* Many of the purposes of curriculum evaluation are long-term because of the nature of much educational change. The nature of the process for evaluation that is established needs to be suitable to both long-term and short-term use.

Conclusion

Curriculum evaluation plays a more important role than ever before. It is also a more difficult role. Its central purpose is to monitor learning achievement of students as the key function of the system. It is no longer sufficient to measure learning achievements solely in cognitive terms. The demands of citizenship have increased. The requirements of employment have become more complex. The decisions needed for individual living are more varied. Thus, evaluation is required to measure a much greater range of human achievement and capacities as well as to monitor the effectiveness of teachers, of schools and of education systems. Over the past three decades, experience and the results of research have delivered the means to increase the power and effectiveness of evaluation. To achieve this increase in practice is the challenge for educators, administrators and politicians.

References

Barber, M. 1996. *The learning game*. London, Victor Gollancz.

Camps, V. 1997. Education for democracy. *Prospects* (Paris), vol. 27, no. 4, December 1997, p. 493-99. (No. 104.)

Darling-Hammond, L., et al. 1993. *Authentic assessment in practice*. New York, NY, National Center for Restructuring Education, Schools and Teaching.

Department for Education and Employment, 2001. *News Centre Release,* 26 January 2001, London, DfEE.

Gipps, C. 1998. Student assessment and learning for a changing society. *Prospects* (Paris), no. 105, March 1998.

McDonald, J. 1996. *Redesigning school: lessons for the twenty-first century*. San Francisco, CA, Jossey-Bass.

Organisation for Economic Co-operation and Development. 1996. *Education at a glance*. Paris, OECD.

Parlett and Hamilton. 1976. Illuminative evaluation. *In:* Tawney, D., ed. *Curriculum evaluaiton today*. London, Macmillan.

Plomp, T. 1998. The potential of international comparative studies to monitor the quality of education. *Prospects* (Paris), no 105, March 1998.

Sizer, T. 1991. *Horace's school: redesigning the American high school*. Boston, MA, Houghton Mifflin.

Stake, R. 1967. The countenance of educational evaluation. *Teachers college record* (New York), no. 68.

Stufflebeam, D., et al. 1971. *Educational evaluation and decision-making*. Itasca, IL, Peacock.

Section 3

Summary of the Proceedings

Summary of the Proceedings

Organization

The seminar on 'The Management of Curriculum Change' for curriculum specialists in the Gulf Region was organized in Muscat with the support of the Omani Ministry of Education, the General Directorate of Curricula and Training and the IBE, in co-operation with the Omani National Commission for UNESCO.

All the Gulf countries (except Qatar) were represented at the meeting: Bahrain, Kuwait, Oman, Saudi Arabia and the United Arab Emirates. The Arab Bureau of Education for the Gulf States (ABEGS) delegated its First Counsellor, Prof. A. Al-Humaidan, while the Director of the UNESCO Bureau in Qatar, Mr. Bubtana, also attended the meeting. Participants included directors and other high-ranking officers from curriculum development centres or corresponding institutions. Three IBE experts—from Australia, India and Malta—presented their reports on one of the themes of the workshop:

- Planning and designing curriculum change or curriculum reforms in the participating countries;
- Management of curriculum change while it is being implemented;
- Monitoring and evaluation of curriculum change or curriculum reform in the participating countries.

H.E. Sayyid Saoud bin Ibrahim Al Bousaidi, Minister of Education, chaired the opening ceremony of the seminar at the Crown Plaza Hotel. Under-secretaries and officials of the Ministry of Education attended the seminar. Dr. Hamed Saif Al-Hammami and Dr. Cecilia Braslavsky delivered speeches at the seminar.

Objectives

This meeting aimed at: sharing experiences and expertise on current changes in curricula; examining common problems and discussing possible solutions relevant to the present situation in the region or foreseen reforms; strengthening co-operation between countries and the IBE and UNESCO; reinforcing the requirements for training curriculum specialists; and discussing the possibilities for animating a networking process for Arab countries.

Highlights of the Seminar

After the inaugural ceremony, the Director of the IBE presented the objectives of the seminar. She explained that the Report of the International Commission on Education for the Twenty-first Century envisaged curricular innovations based on the 'four pillars of learning', particularly on the guiding principle of 'learning to live together'. It is time to broaden our vision in view of the environmental challenges, the emerging global information society and the globalized economy. The Gulf countries could examine their common problems, taking into consideration the cultural sensitivities of each country.

This was followed by exchanging experiences about recent and ongoing initiatives in curriculum reforms in the participating countries. Country reports were presented by Bahrain, Kuwait, Oman, Saudi Arabia and the United Arab Emirates, and, in that order, each country narrated its methodologies of curriculum design and development. Some of the countries also highlighted the areas where improvements are required. A short brief of each country presentation follows.

Bahrain

They have been developing their curriculum for the past twenty years. They have detailed information about measures that could ensure improvements in the field of curriculum development. The curriculum has been implemented according to their needs and requirements. New contents, such as environment and health education, have been incorporated into the school system. They have organized exchange programmes with other Gulf countries for caring and sharing.

They experience a problem with not having specialists in many subjects. Reading is also a basic difficulty, along with the lack of know-how to develop self-learning materials. There is an absence of synergy between the individuals who design the curriculum, draft textbooks and those who are responsible for implementing them. They have separate systems of inspectors and curriculum experts, and their functions are not synchronized, although they are profoundly inter-related.

Kuwait

- In this country new projects and subject contents have been introduced.
- Computer education has been incorporated as part of general education.
- They have developed a competency-based education and training system.

But there is a wide gap between the concept and its actual implementation, since many teachers are not aware of the educational objectives. The weakness of professional capacities among many teachers and a lack of creativity and innovation in their activity are still evident. Improvement is required in classroom teaching. Specialists are not available to make the curriculum enjoyable. There is little contact between the administrators and those who prepare the curriculum. Curriculum development has become an unduly time-consuming process. Discrepancies exist in its implementation and follow up.

Oman

The main features of educational reform are:

- Basic education lasts ten years. It aims to provide students with self-learning skills and to ensure the eradication of illiteracy. There are two years of secondary education in grades eleven and twelve.

- Reforms have been implemented in learning and teaching materials and in the development of new assessment systems.
- New subjects dealing with life skills, information technology (IT) and computers have been introduced.
- Particular importance is given to science and English.
- Educational supervision and inspection have been consolidated.
- In-service training of teachers is provided.
- The country promotes educational evaluation.

There are difficulties in motivating teachers to perform to their full potential. Work pressures are discernable and in-depth coverage in science, mathematics and English is lacking. Teacher training is being imparted based on the cascade system, but this seems to be insufficient as there is a desire to enlarge and strengthen the training system further. Some teachers are not computer literate and require training in IT. Lastly, parents do not appreciate the importance of basic education and sometimes, instead of being of some assistance, they themselves seem to need help.

Saudi Arabia

- Subject matter has been improved and redundancy removed.
- Subject matter related to activity has also been included.
- Computers are accessible in every school.
- Up-to-date educational services, like laboratory equipment and other teaching aids, are also provided.
- There is a system of feedback and suggestions from the teachers, principals and educational administrators, and the necessary revision of the curriculum are made if necessary.

This country did not specify any difficulties, but feels the need for a comprehensive teacher-training programme.

United Arab Emirates

Salient features are as follows:

- Curriculum development is a continuous process and they have created a national curriculum for all subjects. Both interdisciplinary and multi-disciplinary approaches have been adopted.
- They have no problem in implementing English at the elementary level. There is a new national curriculum in English.
- The prepared curriculum has input from indigenous values.
- Technology and environmental education have been introduced in the curriculum at all levels.
- IT is implemented in Grades I and II of the secondary school. Subjects such as life skills and computer courses for girls in secondary school have also been implemented.
- All secondary schools have computers. Computers are also used for school management.

They are in the process of planning for the education sector up to the year 2020. This country has more or less the same problems described by Oman and prevalent in other Gulf countries.

This review shows that most of the Arab region countries are committed to some form of reform of educational processes, involving curriculum design, curriculum change and curriculum evaluation.

It was made clear to the participants that there was no particular need to follow the Western model. It is not necessary to do the same things that originated 200 years ago. We have to stop reinventing the wheel and instead do something relevant to the realities of our present life. For example, with the increase in life expectancy, do present systems of education have the potential to provide lifelong learning? With the human population facing new illnesses, with economic disparities increasing and with global violence, the education system and its implementation needs fine-tuning to confront these challenges. All these relevant points should be included in the curriculum. Do teachers have enough confidence in children, and vice versa? We have to encourage teachers to contribute to these challenging tasks. We have to identify the real situation prevalent in each country and give shape to our strategies accordingly. There is yet another challenge: that of the introduction of new technologies in the curriculum at all levels of education.

The following clarifications were also made to the participants:

- Curriculum management is not simply a technical issue, but is also a very important political issue. Without political intervention, education cannot be made community sensitive.
- Globalization is an accepted fact This must be reflected in the curriculum. We have to avoid isolation. So how do we integrate ourselves with the global community without loosing our individual characteristics?
- It is necessary to develop other means of livelihood and reduce the economy's dependence on oil reserves.
- Criticism should not be a luxury. Constructive criticism is essential to growth.
- We have to be creative.
- Parents need to be convinced of the benefit of reform. For this, systematic research is needed.
- Electronic media may be used to convince the teachers and to raise the teachers' competencies.

Issues Raised in the Seminar

- There is no co-ordination between the people who design the curriculum and the people who implement it.
- The curriculum should be renovated and improved. But how to adopt an integrated/interdisciplinary

approach in the curriculum? How to adopt curricula for living together?

- How to develop the capacity for exploiting new technologies, particularly IT?
- The process of globalization should be taken into consideration alongside the need to adopt curricula that are suitable to the local needs and to the needs of different social and cultural groups.
- Does the curriculum strike a happy balance between life skills, humanistic values, science and technology, vocational and technical education, preservation of traditional cultures, etc.?
- Teachers training and improvements in classroom transactions are needed.
- There is a need to develop self-learning materials and to improve communication skills.
- It is necessary to convince the parents to accept all these changes.

In relation to the question of the implementation of curriculum changes, the key questions discussed were:

- How to handle and manage change?
- How to correlate the implementation of the curriculum with its design and development?
- What are the parameters of change that need management?

All these issues were critical and needed to be addressed with clarity and perseverance. The important point is how changes can be institutionalized. The participants' attention was drawn to the following observations regarding the management of curriculum change.

- Managing curricular change should focus on three aspects of human development: to be knowledgeable; to have a healthy life; and to strive for the three Cs (competence, confidence and commitment).
- Management of change depends upon fulfilment of a few pre-conditions: clarity about the change objectives; detailed processes and strategies to

implement the changes; monitoring and evaluation strategies of changes at various phases (initiation, implementation and institutionalization).

- Emphasis on generic skills in vocational education.
- Integration of academic and career education.
- Development of integrated curriculum, particularly in science and social science.
- An ability to communicate effectively and meaningfully in classrooms will be required, while language skills have to be based on the communicative approach.
- Greater emphasis on the frontline approach, where emphasis is laid on introducing the latest information to about 10 per cent of the existing quantum of the content, without affecting the entire process of curriculum change.
- The role of supportive institutions in the successful management of curriculum change is essential. In this field, ABEGS can play a very crucial role by providing a common platform for curriculum enrichment and identifying resource persons for the training of second- and third-level functionaries. ABEGS can also provide a platform for the periodic exchange of experiences.

Some Comments from the IBE Director

Several points emerged clearly from the discussions and presentations. Reform in education is not seen as an option, but as a necessary response to external factors. However, this still leaves sufficient leeway for individual countries to direct the reforms in ways that suit their specific cultures and values. Further, the effort in reform, as much in the curriculum as in other areas of education, is not a 'one-shot revolution', but involves a continuing effort that calls for a capacity to plan and adapt over long periods of time. A number of factors were identified which were important to resolve in curriculum reform. There were still too few people with appropriate training in curriculum and evaluation. In some places teachers were seen as being resistant to change, while community attitudes to some of the curriculum or organizational changes were not supportive. Better ways of involving teachers and gaining community support were discussed. The universities of the region were notably absent from this meeting and, according to the discussions, play little part in the efforts to implement reform. They were generally characterized as lacking the capacity to contribute to practical endeavours. Changing this attitude seems to be an area where future efforts might be directed.

Where effective curriculum reform has occurred, there has been a co-operative effort involving curriculum specialists from education, teachers from schools and scholars from universities. The interaction between researchers, curriculum experts and those with teaching experience can be a creative one, when the right environment is achieved. Any moves in capacity-building in curriculum reform would need to include the universities, since they have a potentially strong role to play in curriculum development, and in co-operation with other key players, such as teachers and curriculum specialists in education ministries and departments. Among the solutions offered:

- Utilize available expertise (locally, regionally and from outside the region) to overcome the current lack of curriculum specialists—but the priority is to train local people for the necessary tasks.
- Make better use of universities in the region.
- Create a database for curriculum change.
- Use regular surveys to keep track of progress.
- Benefit from studies undertaken by international organizations, such as UNESCO.

Dr. Braslavsky, Director of the IBE, reacted in the following way:

- The country reports provide evidence of the efforts made in the region to assist educational reform in curriculum development.
- In many countries the patterns of Western societies are being used in the implementation of reform. We

need to bear in mind that many Western countries are not proud of their education systems. Are there other choices?

- The reason for this disquiet in Western countries is that they find their systems unable to cope with the magnitude of the changes—social as well as technological.
- Science is providing new possibilities—can we educate people in a manner that they can make better decisions utilizing these possibilities? Lifelong learning is one response to the need to be ready to face continuing change.
- We have heard of your intentions in your countries. What is the situation on the ground? In many countries in South America children are hostile to school and violence often results. Can you convince parents of the value of the changes you are making?
- While science and technology are the more obvious focuses for change, what are the implications for the values you cherish, the values that are part of your traditions? We need to consider how and when to introduce technology. Should we allow market forces alone to decide for us?
- What is the impact of science and technology on culture? We need to keep a wider agenda for change. Languages are increasingly important. Should English be your automatic choice for a first foreign language? Australia teaches 100 languages in an effort to keep alive the cultures of the many groups who make up the nation.
- How far should we go in introducing new technologies at school? The history of education shows the need to take cognizance of new technology, but in order to make of it a servant, and not a master.

Round-Table Discussions

At the round-table discussion, three presentations were made:

- Dr Macelli from Malta on curriculum planning;
- Mr Ganguly from India on curriculum management;
- Dr Hughes from Australia on curriculum evaluation.

These papers are included in full in the previous section.

There was a lively discussion following the papers on practical difficulties in these areas. Among the points made were the following:

- Resistance to curriculum change is a normal response and should not be regarded as necessarily negative. It provides the basis and a starting point for a dialogue with stakeholders, which is an important part of curriculum development.
- A major issue in curriculum reform is the pressure to add more and more content, leading to overcrowding in the curriculum unless other content can be dropped. Many curriculum texts strive to insert new content without reorganizing earlier material or reducing the overall volume to be covered.
- The updating of science education offers particular challenges, given not only the emergence of new knowledge, but also of different perceptions.
- New technology offers great opportunities to add to sources of information, to increase means of access and to vary methods of teaching and learning. Equity of access to this technology will be a major requirement in any change.
- Curriculum evaluation is now more important in the process of development because it offers the opportunity to guide our judgments of past effectiveness and to make decisions on the course of future directions. More varied and realistic approaches need to be included. The paper on curriculum evaluation tabled at the conference outlines the vastly increased range of approaches available for decision-making.
- The preparation of school leaders is now more vital as they play many other roles in addition to

teaching, but may have had little or no preparation or experience for these tasks. Specific provision for training needs to be made both for existing principals and for those who aspire to such positions of leadership. Such programmes need to be continuing, as new approaches and new problems will continually emerge.

- Curriculum management is not a simple choice between centralization and decentralization, but rather a careful study as to where various decisions are best made: centrally, at the district level, nationally or regionally?
- The teacher remains a central figure in curriculum change. Without good teachers no change can be fully effective, but good teachers can be even better given well-designed curricula and support materials.
- Our evaluation needs to take account of the full range of our teaching and learning goals, and to do so in appropriate ways. This provides special challenges in areas such as religious education. These challenges need to be faced because students evaluate and judge our learning priorities through our evaluations.
- In too many curriculum changes, the teachers are aware of the required content but do not fully understand the goals. Without a sense of purpose, the teaching of content is likely to be hollow.

Discussion Groups

Three groups were formed for follow-up discussions on the themes of the meeting to provide recommendations to the plenary. Their findings included notes on the needs and requirements of curriculum reform in the region, on ways and means of preparing curriculum specialists and on capacity-building in different countries. The groups were particularly required to identify means by which they could maintain the integrity of their own cultures and patterns of education, while still adjusting to the needs made apparent through changes in technology. This put particular pressure on the availability of trained and specialized personnel from the Gulf States, where the current supply is limited. The reports from each of the groups are included in Part VI.

The entire approach followed in the seminar was interactive, participative and purposeful. It helped the participants to identify the problem areas, to suggest various solutions and provoked them to come out with new ideas. It is hoped that a new era of co-operation between Gulf countries and the IBE in curriculum design and curriculum implementation at various levels will follow.

The group meeting on curriculum evaluation noted the following points:

1. *Curriculum evaluation* is an integral part of the curriculum. The curriculum is the totality of what happens in the educational process as a result of: intentions/purposes; learning activities; learning outcomes; resources—human and material; evaluation processes; means for change and development; school practices and culture.
2. *Curriculum evaluation* is the means by which the value of this total process is assessed. It involves gathering evidence to judge the degree of achievement of aims and also to enable decisions to be made on future progress. As a guide to decision-making, it needs to be transparent, fully informing the many groups involved in these decisions. Curriculum evaluation has a number of important functions:
   - It protects the quality of educational processes and the standards of outcome.
   - For public accountability purposes, it provides evidence that public money is being well spent.
   - It promotes and improves high-quality processes and outcomes at individual institutions, and provides a basis to disseminate good practice, leading to overall system improvement.
   - If informs student choice, so that students may make sense of a variety of offerings on the basis of their quality and usefulness.

- It informs parents on the progress of their children as students and on how to assist their future decisions and work.
- It provides teachers with comparative data on the effects of their teaching.
- It is the major effective means of curriculum improvement as it provides information on what works well and what is unproductive or even harmful.

Tools for Curriculum Evaluation

Curriculum evaluation has changed greatly in recent decades as a result of studying the experience of the process over that period. A listing of the tools for curriculum evaluation shows the progressive change from simple numerical information to include more descriptive and more revealing forms.

- *Test.* This set of uniform tasks to assess knowledge or ability is the most common form of information provided. It is convenient and easy to control, occurring at a particular time and place and perceived as an evaluation. It provides information in a concise summarized form. Its great strength is its high reliability, given proper design and conditions of implementation. Its major weakness can be a limited validity. Tests may vary from simple and short lists of questions requiring single word answers or a choice among alternatives, to much longer and more elaborate set of tasks in a standardized form. The process of designing and checking on the reliability and validity of such tests is now highly specialized.
- *Examination.* This is usually a long and formal test given under standardized conditions. It has greater flexibility than a test, as long answers are possible, giving more information to the examiner. Short answer tests do not require the student to organize and express complex information. For this reason, validity can be greater but at the cost of reliability.

Essays are difficult to mark with reliability, yet they reveal aspects that are not available from the more reliable short-answer tests.

- *Survey*. A description of a particular topic or institution in a comprehensive way. This might be an examination of the effectiveness of rural schools, both in terms of participation and performance. This may be done through sending out and analysing questionnaires or, more elaborately, through visits, interviews and telephone contacts. The Internet provides new modes of communication.
- *Case study*. A detailed study and analysis of a particular instance to provide insights into characteristics and reasons for them. This is an intensive look at a particular situation to penetrate beneath the surface of test results, for example, and seek to determine reasons. Case studies of both success and failure may provide beneficial information and insights to use in other situations. The case study can concern the work of an individual student or of an entire school. The choice of this approach is made where it is useful to explain the causes of results, rather than just to describe them. It may well use all the tools described here.
- *Interview*. A face-to-face discussion on a particular topic. This approach is frequently used as data for a survey or for selection purposes for a task or job. Reliability is not high for this tool unless the interview is carefully planned and executed. Low reliability means low validity, too.
- *Portfolio*. A collection of work from an individual or group sometimes produced for a particular purpose. The proponents of 'authentic evaluation' see it as a means of access to a representative collection of an individual's work, revealing development over time and the capacity to complete long or difficult tasks. Examinations with their tight time limits can never reveal these characteristics.

- *Authentic task*. An evaluation task that is close to a real-life situation. As mentioned, the portfolio is one of many forms of authentic evaluation. More traditionally, so is the practical examination although this is limited in its reality because the time is usually set and so is the task for completion. An authentic task is a serious attempt to see if the student has the capacity to perform a task of long-term relevance or value. The task must be useful to others and the student is required to present a written report that, in part, requires them to reflect on their own learning experience.
- *Document analysis*. A study of all the documents produced or used in a given programme.
- *Longitudinal study*. A study of a situation, institution or group repeated over a number of years. This is of great value in determining long-term trends but is difficult to maintain over the period needed. While it can never be a universal approach, careful planning and proper maintenance of records can make it possible and the results will always be valuable.
- *Exhibition*. An assessment in which students exhibit for some public audience the results of a project they have undertaken or the understanding they have gained from a set of experiences.
- *Role-play*. An exercise in which people take on defined roles in a play, impromptu or planned. In teaching it is used for students to develop their understanding of diverse viewpoints or new situations. In evaluation it may be used to test a student's capacity to react to a hypothetical but realistic situation, for example, a medical diagnosis.
- *Practical test*. A realistic situation such as an experiment or practical task performed under test conditions. This differs from authentic evaluation in that test situations apply, including a set period of time.

- *Education indicators.* This involves the collection of information on a regular basis to give an appreciation of the system as a whole or some part of it. Such figures may be straightforward such as enrolments, attendance and progress through the grades. In recent years, OECD with co-operation from UNESCO has taken the lead in devising a set of indicators that will give a more complete description of a system including qualitative as well as quantitative measures. There are now indicators covering: the context of education; costs; resources and school processes; participation; staff; and results of education.

The list of evaluation tools shows the gradual changes of emphasis in evaluation in favour of methods revealing more about the student, the programme and the education system than a set of numbers describing performance at a particular point in time. After a long period beginning in the 1950s, when psychometric methods predominated using standardized tests, examinations and other methods directed to produce numerical scores, there was a swing towards more broad-based forms of evaluation. More recent approaches are inclusive of both strands, numerical measures to assess progress in particular areas and also the more descriptive tools which consider the context and seek to give a more inclusive picture. Prominent among these approaches are case studies, portfolios, exhibitions and authentic tasks.

Evaluation of the Seminar

All three external experts and the staff of the IBE made their evaluation of the seminar independently. Their papers are available in the IBE for the reference of interested parties. Part of one of these reports is reproduced here.

The seminar was the first contact with the Gulf Region and was very useful, giving the curriculum development specialists of that region a better insight about what is going on at the international level in terms of adaptation of the education systems to the important challenges of the new century. At the same time, the IBE learned better what the countries of that region are doing to reform their curricula, particularly bearing in mind the reconciliation between their cultural traditions and modernity. The primary school (first cycle) visited in Muscat clearly shows this effort of combining Islamic courses with learning to use computers and having access to the Internet.

The countries of the region have received many suggestions for reform from various institutions and from different consultants (UNESCO Regional Offices, United Nations Development Programme, British Council, ABEGS, etc.). However, they have been facing some problems in the planning, management and implementation of reform projects due to the lack of competent human resources, and sometimes because of the resistance of educational stakeholders, including teachers and parents. There is no doubt that the particular political structures of these countries also have a great influence in advancing or retarding educational reforms.

It seems that universities in the region have little or no role in conceiving and promoting educational reforms. One of the problems mentioned during group discussions was that 'University professors who participate in curriculum planning do not have adequate field experience in education'. No curriculum reform can be successful without the sincere co-operation of teachers. And yet, teachers sometimes need to be trained for this purpose. The university has therefore a crucial role in preparing teachers for the implementation of the new curricula. It has to take this responsibility seriously.

The impression was that countries of the region take a serious interest in basic education. However, the latest statistics show that the illiteracy rate is still rather high (between 13 per cent and 28 per cent). It is assumed that many illiterates can be found among expatriates, the older generation, and possibly among girls and women. UNESCO hopes to help overcome these problems within a reasonable period.

There is also no doubt that the education and training of people to satisfy the human resource requirements of the Gulf countries are considered as a high priority in the region.[1] Technical and vocational education is only one way of responding to the problem of manpower needs. The introduction of productive work and work experience in secondary school is another line of action one may recommend. Most private sector activities seem to be in the hand of expatriates. Gulf region countries should therefore revise their public school programme in order to develop the spirit of entrepreneurship in future graduates, so that all diploma holders do not expect to find a job in the public administration.

Looking at statistics, one finds that Gulf region countries have made tremendous progress during the last thirty years or so in terms of the expansion of education. For example, Oman started with three schools in 1970. Today the country has over 400 primary schools and around 700 secondary schools. Nevertheless, as the representative of ABEGS stated, this expansion has not necessarily been accompanied by an improvement in quality. UNESCO or the IBE can help the educational authorities, perhaps through missions, to find out what quality improvement measures should be adopted in addition to what they have already undertaken. The competition between public (government) school and private school is a beneficial approach that deserves to be promoted.

On several occasions, the issue of the role of the school and of the local authorities was brought into the discussion. It is stated in the seminar's recommendations that local expertise should be used when implementing curriculum changes. Some speakers expressed the wish that the education system should become decentralized and the local authorities should play a greater role in decision-making about how to make the content more suitable to local needs.[2] Greater participation of local resources in financing education was also emphasized.

One has always to keep a balance between local needs and national priorities. National cohesion requires that all children receive the same education. However, at the same time, here is a possibility for the teachers and headmasters to adapt part of the progamme content to the local conditions (in addition to optional courses, the adaptation of content, for example, in geography, is quite feasible; out-of-school activities open large possibilities for local adaptation). If the decentralization approach is adopted, all actors at the local level should receive prior training in curriculum development.

Outcomes and Expected Follow-up

It has been decided that a report will be prepared in English by the IBE. It was agreed that the Omani Ministry of Education would do the same with the Arabic version, helped by the National Commission for UNESCO.

The participating institutions expressed their desire to consolidate their relationship with the IBE. The Director of the IBE discussed with Omani authorities the possibility of networking to be developed in the framework of the worldwide networking commitment on curriculum development that is already taking shape in other countries.

Future strategy

Future activity may include the following steps.

- The IBE may consider the request of one or more of the Gulf countries for closer co-operation on curriculum design.
- Professional support to develop the curriculum, syllabus, textbooks and other instructional material is likely to be extended.
- Training and retraining of teachers, including training in various aspects of classroom transaction, training in educational technology, training in monitoring and evaluation process. The IBE can provide professional support in developing a periodic teacher-training module.
- Capacity-building of resource institutions at various levels.
- Developing learning strategies for providing all learners with common skills.

Summary of the agreement between the IBE and the Omani authorities

- The IBE will help Oman to prepare a special video report on 'good educational practices' in that country to be presented at the forty-sixth session of the

International Conference on Education.

- The IBE will be ready to organize a programme for a high-level study visit for Oman's educationists in Europe and elsewhere, giving them access to a diversity of experience on a special curriculum subject.
- Mrs Al Farsi, Oman's Undersecretary of Education, sought the IBE's co-operation to help organize a major international event on secondary education reform in Oman in 2002.
- The possibility of capacity-building on curriculum management by the IBE and the provision of technical assistance for that purpose were also discussed.
- The Omani authorities expressed their interest in animating a network for the Arab Gulf countries in curriculum development along the lines of the framework of the international networking commitment of the IBE.
- The possibility of the IBE training a young Omani expert was also explored.

Notes

1. If these countries want to diversify their economies in order to become less dependant on oil income, they have to train a large number of qualified persons in various areas of the economy. As many Gulf Region countries have decided to replace expatriates by local people, the development of needed human resources becomes a top priority.
2. See the text of the speech by the representative of the UNESCO Office in Qatar (Part V). Elsewhere, Mr Ganguly also considered the movement toward a decentralized school-based system as one of the main current worldwide trends.

Section 4

Country Reports

23

Management of Curriculum Revision and Change: A Synthesis of the National Reports

Bahrain, Kuwait, Oman, Saudi Arabia and United Arab Emirates have submitted their national reports on the subject of curriculum revision and change. In the following pages, we present a synthesis of these reports that, with the exception of Oman's and the United Arab Emirates (in the latter case, a report of the Centre for Curriculum and Instructional Material Development, dated January 2001), were originally written in Arabic. This synthesis has deleted certain generalized and theoretical statements contained in the reports. The objective is to provide an accurate picture of what is being done in the area of curriculum revisions or changes in each of these countries.

Major Features of Educational Reform

Bahrain

The Ministry of Education in Bahrain has concentrated its comprehensive educational plan for the years 1989-94 on measures to bę adopted to develop the educational process and enhance its efficiency. The Ministry is deeply committed to providing education for all and especial efforts will be made to ensure that this ideal is realized. Efforts are also underway to improve the quality of teaching in order to meet the learner's needs as well as those vital for the socio-economic development of the country.

The following guidelines endowed with their general framework has been adopted with a view to achieving educational objectives:

- viewing education as a gateway to integrated and comprehensive development in all fields. It is appreciated that the development of a society is dependent on its schools as it is education that moulds knowledge, beliefs and attitudes;
- viewing education as constituting a holistic, autonomous system which is also an integral part of the socio-economic system at the macro level;
- the education system in Bahrain is a part of a larger one, namely, the Arab education system;
- the Ministry of Education is responsible for both formal and non-formal education;
- in view of the fact that education is a shared responsibility, new initiatives such as the Educational Council for Planning and Co-ordination and Parent-Teacher Council need to be encouraged to ensure wider participation;
- viewing education as a co-operative enterprise and gradually delegating more functional powers to the schools to achieve greater decentralization;
- ensuring that the educational reforms constitute a comprehensive change rather than a partial one.

Current educational policy focuses mainly on three elements:

- education for all;
- improving the standard of teaching through major reforms in the content of education and teaching methods:
- linking education with the requirements of the job market.

During the last five years, Bahrain has placed especial emphasis on upgrading the academic curriculum in the light of the requirements of the twenty-first century. New systems of evaluation have also been instituted in grade one since 1995-96. The objective is to encourage those who excel to continue their upward mobility and sustain improved performances.

Kuwait

The Ministry of Education has formulated its orientations, according to a previous report (see Kuwait Profile, revised version, (1995-2000), which encompass changes at all levels of education.

At the elementary and secondary levels, the new objectives include:

- broadening the scope of formal education by introducing information technology and practical skills;
- fostering individual development in students while stressing Islamic, Arab and humanitarian values along with a sense of civic duty;
- directing formal education towards continuing studies at institutions of higher education and applied knowledge to generate supplies to fulfil the demands of the labour market;
- maintaining the student/teacher ratio at optimum levels;
- ensuring balanced distribution of schools in the geographically distanced residential areas;
- strengthening relations with the Arab as well as the international educational institutions; and
- implementing schemes to adequately finance formal education. Raise the standards of performance and diversify sources of financing. Education development programmes would be assisted in sourcing financial as well as popular support.

The objectives for post-secondary education are:

- ensuring specialized human resource training and development. Young people should learn to respect societal values and traditions and acquire the qualities necessary to play the role of future leaders in society;
- keeping track of and contributing to scientific progress through research in economic, social and cultural development;

- playing a leading role in serving society and ensuring development, even while safeguarding the values and ethics of society;
- reinforcing the Arab/Islamic cultural heritage;
- enriching Arab civilization by encouraging research in the field of arts and sciences;
- ensuring that the global culture remains accessible to Kuwaiti learners in the areas of arts and sciences.

Oman

Educational reform encompasses several aspects in Oman: one of them is re-structuring the educational hierarchy that is divided into two levels:

1. Basic education for ten years. This is divided into two cycles—cycle one includes grades one to four and cycle two contains grades five to ten;
2. Two years of education (secondary education) in grades eleven and twelve.

The introduction of the basic education system necessitated implementing several fundamental changes to achieve various important objectives such as:

- to provide equal education opportunities for all children;
- to remedy the shortcomings of the elementary level and to provide students with the necessary knowledge and skills:
- to cope with the information explosion and new trends in education the time devoted to basic education may have to be extended;
- to extend the duration of the periods and lengthen the school day at the level of basic education;
- to ensure the eradication of functional illiteracy.

In relation to curriculum, reforms were implemented in several fields such as:

- developing organizational structure of the Ministry and designating a Directorate General for curriculum and training;

- revising the general objectives of curricula and educational levels;
- reforming the study plan;
- reforming the learning and teaching materials of the educational subjects;
- introduction of new curricula and courses;
- development of learning and teaching materials;
- development of new systems of assessment (evaluation);
- development of educational supervision;
- development of educational activities; and
- upgrading the quality of teachers.

Saudi Arabia

The country profile of Saudi Arabia reveals that in general terms, the education system in the country is presently focused on:

- raising the efficiency of professional and administrative performance in the educational institutions to enhance the standards and content of the educational process;
- ensuring that the education system meets the religious, economic and social goals;
- reducing the rate of illiteracy;
- integrating the activities of the institutions of higher education to fulfil the needs arising from socio-economic planning;
- broadening the base of higher education by diversifying its programmes to cope with the Kingdom's requirements to achieve overall development;
- ensuring that qualified citizens enjoy the opportunity to continue their education at the university level.

The Kingdom of Saudi Arabia places special emphasis on religion so that Islamic values permeate all aspects of students' life, without compromising the capacities to acquire production-oriented skills, attitudes and the development of the country's economy.

The Saudi Arabian report underscores the importance of preparing appropriate textbooks for various fields of studies in schools: Islamic studies, Arabic language, science, social sciences, technical sciences and computer. Staff, teacher training and exchange of experience with other Gulf Region countries also receive considerable attention.

We learn through the country profile that the Ministry of Education tends to delegate all operational and administrative responsibilities to the regional and provincial bodies in charge of education. The Ministry concentrates on the strategic issues, besides planning and supervising developmental and promotional activities. Thus, the decision-making processes are speeded up and the procedures simplified.

United Arab Emirates

With regard to the United Arab Emirates, some of the focal themes underlying the reform process are:

- creation of a kindergarten development centre;
- development of curricula and preparation of textbooks for Islamic education, Arabic language, social studies, etc.;
- creation of school administration programme at the university;
- promotion of English-language learning at the primary level;
- teaching of computer science at the secondary school;
- providing private schools with select educational materials;
- launching various programmes to develop and improve the professional skills of the teachers;
- developing educational planning and improving the Ministry's efficiency;
- manpower planning and research.

The computer is being used not only as a teaching aid, but also for improving the school administration. From 1998 to 1999, a project has been launched to transform traditional school libraries into learning resource centres having at their disposal a specialized database of school subjects. Improvement in the use of science laboratories by the secondary-level students is another effort that is being undertaken. Language laboratories are also being equipped and promoted. Since 1992 special emphasis has been placed on the improvement of schoolbooks and related materials. The quality of the printing of books is enhanced to make them more attractive to students.

The Centre of Curriculum states that, from 1999, a programme for learning essential life skills has been introduced in grades 4 to 9 of primary and preparatory stages, which includes study skills, thinking skills, communication skills, social interaction skills, skills related to recreation and to proper use of spare time, and finally some elements of career education.

Organizational Structure for Curriculum Development

Bahrain

Curriculum is being considered in Bahrain as part of the education system in its entirely, and as being integral to its goals, content, learning, educational strategies, school activities, evaluation and feedback.

Curriculum has its inputs, processes and outputs that are influenced by the school environment and culture—values, attitudes, knowledge and the behavioural aspects that characterize teachers, administrators and pupils. It includes the educational experiences of the learner in and outside the school. It is perceived to reflect the society and its modernization. It is 'all what happens in the educational establishment ... to enable the learner's social adaptability'.

The Curriculum Department deals with the design and development of objectives and strategies. It undertakes research and project planning, reviews the progress and works towards continuously improving the efficiency of the education system. One of the primary functions of the Curriculum

Department in the Ministry is to be alert to changes taking place and around us, in order to update the programmes to keep them in tune with the changing realities. The Curriculum Department has to go through the following phases in the course of performing its major task:

- study and research (about actual development needs);
- examining alternative strategies and preparing development projects;
- consultations with specialists and partners, and submission of results to the Curriculum Committee and the Minister for approval;
- planning the implementation of the approved project(s);
- consultations with subject advisory committees, experts and teachers;
- once the new curriculum or new project is put into execution, and then generalized from experimental schools to all schools, the stage of follow-up and evaluation will start.

Kuwait

In Kuwait, there exists a Curriculum Department in the Ministry of Education. It received its inspiration first from an evaluation study of the Kuwaiti education system in 1978, following a general conference on school curricula held in 1972.

The adaptation of a new curriculum undergoes three stages:

1. Introductory phase: preparation of the suggestion, its presentation to a higher committee, identifying priorities and undertaking relevant research;
2. Execution phase: includes the experimental phase in the sample schools and subsequent evaluation;
3. Post evaluation of the applied programme, review of the curriculum and its adaptation. Several committees take part in adopting, executing and evaluating the new programme along with some

departments of the ministry that are oriented toward preparing materials, techniques and teaching aids.

The creation of a curriculum requires the formation of special committees by the Ministry in relation to various subjects. Development committees participate in experimenting and improving the new curriculum in co-operation with the concerned groups. Their members may be both from the Ministry and from outside.

Oman

Recognizing the importance of curricula and training in achieving the goals of educational reform, the Directorate General of Curriculum and Training was established to assume responsibilities in the following areas:

- development of course materials and books for every subject at different educational levels;
- development of teachers' guides for all subjects;
- preparing a plan to implement the new curricula in schools;
- evaluation of the curricula implemented, by assessment data, inspectors' reports and teacher-training programmes;
- studying, in collaboration with the Department of Private Education, the curricula of private schools to determine their suitability;
- direct supervision of regional subject inspectors;
- identification of educational innovations, methodologies and computer programmes;
- identification of the types of training needed to support curricula, preparation and supervision of an annual training programme based on these needs;
- development of inspectorate to ensure that the inspectors are familiar with the new curricula;
- development of evaluation and assessment systems to measure the achievement of curriculum objectives;

- designing and producing educational aids to serve curricula;
- collecting and updating of reference materials to support curricula;
- maintaining a computer database for teachers to meet their particular training needs.

The Directorate General of Curriculum and Training comprises the following departments:

(a) Book Production Department;
(b) Education of Young Learners Department;
(c) Department of Islamic Studies;
(d) Arabic Language Department;
(e) English Language Department;
(f) Mathematics and Science Department;
(g) Social Studies Department;
(h) Life Skills Department;
(i) Training Department;
(j) Educational Aids Department;
(k) Informational Technology Department.

The precise role of each department was defined according to the goals of the Directorate General of Curriculum and Training.

Saudi Arabia

Since 1960 the Department known as the Presidency General for Girls' Education was instituted in the Kingdom of Saudi Arabia. Its objective was to define the study programmes and curricula for girls' education in accordance with the teaching of Islam. The Presidency controls kindergartens, general education (elementary, intermediate and secondary), teacher training, college education, adult education and literacy, vocational education and training in relation to girls. The basic credo is that God has created the female of the species different from the male not only in their physical aspects but also from psychological and behavioural points of view. However, the curriculum development authorities try to formulate the programme in science, mathematics, etc., in a manner that is comparable to what is being taught in Germany, Japan the United Kingdom and the United States of America.

The Curriculum Department in the Ministry has embarked on two types of development: 'particular development' or the improvement of a specific subject in the learning process; and 'comprehensive development' which embraces all aspects of curriculum, finalized recently by the highest authorities. Committees were then formed to plan strategies for developing and procedures for executing such essential endeavours. For such a comprehensive approach, the inspiration comes not only from the new educational and scientific advancement, the recent technological and informational progress, but also from traditional beliefs in Saudi Arabia. The application of the comprehensive curriculum development was foreseen for the year 1419 (=1998 AD) to the year 1425 (=2004).

Another aspect particular to the Kingdom is the formation of an educational development centre for a comprehensive reform. An educational development team comprising the general curriculum department, technical department, evaluation department and a number of advisors, researchers, headmasters and teachers who have been especially trained have also been established under a Depute Minister.

United Arab Emirates

The national curriculum committee, with a Deputy Minister as Chairman, was established in 1975 in the United Arab Emirates. In 1980, the preparation of curriculum for basic education schools was underway. In 1989, a higher committee for the curriculum was formed in the Ministry to examine education in general, and textbooks and syllabi in particular. The higher committee was composed of the deputy minister, the director of the curriculum department, a number of professors from the faculty of education in the United Arab Emirates and specialists from the ministry. The development of national curriculum passed through a number of phases:

- Field study and research for testing the effectiveness of teaching methods with regard to various subjects;

- Documentation of different subjects taught in schools (Islamic studies, Arabic language, social studies and psychology);
- Transformation of curriculum documents into teaching materials and manuals (in 1994 a review committee for textbooks, manuals and related materials was created by the respective ministries);
- The stage of producing and printing books of a better quality;
- To evaluate the new programme, a high level committee was set up in 1998. Subsequently, a decree was issued to establish a co-ordination committee for general education curriculum. A national conference was organized in 1999 to discuss the development of curriculum in general education. In the year 2000, the Ministry assigned a number of experts and advisors to scrutinize the vocabulary used in basic general education subjects or texts and reject whatever was found to be unsuitable or redundant.

Some Basic Principles of Curriculum Adaptation and Change

The reports from all countries of the region show that the authorities are quite aware of the necessity of a substantial reform in the school curricula to meet the challenges of the twenty-first century. We read in the Oman report, that motivated by a firm belief in the importance of education to social and economic development, the Sultanate is keen on rejuvenating the education system. They look forward to revising the educational structure so as to make it relevant to this century and fulfil their objectives of attaining overall development.

Kuwait is keenly aware that the curriculum should inspire behavioural change among the students and contribute to their wholesome development. One of the foremost characteristics of the curriculum change in Bahrain is *'to develop the learner physically, mentally, socially and spiritually through the acquisition of knowledge, skills, values and positive attitudes drawn from Islam, which can develop the capacity of contemplation, thinking, and being creative, making the learner an effective member of society'.*

With respect to the basic principles that guide curriculum adaptation and change, the country reports provide the following information.

Bahrain

In adapting the curriculum, Bahrain is primarily guided by four basic tenets that relate knowledge to the service of humanity:

1. *Philosophical basis*—the curriculum should be guided by Islamic perceptions of man and religious views on education;
2. *Social basis*—being an Arab and Muslim country, Bahrain seeks to inculcate the noble principles of Islam, and Arab-Islamic values in the minds of the younger generation, to enrich them with the past tradition. They also seek to enlighten the students about the world around them and the unfolding future, so as to equip them with the knowledge essential to facilitate efficient communication with the world;
3. *Psychological basis*—sensitivity towards the learner's need for character building and a holistic development of personality;
4. *Educational or pedagogical basis*—inspired by the Islamic philosophy of education against the backdrop of recent research and discoveries in human sciences.

Bahrain's report also presents the nineteen points mentioned below as constituting the basic principles underlying curriculum development:

- to consider the development of education as a holistic process and the curriculum as being integral to that process;
- to direct the development of education with the vision necessary to cope with future challenges;
- to rely upon an explicit philosophy of education with adequate attention being paid to the characteristics

of learners, their stage of growth and attendant problems by adopting a scientific approach;

- to facilitate the involvement of schools, their headmaster and teachers in the efforts aimed at renewal and change;
- to improve educational performances in schools through the introduction of new methods and approaches more suitable to the environment in Bahrain;
- to enhance the role of learners in the education process and ensure continuous training and upgrading for the educational personnel;
- to better organize the schools, encourage an innovative administration and provide for a healthy relationship amongst the staff as well as between the staff and the students;
- to make the school more responsive to the requirements of the new curriculum and the challenges of environment;
- to create a flexible mechanism for effective participation of all stakeholders in the educational process, and ensure its continuity by regular monitoring and evaluation;
- the curriculum should assimilate contemporary science, ensure the students' understanding of modern technology, develop capacities related to thinking, creativity, problem-solving and fostering social adaptability;
- to construct the curriculum on a flexible basis to allow for the introduction of new inputs;
- to facilitate self-learning;
- to create an comprehensive information system encompassing aspects such as the school's strategy, activities, methods and related statistics;
- to prepare schools to accept the risks involved in implementing the new curriculum, initiate appropriate action to ensure proper adaptation, and

inspire them to face any setbacks with a scientific spirit;

- to develop an evaluation system to help continually improve the teaching and learning processes;
- to ensure the participation of the public sector and other concerned establishments and co-ordinate their activities with the school in order to attain the objectives of the curriculum;
- to emphasize the role of the family in the process of teaching/learning and enlisting the participation of parents in realizing the functions and the objectives of school. It is necessary to make the family understand that *the new axis in education is the learner himself* and it is in the learner that the capacity of thinking and innovating needs to be developed;
- to undertake research and field studies in order to evaluate the new programme before its generalized adoption;
- to sensitize media as to its role in informing the public about the new curriculum and its objectives, and convince them about the need for adaptation and change.

Kuwait

The different phases involved in the development of a new curriculum in Kuwait have already been detailed above. Only a few guiding principles have been mentioned in the country report and they are as follows:

- Implementing the new curriculum in a few experimental schools before its large-scale adoption;
- Improving and adapting the curriculum in keeping with the results of ongoing evaluation;
- The introduction of a new curriculum should be preceded by surveys that identify the needs and policies that are formulated to respond to these needs.

The national report of Kuwait remains silent on most of the basic principles governing the curriculum change. The same is the case with respect to the report on Saudi Arabia.

Oman

In the case of Oman the curriculum reformers have projected the following activities:

- revision of general objectives of curricula and educational levels;
- reform study plans;
- reform the learning and teaching materials used in the various educational disciplines;
- introduction of new subjects and courses, including those aimed at developing life skills, familiarizing students with the new communication and information technologies, helping them gain fluency in an international language (English), or to understand the basis of economy and business. Other steps or actions include: production of books; development of other teaching/learning materials; development and application of tools for assessment and evaluation; development of educational supervision; promotion of extracurricular activities to support the curriculum.

Substantial significance is attached to the decision involving the overall objectives of the curriculum as well as the specific objectives of each subject in the new curriculum. The following is the *list of the objectives* set in the Sultanate of Oman:

- develop the physical, intellectual, social, spiritual and emotional personality of students in a well-adjusted manner at the basic educational level;
- augment Islamic faith in students and encourage Islamic behaviour;
- develop students' competence in learning and using Arabic language;
- stimulate Omani cultural identity in students;
- increase awareness of social laws and regulations and respect for public and private ownership;
- develop students' communicative skills in a foreign language (English);

- develop students' willingness to engage in ongoing independent learning;
- develop their capacity in the use of scientific thinking and research abilities;
- develop students' basic skills in science and modern technology;
- develop students' creative abilities;
- develop appropriate work ethics in students;
- provide students with basic life skills and improve vocational preparedness;
- inculcate in students an awareness of environmental issues;
- sensitize the students to contemporary problems facing the world and ways of coping with them;
- encourage students to acquire the saving habit and moderate consumerist tendencies;
- awareness of the importance of time management;
- awareness of truth and beauty;
- develop students' ability to deal with global issues; and
- enhance students' awareness of the need for peace, tolerance and living together in harmony.

These objectives inspire and guide the preparation of the programme for each level, both basic as well as general education.

United Arab Emirates

In the case of the United Arab Emirates, the Centre for Curriculum refers to the following twelve general objectives, which are found in the United Arab Emirates' educational policy document:

1. To build in students an integrated personality involving faith, behaviour, skills and performance;
2. To foster a sense of belonging to the United Arab Emirates as a country, the Arab world and Islamic world;
3. To continue and further promote the use of the Arabic language;

4. To encourage contact with people of other cultures;
5. To meet the needs of society by preparing the required numbers of appropriately trained people;
6. To expand compulsory education to the end of the secondary stage;
7. To promote equality of educational opportunity;
8. To offer educational opportunities suitable to the interests and needs of learners;
9. To upgrade the quality and effectiveness of education to help achieve society's goals and to make instructional programmes relevant to society's current and future needs;
10. To provide education for creativity and innovation;
11. To base education on an advanced technological foundation;
12. To achieve a status where society becomes both teacher and learner with full co-ordination among all institutions, to assure opportunities for life-long learning.

As the national report of United Arab Emirates is not always explicit about the principles guiding the curriculum adaptation in that country, we may refer to some indications in the country's profile, which states that the curricula and syllabi of general education are currently being developed, especially the curricula of the liberal arts. This also involves enhancing the role of technology, computer usage, extra-curricular activities, as well as raising the standard of the English language. Also being prepared are guides to the liberal arts, English language, computers, as well as books on the three stages of education.

The Ministry aims to strengthen the relationship between education, the community and the environment through a number of subsidiary studies that support the curriculum. These studies cover technology, health education, environmental education and security education. Future prospects for curricula aim at changing the quality of education by concentrating on skills and values, as well as inference and discovery methods, and by bridging the gap between subject matter, life and abstract knowledge—instead of isolated information, repetition and traditional education.

The United Arab Emirates is also aware of the necessity to improve the efficiency of the educational process including that of the teachers.

In the case of technical education, effort is being made to ensure an organic correlation with work opportunities in the labour market and their requirements.

The report of the Centre for Curriculum provides us with the following indications about how educational policy and curriculum planning and implementation have to respond to the new challenges facing the country. It says:

1. Education should be free from rigid patterns and conventional systems, and should be based on promoting understanding, analysis, evaluation and other thinking skills;
2. Education should contribute more effectively to fostering national loyalty and competent citizenship;
3. Education should focus on preparing students for a productive life;
4. Education should encourage the broadest possible framework of knowledge, skills, values and attitudes. This framework should also combine knowledge of the past, awareness of the present and anticipation of and preparation for the future;
5. Greater attention should be given to the teaching of science, mathematics, and languages;
6. Innovative techniques must be developed to teach students, not just managers and administrators, the methods of effective decision-making.

Specific Measures to Improve the Curriculum

The general principles of adaptation and reform applied in various Gulf countries are best illustrated by the specific measures each country has undertaken to improve their school programmes.

Bahrain

The last couple of decades have witnessed several measures being taken to help decentralize the education system. The country profile states that since the early 1980s, the Ministry of Education has promoted decentralization alongside a consultative democratic policy. They are creating channels of expression and interaction amongst educational officials and involving all educational personnel in developmental committees in order to take appropriate decisions that will help raise educational efficiency. Several advisory committees have also been established. Membership is not confined to the Ministry's officials, and assistance can be sought from experienced personnel from other Ministries and universities in Bahrain. Students are involved in the decision-making process by participating in a number of these committees.

Institutions of higher education generally enjoy considerable autonomy in administrative and technical matters. However, the Ministry of Education is the superior official authority responsible for the University of Bahrain and the Arabian Gulf University. The Minister of Education is the chairman of their Board of Trustees.

In 1990-91, the Ministry adopted the system of each school becoming an autonomous educational unit, according to a ministerial decision of 24 April 1990. The document attached to the ministerial decision has defined the basic proceedings, the new organizational chart of school administration, educational and administrative tasks, as well as the evaluation process.

This new organizational structure of the school as an autonomous educational unit consists of the following: the school principal, the school council, the assistant principal, the teacher, the social worker, the learning resource centre specialist and the secretary in-charge of administration, accounting and financial matters. Even if curriculum development is a centralized issue, the school council is entitled to discuss the suggestions and projects presented by the school staff regarding curriculum development and teaching methods. The results of these consultations will be submitted to the Ministry of Education.

An interesting procedure followed in Bahrain in relation to the adaptation of a curriculum reform is to consult not only with specialists, teams of senior teachers and university professors, but also with people who have some stake in the development of education, besides the representatives of the private sector (see country report). A seminar is held to discuss reforms by those concerned; the outcome will be presented to a higher committee for academic curriculum and to the education committee for approval or improvement. The proposal will then be forwarded to the higher curriculum committee for adaptation or rejection prior to the ministry's final decision.

Kuwait

Several measures such as the teaching of swimming skills to children and the initiation of computer literacy have recently been introduced at the kindergarten level in Kuwait. The report says that these measures have been expanded to cover all educational institutions since the year 2000-2001.

Kuwait is co-operating with UNESCO in the area of 'associated schools'. The aim is to introduce human rights, peace, tolerance and related subjects in school programmes. Twenty intermediate and ten secondary schools are considered as UNESCO associated establishments.

Oman

The national report of Oman indicates that there has been an effort to do away with the 'two shifts' systems in the school day. The use of the school premises enables extension of the school day to eight periods instead of six. This amounts to an increase by about 33% of the work hours at school. The duration of the periods were increased to forty minutes from thirty-five minutes. The academic year was extended to 180 days from 160 days to allow more time for important educational extra-curricular activities. This has encouraged the inclusion of new subjects, not taught hitherto, such as life skills, computer science, information technology and the introduction of English-language teaching from grade one, rather than grade four.

New learning and teaching techniques were introduced to overcome the limitations of the older ones. The Ministry was keen to introduce modern equipment and tools in the schools. Learning resource centres were established and equipped with modern computers, reference books and audio-visual aids. These centres provide students with opportunities to operate the different equipment and subsequently acquire manual skills and be prepared to exploit the labour market. Cycle two of basic education schools shall be equipped with science and computer laboratories.

The introduction of life skills as a subject in the curriculum can be considered as yet another innovative measure. Life skills include skills to deal with family affairs, management skills, commercial skills. communication skills, etc.

In Oman especial care is devoted to the writing and the preparation of course books and teachers' guides as well as to their printing and publication.

Saudi Arabia

A noteworthy initiative emerging from the Kingdom of Saudi Arabia has been the idea of instituting 'pioneer schools' involving both elementary and intermediate levels, on a trial basis. If these 'tests' are seen to be successful, then these schools could serve as models for future education establishments. This project has been underway since 1420 (=1999 AD) and lasts for a period of five years. The project will help to train the necessary staff, to supply the required equipment, to prepare evaluation tools, and also to carry out an awareness campaign among the population.

Saudi Arabia is also active in reviewing school textbooks, in promoting modern laboratories and libraries, in introducing computers, and in considerably improving the printing process.

Mention needs also be made of extracurricular and cultural activities for students, and of retraining programmes for teachers, supervisors, administrators and other staff that are being regularized.

United Arab Emirates

A notable success has been its initiative to introduce the English language from the first year of elementary school. After several rounds of trials in experimental schools underway since 1987, the generalization was effected in 1992-93. The curriculum has been subjected to review and scrutiny in recent years and recommendations were made for the improvement in the following fields: Islamic studies, Arabic language, social studies and philosophy.

On the basis of the proposed changes, manuals and reading materials have been under preparation since the year 1994. The University of the United Arab Emirates had a considerable role in that process along with the Ministry of Education. The latter created a technical committee in 1996 to supervise the preparation of textbooks and other learning/ teaching materials. The committee had a Deputy Minister as its chairman.

Another important project in the United Arab Emirates was the transformation of school libraries to learning resource centres equipped with computers and audio-visual facilities. Language laboratories, both for Arabic and English, have also been established. The report refers to around sixty-nine existing language laboratories.

Teachers have been trained to become familiar with the new educational and information techniques and devices. The project was started in 1998-99 and is being implemented today in around forty schools.

However, the Centre for Curriculum refers to some constraints which make it difficult to improve sufficiently the quality of instruction. The inadequate availability of instructional resources (textbooks, teachers' guides, maps, wall charts, audio-visual materials, computer-based materials) is considered as the main bottleneck.

Obstacles to Curriculum Reform

In the majority of the national reports, references are also made in more or less details to the obstacles in the path of curriculum reforms. These obstacles are at times shared problems facing the education system in a large number of countries. Without indulging in any value judgements, issues raised in the national reports, with especial emphasis on problems curriculum reform is facing in the Gulf Region, are reproduced here.

Bahrain experiences a number of obstacles in the path of implementing a new curriculum. Despite the great role the school in general and the teachers in particular have in the implementation of a new curriculum, they face some difficulty in discharging their responsibilities. The primary reasons are:

- teachers may be insensitive to the development process and once given the responsibility may even resist change fearing that it would only add to their burdens;
- lack of sufficient time to retrain teachers in the new curriculum and new reading materials may be another obstacle; teachers are sometimes very busy during the day and cannot attend on a regular basis the training workshops organized for them;
- there are few educational advisors to help and advise the teachers in understanding the requirements of the new curriculum;
- the teachers are not obliged to apply all related teaching materials and may lack of the necessary motivation to read and digest documents which indicate how the new programme should be applied.

The national report of the United Arab Emirates does not speak about the problems and difficulties faced in the application of a curriculum change. On the contrary, Kuwait has presented a long list of problems facing curriculum specialists in designing and reviewing the curricula. Directors of schools, teachers and advisors are those who apply the new curriculum. It cannot be said with certainty that they always understand the objectives and the intention of curriculum planners. The process of application may well be full of surprises and produce unexpected results. It would be productive if review and evaluation were to make a parallel progress alongside the execution. This necessitates:

- the continuity of pre- and in-service training of teachers;
- the continuity of information collection to recognize defects;
- regular and frequent follow-up of aims and objectives;
- continuous evaluation of all elements in the educational process.

In light of the above, we find the unity of the three elements (design, execution, review) as one major factor that requires the co-operation of all concerned. It is not easy to place limitations or draw lines of separation between the technical and the administrative decisions regarding the educational process. The gulf between theory and practice with respect to education results from a misunderstanding involving the unity and mutuality between the technical and administrative dimensions.

Sometimes the lack of understanding of the interconnectedness between plans and their implementation leads one to concentrate on the short term to the detriment of long term. Policy-makers are sometimes in a great hurry to revolutionize education while they are still in office. This may lead to the misapplication of the reform due to lack of adequate time. Some other problems mentioned in the Kuwaiti report are:

- lack of strong co-operation between administrators and curriculum designers;
- lack of co-ordination between the curriculum development committee and the education departments of the ministry;
- lack of harmony among the committee members and improper working styles of these committees;
- lack of interest in familiarizing future teachers during their pre-service training with modern techniques;
- dependence on external sources for maintenance of equipment and machines;
- inadequate awareness on the part of teacher trainers with regard to educational priorities and obligations;
- too much emphasis of teachers on theory rather than on reality and on practice;
- lack of participation of the majority of teachers in decision-making about the educational development process;
- too much work assigned to the teachers prevents them from reading or research;

- problems faced by teachers due to the large number of pupils in each class, which, in addition to the administrative burdens, affects their performance.
- concentration of the syllabus on the cognitive side and negligence of skills (behavioural skills). The present examination and evaluation system is based only on measuring success in terms of storage and retrieval of knowledge;
- the application of a new and modernized curriculum requires classrooms, labs, playgrounds, learning materials, good equipment and a suitable teaching environment. Any limitations placed on these requirements would be unhelpful.

Some of the obstacles reported by Oman as being in the path of the developmental processes are:

- despite efforts made to train teachers in modern methodologies, some of them unconsciously use the old methodology and 'spoon feeding' techniques without involving the learner in the learning process and ignore educational aids;
- the process of writing textbooks is completed within five to six months. This increases the pressure of work and results in inefficiency. Continuous evaluation of the materials that will be reprinted after two years and after obtaining feedback from the field help resolve this problem;
- some teachers are not conversant with computer use and thus cannot benefit from the learning resource centre in implementing some of the course tasks. Moreover, they cannot encourage their students in the use of computers; and
- some of the parents misunderstand the philosophy of the basic education system in this country. This problem can be solved by activating the role of parents' councils through seminars to be attended by Ministry officials and parents to familiarize them with the philosophy and objectives of the basic education system. Mass media can also spread awareness among individuals about education, its goals and values.

Section 5

Reports from Regional Institutions

24

The Role of ABEGS in the Development and Renovation of School Textbooks and Curricula

Humaidan A. Al-Humaidan

Background

About a quarter of a century ago, educational leaders of the Arab Gulf States realized the importance of co-ordinating and integrating their efforts in order to develop educational methodologies, pedagogy and school curricula. Owing to the shared characteristics of these countries, educationists in the Arab Gulf States recognized that such a development could only be realized through strengthening the existing ties and the enhancing co-operation and co-ordination among these countries.

The First General Conference of the Ministers of Education in the Arab States of the Gulf (Riyadh, 1975) came to conclude that these facts and aspirations should be embodied in a specialized organ that aims to encourage, strengthen and develop co-ordination and co-operation among the six member states (Bahrain, Kuwait, Oman, Qatar, Saudi Arabia and the United Arab Emirates) in the fields of culture, education, science, information and documentation.

The Ministers of Education in the Arab States of the Gulf therefore adopted a resolution establishing the Arab Bureau of Education for the Gulf States (ABEGS) and indicating its duties and major objectives.

In accordance with its capacity as the highest authority of the Bureau, the General Conference resolved that ABEGS should introduce, update and promote educational reforms and modern techniques consistent with the spirit of Islam and the traditional values of the region. These duties could only be realized through the implementation of its programmes and activities, the promotion of educational development and the unification of school curricula and textbooks among the six member states.

The Bureau, through its main affiliate organ, the Gulf Arab States Educational Research Center (GASERC) in Kuwait, has exerted a lot of efforts in the field of the development and unification of school curricula and textbooks. Thanks to the center, special attention was paid and major breakthroughs were achieved in the field of curriculum development and unification, especially in the domains of mathematics and sciences textbooks and school curricula. The Bureau and its sub-organ have managed to attract and benefit from a lot of regional as well as international sources of experience and expertise.

Since its establishment, ABEGS, through its programmes and activities and those of GASERC, has launched several initiatives towards the development and unification of school curricula and textbooks. Undertaking and publishing a study of 'educational aims and the general bases of school curricula' (in 1403 H. = 1982) was one of the most prominent initiatives in this domain. In 1404 H., ABEGS organized and held the first International Conference on Mathematics in the Gulf Region. During the following years, the Bureau carried out several studies on mathematics and science in the various stages of education in the Gulf Region.

Throughout its endeavor, ABEGS was open-minded and receptive to various sources of experience and expertise. Thus, it translated the report of the National Commission on Excellence in Education of the United States—*A nation at risk*. It also translated an important study on education in West Germany. Later on, the Bureau carried out a translation of *Educational renovation in the United States*. ABEGS undertook the translation of several studies on natural science education worldwide.

Moreover, the General Conference of ABEGS established a special commission to follow-up and assess the efforts and results achieved in the field of curriculum development and unification. The special commission comprised experts and specialists from within ABEGS and GASERC, and from outside sources as well.

The efforts exerted in the process of curriculum development and unification progressed along two parallel streams. The major educational aims, the general basis of school curricula and the unified objectives of educational phases, school subjects and curricula were defined. The Bureau also launched a number of initiatives to reform, develop and unify the current school curricula and textbooks. To pave the way for these essential educational reforms and major changes, it carried out several studies to evaluate and assess the status quo of education in the region. Within this framework, the Bureau issued new unified textbooks, carried out case studies, field evaluation research and made the necessary modifications and changes based on these evaluative measures.

The Development Strategy

ABEGS set up a clearly defined strategy for managing the process of development and unification of school curricula and textbooks. One of the major aspects of this strategy was its dependence upon the contribution and participation of specialists from the member states in composing, reviewing, evaluating the newly developed, unified school curricula and textbooks. The Bureau also decided that these unified textbooks should have trial periods, during which they should be reviewed and evaluated.

In its documents on the development of unified school curricula in mathematics and the development of unified school curricula in science, GASERC pointed out several important issues and challenges. Among the major issues relating to the currently applied school curricula, there is an obvious gab between the general aims of mathematic education and the specified grade objectives. This might be due to the absence of a coherent and comprehensive structure outlining major aims and objectives. With respect to the development of unified school curricula in science, GASERC highlighted the need for exerting our utmost efforts in order for the member states to cope with the changes and challenges of the information technology revolution.

The document also underscored the importance of preserving the cultural and spiritual identity of the region in the face of the current threats of globalization and the dangers posed by new means of communication, e.g. the Internet and web-based means of communication.

Thus, the document laid down the basic general aims, objectives and terms of reference of the development process of the unified school curricula in science for the Gulf States. GASERC also launched a unique initiative in the development and unification of Arabic curricula and textbooks for basic education in the member states. ABEGS took great pains to review and evaluate the process and outcomes of curriculum development and unification, especially in the domains of mathematics and science textbooks and school curricula.

Indeed, the Bureau brought about curriculum development through its activities and major breakthroughs in the field of curriculum development and unification, as a specialized organization conducting programmes and activities geared to the needs of schools in its member states, in the field of education in general, and school curriculum, in particular.

The Major Factors Influencing Curriculum Development

It is almost impossible to conduct curriculum development and unification without taking into account the following factors.

The political factor

Today's world witnesses an ardent race in which all runners try to achieve higher standards of planning and projecting into the future to cope with the ebbs and flows of a rapidly changing world. The scope and pace of change in today's world are such that any society that does not join the race now may never be able to meet the challenges of the future. Therefore, we should take part in the current process of transformation, which involves all aspects of our lives.

ABEGS carries out its programmes and activities, including the development and unification of school curricula and textbooks, taking into account the various regional as well as international political factors. Great breakthroughs were achieved in the field of curriculum development and unification, owing to the wise directives and instructions of the political as well as educational leadership of the Gulf Co-operation Council (GCC) countries.

The economic factor

Education is the main vehicle of human as well as economic development. The economic factors play a major role in the ABEGS programmes and activities, including the development and unification of school curricula and textbooks. Specifically speaking, the economic changes taking place in the GCC countries made it necessary for the secondary school graduates to join the labour force and participate in the economy, especially with the growing trend towards nationalizing the labour force and providing jobs for the entire population at a time which witnessed unemployment rising to unprecedented heights.

The social and cultural factor

The social and cultural factor creates the main framework in which the newly developed curricula should be received, applied and evaluated. Accordingly, any successful plan for the development and unification of school curricula and textbooks should take into account the social and cultural factors—namely the needs, expectations and major aspirations of education stakeholders.

The educational factor

There was one key principle underlining the efforts made by the Bureau in its major initiatives to undertake reforms, develop and unify the current school curricula and textbooks: although the Arab Gulf States achieved great success and major breakthroughs in the field of education, from a quantitative perspective, providing free education to all their citizens, they have hardly achieved the same kind of success from a qualitative point of view.

Due to the increasing challenges facing these countries during the last two decades, the GCC countries have strived hard to implement the most urgently needed economic, social and educational changes.

Since as education system should aim to create better understanding of the demands and potential of our world and to form new patterns of thought and behaviour which are not contrary to the spirit of Islam and our social traditions, ABEGS saw the need for a quality education so as to cope with the daunting challenges facing these countries.

Thus, we embarked on a major project for previewing the future of education in the Arab States of the Gulf. The project resulted in a pioneering and profound document focusing on the major aspects and conditions required for achieving the goals of 'education for the future'. Education for the future must be part of a long-term strategy, presupposing continuity in the choices made and in the implementation of educational reforms. Although priorities will naturally vary from one country to another, educational preview should be carried out according to the basic conditions that are common to all.

In order to ensure the correct application of the new advanced curriculum, their Royal Highnesses, the leaders of the GCC countries, set up a committee comprising the education under-secretaries responsible for school curricula in their respective countries. It was their duty to supervise the developmental programmes, set up the frameworks and guidelines, and ensure that the result is appreciable and practical. After the special committee adopts the new curricula, the Ministries of Education in the GCC countries would implement the new curricula in their schools, taking into consideration the individual needs of each state and its ability to carry out the necessary changes.

The wise leadership of the GCC countries underscored how important it is for the product of the development programme to be defined within the framework of the overall strategies of these nations. The new content of education should reflect the knowledge and skills necessary for individual personal growth, young people's capabilities and their ability to join the labour force and meet the new challenges, especially the influence of the globalized economy and the rapid advances in science and technology.

Conclusion

To sum up, educational reform is not the only precondition for bringing about an inclusive, comprehensive revival of our society. There are other important issues at stake: economic, political and social. Yet, education for the future is the spinning wheel that transforms all fibres into a long yarn and leads us to cross the cultural gap between our developing societies and the developed ones. Hence, ABEGS saw the need for a quality education to cope with the enormous challenges facing these countries.

In conclusion, I would like to say that although the Bureau cannot be an alternative to the Ministries of Education in the Arab Gulf States, it has significantly influenced curriculum development through its activities and major breakthroughs in the field of curriculum development and unification. As a specialized organization, conducting programmes and activities geared to the needs of its member states in the field of education in general, and school curriculum, in particular, it has a critical role to play in the new millennium.

25

The Role of UNESCO in the Promotion and Implementation of Contemporary Trends in Education

Abdalla Bubtana

Globally, the development of education systems had passed, during the last century, through four distinct periods when efforts were concentrated on their reform and renovation.

The collapse of the economic systems during the 1930s resulted in a need to review the social, political and economic aspects of societies. A large number of nations gained independence after the Second World War and they began to lay especial emphasis on quantitative expansion of systems with a view to satisfying rising social expectations. This has a negative effect on the qualitative aspects of developmental activities. Even today, a number of developing countries are trying to overcome this imbalance.

During the 1980s, concentration was placed on restructuring systems and on the mobilization of financial resources through reforms. The 1990s witnessed the Jometen Conference, during which basic education for all and the provision of additional resources represented a universal commitment to education.

During these periods, especially in the light of drastic quantitative expansions, three main issues relevant to reform of education systems were highlighted:

1. the objectives of education and suitable pedagogies;

2. access to education and equality (democratization);
3. quality, relevance and financing of education.

During the recent decades, the reform and renovation processes targeted five areas of education:

Decentralization: this was intended to provide flexibility and incorporate relevance to different socio-economic contexts.

The nature of school: non-traditional forms of educational institutions were adopted, i.e. comprehensive schools, distance learning, etc.

Renovation of the content of education: to renovate curricula, strengthen science and technology, incorporate new contents, etc.

Evaluation and measurement: reform of the testing and examination systems, institutional evaluation, quality control, etc.

Teacher education and training: this aspect required considerable attention brought about by the in-service training of huge numbers of unqualified teachers employed during the post-colonial period.

Two developments that have taken place recently will have a major impact on the future of education systems worldwide.

In 1996, UNESCO issued the report of the International Commission on Education for the Twenty-first Century, entitled *Learning: the treasure within.* In addition to confirming the four pillars of education, i.e. learning to know, learning to do, learning to live together and learning to be, the report contained numerous ideas and principles for the reform and renovation of all levels of education.

In April 2000, the Dakar Conference was convened under the theme of education for all. The conference renewed the commitment to this principle and called upon all partners to provide the necessary resources to achieve this objective. New means and modalities were also proposed.

UNESCO, in addition to its active role in initiating innovations and reform through its different modalities and mechanisms, conferences, meetings, advisory and consultancy services, etc., has established a number of innovative networks to stimulate and implement reform projects in all regions of the world. The Educational Innovation Programme for Development in the Arab States (EIPDAS) was the network created for the Arab Region.

In addition to the provision of financial and human resources for these networks, UNESCO was able to mobilize funding from extra-budgetary sources to implement innovative experiences in a number of countries around the world.

Section 6

Contributions and Recommendations of the Three Discussion Groups

The Three Discussion Groups

GROUP I: CURRICULAR PLANNING

Problems

1. Shortage of capable manpower to undertake curriculum planning.
2. Inadequate information and databases essential to facilitate decision-making regarding the curriculum.
3. Specialists who are neither able to implement the curriculum nor comprehend the philosophy underlying curriculum planning.
4. Resistance from teachers and society.

Solutions

1. Inviting overseas experts to train the national planners.
2. Seeking assistance from local universities.
3. Creating a database under the supervision of the UNESCO Regional Office in the Gulf Region.
4. Undertaking surveys on different aspects of the curriculum.
5. Creating associate programmes that facilitate the implementation of curriculum.
6. Utilizing studies carried out by UNESCO regarding curriculum.
7. Clarifying the philosophy of change in curriculum and concentrating on its various aspects.

Needs

1. Preparing and providing proper budgets.
2. Training national manpower to enhance their capabilities in dealing with the technical aspects of curriculum development.

3. Approaching international and regional organizations to obtain technical assistance.
4. Co-operating with establishments working on educational programmes.
5. Facilitating co-operation with the media to disseminate with clarity the aims and objectives of development.

Facilitator's Report on the Working Group

An Arabic speaking chairperson and rapporteur were selected at the beginning of the working group's session.

Problems of curriculum planners

The participants were concerned about the shortage of curriculum planning specialists in Gulf countries. It was observed that in many cases the existing curriculum specialists were not familiar with the techniques of planning and found it difficult to develop a curriculum in a systematic manner. Concern was also expressed about the fact that appropriate information regarding social and education needs—essential for curriculum planning—was neither collected nor available in many countries. This meant that a basic requirement was lacking, and resources and skills had to be diverted to gather the necessary information. Resistance to changing the existing curricula from individuals and communities, especially hailing from the remote areas of certain countries, dampened the enthusiasm of some participants.

Solutions proposed

The participants came up with solutions that fell into three broad categories: seeking international help; seeking assistance from within the countries; and doing the required work oneself.

With regard to seeking external assistance, proposals were made to request experts from abroad to help train the national planners. It was also suggested that curriculum related studies carried out by the IBE and UNESCO should be utilized to help reduce the information gap. It was suggested that a regional database be set up and run by the UNESCO regional office to serve as a clearing-house for information concerning experts and trainers within the Gulf Region. The services of these experts could be utilized, as they would probably be willing and free to travel on request to the countries within the region.

The utilization of existing national resources was discussed and it was decided that the universities of respective countries could be engaged in the systematic collection of the information required by curriculum planners. Some participants suggested that they themselves, in their own countries, could initiate surveys to gather the requisite information regarding various aspects of the curriculum. It was felt that a scheme outlining the methodology of curriculum change in simple steps would facilitate the task of implementation in several countries.

Felt needs

The participants identified a variety of needs with respect to curriculum development. Some emphasized the particular need to allocate an appropriate budget for the project. It was felt that there was a need for technical assistance from regional organizations of the Gulf Region, as well as from several international organizations with wider exposure and expertise. Others believed that a training programme should be conceived and organized to help develop the national capacities for curriculum development.

It was noted that there was a need for curriculum development planners to work with educational establishments that are in the process of developing their own educational programmes. It was also suggested that there was a need for special contacts with the media so that a dialogue could be established with the public regarding the aims of curricular changes.

Comments

Participants were keen to describe the conditions prevalent in their own countries, as well as the felt needs and views in the area of curriculum-related planning. However, the exercise was hampered by the extreme brevity of the time allocated, as well as by the seating arrangement imposed by the fixed chairs. The participants were very enthusiastic, and it is probably correct to say that all of them were frustrated by the limited time allotted. Several participants may have found it difficult to avoid the impression that this brief session was just a token interactive session involving a small group.

Recommendations

In future workshops, a similar session with participants from a number of countries in a region may have some usefulness, but its value will be seriously limited if the following recommendations were to be ignored.

1. Loosely structured small-group session(s) should have preceded this type of session to encourage the informal sharing of views and experiences, and to improve group dynamics.
2. The present type of session should have been accompanied by a series of other participatory sessions involving smaller groups, as well as by other plenary participatory sessions—all linked to each other in an overall framework for generating facts, opinions and suggestions.
3. Most of such sessions should be of a longer duration. Some of them would benefit from participants' written suggestions during the session, and they could then be integrated into a report together with the rapporteur's discussion notes.
4. Future sessions should permit actual creative or constructive work to be done by the participants together, preferably using in some way real or simulated data from the home country or the region.

GROUP II: MANAGEMENT OF CURRICULUM CHANGE

Problems

1. University professors who participate in curriculum planning do not have the requisite field experience.
2. Budgets for developing curriculum are either unallocated or inadequate.
3. Curriculum development objectives are ill-defined, leading to wastage of time and money.
4. Therefore, a curriculum needs to be reviewed from time to time.

5. The manpower needed for curriculum development is inadequate.
6. There is insufficient time for in-service training of teachers and inadequate motivation on their part to attend training courses.
7. Co-ordination between committees involved in curriculum developments and those in charge at the Ministry of Education is not satisfactory.
8. New syllabuses are imposed on teachers who are ill-prepared to handle them.
9. Teacher-training programmes at universities focus on theoretical aspects to the exclusion of practical applications.
10. There is resistance to curriculum development from society and other quarters.
11. Media programmes to spread awareness regarding the objectives of curriculum development are needed.
12. Allowances should be made for raising awareness among teachers before contemplating curriculum changes.
13. A system of developmental evaluation should be introduced during the implementation phase to help overcome obstacles and receive feedback.

Needs

1. Provision of budget.
2. More specialists in curriculum and training departments.
3. Experts and technicians in curriculum design and educational media.

Evaluation of the Work of Group II

The presentation on various issues of management of curriculum change was followed by intensive discussions. The delegates presented their views on the prevalent local realities and problems of curriculum development and implementation in their respective countries. Some of the problems highlighted were: a shortage of qualified teachers; lack of teaching/learning materials; the need to upgrade teachers' competency; and the lack of connection between political wisdom and grassroot realities. The delegations also observed that it was becoming very difficult to translate the intended curriculum into reality and some of them even mentioned resource constraints.

Further discussions highlighted the importance of a training programme on the management of curriculum change. The delegates expected two types of training materials: one for the curriculum develops at the national level, and the other for the curriculum implementers at the field level. It was felt that, while discussing such issues, the knowledge base at the global level should be borne in mind.

It was felt also that as most of the curriculum development problems were common to all countries, the training of a curriculum development and planning team could be arranged at an inter-country level with the assistance of the IBE. It was also proposed that the training activity of curriculum implementers, including teachers, be integrated with similar ongoing activities in these countries. Active co-operation was expected by the member countries regarding the methodologies to be adopted and the expected outcomes of such a training programme.

One of the major issues highlighted was that of the wide gap existing between the intended curriculum and the actual curriculum. Effective strategies need to be adopted to reduce this gap.

The priority need is that all member countries should focus on a quality curriculum with innovative practices, such as an integrated approach, an inter-disciplinary approach, a front-line approach and interactive classroom transactions aimed at higher levels of achievement.

Capacity-building programmes in management of curriculum change may focus on three phases of activities: preparatory meetings; training; and follow-up. The preparatory meeting is intended to discuss and identify the training needs and suggest strategies for the proposed training programme on the management of curriculum change. It may be undertaken with all the member countries forming a collective group, or with the countries participating individually.

The management of curriculum change covers three critical issues: one relates to change, another to the curriculum and the third to links between management and change. The parameters of change that need to be managed are syllabus, production of study material, training of teachers and other concerned functionaries, fine tuning of delivery systems, and ensuring that the management system remains responsive, participative and forward looking. The implementation of the curriculum depends to a great degree on the classroom teaching strategies that, in turn, depend on teachers' training, competence and commitment.

The approaches to the curricular interventions could be several, but care should be taken that these interventions are fine-tuned with existing structures. These may be frontline areas of learning, the constructivist approach, and the communicative approach to the teaching of language, the modular approach and interdisciplinary approaches to learning.

GROUP III: EVALUATION OF CURRICULUM CHANGE

A Definition of Curriculum Evaluation

- *Curriculum*: all educational experiences prepared and planned by the school and offered to students in order to modify their behaviour and encourage them to achieve total development—growth.
- *Evaluation*: procedure followed by specialists to study to what extent the objectives of the curriculum have been achieved and to know the obstacles faced during implementation in order to overcome them.
- *Curriculum evaluation*: a continuous process for collecting information about all the elements and outcomes of the curriculum to help arrive at an understanding of the extent to which they have been achieved and subsequently take decisions to improve their efficacy.

Why Evaluation?

We evaluate in order to:

- avoid existing mistakes;
- expand knowledge;

- involve society in education and encourage interest in the importance of the curriculum;
- keep pace with the social changes;
- deal with societies in acceptance of results and outcome of education; and
- insure the importance of education reforms.

The Functions of Evaluation

- To provide us with a database of information regarding pedagogical processes.
- To provide us with information and to facilitate decision-making regarding the curriculum and its elements.
- The outcomes of evaluation are the basis for developing and modifying the curriculum.
- To discover ways of learning and finding the points of strength and weakness in the curriculum.
- To show students a productive pathway to learning.
- To discover the students' areas of strengths and weaknesses.
- To discover the aspects of teaching that require greater focus and efforts.
- To share with teachers all they need to *learn* to teach students better.

Characteristics of Evaluation

- Conformity with objectives.
- Complementarities.
- Credibility.
- Continuity.

Evaluated Elements

- *Objectives*—clarity; limits achievable and suitable for evaluation.
- *Contents*—appropriate levels for the students; modern integration with other elements; achieving

the objectives, infusing variety and information dissemination so that it is able to cope with the individual differences. Some elements used for evaluation of content include: probing, teachers' reports, meetings, and views of inspectors, parents, as well as specialists.

- *Methods of teaching and educational aids*—asking students and teachers about the efficiency appropriate to the methods through questionnaires, surveys, studies, and other evaluating teaching aids.
- *Evaluating students*—there are targeted classes to ensure achieving the objectives through essays, trends and attitude tests.
- *Evaluating teachers*—teachers are evaluated with regard to their efficiency, extent of achieving and implementing the curriculum, weakness in scientific and methods of teaching aspects, knowledge and information. They are evaluated by: inspectors, reports, student opinions, self-evaluation, written tests to discover competencies.

Needs

- A way to test a teacher's efficiency.
- Follow-up for developmental evaluation.
- Comparing results of the previous and the new curriculum.
- Involving members of the society, parents, teachers in evaluating the new curriculum.
- Evaluation must be comprehensive, covering all the elements of the curriculum.

Evaluation of the Work of the Group III

The group first considered the definitions of 'curriculum' and 'curriculum evaluation'. Curriculum is seen as being inclusive of not only goals, content and learning processes, but also that which is 'implicit curriculum' derived from the culture of the institutions themselves. Curriculum evaluation is the collection of information to arrive at judgements and decisions on the value of the curriculum.

Given these concepts, the task of curriculum evaluation, like the curriculum itself, is a continuous process. Evaluation is the process that enables continuity, as it provides the judgemental inputs regarding the efficiency and effectiveness of the various elements constituting the curriculum. With this approach, curriculum change is not a simple revolutionary operation, but an evolving, self-correcting and self-guiding process.

It was emphasized that the purpose of curriculum evaluation was to improve the quality of student learning and that, finally, the worth of evaluation must be assessed by the extent to which it succeeds in promoting such an understanding.

A variety of evaluation tools were discussed and it was noted that tests and examinations alone were inadequate to give a whole picture of the curriculum. Surveys, interviews, portfolios and other forms of evaluation were seen as valuable and authentic extensions. The role of teachers was seen as being crucial to the success of the curriculum and the means of appraising the effectiveness of teaching were discussed. These included visits to the classroom by principals and inspectors, interviews with teachers and obtaining the responses of students.

Major difficulties in developing good processes of curriculum evaluation arose from the shortage of people who were knowledgeable about the wide variety of evaluation tools. Capacity-building was seen as a major need, both through local institutions where there were suitable staff and through international organizations such as the IBE.

It was agreed that the development of indigenous capacity in evaluation was of the highest priority. The IBE could assist in this respect by providing consultants who might work with the Gulf States to produce a nucleus of evaluation specialists who could then work in their own countries to further develop and share their expertise.

Curriculum evaluation is an integral part of curriculum development and of especial importance to curriculum reform. It has today developed and designed a number of tools to deal with the complexities of the task. Enhancing the learning experience of students must always remain pivotal to any form of evaluation.

Section 7

Final Report and Recommendations Approved by the Plenary

Final Report and Recommendations

Seminar Participants

The following educational institutions participated in the workshop:

- International Bureau of Education (IBE);
- Arab Bureau of Education for the Gulf States (ABEGS);
- Arab Gulf Co-operation Council Bureau of Education;
- Ministry of Education, Oman;
- Curriculum experts from Australia, India and Malta;
- Curriculum experts for the countries of the Arab Gulf Co-operation Council (AGCC).

Seminar Management

The seminar's activities and operations were managed as follows:

1. Workshop General Rapporteur: Mr Khalifa bin Ahmed bin Humaid Al Kassabi, Oman.
2. Drafting Committee
   - Mr Khalifa bin Ahmed bin Humaid Al Kassabi, Oman.
   - Mr Abdullah Ali el Faizi, Saudi Arabia.
   - Mr Mohammed Ben Saif Ben Musbeh al Bousaïdi, Oman.
   - Mr Mohammed ben Shames el Husni, Oman.

- Mrs Jeanine Thomas, IBE.
- Mrs Sabine Ferra de Cerda, IBE Consultant.

Management of daily sessions

- Saturday, 17 February 2001: Mrs Latifé Mohamad el Mahmoud, Bahrain.
- Sunday, 18 February 2001: Dr Obeid bin Butti Al-Muhairi, UAE.
- Monday, 19 February 2001: Mrs Aïcha el Redwan, Kuwait.
- Tuesday, 20 February 2001: Prof. Humaidan Al-Hamaidan, ABEGS.

The discussion was directed so as to benefit from the experts' opinions and to upgrade local capabilities

Presentations

Country reports were presented as follows:

- *Bahrain:* Mrs Latifé Mohamed el Mahmoud presented the Bahrain paper, indicating that educational development in Bahrain was based on introducing learning through efficiency, and a list has been established of efficiencies that it is to be achieved at every stage, specifying the efficiency level as a reference for evaluation.
- *Kuwait:* Mrs Abla el Issa presented the Kuwaiti experience, which concentrated on new themes and projects, and on their introduction into the curricula, such as celebrations, elimination of illiteracy, swimming, computers in kindergarten, advanced educational management and teaching about computers.
- *Oman:* Dr Hamad Seif Al Hammami, Director-General of Curricula and Training, presented the paper 'Curricular development in Oman and the challenges of the twenty-first century', saying that the objectives for developing the Omani curricula were: to eliminate evening classrooms, to concentrate on quality and not quantity, to consider

practical aspects of education, to develop higher mental capabilities and thinking for students, and to achieve complete basic education. He indicated that the development concentrated on the organizational structure of the Ministry, reconsidering the general objectives of educational stages and materials, developing an education plan, developing a syllabus, and introducing new syllabi and materials.

- *Saudi Arabia:* Mr Abudullah Ben Ali el Faiza presented the Saudi paper, saying that the production of schoolbooks passes through several legal, political, educational, scientific and linguistic reviews. Development has concentrated on the syllabus. The education plan was amended in terms of the number of classrooms and the introduction of the computer.
- *United Arab Emirates:* Dr Obeid Al-Muhairi talked about the role of the UAE in developing its curricula through several projects, including teaching English language from grade one, a computer teaching project, transforming libraries into teaching resource centres, creating language laboratories for English and Arabic languages, setting up Islamic studies laboratories and the rehabilitation of the classroom teacher.

Final recommendations

After the discussion of various reports and presentations, the Plenary Session adopted the following twenty-five recommendations to be submitted to the respective authorities:

1. All the papers are considered as official documents to be published by the IBE so that the experiences can be shared.
2. The importance of maintaining the national identity and Islamic customs, culture and values when implementing changes in the curricula.
3. The importance of finding a specific mechanism to introduce changes in a way acceptable to the teacher,

not neglecting the training point of view, preparing the teacher to participate in the change and encouraging them by providing financial incentives and rewards.

4. There must be more co-ordination between the teacher-training faculties, ministries of education and schools.
5. To depend on local expertise when implementing changes, and utilize local consultants and the Internet.
6. Curricula should be directed to benefit from the new technology, such as computers in education, and not concentrate on learning about the computer itself.
7. Development plans should be prepared on a short-term basis—not more than five years—in order to keep pace with rapid developments around the world.
8. When changing curricula, the change should be planned in a manner that satisfies all the stakeholders.
9. When changing the curricula, it is important to carry out a proper training analysis for the teachers.
10. Constructive evaluation should be carried out while implementing, identifying problems and obstacles as they occur and monitoring the most important positive and negative aspects. The impact of the change on the various components in the curriculum, the teachers, students, educational activities and teaching strategies should be monitored and feedback provided to modify the process.
11. When contemplating changing the curricula, there should be a space for the reaction of various social groups (teachers, parents, public institutions, etc.). This is looked upon as a positive and healthy sign towards change, which indicates the community's culture and awareness towards modernization.
12. It is important to benefit from regional co-operation when implementing change in the curricula in order to share the experience.
13. The teachers' time should be reduced in order to give them opportunities for in-service training so as to implement the developed curricula.
14. A number of field operatives should be trained to prepare curricula, and to implement, supervise and manage the changes.

15. Teachers should be prepared to teach in the new field before introducing the syllabus, such as in economic and life skills.
16. Train teachers before introducing the syllabus.
17. Prepare a media campaign to raise public awareness of the objectives of change in the curricula, and the role of society in relation to the change.
18. Include the use of the UNESCO Internet site when training teachers for the management of curriculum change.
19. To take advantage of workshop and training sessions organized by the IBE to improve the skills of supervisors and implementers of curriculum change.
20. To organize local workshops inspired by this workshop.
21. During the International Conference on Education organized by the IBE in Geneva, to raise the topic of introducing international exchange concerning curriculum change.
22. To set up a networked database in ABEGS similar to that of the IBE.
23. To give enough time for planning in connection with curriculum change.
24. To ask the Ministries of Education of the Arabic Gulf countries to share with the IBE their experiences and innovations in the field of education which have been already carried out and those that are planned for the future.
25. To ask the participants of this workshop to send an official letter thanking the Omani Minister of Education.

Annex: The Gulf Region at a Glance

Some Statistics

Table 1. Population, schooling and illiteracy

Country	Total population	GNP per capita ($)	Gross enrolment ratio: primary (%)	Gross enrolment ratio: secondary (%)	Gross enrolment ratio: third level (%)	Illiteracy rate (%)
UAE	2,100,000	17,400	89	79	11,9	20,8
Kuwait	2,100,000	17,390	77	65	19	21,4
Oman	2,070,000	4,820	77	66	6,4	28.1
Qatar	539,00	11,600	97	81	27	22,9
Saudi Arabia	16,900,000	7,150	76	61	16	29,2
Bahrain	538,000	7,840	106	94	18	17,7

Source: IBE. *World data on education,* 2000; *The Europa World Yearbook,* 2000; *UNESCO Statistical yearbook,* 1999.

Table 2. Illiteracy rates according to the *UNESCO statistical yearbook, 1999*

Country	Year 1995 Mean	Year 2000 Mean	Year 2000 Mn	Year 2000 Women
Bahrain	14.7	12.4	17.3	9.0
UAE	26.2	23.5	20.5	24.8
Kuwait	20.7	17.7	20.1	15.7
Oman	36.0	28.1	38.3	19.6
Qatar	20.7	18.7	16.8	19.5
Saudi Arabia	27.8	23.0	32.8	15.9

Note: According to the *UNESCO statistical yearbook,* the overall illiteracy rate in the Arab States was 31.0% for men and 57.2% for women in 1995.

Degree of Dependency on Oil Revenue

Bahrain:	Petroleum and natural gas are nearing exhaustion (1998: petroleum production around 37,600 barrels per day; output of natural gas was 7,900 m. cu. per year).
Kuwait:	Petroleum refineries account for 68.4% of manufacturing activities in 1998. The production of petroleum and its derivatives is the most important industry in Kuwait, providing 88.7% of export revenue in 1998.
Oman:	Petroleum and natural gas provide 30.1% of total GDP in 1998.
Qatar:	Petroleum and natural gas provide 36.8% of total GDP in 1998.
Saudi Arabia:	Petroleum and natural gas provide 27.5% of total GDP in 1998.
UAE:	Petroleum provided 45% of total export revenues in 1994 and 34% of GDP in 1995.

(Source: *The European world yearbook*, 2000.)

Three Aspects of Curriculum Development in the Region

- Emphasizing traditional values of education;
- Promoting science evaluation; and
- Taking innovative measures.

Emphasizing traditional values of education

Countries of the region are quite conscious of the value of their cultural heritage. Islamic studies have a particular place in a school's curriculum. They also pay particular attention to strengthening relations with other Arab and Islamic countries of the Gulf Region as an integral part of their education policy.

We read in the *National report* of the United Arab Emirates on the development of education (1993-96) that among the objectives of the education system are (1) inculcating faith in God, his prophets, moral and human values; (2) inculcating pride in Arab nationalism, the nation itself and the homeland.

Qatar in its *National report* of 1996 puts the two following principles among the main principles of education: inculcating belief in Allah and developing sense of affiliation and loyalty to homeland, to religion and to the whole Arab nation. In Oman's *National report* (1996), see the section on Omani characteristics.

Promoting science education

The access to the most advanced scientific and technological knowledge is emphasized in all these countries in addition to creating stronger links between education and the labour market.

We read in Oman's *National report* (1996):

> The Ministry of education is busily engaged in innovating and developing the educational system in Oman in order to cope with the scientific and technological innovations of recent years of this century and to be prepared for the next century (pp. 2-3).

The Ministry of Education in Kuwait (*National report*, 1996) considers five main objectives for its action in facing the challenges of future including:

> Realizing the aspiration of developing the Kuwaiti citizen in keeping with modern scientific concepts and developing the students' capabilities at all levels of education so that they may absorb the necessary scientific methods and their practical applications in all areas required by society.
>
> To make world culture accessible to Kuwaiti students within the framework of the ongoing scientific and technical revolution, while stressing the importance of the Arab and Islamic heritage in developing spiritual values, in strengthening basic principles and the sense of belonging to the homeland.

We read in the 1996 *National report* of Qatar among the main objectives of the education:[1]

> Providing students with an access to the advanced knowledge and useful sciences, promoting the love and acquisition of knowledge, the attitudes and skills of self-learning; the constant search for knowledge and investing its resources to create an ever learning society (p. 11).

Innovative measures

It seems that most of the Arab Gulf Region countries are committed to some form of reform or improvement of educational process. Some of them have already asked a group of external experts to visit the country and its educational institutions in order to offer suggestions for reforms. For example, UNESCO's Regional Bureau of Education in the Arab Countries (Lebanon) sent in 1999 some experts to Kuwait who proposed 'a strategy for discipline and education in Kuwait to the year 2025', with particular emphasis on curriculum change and improvement of education's contents. The British Council has submitted in 1998 to the same country a set of ideas about the 'development of a competence-based education and training system in Kuwait'.

The report of the Working Group for Educational Innovations Project, under the title of *Educational innovations in Bahrain* (1995), contains a wealth of information about improvement measures taken in this country, including those in the field of curriculum development. The report shows that the new contents, such as environment, health education and family life education, have entered into the school system and that there is a course at the secondary school level on 'computer as a subject and a tool'.

The Kingdom of Saudi Arabia, as the report of 1996 testifies, is also keen on 'providing schools with up-to-date educational services including computers, laboratory equipments and all other sophisticated apparatus'.

The national report of Saudi Arabia (1996) informs us that curriculum development directorates receive the comments and suggestions from the teachers, principals and inspectors and make the necessary evaluation and revision if required in line with scientific research' (p. 20).

Development of technical education and linking it with national development plans and building up of comprehensive schools have been the target of another project undertaken by the United Arab Emirates, Ministry of Education between 1997 and the year 2000. The integration of disabled students into mainstream education has received attention since 1995-96 in the same country.

The United Arab Emirates in its 1996 *National report* refers to some of the reforms undertaken there in various aspects of the educational systems. This report says:

> It is generally agreed that the principal basis for present and future reforms is the respect and esteem given to the teachers, because of their role in improving the education process and realizing the objective of those developments. Various programs have to be prepared to develop their professional skills and scientific background (p. 30).

Another measure of reform in the same country is the 'introduction of technology and environmental education in the curriculum at all levels of education' (p. 32).

We learn from INNODATA that the United Arab Emirates embarked from 1991 to 1997 on a revision of its school curriculum for the primary, preparatory and secondary stages so as to include topics of international education. To that end, both interdisciplinary and multidisciplinary approaches have been adopted.

Kuwait has also launched from 1994-95 an ongoing project to develop the abilities of slow learners and handicapped children.

Already in 1990 Qatar had introduce a reform intended to diversify the secondary education programme (*National report,* 1996, p.13). Curriculum development in Qatar aims at both the improvement of content and of methods; computer science has been introduced in the curriculum; school libraries have been established; and educational research has been promoted.

According to INNODATA, Qatar introduced female teachers in a number of primary schools (from 1990 on) and transformed them with the creation of an attractive environment to model schools, an experiment that proved to be successful.

In co-operation with ABEGS, the country started (1990-91) to examine curriculum and textbooks development in the other Arab States in order to raise the standard and effectiveness of Qatari curricula.

The improvement measures taken in Oman according to its *National report* of 1996 are directed toward: (1) qualitative improvement; (2) participation of parents in school affairs; (3) training of school headmasters; (4) consolidation of educational supervision and inspection; and (5) promotion of 'educational evaluation' (pp. 11-15).

Another important feature of the Gulf Region is the existence of regional institutions that contribute to furthering co-operation between the respective countries in a number of fields, including education, such as ABEGS. In addition to that, as far as science and technology are concerned, bilateral relations with the most advanced countries in the West bring fresh ideas to this vital region of the world.[2]

Some Initiatives in the Field of Teacher Training

One of the fundamental problems in the Gulf Region is the inadequacy of both the quantity and the quality of teaching staff. A 1999 report of the UNESCO team to Kuwait refers to the following problems:[3]

(a) the weakness of professional and technical qualifications and capacities among many teachers;

(b) an insufficient number of Kuwaiti teachers in many specialized fields;

(c) an insufficient professional commitment among the teachers and a lack of creativity and innovation in that job;

(d) an improper distribution of teachers in both private and public sectors and at different educational levels.

In the case of the United Arab Emirates, most of the teachers are from other Arab countries.[4] Oman has taken energetic measures to overcome that problem. In 1994-95, there were eight teacher-training colleges in that country. In Bahrain, it is the university that plays a major role in pre-service training of educational staff, but it is the Directorate of Training at the Ministry of Education that is responsible for further in-service training of teachers.[5]

Saudi Arabia has no other alternative than recruiting non-Saudi teachers of different nationalities 'who are mostly working in the distant villages and towns where most of the Saudi teachers are reluctant to work' (*National report,* 1996 p. 5)

Moving Toward Lifelong Education

Bahrain (*National report,* 1994-96) organizes some language courses as continuing education. Some secretarial courses (such as computer and typewriting) and a programme of family life education (for women only) are also offered. A post-literacy programme is also organized in some countries. In addition to non-formal education the United Arab Emirates organizes literacy courses for street children and other disadvantaged children and offers some adult education and community programmes (*National report,* 1996, pp. 67-68). There exists nowhere a real overall structure for lifelong education.

Educational Research

In the areas of educational research and planning, all these countries are faced with the scarcity of high-level human resources. In UAE, the Department of Information and Research within the Ministry of Education is entrusted with part of research responsibilities. The Ministry of Education in Qatar has established a special sector for educational planning and curricula. All these countries seem to need exchange of information, experience, and even management between themselves in those two areas. [6] At the same time, they have to benefit from the larger world experiences directly or through the Internet (the IBE's INNODATA could be of great help to them).

There is hope that, with the strengthening of national universities, greater progress will be achieved in the field of educational research indispensable for any educational planning.

Comparative Tables Concerning Curriculum in the Gulf Region Countries

Table 3. Number of weekly periods devoted to Islamic and science education in each year

Country	Grade 4	Grade 5	Grade 6	Grade 7	Grade 8	Total periods (weeks)
Kuwait	3	3	3	2	2	30-32
Oman	5	5	5	4	4	30
Qatar	6	6	6	5	5	33-36
Saudi Arabia	9	9	9	8	8	30-34
Number of weekly periods for science education in each year						
Kuwait	-	-	3	3	3	30-32
Oman	-	3	3	4	4	30
Qatar	-	4	4	4	4	33-36
Saudi Arabia	-	3	3	4	4	30-34

Table 4. Place of physical education in the yearly programme (Number of weekly period)

Country	Grade 4	Grade 5	Grade 6	Grade 7	Grade 8	Total periods (weeks)
Kuwait	-	2	2	2	2	30-32
Oman	-	2	2	2	1	30
Qatar	-	3	2	2	2	33-36
Saudi Arabia	-	2	2	2	1	30-34

Includes biology, geology, physics, chemistry and general science.
Source of data: IBE. 2000. *Draft educational profiles.*

Notes

1. Similar objectives can be found in other national reports (Oman, p. 4; the United Arab Emirates talks about bridging the gap in technological achievements, p. 19).
2. Reference has already been made to the report of the British Council about technical education in Kuwait (1998). There also exists a report of an ILO mission to Kuwait on 'development of strategic planning for applied education and training' (1993).
3. Shapour Rassekh: *Kuwait at the threshold of a new millennium* (report of a mission to Kuwait), 1999.
4. Egypt, Iraq and Palestinian Autonomous Territories have been providing teachers for the Gulf Region before recent events.
5. See *The development of education in Bahrain 1994-96,* pp. 80-84.
6. The following regional institutions can be of great assistance: Arab Bureau of Education for Gulf States; Arab League Educational, Cultural and Scientific Organization; Islamic Organization for Education, Culture and Science; Arab Gulf Programme of the United Nations Development Programme; and the Regional Bureau of UNESCO.

Annex: Opening and Closing Speeches

Speech at the Opening Ceremony, Muscat, 17 February 2001

By Dr Hamed Saif Al Hammami
Director-General of Curriculum and Training, Ministry of Education, Sultanate of Oman

It gives me great pleasure to welcome you all, especially those who have come from outside Oman to participate in this workshop about 'The Management of Curriculum Change and Adaptation'. I would like to take this opportunity to wish you all a pleasant stay in our lovely country.

It is a great honour for us to host this valuable and important workshop in collaboration with the International Bureau of Education. This workshop is similar to other workshops that were held in Geneva in 1998, in New Delhi in 1999 and in Beijing in the year 2000. In the next five days, this workshop will address the following six topics:

- strategies of managing changes and revisions in curricula, focusing on international experiences. We shall also discuss developing and planning curricula with regard to the selection of course content and the ways of integrating these curricula;
- the development of curricula taking into account feedback and evaluation obtained from the field;
- learner-centred teaching methods that aim to activate the learners' participation in a learning situation;
- methods of introducing extra activities that will enrich the school curricula;
- training teachers on how curricula are implemented and developed; and

- a review of the experiences of other countries in the Gulf Region in developing and revising curricula, their management of the change and development processes, the difficulties that have faced these countries during the process, and the methods used to overcome these difficulties.

Developed and developing countries from all over the world are currently engaged in advancing their education systems to cope with the knowledge explosion, developments in technology and globalization.

Curriculum occupies an important position in educational development and is considered as being the backbone of the process. If the education system is to continue to be effective and to achieve its projected objectives and outcomes, development and revision of the curricula is inevitable. Concerns over the various processes of curricula—such as developing, planning, organizing, implementing and evaluating—have been increasing in recent years. This is mainly because of the role these processes play in forming of children's characters to cope with the requirements and changes of life today and in the future.

Based on our appreciation of the importance of the role played by education in social and economic development, we are prepared for the twenty-first century with all its scientific, cultural and technological challenges. The Sultanate of Oman endeavours to develop and innovate general education in a way that matches modern life and copes with the objectives of comprehensive development of our future generations. Observers of educational developments in the Sultanate of Oman realize the achievements that have been made over more than a quarter of a century. History witnesses and records the birth of this educational development which started with the great Omani renaissance in July 1970, which has placed Oman in its strong position in the same level as countries who started their development many years ahead of us.

The Ministry of Education has set up an ambitious plan to develop education. The objective of this plan is to develop the abilities of individuals and prepare students to play their designated roles effectively and efficiently in an age that is marked with scientific and technological developments in all aspects of life. The development plan has adapted the concept of basic education, a type of education that involves integration of theory and practice, ideas and work, and education and life. With its comprehensive view, basic education works to develop all aspects of the individual's character and to provide the student with independent learning skills within the framework of the concept of continuous lifelong education. It also develops values and practices necessary for achieving skilfulness in teaching and learning. In addition, it meets the needs of human development as part of comprehensive social development.

Development of curricula has also included several related areas, some of these being:

1. the development of the organizational structure of the Ministry that has resulted in the formation of a Directorate General of Curricula and Training;
2. a review of general objectives of educational levels and school subjects;
3. the development of school programmes and plans;
4. the development of courses and the introduction of new school subjects;
5. the development of stages of writing and producing textbooks;
6. the development of educational evaluation; and
7. the development of educational supervision and inspection.

This workshop is concerned with the 'Management of Curriculum Change and Adaptation'. In our opinion, it is difficult to define the concept of 'curriculum' as many concomitants have been attached to this concept, not only among lay people, but also among specialists. Some specialists have defined 'curriculum' as the school programmes, courses or subjects that are learnt by learners. Others have added on further activities that could complement the curriculum, while yet others have defined curriculum as a set of facts, concepts and information relevant to a certain school subject. In fact, 'curriculum' is all educational experiences that learners are involved with inside and outside the school in order to acquire these experiences to develop themselves in all aspects of their characters, and to build and adjust their behaviours in accordance with the educational objectives.

According to this concept, the curriculum is much more than a school textbook. An integrated process includes the written curriculum, the hidden curriculum, the taught curriculum, and the learnt curriculum. In addition to the subjects' written curricula, we have to include learning multimedia, technology and the environment in which we live.

It is not an easy task to develop an education system and corresponding curricula. A very complicated process, it affects and is affected by all political, social and economic systems within society, as well as systems outside. The influences of globalization and its requirements of development are not concealed. The distances between different ends of the global village are getting shorter by the day.

The vast quantum of knowledge and the development of technological systems that accompany it will embarrass education systems if these systems do not keep pace. Education systems, from our point of view, should prepare students to obtain information that meets their individual requirements for development and for entering the labour market.

At the end of this address I pray to Almighty Allah to crown our efforts with success, and that all of us shall benefit from this workshop.

I would like also to seize this opportunity to thank—on behalf of the Ministry of Education—the International Bureau of Education for the support and help that it offers Gulf countries to promote and develop their education systems. Our thanks also are extended to the Omani National Committee of Education, Culture and Science and to all those who have contributed to the preparation of this workshop. I would like also to thank our honourable guests for their participation in this gathering, and all those who have responded to our invitation.

Speech at the Opening Ceremony, Muscat, 17 February 2001

By Ms C. Braslavsky
Director, International Bureau of Education

It gives me great pleasure to address you briefly at the opening of this Regional Seminar on management of curriculum adaptation jointly organized by the Omani National Commission for UNESCO, high-level educational authorities of this country and the International Bureau of Education.

This seminar follows in the footsteps of a number of seminars, workshops and training courses that have taken place in different regions of the world[1] as part of the new focal programme of the IBE. Our key objectives in augmenting the educational contents to encounter the challenges of the twenty-first century are:

- to make participants from different countries aware of common concerns about the curriculum;
- to introduce them to modern approaches to curriculum design and implementation;
- to launch a dialogue on possible regional co-operation; and
- to analyse the needs and possibilities of improving the practical and conceptual skills in these matters.

Only a couple of years ago, the IBE was designated as the UNESCO centre for the content of education and we have since been reorienting its activities towards the adaptation of curricula to cope with the challenges of the twenty-first century, with specific focus on education for learning to live together. UNESCO and IBE consider that education based on the four 'pillars'[2] advocated by the Delors Report is quintessential in view of the prevalent global situation, where, despite phenomenal socio-economic, scientific and technological progress, human-kind's flirtation with wars, conflicts and arbitrary inequities continue unabated in many parts of the world.

Asia received our particular attention because of its vastness. It is time to enlarge the vision. The present seminar follows on three previous ones in Asia organized in Delhi

(March 1999), Beijing (March 2000) and Thailand (December 2000). In keeping with its innovative focus, the IBE has been organizing a series of seminars both for the exchange of experiences and training on matters related to curriculum development and adaptation in various geographic regions, as one of its principal activities.

In addition to seeking to identify trends in curriculum development in the different regions to help build a better knowledge base from which to work with the Member States, the IBE wishes to evolve a series of training modules for the strengthening of transversal skills for curriculum development. Rather than focusing on the more traditional aspects of curriculum development, that of content and its renewal and adaptation to new trends and needs, the IBE, through its capacity-building seminars wishes to develop and fortify transversal skills/competencies, the mastery of which it is felt will give a boost to the curriculum development process.

We are aware of the fact that many countries in this part of the world are already committed to some degree of reforms in their educational curricula. It is therefore an ideal opportunity for the IBE to collaborate more closely not only with Regional Bureaux of UNESCO in Qatar and Lebanon as well as with ABEGS, but also with individual countries in the Gulf Region.

All these experiences will be of great interest to ignite the debates at the forthcoming International Conference on Education that is going to be held in Geneva in September this year. The theme of this session will be 'Education for all for learning to live together: content and learning strategies—problems and solutions'.

The choice of venue was due to the great generosity of the Omani authorities. The Oman Sultanate, which has been a member in the IBE's Governing Council, offered sometime back to host an IBE meeting on curriculum issues. We are very grateful to all persons in high positions who made possible this excellent choice for such a meeting.

The IBE sees the development of networking among institutions and individuals in the different regions to be an essential component of capacity-building, and seeks to promote this among participants attending its workshops. Sharing of information and expertise among curriculum professionals on regional and international levels amplifies resources and reinforces professional and institutional developments. However, networking only takes place if there is a felt need experienced by those it benefits.

The new Director-General of UNESCO, in a recent speech, referred to five top priority areas for the Organization: education for all throughout life and learning to live together; the preservation and enhancement of cultural pluralism; the ethics of science and technology; solution to environmental problems; and finally, movement towards a global information society. Mr K. Matsuura suggested a range of imperative reforms in the Organization to empower it to take on these new global challenges. As he indicated 'framing effective policies in these areas calls for much more interdisciplinary research and for information exchanges, capacity-building, better training and sustained partnerships with the academic and scientific communities, in order to assist the search for integrated approaches' (see *INNOVATION,* no. 104). The IBE intends to apply these policies to its own areas of activities. Healthier communion with countries, concerted work ethos, capacity-building in closer proximity and with a collaborative spirit, greater emphasis on interdisciplinary and transversal approaches, and finally, an assiduous exchange of information on successful experiences and best practices in the area of curriculum are some of the core policy guidelines that will be pursued.

I sincerely hope that during this five-day seminar, our sharing of experiences and expertise, exploration of shared problems, and discussion of promising solutions will result in consolidating the process of curriculum development in the countries of the region, and lead to fertile and lasting working relationships.

Thank you very much.

Notes

1. In South and South-East Asia (1999), in Latin America (1999 and 2000), in the Mediterranean region (1999 and

2000), in East Asia (2000), in Africa (2000) and in Thailand (2000).

2. Learning to know, learning to do (acquisition of skills and competences), learning to be (acquisitions of human qualities and virtues) and finally learning to live with other people in peace and harmony (co-operation, solidarity, etc.).

SPEECH AT THE CLOSING CEREMONY, MUSCAT, 21 FEBRUARY 2001

By Mr Shapour Rassekh
IBE Consultant

On behalf of Ms Cecilia Braslavsky, Director of the IBE, and my colleagues, I should like to convey to the distinguished authorities of the host country our deep gratitude for their most appreciated co-operation in organizing this seminar. All of us felt grateful to his excellency the Omani Minister of Education, her honorable under-secretary, Mrs. Fuzia Nasser Al Farsi, his honorable under-secretary, Mr. Muhammed Attoubi, present today, as well as to the eminent members of the National Commission for Education, Science and Culture, for having offered such generous hospitality to the seminar's participants. Our warm thanks go also to the respected representatives of the regional institutions, ABEGS and UNESCO's Office in Qatar, who participated so actively and constructively in the deliberations. We also thank wholeheartedly all delegates of various Gulf countries who brought to this seminar not only their vision but also their rich experience in matters of curriculum development. I should like to express our feeling of appreciation to our three knowledgeable experts from Australia, India and Malta, who gracefully shared with us their huge experience and wisdom.

It was the first experience of working contact of our institution, IBE, with this important region of the world. Therefore, we learned lots from you, benefited greatly from your analysis of problems, solutions and needs in the area of curriculum adaptation in this region. The signs of will-power and courage of your political leaders have impressed us, who are pushing education towards being relevant to the growing needs of our times. We became acquainted with the efforts the educational authorities, teachers and other stakeholders in this area are devoting to the renewal of your education systems and to the adaptation of school curricula to the challenges of modern time. Our visit to a basic education school today created in all of us a sense of admiration for your achievement in modernizing schools, but at the same time promoting basic moral and spiritual values. You, as experts in education and curriculum development, are quite aware of inadequacies, but you are also searching courageously for solutions and remedies. Be sure that the IBE will be at your side and will help you to the extent of its capacity to develop your expertise and your skills in making the curriculum adaptation a success, whenever the need is felt. Our information network will be at your disposal in a number of areas, which might be of interest for your work. We will expect also your collaboration in providing us with adequate and regularly updated information regarding the situation of education in your respective countries.

Concerning innovating ideas, lots can be obtained through workshops and seminars like this one, and through INNODATA that the IBE has established and put at the disposal of all countries. No doubt, it is vitally important that you consolidate co-operative relations within the region, but at this time of globalization, the region will benefit also from interaction with the outside world. We hope that our experts present here from different parts of the world have given you an idea of what we can learn from the experiences of other nations.

I feel happy that this seminar led to a useful report on the results. We can build our future relations of co-operation on that basis. Our intention is to prepare a comprehensive report of this seminar, including all the contributions already made, and publish it, in co-operation with you, in the course of this year for the benefit of all. We hope that specific characteristics of the region will be reflected in this publication, as well as its common problems with the rest of the world. We should also consider this seminar as a preparation for the active participation of your respective countries in the forthcoming International Conference on Education next September on the theme of 'living together in the twenty-first century'.

In the course of the seminar, we said and repeated that the emphasis in 'education for the twenty-first century' will be increasingly on learning instead of teaching. It is therefore appropriate to quote the following sentence from the beautiful book *Oman 2000* you offered us: 'The major shift in the curriculum will be away from rote learning, and emphasis will be put on encouraging students to develop scientific and logical thinking, as well as acquiring skills of analysis and problem-solving.' It is our hope that not only Oman but all countries of the region, through the continuous efforts of their educationists, their curriculum designers and their teachers, will succeed in reaching that sort of ambitious aim, forming a more competent, skilled, thoughtful, responsible and co-operative generation to face the challenges of the century ahead of us.

Thank you for your attention.

Annex: List of Participants

Bahrain

Mrs Mariam Mohamad Matar
Specialist of Mathematics Curricula
Direction of Curricula
Ministry of Education and Teaching
BP 43
Manama

Mrs Latifé Mohamad el Mahmoud
Specialist of Arabic Language Curricula
Direction of Curricula
Ministry of Education and Teaching
BP 43
Manama

Kuwait

Mrs Abla el Issa
Head of Progammes Unit
Ministry of Education
P.O. Box 7
Safat

Mrs Aïcha el Redwan
Head for Technical Guidance for Arabic Language
Ministry of Education
P.O. Box 7
Safat

Oman

Mr Mohamad Ben Saif Ben Musbeh al Bousaïdi
Deputy-Director of Science and Mathematics Department
Ministry of Education
P.O. Box 3
Muscat

Mrs Mahssoumah Bint Habib el Ajami
Responsible of Curriculum Development
Department of Arabic Language Programmes
Ministry of Education
P.O. Box 3
Muscat

Mr Hadi Ahmad el Faraji
In Charge of the Geography
Department of Social Sciences
Ministry of Education
P.O. Box 3
Muscat

Mrs Shehira Issa Bint Nasser el Ismaïili
Head of Section for English
Department of English-Language Programmes
Ministry of Education
P.O. Box 3
Muscat

Mrs Charifa bint Zahrane Bint Mohamad el Kanadi
Member of the Department for Family Education
Department of Social Sciences
Ministry of Education
P.O. Box 3
Muscat

Mr Kassen Ben Mohamad Ben Massoud Al Khalifein
Member of the Mathematics Programme
Department of Sciences and Mathematics
Ministry of Education
P.O. Box 3
Muscat

Mr Yime Mounes
Expert in the English Language Programmes
Department of English Language Programmes
Ministry of Education
P.O. Box 3
Muscat

Mr Abdullah ben Marhoon ben Muhammad-el-Isaï
Chief
Department of Islamic Education
Ministry of Education
P.O. Box 3
Muscat

Mr Muhammad ben Saoud ben Salem el Hazrami
Training Section
Ministry of Education
P.O. Box 3
Muscat

Mr Salim ben Muhammad el Jaberi
Ministry of Education
P.O. Box 3
Muscat

Mr Rashid Hamed Saleh el Ghanbossi
Ministry of Education
P.O. Box 3
Muscat

Mr Rashid ben Saïd el Hinaï
Technical Section
Ministry of Education
P.O. Box 3
Muscat

Mr Muhammad ben Shames el Husni
Supervision
Ministry of Education
P.O. Box 3
Muscat

Mr Ibrahim ben Saïd ben Hamd-el-Ravahi
Teacher of History
Muscat

Mr Hamad ben Salem el Rajahi
Responsible of Curriculum Development
Department of Islamic Education
Ministry of Education
P.O. Box 3
Muscat

Mrs Jane Noates
Project Manager (English)
Ministry of Education
P.O. Box 3
Muscat

Mrs Asma Bint Salem Bin Rached Al Belushi
Director of the Technical Office for Studies and Development
Department of Science and Mathematics
Ministry of Education
P.O. Box 3
Muscat

Omani Observers

Mr Al Bahrani Mahir Ahmed
Education Planner
Ministry of Education
Muscat

Mr Suleiman Mohamad
Expert in Statistical Analysis
Examination Department
Ministry of Education
Muscat

Mr Al Rayad Osman Talballa
Expert in Education
Ministry of Education
Muscat

Mr Rashid M. Khalfan Al Khaifi
Director
Training and Professor Development
Ministry of Education
Muscat

Mr Hamood Khalfan Said Al Nasseri
Deputy Director of Training
Department of Mathematics
Ministry of Education
Muscat

Mr Rashid M. Khalfan Al Khaifi
Director
Training and Professor Development
Ministry of Education
Muscat

Mrs. Nahla Hamed Al Kindi
Director of Science and Mathematics Department
Ministry of Education
Muscat

Mrs Janet Mohammed Al Lamki
Director of English Language Curriculum Department
Ministry of Education
Muscat

Mr Mofreh Mahmod Ajlan
Educational Planner
Ministry of Education
Muscat

Mr Musa Gasn El Seed Al Malik
Educational Expert
Systems and Performance Follow-up Department
Ministry of Education
Muscat

Mr Al Tayib Mustaffa Al Nour
Science Curriculum Specialist
Private Education Department
Ministry of Education
Muscat

Saudi Arabia

Mr Abudullah Ben Ali el Faizi
Responsible of Cultural Relations for Girls Department
Ministry of Education
Riyadh

United Arab Emirates

Dr Obeid bin Butti Al-Muhairi
Director
Centre for Curriculum and Instructional Materials Development
Ministry of Education and Youth
3062 Dubai

Dr Ibrahim Ahmed Ali Alnaqbi
Educational Expert
Curriculum Development Center
Ministry of Education and Youth
Khorfakkan

UNESCO Office in Qatar

Mr M. Bubtana
Director
UNESCO Office in Qatar
P.O. Box 3945
Doha

ABEGS

Prof Humaidan A. Al-Humaidan
First Counsellor
ABEGS Office
P.O. Box 86386
Riyadh 22614
Kingdom of Saudi Arabia

IBE

Mrs Cecilia Braslavsky
Director
IBE
P.O. Box 199
1211 Geneva 20
Switzerland

Mrs Jeanine Thomas
Programme Specialist
IBE
P.O. Box 199
1211 Geneva 20
Switzerland

Consultants

Mr Shapour Rassekh
5, rue Albert Gos
1206 Geneva
Switzerland

Mrs Sabine Ferra de Cerda
3 Chemin des Floralies
Cointrin
Switzerland

Contributors

Mr Mohammed Saleem Al Yacoubi
Vice-Secretary-General
Omani National Commission for UNESCO
Ministry of Education
P.O. Box 3
Code: 112
Muscat

Dr Hamed Saif Al Hammami
Director-General
General Directorate of Curricula and Training
Ministry of Education
P.O. Box 3
P.C. 113
Muscat

Experts

Mr. Ashok Ganguly
Chairman
Central Board of Secondary Education
Shiksha Kendra
2, Community Centre
Preet Vihar
New Delhi-110092
India

Mr Phillip W. Hughes
Professor
Australian National University
5 Liversidge St.
Canberra 0200
Australie

Mr Anthony Macelli
Adviser to Minister
Ministry of Education
Great Siege Street
Floriana CMR02
Malta

Part 3

Capacity Building for Curriculum Specialists

* The Final Report of the Training Seminar on 'Capacity Building for Curriculum Specialists in East and Southeast Asia" held in Bangkok, Thailand. © International Bureau of Education.

Introduction

Cecilia Braslavsky, Director of the IBE

In December 2000, the International Bureau of Education (IBE), in partnership with the UNESCO Principal Regional Office for Asia and the Pacific (PROAP) and the Thai Ministry of Education, organized a seminar on Capacity-Building for Curriculum Specialists for East and South-East Asia, in Bangkok. Participating countries included: Cambodia, China, Indonesia, Japan, Laos, Malaysia, Mongolia, Philippines, Republic of Korea, Thailand and Viet Nam. This was the third meeting on curriculum development issues which the IBE has held in Asia, the first two taking place respectively in New Delhi in March 1999 and Beijing in March 2000.[1] These seminars are principal components of the IBE's programme of capacity-building for curriculum development and renewal in all Member States. The Bangkok seminar was organized as a follow-up activity to the outcomes of the New Delhi meeting, at which the possibilities of developing an Asian Network for the Management of Curriculum Change had been discussed, and proposals put forward for such an eventual undertaking. While, to date, there has been no official launching of such a network, the Bangkok seminar was intended to build on some of the concerns and suggestions coming out of the New Delhi seminar, while introducing the new training approach of the IBE which will focus on the strengthening of professional competencies for more effective curriculum development. This approach was piloted through a component on communications skills for curriculum specialists.

The objectives sought by the IBE were complemented by those of PROAP, which had just launched a project entitled: Curriculum Innovations in Basic Education: Preparing the Learners to meet the Challenges of the New Millennium. This project, funded by Japanese-Funds-in-Trust, initially targeted six Asian countries, namely, China, Japan, Philippines, the Republic of Korea, Thailand and Viet Nam. With the collaboration of the IBE, it was possible for the other participating countries to be included in some aspects of the project. The broad goal is to 'provide some assessment of the quality of learning at the basic level and the effectiveness of this in preparing learners for the challenge of the twenty-first century, with lifelong learning as the ultimate goal. Considerations would be based [...] on the Four Pillars of Learning advocated by the International Commission on Education for the Twenty-First Century'.[2] The project has a number of objectives, which include a critical analysis of the curriculum development/reform process in the participant countries using prescribed guidelines, and the formulation of a regional framework for curriculum development and renewal based on the four pillars of learning.

Thus, as part of on-going collaboration between IBE and UNESCO-PROAP, it was agreed to merge the two institutions' similar interests in capacity-building for curriculum development, through jointly organizing this seminar, assisted by the very generous hosting of the event by the Ministry of Education of Thailand.

In preparation for the seminar, delegates were asked to prepare reports on their countries' curriculum development processes and trends. A reading of these reports showed a number of similar concerns within the region, despite the great diversity in economic development, cultures and political systems. The search for improved quality and relevance of school curricula is an overall preoccupation, manifested by a range of reform efforts. Expressed needs include: a more integrated curriculum with reduced content, improved teacher education for the effective implementation of reform, greater involvement of parents and the wider community in the educational process, and an improved balance between academic and practical elements of the curriculum.

As a key aspect of the proceedings, a specialist from the Asia Pacific Social Science Research Council (ASSREC) presented criteria for a situation analysis of the national curriculum for basic education and a proposed new framework for revising and updating the existing curriculum. These were discussed, modified and approved by the participants. As a follow-up to the seminar and continuation of the project, an in-depth study is being undertaken of the process of curriculum reform in the countries of the region. It is also hoped that the proposed framework will serve to direct/inform future curriculum development and change in East and South-East Asia.

The report is divided into three sections. Section One, entitled 'Rethinking the framework and the capacities needed for curriculum reform', gives some perspectives on trends and issues in curriculum change for the twenty-first century, both internationally and within South-East Asia. Cecilia Braslavsky, Director of the IBE, describes the inadequacy for contemporary societal needs of the traditional education systems developed in the nineteenth century, which are still largely followed in much of the world. She identifies key trends in contemporary society and corresponding societal needs which make new, urgent demands on education, looking at some of the risks and tensions these imply for the educational process, and referring to some current efforts at reform. Zhou Nanzhao, Acting Director of the UNESCO Principal Officer for Asia and the Pacific, outlines further the challenges for education in today's world, applying this both to the global and Asian contexts, recommending the 'Four pillars of learning' described in the Delors Report as the basis for curriculum reform and renewal.[3] Tan Khun, Director of the Southeast Asian Ministers of Education organization Regional Centre for Education in Science and Mathematics (SEAMEO-RECSAM) provides a brief overview of SEAMEO and of its role in curriculum reform in the sub-region.

Section Two, 'Strengthening capacities for curriculum reform', looks at some specific practical means of improving the curriculum development and reform process. Lucille Gregorio gives a summary of the recently launched PROAP project, 'Curriculum Innovations in Basic Education: Preparing the Learners to Meet the Challenges of the New Millennium'. This is followed with chapters by Isabel Byron and Liliana Jabif on the roles of information, communication skills and networking in improving the process of curriculum reform.

Section Three, 'Curriculum changes and reform in East and Southeast Asia', focuses directly on the region in question. Virginia Miralao looks briefly at the socio-economic and political issues which have implications for curriculum changes in Asia and the rest of the world, followed by a synthesis of the country reports presented to the seminar on curriculum development processes, trends and needs in the participating countries.

Notes

1. See: (a) International Bureau of Education; India, Ministry of Human Resource Development, *Globalization and living together: the challenges for educational content in Asia,* Geneva, IBE, 2000. (Final report of the sub-regional course on curriculum development, New Delhi, March 1999); (b) International Bureau of Education; The Chinese National Commission for UNESCO, *Science education for contemporary society: problems, issues and dilemmas,* Geneva, IBE, 2001. (Final Report of the International Workshop on the Reform in the Teaching of Science and Technology at Primary and Secondary Level in Asia: Comparative References to Europe, Beijing, March 2000.)
2. UNESCO Principal Regional Office for Asia and the Pacific, Project proposal for extra-budgetary funding, Bangkok, 2000, p.4.
3. Jacques Delors, et al., *Learning: the treasure within,* Paris, UNESCO, 1996.

Section 1

Rethinking the Framework and the Capacities Needed for Curriculum Reform

The Education System of the Nineteenth Century: The Direction, Trends and Tensions of Curriculum Reforms in the Twenty-first Century

Cecilia Braslavsky

Some Major Trends of the Social Development and the Need to Review Education

The need for curriculum change is based on the recognition that there has been a consolidation of a number of trends that began at least twenty years ago. These trends relate to the demand for education, to the components and resources of educational processed and to the current provision of educational services.

There are at least six noticeable trends in the demand for education: (i) the changes in occupational profiles in the context of a world of work that is increasingly heterogeneous, in many cases shrinking, swiftly changing and ever more globalized; (ii) the need to counteract deepening social inequalities and increasing marginalization and violence; (iii) the need to recognize that the diversity between individuals and communities is a valuable resource that is different from social inequality; (iv) the need to educate individuals so that they are able to satisfy their need for better forms of representation as citizens in society; (v) the increasingly broader spectrum of issues arising, for example, from advances in biotechnology on which individuals may take decisions; and (vi) the coexistence of advantages and disadvantages resulting from the impact of technical progress on the environment and the quality of life of individuals and communities.

These trends bring different opportunities and new risks for education and education systems. The existing education system was invented to cope with a society organized in classes but giving at the same time opportunities for the majority to be integrated. It was improved to cope with an economy organized in sectors and seeking for specialization. In that economy, society expected that some people learned to think and to take decisions and some others to act without thinking. Especially the non-specialized working positions could be occupied by skilled trained workers having less general knowledge and capacities for lifelong learning.

The current situation makes it necessary to learn both: to act and to think. People who have not been educated in this sense are probably not able to maintain good jobs, or invent new ones, and even to have some possibilities to direct their lives. The speed of economic and social changes makes it also necessary to learn to tackle the stress of constant changes, for one to take advantage of the changes.

It is also necessary in this current situation to strengthen the teaching of values that could be understood and internalized. The attempts to react against marginalization using violence would not solve the problems, and more than that, the unequal and haphazard distribution of opportunities are threats to the survival of humankind.

With regard to the components of the educational processes, there are also at least four important trends to be considered: (i) the constant restructuring and the accelaration of scientific and technological knowledge, and the emergence of an authentic scientific and technological system that is rapidly making educational contents obsolete based on the provision of information; (ii) the growth of milieus outside the school for cultural creation and consumption by children and young people; (iii) the ever-widening use of the new information and communication technologies; (iv) the decline in the effectiveness of the teaching and school models developed in the previous centuries.

Special attention has to be paid to the first of those for trends in the framework of the need to shift the educational paradigm in relation to one of the basic educational principles. Education was supposed 'to transmit the culture of adult generations to younger generations'. Behind this principle is a hypothesis of stability and homogeneity that is not later acceptable. This hypothesis of stability involves generations—every generation and every culture. During the past centuries it was assumed that the young generation did not have a culture of its own and would accept willingly what was imposed by adults, that young people from an homogeneous group, where the only differences were biological or attributable to social class and that adult culture, and the way in which knowledge was produced and structured was stable over time.

The speed of current changes led to a rediscovery that each generation possesses its own culture, that there is wide diversity within each generation and that the way in which knowledge is produced and structured changes in relation to changing times. These rediscoveries and the evolution of educational psychology lead to the acceptance that children and young people have to be active participants in the educational processes and that even the diversity has to be encouraged. The increasing evidences about the instability of knowledge added elements to face the challenges of 'learning to learn'.

As a result of the concurrent actions of these trends, there is a growing contradiction between progress in incorporating individuals into formal education and the deficiencies in its quality, understood as its capacity to respond to new educational demands. Some of the above mentioned trends—for example, the demand for new profiles for economic, social and political participation, greater recognition of diversity, and the new dynamics of knowledge production—are posing renewed challenges to the meaning of education. In any case, this issue concerns the content of education, defined in the broadest sense of the term. The content of education is, in fact, all that should be taught or which is effectively 'contained' in educational practices: values, concepts and processes for learning, being, doing and living together.

The contradictions between quantitative advances and problems in the quality of education, the increasing use of the new information and communication technologies (ICTs), the growing demand from children and young people to learn actively and creatively, and a deeper understanding of the importance of links with communities so that education may be of better quality and more effective, also present new challenges to the issue of teaching methods and school management.

Increasing interconnections and the globalization of many economic decisions and processes, intensified migration, and the international scale of many communication media provide populations with new standards and parameters. There are attempts to counterbalance these through local and national production, and they also provoke resistance. This context produces tensions reflecting different attempts at achieving membership and constructing identities. These tensions make demands on education in terms of acquiring skills to facilitate their peaceful, creative resolution.

The new scenario at the beginning of the twenty-first century thus provides more opportunities and more risks for each and every individual to have access to a living wage, for the redistribution of the benefits of economic growth, for social cohesion, democracy and cultural diversity. It also provides more opportunities and risks for peace at the international, regional and local levels.

Education can be a powerful tool for exploiting the opportunities and avoiding the pitfalls of this new scenario. But not the same education as in the nineteenth century, which is still widespread today. This education has also just offered all that it could offer, to integrate to the new social and age groups.

Some Current Attempts at Reforming Education

In the 1980s and 1990s many countries worldwide introduced educational reforms focused on the above-mentioned concerns. These countries have implemented their reforms from national, provincial, to community levels. But there are still other countries that have not undertaken educational reforms. In the current context, there is no guarantee that carrying out a number of unconnected national, provincial or local reforms is a sufficient strategy for social cohesion and world peace. For example, even countries with a high degree of educational development and well supplied with resources are dissatisfied with the quality of education and the way the reforms are taking shape. Some prominent representatives of the efforts to introduce reforms are going so far that they write about the 'impossible reform's (Meirieu, 2000).

It maybe possible to mention that these feelings do not arise because of the difficulties of finding the direction of the changes, but rather due to the difficulties in finding ways of managing those changes.

There is in fact a general agreement that there is a need to strengthen the competencies and identities in order to empower the young and adult people to find best solutions to problems that are existing and known, and to new and unknown problems that are going to emerge. There is also general agreement to the fact that to do it, it is necessary to count on old and new knowledge, to be able to learn today unknown knowledge and acquire the awareness of the consequences of actions in the short, medium and long terms. In other words, there is a general agreement with the needs of learning to do, to be, to live together, and to learn.

The ongoing reforms to tackle the challenges refer to the educational structure, curriculum and system, and school governance.

Concerning the educational structures many countries are trying to move from what can be called a 'pyramid for the pyramid' invented in the nineteenth century, to a more flexible one, structured according to the stages of life and admitting different ways of using the educational opportunities. They are also trying to move from streams for the different sectors of the economy in a modern industrial society (primary, secondary and higher), to a diversity that accepts and caters to different identities without aggravating social inequalities. They are trying to preserve spaces for lifelong basic education and to offer supplementary training for skills, that can be rapidly outdated.

But from day to day it seems clear that curriculum reform is becoming the axis of the next reform period. Many countries are trying to move from rigid programmes to flexible frameworks. In fact, after years of being obsessed about updated information, the educational community realises that a continuously updated curriculum is impossible, and that to improve the quality of education, it is much more important to reform the curriculum concept and structure.

It is quite impossible to explain in a short presentation all the aspects involved in this new approach. There is not enough information to do it. But it is possible to anticipate at least four trends of the new curricula: (i) it should really try to orient the selection of contents to make possible the promotion of the competencies 'to do, to learn, to live together, and to be'; (ii) it should try to change the logic of integration at the primary level and differentiation by 'academic disciplines' at the secondary level, going into a logic of a tension between integration and differentiation throughout childhood and adolescence, allowing schools to combine the disciplines, workshops, projects, etc.; (iii) it should suggest replacing methods oriented towards transmission, by methods towards the 'construction' of skills and the use of knowledge in context as a way to learn; and (iv) it should include proposals to evaluate procedures and competencies instead of measuring the amount of information learned.

There are mainly two changes that are being introduced between system and school governance. The first one concerns internal processes. This consists of a shift from the top-down control of well-established processes to the promotion of the institutional capacity to learn through networking. The second one concerns external processes. This consists in a shift from an isolated way of doing to a partner-oriented action.

Tensions in the Process of Educational Change

In talking about comprehensive reforms and, especially, about curriculum reforms, there is a general tendency to over emphasize or interpret result and products. The government representatives reinforce the perceived successes. Frequently, university representatives and unions prefer to emphasize criticism. But in fact those products and impacts are the results of very complex processes that suffer from a number of tensions. For the purpose of an orderly presentation, these tensions can be classified as political, conceptual and institutional ones, although in practice, the political, the conceptual and the institutional tensions are rather closely interwoven aspects or dimensions of same process.

Table 1. An overview of the reforms mentioned in the text

Horizontal structure	Countries of Northern Europe Brazil, San Pablo	'Comprehensive school' School for children for young people
Vertical structure	Australia	Secondary—'Taffies'.
Curriculum	Argentina	'Basic content' (CBC), by level and not by year.
Content	Canada	Concepts, procedures
Methodologies	Australia	Primary school class with 100 children
Evaluation	Baccalaureate, Abutter, Maturity	PISA
Links	Portugal Mozambique	Secondary schools in partnership with business teacher training institution with Danish NGO.
Management	UK (Scotland) Uruguay	School projects Flexibility of time

The acceleration and focus of the education reform and especially of the curricular transformation processes were made possible by the pressures when knowledge become a core item on the public agenda. This shows that there is a new consensus regarding the role of knowledge in the future development of societies and individuals. However, apart from the highly abstract question, the degree of consensus with regard to what, how, and when teaching should take place can be relatively limited.

Consequently, when reforms begin, it is necessary to deal simultaneously with at least two needs that tend to impose two different speeds on the processes. On the one hand, it is known that all consensus-building processes require a great deal of time. On the other, the possibility of legitimizing government teams depends on the speed with which they can provide responses to the felt needs of different social groups and segment, in the case of curriculum reforms, the need to have available frames of references and appropriate tools to improve the quality of education. In short, in all reform processes, it is necessary to resolve adequately the tension between achieving consensus and being efficient, to mediate between different positions and quickly provide appropriate products.

Furthermore, this has to be done frequently, in a context of dissociation between criticism and action. In fact, in many countries a factor which on occasion restricts the spectrum of participants in the processes seeking consensus and efficiency is the way in which some academic and intellectual sectors in the one hand, and political sectors on the other, interpret the role of criticism. Numerous academics and intellectuals consider the critical role that can be played within the framework of republican democracy to be the same as under military authoritarianism and attempt to monopolize this role. The paradoxical results of these attitudes are the abstention from the relevant decision-making processes relating to specifically professional aspects. Some politicians, for their part, reject all criticism of their administration, discrediting it as press manipulation, products of the opposition parties, or something of that nature. The result of this attitude is paradoxical, because they deprive themselves of external views which could provide them with interesting suggestions for an improved monitoring of their transformation. It fact, in both cases there is a lack of recognition of many personal and institutional efforts.

The tension between guaranteed national unity, federal power and local empowerment is also always present in reforms, and especially in the curriculum. Frequently, the professional teams tend to loose them when deciding percentage of contents, whoever has the power. But..., is it possible to establish a percentage of local mathematics contents? Most working teams are moving towards a recognition that in each content is a global, a national, a provincial or regional and a local dimension and that decisions have to be taken differently in each dimension.

In the constellation of situations, there are on occasions certain pressures from some decision-makers to restrict and accelerate the processes of consultation and participation to the minimum required to validate the activities, alternatives and proposals generated by the nearest available technical teams. This led dot a loss of opportunities for improving quality and directing collective actions that can be provided by, for instance, curricular materials produced by genuine processes of consultation and participation.

Political tensions are not dissociated from ideological and conceptual tensions. Some requirements for political monitoring arise from conceptual decisions, such as how to manage the tension between discipline-centred or child-centred curricula. In fact, one of the most difficult decisions in curriculum reforms is whether or not to reproduce the discipline-based structure of academic and university research areas as a curricular structure. The result of this decision involves many teachers and pupils. Sometimes it is not easy for them to understand why some disciplines have to disappear, be merged or split.

There are also at least four other ideological or conceptual tensions to be managed in curriculum reforms. The first, refers to the interests of religious, ethnic and cultural groups; the second, refers to the interests of professional groups having different languages and also interests; the third, refers to promoting skills or knowledge; and the fourth, refers to indicating information that has to be communicated and focuses on values and procedures to be learned—both of which are linked to one of the most important institutional tensions, between decision-makers at governmental and school levels.

In fact, one of the most relevant tensions that takes place during reforms, and specially during the current curriculum reforms, relates to what should be laid down by the authorities to educational institutions which—conceptually—everyone accepts should be increasingly autonomous.

Educational institutions and teachers go through very important experiences, but experiences are not necessarily synonymous with competency to create the education needed in the twenty-first century. Therefore, another two tensions that emerge during reform periods are those between experience and competency on the one hand and experience and capacity for innovation on the other.

It is also necessary to mention at least some of the many other institutional tensions. In all complex reform processes, it is necessary to manage different timings, which can be described as political, technical, bureaucratic and pedagogical. In poor countries, it is necessary to count upon the existence of career functionaries having stability but low salaries on one side, and the hiring of highly paid consultants but with unstable positions, following the demands of the donors.

To go through all of these tensions, reform leaders have to be very clear that if the timing, needs, languages and interests of each actor are considered separately, everything will lead to conserving the nineteenth century education. Only a new vision of educational reform can help the reformers go through these complexities.

Four Pillars for a New Vision of Educational Reform: Ideas, Information, Capacities and Resources

Expanding education, and especially improving the quality of educational processes throughout curriculum reform on the one side and innovation on the other side, needs a new vision for action.

This new vision assumes the centrality of empowerment, politics and policy. It promotes the access to four pillars: ideas, information, capacities and resources.

The available resources for education are not always enough and have to be increased. Whatever resources are available should be efficiently used.

Oftentimes, it is amazing how the same ideas are repeated in very different contexts. It is also amazing to see very interesting ideas, which could be useful in one special context, are not known or recognized elsewhere. The strengthening of dialogue and, as far as possible, of certain basic political and social consensus on educational contents and methods, can really help to both find new ideas and also utilize the old ones better.

Nowadays, an enormous amount of information exists, however, it is not always available. In order to direct reforms, the different teams need swift and smooth availability of relevant information on contents, methods, as well as on processes of consensus building, which may also be systematically articulated with quantitative, structural and qualitative information.

Lastly, it is said that there are not enough skilled people for undertaking the reforms. It is for this reason that the most important pillars to improve the capacities seem to be the strengthening of the collective and individual capacity of the actors at all levels of educational management and in the day-to-day activities of schools. This will allow the education personnel to participate in the processes of educational dialogue and consensus, to produce and use relevant information and to promote coherent reforms, especially curriculum reforms.

In other words, it is a question of promoting a virtuous circle between policy dialogue, availability, analysis and constant improvement of key information and the strengthening of the skills to mange the tensions. But there are two possibilities of managing the tensions. The first one, is to avoid complaints—letting things go on. The second one, is conducting the reforms in the decided direction, bearing in mind that reforms and especially curriculum reforms involve political, social and professional commitments.

The IBE intends to contribute in the construction of this virtuous circle, organizing opportunities for methodologies of exchange, information sharing and capacity-building through the promotion of networking in all the regions of the world. Networking could be in the form of ideas, information and capacities, which are available but unequally distributed. It is just a question of mobilizing them.

Reference

Meirieu, P. 2000. *L'école des parents: la grande explication.* Paris, Plon.

30

A Reflection on 'Learning to Learn': The Four Pillars of Learning and their Implications for Curriculum Reforms

Zhou Nanzhao

Introduction

The IBE-PROAP Capacity-Building Seminar for Curriculum Specialists is part of UNESCO's endeavour, in close co-operation with its Member States, to develop a broadened vision of educational contents and methods in emerging knowledge-based society and to facilitate a holistic approach to curricular reform/renewal in light of the guiding principle of learning throughout life.

In an information-intensive age, education is mandated to respond to demands in two directions: on the one hand, it has to transmit an increasing amount of constantly evolving knowledge and know-how adapted to a knowledge-driven civilization; on the other hand, it has to enable learners not to be overwhelmed by the flows of information, while keeping personal and social development as its end in view. To quote from the Delors Report, *Learning: the treasure within,* 'Education must ... simultaneously provide maps of a complex world in constant turmoil and the compass that will enable people to find their way in it' (p. 85).

The reform of curriculum content has become increasingly important, inasmuch as it is essential that what students learn is relevant to them as individuals and citizens, in their present and future context, as well as to community and societal development. It is not so much based on the delivery of 'facts' and knowledge, but rather on the skills of learning that can be consistently applied in an ongoing manner, long after leaving the formal education setting.

This presentation focuses on the changes in education emerging over the very recent past, which have mandated fundamental rethinking on roles of education and fundamental changes in the content of education. It is intended to contribute an alternative to the world-wide efforts in the reorganization of education. It is argued, as in the Delors Report, that if education is to succeed in its tasks, curriculum as its core should and could be restructured and re-built upon the four pillars of learning: *learning to know* for acquiring the instruments of understanding, *learning to live together* for co-operation with others in all human activities, and *learning to be* for the full flowering of human potential and multi-dimensional development of the 'complete person.'

The Context for 'Capacity Building'

With all the current rhetoric around the region relating to the reform of educational content, delivery and systems, it is essential to understand the content of and need for 'capacity building', as it has become known. In order to complete the process of educational reform, the following contextual factors articulate important pre-requisites for building the capacity of our education systems to deliver high quality and relevant curriculum to learners of all ages.

- Important new policy perspectives are emerging, and required, in the light of the changing nature and trends of development around the region.
- At the same time, these changes have led to a need for revision and improvement of the educational content provided to learners, so that what they learn is relevant to their lives and contexts.
- A broad understanding of the structures and theories of knowledge by those responsible for building the capacity of our education systems is fundamental, so that sound decisions are made.

- Similarly, specialized knowledge of the specific content and contexts of the various disciplines and subject areas is essential before changes can be properly made.
- No one can safely make changes to build the capacity of education without understanding the psychological characteristics and learning needs of the target groups.
- Finally, education policy-makers must have a thorough understanding of the pedagogical principles of organized teaching and learning.

The Need for Curriculum Reform

In essence, there is now a need for the fundamental reorganization and re-packaging of the educational content made available to learners.

School curriculum in most Asian education systems has been much over-loaded, and yet many educators have continued to attempt to include new content in the curriculum in order to reflect changes and new needs. Therefore, there is now widespread overcrowding of the total curriculum in most systems. Too much material is competing for a finite time available for delivery, with the result that some material is of necessity ignored or brushed over.

Further, education has traditionally not so much involved imparting the skills of learning, but rather the cramming of information and facts, often unrelated to the learners' needs, and largely due to the overcrowded curriculum. The content has also suffered from being narrow in focus and single-discipline oriented, without the benefits of establishing and building on links with other disciplines in an integrated approach for a broad education. Traditionally, there has been a bias against the affective, ethical and values dimension of curriculum content, now seen as vital for a balanced education.

The design and organization of education systems has usually been centralized, with the head offices directing in a top-down, one-way flow of education delivery in a unified and single-style approach. Tragically, the product delivered is all too often also irrelevant to the contemporary needs of learners.

The teaching of life skills and social skills has not previously been recognized as important, nor indeed defined. Life is infinitely more complex in the world of the twenty-first century, and it is important to ensure that learners are adequately equipped to deal with them.

It is also widely observed the that school system tends to cram a narrow range of information into students that specifically prepares them to gain admission into some tertiary course with its restricted entry criteria. This limited approach does not adequately prepare students for life after students leave the security of the formal learning centres and systems.

Changed/Changing Contexts in Curriculum Reform

A wide and very significant range of contextual changes combine to emphasize the importance of curriculum and education renewal. Several major factors can be identified:

- With the explosion of information and communication technologies around the world, we are witnessing the emergence and consolidation of a knowledge-based economy and society. Such a major change requires important and expanded roles for education.
- The rift between the rich and the poor around the region is not decreasing, but widening. The Asia-Pacific region has approximately 1.3 billion of its people living below the poverty line, living on less than US$ 1 per day, and increasingly helpless to alleviate this gap. Policy-makers now see education for poverty alleviation as one way of making some inroad into this dilemma.
- As an extension to this last scenario, we now have a new phenomenon described commonly as the 'digital divide', whereby the huge gap between those who have access to information and communication technology and those who do not is exacerbated. Strategic education policies and planning can go some way to reducing that gap.

- As signaled in the Delors Report, several tensions are emerging. One key example is the threat to the preservation of cultural identity and traditional indigenous knowledge in many communities, due to the overpowering globalization impacts of the knowledge society. There is a growing need for intercultural learning and international understanding, in order to redress this impact.
- Despite the many obvious progressive developments around the region, there are still many people who suffer from what can best be described as social exclusion, due to economic inequity. For instance, 800 million people are under-nourished, 1.3 billion are living without safe water, 880 million adults are functionally illiterate, and around 113 million children still have no access to primary education. Therefore, the absolute priority the UNESCO places on social equity and education for all (EFA) to reach the unrecalled is very soundly based.
- As a direct consequence of the emphasis around the region on economic growth at any cost, severe environmental and ecological degradation has occurred in many countries. The importance, therefore, of environmental education programmes that articulate sustainable growth and development cannot be over-emphasized.
- The processes of material progress and technical change have in many instances led to the alienation and de-humanization of many people. Introducing education programmes that focus on humanistic values can lessen these tragic effects.
- The increasing AIDS epidemic (18.8 million people in the region have died since 1983) shows the clear need for preventive education and culturally-based approaches to prevention and teacher training for 'life-skills' programmes.

A New Educational Vision for Action

These changing contexts demand a new vision for education, a vision that accepts the inalienable right for all people to have access to a relevant education, and that many problems and issues can successfully be addressed through appropriate educational policies and programmes.

In a broadening vision for education, it is increasingly accepted that education has expanded roles:

- as a fundamental human right;
- as an investment, for economic, social and political advantages;
- as a tool of empowerment for disadvantaged groups;
- as a principal means for the full development of human potential and individual talents;
- as a cornerstone for a culture of peace;
- as a major avenue towards the sound development of learning societies.

Major Shifts in Education

Over the past few ears, several major directional shifts in education have become apparent, which will have major implications for curricular changes:

- From 'schooling' (with the expectation that people only learn during their relatively brief time in the formal school system) to continuous lifelong education.
- From teaching as the delivery of curriculum content, to learning as an active role by the learner.
- From inequality of access to equality of education, or on other words, from 'the best education for the best' (most privileged students) to 'the best education for all'.
- From a focus on financial/material inputs, onto the learning process and the resultant outcomes.
- From a narrow, discipline-based curriculum and teacher-centred education, to a learner-centred, integrated, inter-disciplinary learning.
- From purely quantitative evaluation of cognitive learning achievements in teams of test scores, to qualitative as well as quantitative evaluation of all dimensions of learning outcomes.

- From rigid assessment of individual students/ teaches, to a broader assessment that includes school and system performance indicators.

The Four 'Pillars of Education' as Fundamentals

In order that educators and policy-makers understand the relevance of the four pillars, a brief snapshot follows of what each relates to in terms of educational context.

Learning to know

This pillar focuses on combining sufficiently broad general knowledge and basic education, such as might be experienced in elementary schooling, with the opportunity to work in depth on a small number of subjects, in the light of rapid changes brought about by scientific progress and new forms of economic and social activity. Specific aims include.

- to master the instrument of knowledge;
- to learn how to learn and to discover, so as to benefit from ongoing educational opportunities continuously arising (formally and non-formally) throughout life;
- to develop the faculties of memory, imagination, reasoning and problem-solving;
- to understand about his/her environment;
- to think in a coherent and critical way;
- to communicate with others;
- to acquire a knowledge of the scientific method and instruments;
- to develop a scientific spirit and an inquiring mind;
- to acquire independence of judgement.

Learning to do

Emphasis is on the learning of skills necessary to practice a profession or trade, including all schemes in which education and training interact with work. People also need to develop the ability to face a variety of situations, often unforeseeable, and to work in a team approach. Partnerships between education, business and industry are encouraged.

Key aims are:

- to apply in practice what has been learned;
- to develop vocational/occupational and technical skills;
- to develop social skills in building meaningful interpersonal relations;
- to transform knowledge into innovations and job-creation;
- to develop competence, a mix of higher skills, of social behaviour, of an aptitude for team work, and initiative/readiness to take risks;
- to develop personal commitment to work;
- to enhance the ability to communicate and to work with others;
- to manage and resolve conflicts.

Learning to be

The development of human potential to the fullest is the major priority of this pillar. As we go forward in the twenty-first century, everyone will need to exercise greater independence and judgement, combined with a stronger sense of personal responsibility.

An underpinning principle could be said to be 'the aim of development is the complement of man, in all the richness of his personality', with education contributing to the all-round development of each individual, in the face of the 'dehumanization and personality-alienation' that comes as a result of technical change. Education is above all an inner journey, the stages of which correspond to those of the continuous maturing of the personality. Education as a means to an end of a successful working life is thus a very individualized process. At the same time, it represents a process of constructing social interaction. Fundamental aims of learning to be include:

- cultivating qualities of imagination and creativity;
- developing diversified talents and dimensions of personalities—*aesthetic, artistic, literary, sporting, scientific, cultural and social;*

- developing critical thinking and exercising independent judgement;
- developing personal commitment and responsibility for the public good;
- tapping fully the talents (treasure) hidden within each individual.

Learning to live together

In the current content of globalization, the Delors Report places particular emphasis on this pillar. We must come to understand others, their history, traditions and cultures, living and interacting peacefully together. Aims of this pillar include:

- to discover others;
- to appreciate the diversity of the human race;
- to know oneself;
- to be receptive to others and to encounter others through dialogue and debate;
- to care about others;
- to work toward common objectives in co-operative undertakings;
- to manage and resolve conflicts.

Approaches to Curricular Renewal and Reform

Given that we have now entered the twenty-first century, it is absolutely essential that educators and policy makers use the broad framework of the four pillars of education and learning to develop a relevant education that will effectively meet the needs of the region's people. In summary, it is advocated that:

- the four pillars of education be used as guiding principles for educational content and practice, in line with the principle of lifelong learning.
- the four pillars of education be used as integrated components of teaching units in individual subjects;
- the four pillars of education be used as themes for inter-disciplinary studies and programmes on major

societal or scientific/technological themes, such as in the International Baccalaureate Organization's *Approaches to learning; theories of knowledge (modules as 'building-blocks' of learning);*

- diversification of curricular and extra-curricular activities be developed;
- decentralization of curriculum planning be implemented, taking into account the various needs of local learning communities:
- utilizing educational resources in virtual learning environments, in addition to traditional settings.

Conclusion

The four pillars of education, as articulated in the Delors Report, provide an excellent basis for the reform and renewal of the basic education curriculum in the Asia-Pacific region. If applied appropriately within the contextual settings around the region, these pillars will add great value to the relevance of curriculum content and the delivery of a quality education that is designed to meet the lifelong needs of learners in their communities.

31

Capacity-building for Curriculum Reforms: A South-East Asian Perspective

Tan Khun

Introduction

The new millennium has brought with it a heightened sense of urgency for a greater regional co-operation in virtually all spheres of human activities. This urgency is a gift of 'globalization', which began to gain momentum towards the end of the twentieth century to become the gospel of the twenty-first century. It also carries with it, its own share of novelties, problems, opportunities and complexities that call for responses and resolutions which transcend national boundaries. Education is one area of activity that has been among the earliest to recognize the value of and need for regional co-operation. Some thirty years before the term 'globalization' came into vogue, the countries of the Southeast Asian region formed SEAMEO (Southeast Asian Ministers of Education Organization, established on 30 November 1965, with the Secretariat based in Bangkok, Thailand). The objectives were to work towards 'strengthening regional understanding and co-operation in education, science and culture for a better quality of life.'

In keeping with its mission statement, SEAMEO is geared towards:

- The establishment of networks and partnerships;
- The provision of an intellectual forum for policy makers and experts; and

- The development of regional 'centres of excellence' for the promotion of sustainable human resource development.

Since its establishment thirty-five years ago, SEAMEO has achieved remarkable progress in human resource development among its member countries in the areas of education, science and culture. This has been made possible by the close links and spirit of co-operation that has prevailed over the years among the member and associate member countries. This spirit of co-operation can provide the foundation on which curricular reform in education could be built to enable the region's education systems to meet the challenges of globalization.

Current Status of Curricular Reforms in the Region

The term 'curriculum' as used here, refers to 'school' curriculum, or curriculum that constitutes a child's first eleven or twelve years of basic formal education—in the primary as well as secondary school environment. Within this setting, a comparative overview of the region's diverse school curricula becomes possible and meaningful.

A study of the region's new or 'about-to-be-adopted' national school curricula will reveal some common trends in the curricular reforms expected to be implemented by the respective countries. The following are some of the common trends:

Increased democratization of educational opportunities

In all countries of the SEAMEO region, serious efforts have been made towards providing free and/or compulsory education up to the ninth or even the twelfth year of school education. This augurs well to increase literacy rates and usher in an era where an educated population is receptive to concepts such as lifelong learning, continuing education self-improvement.

Raised profile of selected components of the curricula

This is especially true in science and mathematics, information technology usage and application, and the acquisition of an international language—especially English.

Serious efforts have been made towards a balanced curriculum in each country, such as, integrating elements of various components across the curriculum. However, it is quite apparent that the above three components stand out in all the reformed curricula or 'about-to-be-reformed' curricula. The rationale behind these components' prominence is in line with global trends as the looming dominance of the k-economy would invariably require that the human resources of any region be scientifically literate, and IT-functional.

Pedagogical shift towards child-centered, activity-based methodology

Increasingly, the curricula of the countries in the region advocate a shift from the traditional teacher-centred methodology towards one that is child-centred and activity-based. This move is not entirely a new one but it does differ from the previous ones in that it goes beyond mere child-centred activities (such as lists of procedures in science practical) towards involving students in problem-solving and investigative work. Such a trend would entail the employment of a wide selection of teaching strategies, such as co-operative learning, higher-order of thinking skills and active learning.

Assessment, move towards alternatives

While the traditional paper-and-pencil tests still prevail in the regional curricula, such traditional notions of academic assessment through a single valid way are increasingly giving way to the application of alternative instruments of assessment. These alternatives, designed in forms such as portfolios, projects, self-assessment, etc., would provide a more holistic representation of the students' knowledge and progress. Thus, this move represents a shift from the traditionally upheld instruments based on verbal-linguistics and logical-mathematical skills towards assessments that include a greater range of human capacities and intelligences, in tune with prevailing global trends on school assessment.

SEAMEO'S Role in Curricular Reform in the Region

'Curriculum', whether taken in its narrow sense or viewed in a broader perspective, has to in any case be effectively implemented to produce the desired outcome. Effective implementation entails aspects of: planning, teaching, learning and assessing. All these aspects constitute major domains of teachers education and training programmes—for the professional development of teachers. Successful implementation of a curriculum would require efficient and well-equipped implementers—the professional teachers. In the same vein, any curricular reform depends greatly on the implementers at the school level: the quality of the school managers and teachers. In this respect, the emerging scenario in some member countries of the SEAMEO region is cause for major concerns. In the countries of the Indo-China region, for sample, there are shortages of teaching staff— the untrained teachers and the under-trained teachers implement the curriculum without sufficient understanding, thus compromising the curricular reform.

SEAMEO, as a regional organization committed to promoting regional co-operation in matters related to education and human resource development, plays a positive role in helping the member countries to overcome difficulties faced in implementing their curriculum so that they may maximally benefit from these reforms. SEAMEO has currently fourteen centres of specialized institutions hosted by member countries. Each centre's primary focus is on training educational personnel, besides engaging in research, consultancy and training capacity that go beyond its 'core' mandate. These centres are structured in three groupings, namely: (a) learning, (b) health, (c) agriculture, natural resources, environment. Of the three groupings, three centres oppropriately support curricular implementation and reforms in basic education. These three centres have a direct impact on and contribute to capacity-building towards curricular reform. These are: (i) Regional Centre for Education in Science and Mathematics (SEAMEO-RECSAM); (ii) Regional Language Centre (SEAMEO-RELC); and (iii) Regional Centre for Educational Innovation and Technology (SEAMEO-INNOTECH).

The above-mentioned centres have, over the past three decades, built up a wealth of experience and expertise in training and professional activities aimed at enhancing the skills of teachers, educators and school managers in their respective fields. Their specializations correspond to the core concerns of the member countries' curricular reforms in science and mathematics, English language, educational leadership and innovations for development.

Building the capacities of teachers and school managers is essential to fully realize the potential of any curriculum implementation and reform. The three SEAMEO centres that have been singled out to be in the forefront of the organization's involvement in the region's curricular reform have been making tireless efforts at enhancing the skills of the grassroots workers at school level for the past three decades or so. These workers are none other than the teachers and managers of the countless schools in the region. As the region progresses, societal demands and expectations on the schools become greater, making their tasks more complex and multifarious. These three centres with their specializations are by no means adequate to successfully meet the targets set in relation to curricular reforms by each country. However, as their specialized expertise is directly relevant to the core-elements of the reforms, it is hoped that their efforts and contributions in basic capacity-building towards effective curricular reform in the region's education systems would be significant. SEAMEO, as a whole, is sensitive to the need to continuously re-orient and adapt itself to new situations in order to stay abreast of new developments and changes in the new age. The centres' activities reflect this philosophy, and their training programmes are continuously upgraded to meet new requirements. Presently, all of the three centres have sufficient room and training capacity to accommodate an increase in the number of trainees. The good news is that a certain momentum has already been generated and no longer are prohibitive external inputs required to take the great strides necessary to keep pace with the ceaseless changes that characterize our times.

Section 2

Strengthening Capacities for Curriculum Reform

Analyzing Existing Curriculum Frameworks for Change

Lucille C. Gregorio

Background

A project—'Curriculum Innovations in Basic Education: Preparing the Learners to Meet the Challenges of the New Millenium'—has received extra-budgetary support from the Japanese Funds-in-Trust grant to UNESCO. The implementation of the project was initiated in September 2000, with the preparation of a concept paper for joint programming between the International Bureau of Education (IBE) and the UNESCO Principal Regional Office for Asian and the Pacific (PROAP). The partnership with IBE took concrete steps during the Seminar on 'Capacity-building for Curriculum Specialists in the East and South-East Asia Region,' held in Bangkok, Thailand in December 2000. This was hosted by the Ministry of Education, Thailand, with eleven countries and one SEAMEO Regional Centre participating. These were: Cambodia, China, Indonesia, Japan, Lao PDR, Malaysia, Mongolia, Philippines, Republic of Korea, Thailand, Viet Nam, and SEAMEO RECSAM. The seminar was aimed at building capacities in the areas of curriculum reform and innovation at primary and secondary levels, and also to prepare the participating countries in undertaking the 'Situation Analysis of the Existing Curriculum,' as a basis for pursuing curriculum reforms.

Rationale of the Project

The South-East and East Asian region is faced with a difficult situation as a result of the economic downturn leading to a new economic and social order. The region is also challenged to cope with the scientific and technological progress and the advances in information and communication technology, which are mostly happening in the developed world. Despite continuous efforts to improve the science education programmes, society believes that the reforms taking place are still slow. Curriculum structure and content and the teachers' skills become increasingly out-dated. Even in cases where formal educational institutions succeed in keeping up-dated with the advances in knowledge, information learned in school soon becomes obsolete in a short period of time. Furthermore, educational reforms are not implemented effectively.

Both regionally and internationally, there have been trends toward curricular reforms and innovations to introduce learner-centred educational content and systemic changes responding to national/regional development needs. However, a large gap needs to be filled to build national capacities for curriculum reform through intellectual guidance and advisory services, UNESCO intends to fill this gap.

In August 1999, *Asiaweek* mentioned twenty trends for the new millenium that are expected to shape developments in the Asian region and the world, and the lives of people in the years ahead—both positively and negatively. Most of these are attributed to science and technology advances, and the introduction of new forms of technology, i.e. 'the power of the microchips.'

We are wondering, however, how the advances in science and technology will affect a region characterized by a wide range of diversity—economically, politically, geographically, culturally, etc. In 1995, the Asian region had 60% of the world's population, 625 million out of the 885 million adult illiterates of the world, 74 million children, comprising 50% of the world's unschooled children. Some 64% of the illiterates are women, and 66% of children not enrolled in schools are girls. Of course, most of these are in Southern Asia. Many countries are predominantly rural and agricultural with low per capita income and high population growth rate; high unemployment; and with a high incidence of HIV/AIDS, and generally live below the poverty level. The World Forum on Education of All (Dakar, 2000) showed some improvements in the above figures, but these are not significant enough. Besides, the 'quality of education' has not been given enough emphasis.

In 1993, Project 2000+: Scientific and Technological Literacy for All was launched at the UNESCO Headquarters in Paris, within the framework of 'Education for All'. The provision for providing basic learning needs of youth and adults recognizes the need for a scientifically and technologically literate society. Scientific and Technological Literacy will provide learners with an understanding of the positive use of science and technology for the social good, provide opportunities for rational decisions to prevent destruction of the physical environment, to preserve and ensure the survival of the future generation, and allow cultures to renew cultural traditions with scientific wisdom.

The 30C/5 (UNESCO's Draft Programme and Budget, 2000-2001), stresses the need for 'renewal of curricula, focusing on integration of various curricular elements,' and the need to intensify science and technology education (STE), with emphasis on scientific knowledge and technical skills necessary for meaningful participation in the knowledge society of the future. The activities envisioned in this project would closely link to UNESCO's regular programme and would be included in the 'monitoring and evaluation plan.'

The World Conference on Science organized by UNESCO and the International Council for Science, help in Hungary in June 1999, recommended that gender and cultural diversity, and response to educational and societal needs be considered in curriculum development. The conference also recognized that science education reforms will not solve problems without 'social change', and therefore, the participation of social science and humanities was well applauded. It was during the Conference that the World Social Science Report was launched.

The Delors Report, the main sources of inspiration on education for the twenty-first century, proposed reorientation and reorganization of education systems based on the guiding principle of 'learning throughout life,' building on the 'four pillars of learning' (learning to know, learning to do, learning to be, learning to live together) through curricular innovations/reforms.

The 6 September 1999 issue of *Asiaweek* points out the 'Asians have always been proud of how well they educate their children'. The Third Science and Mathematics Study has shown that Japan, Korea and Singapore scored highest in science and mathematics compared to the rest of the countries participating in the study. However, governments are realizing that the young learners are not at all prepared to meet the new millenium—'where thinking and creativity' would be the most important attributes.

There are also questions being raised today, as to whether the present teaching/learning in school and out of school provide learners with opportunities to create their own abilities to develop skills and competencies in acquiring and processing information, in risk taking, and develop self-confidence in solving problems and decisions-making.

This project, therefore, seeks to look into the strengths and weaknesses of the curriculum for basic education of the eleven participating countries in East and South-East Asia, moving towards a sub-regional strategy for developing a curriculum framework for the learners of the twenty-first century.

The Project Goal and Outcomes

The project will provide some assessment of the quality of learning at the basic level, and the effectiveness in preparing the learners for the challenge of the new millenium, with 'lifelong learning' as the ultimate goal. Considerations would be based not only on the recommendations of the world conferences held from 1990, but more so in the "our Pillars of Learning,' advocated by the International Commission on Education for the Twenty-first Century.

To attain this goal, a regional framework and guidelines were agreed upon by the participants of the capacity-building seminar.

The Situation Analysis Guidelines and Framework

Part I: A situation analysis of the National Curriculum for Basic Education

1. *Brief introduction / background on the national curriculum:*
   (a) Pertinent laws and policies bearing on the national curriculum for basic education;
   (b) The underlying philosophy and rationale of the national curriculum;
   (c) Major goals and objectives of basic education;
   (d) Vision of a student completing primary-level, elementary-level, and secondary-level education (as expressed in terms of specific knowledge and competencies learned and acquired by the student).
2. *Curriculum development and design:*
   (a) Description of the prevailing organizational structures and mechanisms and consultation processes involved in curriculum;
   (b) Development (the role of ministries/departments of education, other national bodies, regional agencies, and local schools and communities in curriculum development; balancing the demands of the prescribed core curriculum with local needs and circumstances or the autonomy of schools in translating the core curriculum into a school-based curriculum);
   (c) An overview of the existing curriculum design for basic education describing the subject matter or topical coverage by grade level or year and the number of hours/minutes devoted to each subject or topic at the primary, elementary and secondary grades.
3. *The implementation of the national curriculum:*
   (a) The adoption of the national curriculum in the formal school system (or by public and private schools);

(b) Existing infrastructure support for the national curriculum (i.e. the adequacy of classrooms and physical facilities, and of equipment, laboratories and libraries in schools and learning centers);

(c) The state of textbooks and instructional materials;

(d) The training of teachers in subject matter/topical content, pedagogy updates, and the use of textbooks and other instructional materials.

4. *Feedback (monitoring, reporting and evaluation) mechanisms on the implementation of the national curriculum:*

(a) Institutional supervision and reporting systems adopted by schools, regional bodies and national ministries/departments of education;

(b) Achievement indicators (enrolment rates and drop-out rates by grade/year level; per cent passing of national achievement tests or qualifying examinations at primary, elementary and secondary levels);

(c) External or commissioned reviews regularly or periodically undertaken by special committees or task forces on the curriculum or the education sector;

(d) Research-based studies on the state and effectiveness of various aspects of the national curriculum and its implementation, i.e., as research on the effectiveness of curriculum content, existing pedagogies and instructional approaches, teacher training, and of textbooks and instructional materials).

5. *A discussion on the specific strengths and weaknesses of the national curriculum and its implementation:*

(a) Its strengths;

(b) Its weaknesses;

(c) Summary of the major recommendations for improving the national curriculum.

6. *Recent and ongoing curricular reform initiatives:*

(a) Status of implementation;

(*b*) Factors facilitating and/or constraining the implementation of curricular reform initiatives.

7. *Summary and conclusions: assessment of the National Curriculum for Basic Education.*

Part II: Proposing a new framework for revising and updating the curriculum in basic education

1. *Revisiting the goals and objectives of basic education against the background of current-day demands and realities.*
2. *Visioning or imaging the growth and development of students in the new millennium as they go through the various levels of basic education.*
3. *Integrating the principle of learning/education throughout life (as against simply education for higher learning or education for work, cf. the Delors Report) into the underlying rationale and philosophy of basic education.*
4. *Integrating/incorporating the four pillars of learning expounded in the Delors Report (learning to live together, learning to know, learning to do and learning to be) into the learning outcomes of the basic education curriculum along with the following:*

   (*a*) The knowledge and concepts to be learned/acquired by students (learning to know);

   (*b*) The mental (thinking, reasoning, etc.) faculties, emotional skills and qualities, the creative/aesthetic sense, the spiritual well-being, or the self-knowledge, discovery and development to be encouraged among students (learning to be);

   (*c*) The attitudes and values to be imparted to students with some emphasis placed on those supportive of tolerance and peace, respect for others and social cohesion and harmony (learning to live together); and

   (*d*) The practical application skills and work-related experiences and competencies to be similarly developed among students (learning to do).

5. *Promoting interdisciplinary in the basic education curriculum:*
   - (a) Reconceptualizing subject-matter contents into interrelated themes or topics (as against dividing these into separate subjects or fields of studies) and highlighting their coherence and connectedness;
   - (b) Reorienting instructional methods and pedagogies towards interdisciplinary and more holistic approaches.
6. *Proposals (for workshops, training seminars, development of new teaching modules and materials and other activities) for further advancing the new framework for a basic education curriculum.*

Future Plans

The participants from the eleven countries went back to undertake a 'Situation Analysis of the Existing Curriculum,' in their respective countries. By the middle of 2001 we expect to publish the eleven country situation analyses and a regional synthesis.

Based on the outcome of the country situation analysis, a sub-regional strategy for developing a curriculum framework for the learners of the twenty-first century will be formulated. This will be latter utilized for the 'Training of Curriculum Developers and Teacher Trainers of Curriculum Change.'

The Role of Information and Knowledge in Curriculum Development

Isabel Byron

The New Demands for Education

Curriculum development is a complex ongoing process, which must constantly change to reflect changes in broader society and to take into account evolving knowledge about learning and developmental processes. Effective curriculum development for adequately meeting learner needs should involve constant reflection, debate and decision-making about what is to be learned and why, how it is to be learned, the roles of teacher and learner in the educational process, the roles of other stakeholders, and the relationship between the school and the community.

Regular curriculum renewal is considered increasingly necessary in education systems around the world due to the rapid changes taking place in contemporary society. According to Skilbeck (1998), curriculum renewal may be defined as 'the gearing of educational contents and procedures to a changing and uncertain world'. This world is characterized, among other things, by evermore-rapid technological and scientific development; a growing dependence on information and knowledge as the most important resources for economic advancement; an increasingly globalized economy leading to growing inequality between rich and poor countries; an ever greater intermingling of peoples and cultures; severe ethnic, cultural and political conflicts in many countries; and an erosion of traditional value systems in nearly all societies.

The issues listed here along with a number of others discussed in other chapters of this report indicate the great challenges posed to the process of curriculum development and reform in today's society. The rapid pace of change, and the central role played by information and knowledge in development, have led to an ongoing debate about the nature and purpose of learning in school and in society, with the meaning of education being re-examined and redefined. Traditional education has proved to be inadequate for the needs of the 'postmodern' society. As discussed elsewhere in this report, acquiring the four pillars of knowledge—learning to know, learning to do, learning to be, and learning to live together—is advocated as the desired objective of the educational process, equipping individuals with the knowledge and skills needed to learn throughout life, to be productive and active citizens, enabling continued personal growth, enhanced economic and social development, and fostering social cohesion (Delors at al., 1996). The concept of 'learning to learn' has come to dominate educational discourse, being seen as the ultimate outcome of learning.[1]

To equip young people in this way requires a huge shift in the traditional contents and methods of education as they continue to exist in the majority of schools around the world. The concept and meaning of knowledge has altered. It is no longer considered finite and unchanging, but is seen instead to be continuously evolving. New discoveries are constantly being made and new ways of interpreting and doing things are being found, with some knowledge rapidly becoming obsolete. Knowledge is also no longer seen as compartmentalized in rigid disciplinary fields, but rather the relationships and interrelationships between different fields are recognized. The learner is acknowledged to play in active role in constructing knowledge as he/she interprets and interacts with the surrounding world.

Furthermore, the learning of a range of skills, attitudes and behaviours needed for living in contemporary society is considered as important as the acquiring of knowledge itself, and they are, in fact, seen as an integral part of knowledge. Many of these skills and behaviours focus on preparation for the needs of the labour market.[2] Others are concerned more generally with fostering personal and social well-being. These changes have great implications when deciding what and how to teach in schools.

To respond to these new concepts of education, much emphasis is being placed on interdisciplinary learning and integrated curricula, as well as on student-centred, activity-based approaches.

In light of the new demands on the curriculum development process, it is increasingly agreed that it should involve a wide range of actors or stakeholders, not just educational policy-makers, researchers and curriculum specialists, but community leaders, representatives from economic sectors, future employers, parents, students and, most importantly, the teachers themselves. In this overview of the role of information in curriculum development, the target group being considered is those primarily responsible for curriculum design. This would include directors of curriculum development units and curriculum/subject specialists working in such institutions or in schools, as well as academic faculty working directly with education departments and schools in this field, teacher educators, school principals and some teachers.

Curriculum developers have the task of translating educational policy decisions into detailed curriculum plans for individual subject areas, specific grades and levels of education. The level of freedom or autonomy given to them in this task varies from country to country, as does the degree to which the curriculum development process is a truly participatory one. Whatever the situation, the main actors in the process should be equipped to make suitably informed decisions about what and how children learn in schools.

What Type of Information is Needed?

Decision-making for curriculum developers is often dictated by external forces and pressures: political decisions, world economic trends, the increasing urge to be competitive and to respond to the international drive for change. Often, there is insufficient time for reflection and considered use of research findings and other documented knowledge. Nevertheless, systematic use of information is felt to be essential to quality educational provision (Reimers and McGinn, 1995, 1998).

Curriculum developers need access to information which is up-to-date, reliable, relevant, and expressed in language which is easily understood. Educational professionals ideally need orientation towards quality information suitable for their specific needs. They will want information packaged in a way which concisely presents solutions or practical approaches to specific issues. In an information age, skilled management of information and knowledge is considered vital to the success of any sector, including education. In order for knowledge to be managed effectively, educational professionals themselves need to understand the processes of knowledge creation, dissemination and application (OECD, 2000).

Reimers and McGinn define information as 'knowledge that reduces uncertainly' (1995, p. 20). The OECD distinguishes between information and knowledge, establishing the latter as 'a stock of experience', rather than a mere product (2000, p. 57). Knowledge is classified into four categories, namely, 'know what' (facts or information); 'know why' (principles that explain phenomena); 'know how' (competence and skills); 'know who' (who knows what and who knows what to do) (ibid., pp. 14-17). Curriculum professionals need all of these types of knowledge, which will come from different sources and may be more or less easily obtained. As the OECD publication explains, while 'know what' and 'know why' may be recorded in databases and various published media, 'know how' and 'known who' depend not only on recorded data, but also on huma interaction and social relationships. To obtain access to these types of knowledge, training, interaction with a range of actors and effective professional networking are vital.

There is a wide range of educational information arising from a multitude of sources. Listed below are a number of types of information felt to be necessary or useful for effective curriculum development, although the list is not intended to be exhaustive:

- Major political, social, economic, cultural trends at national and international levels;
- Specific information about the labour market, predictions of future training needs;
- Educational policies at national, regional and international levels;
- Curriculum development and reform processes and trends in other countries (in the same region, in countries at similar levels of development, in more developed countries);
- Recent research findings on learning and development, curriculum development and student achievement;
- Recent research in fields central to curriculum development: philosophy of education, psychology of education, sociology of education;
- Comparative research and studies;
- Curricular approaches within specific subject fields;
- Innovative teaching/learning methods;
- Information on students' needs and interests;
- Information on existing classroom practices, teacher attitudes and behaviour;
- Information on community needs and interests;
- Approaches to avoid in curriculum development; what hasn't worked nationally or in other contexts—and why;
- Information on the nature of knowledge and its effective management;
- Information on the process and management of innovation and change.

In addition to information for making decisions, curriculum specialists need to know how to communicate their own decisions to others, to teachers in particular, but also to parents and other key stakeholders in the educational process.

At the same time, it should be recognized that curriculum developers are also producers of information and knowledge themselves. They may be researchers in their own right and may have been teachers in the past. Their professional experience has given them very significant knowledge, but they also need the skills to put this to effective use by passing in on to others.

Curriculum specialists need to understand the process of change in order to implement innovation. Successful curricular innovation can only come about through carefully planned collaborative efforts involving all key partners in the educational process. Anderson (1992) observes that effective curriculum reform requires systemic change, that the various elements of the education system are dynamically interconnected and are also linked to other social systems. Curriculum change will have impacts throughout the system and all those involved in reform should be made aware of and be prepared for their role in the process. Anderson further stresses that, in today's context, curricular change is likely to be ongoing and long term, while those involved in the process need to understand the dynamics of this situation.

Sources of Information for Curriculum Development

Electronic sources

The information technology revolution has transformed the possibilities for disseminating and accessing information. Key sources of information of potential use to curriculum developers, to be found through electronic means include: databases and databanks; and on-line journals and websites of numerous institutions working in education. The Internet also provides access to fora and discussion groups — a new medium which is potentially very useful for sharing information, views and expertise among curriculum professionals on an international level.

Networking

Interacting with others, both within and outside one's profession, is a very important means of obtaining information and increasing one's knowledge. Networks, now revolutionized by the new information technologies, are strongly recommended as means of crating, disseminating and applying knowledge. Ideally, they provide opportunities not merely for exchange of information, but for collaborative efforts which allow the learning and practical application of new knowledge (OECD, 2000, pp. 74-76). Interaction with sectors and professionals outside the education sector can bring in new ideas and approaches which can enhance the quality and accelerate the pace of the change process.

Training

Training opportunities provide an ideal means of obtaining new knowledge, and making new contacts. Training tends, however, to be expensive and time-consuming. The type of continuous training which would be available to curriculum professionals would normally be short-term intensive seminars or workshops. Often opportunities for follow-up are limited or non-existent. In this regard, networking is all the more recommended.

Impediments to the Use of Information

The extent to and ways by which information and new knowledge are used by curriculum specialists in the regular course of their profession is an area which needs to be studied in detail, in order to improve the management of information and knowledge. There are a number of challenges relating to the effective provision of information to meet the new demands for curriculum development and reform.

1. In most developing countries, those involved in curriculum development find it hard to obtain adequate up-to-date quality information to carry out their work. Educational documentation centres in ministries and curriculum development centres, if they exist, may be poorly stocked and badly run. Libraries in universities and research centres may have limited resources. Access to the Internet is often still difficult, irregular and requires considerable investment. Pertinent publications listed on the Web are likely not to be available in local libraries, or exist only in English, the principal language for the reporting of research.

2. Even where Internet technology is readily available, it does not yet provide unlimited access to knowledge. Furthermore, even in contexts where information is readily available, there is no guarantee that it will be adequately exploited. Studies into information utilization by educational policy/decision-makers and practitioners cite a number of reasons for this, one being the limited time these professionals have to access, read and assimilate information. They typically have very busy schedules, which means that opportunities for regular, in-depth reading on educational issues, and in particular research findings, are very limited (Anderson, 1992).
3. It is argued that education as a field of academic study is not properly grounded in scientific principles, and has depended on social science disciplines, such as sociology, psychology and philosophy, for its academic base, a practice that has led to the neglect of the study of actual educational phenomena. Despite advances in cognitive psychology, it is felt that much is still not known and misunderstood about the learning process essential knowledge if students are to be taught to learn how to learn and become lifelong learners (OECD, 2000).
4. Research-based information is felt to be indispensable to improving educational provision. (Reimers, McGinn & Wild, 1995; OECD, 2000). However, educational research has had limited impact on either educational policy making or practice in systems around the world. There are a number of reasons offered to explain this:
   (a) *Irrelevance:* Educational research tends to be largely restricted to academic institutions, with limited involvement on the part of decision-makers or practitioners. Much research is not undertaken with the decision-maker or practitioner in mind, but primarily to serve the interests of the researcher and the institution where he/she works. Reimers and McGinn (1998, p. 20) observe that, 'in many countries, much of the educational research is produced in universities and is conceived, funded and carried out in ways that have limited links to potential users, and which do not take into account

the perspectives of users in drawing the implications of findings.' The findings often have little direct relevance to curriculum design or classroom practice.

(b) *Inaccessibility:* Research findings tend to be published in academic journals and presented in recondite, technical language (Reimers, McGinn & Wild, 1995). According to one writer, 'researchers often have greater interest and experience in the generation of new knowledge than in its communication to others' (Anderson, 1992, p. 1).

(c) *Lack of sufficient authority/persuasiveness,* (OECD, 2000). The findings of much educational research are inconclusive and do not answer the practical questions being sought by those making decisions about what to teach and how.

(d) *The inadequacy of the education system itself,* which may make it resistant to or incapable of change (ibid.). This last point is fundamental issue in the whole process of reform, and not merely related to issues of research use.

5. A further challenge to the accessibility of knowledge about the educational process is that a lot of it tends to be what is termed 'tacit' knowledge. This means that it is not explicit and clearly recorded or codified, allowing for easy transfer, dissemination and integration into professional practice. Much tacit knowledge is of the 'know how' variety. Teachers' knowledge, in particular, is felt to be largely tacit. While some of this knowledge is tacit by nature, some is so because no efforts have been made to document it (OECD, 2000). This has implications for curriculum developers. Who need to work closely with teachers in producing and disseminating knowledge about good instructional practice.

Responding to the Challenges

It is clearly necessary not simply to improve access to information, but to increase opportunities to use and reflect on this information, as well as to create new knowledge, and apply it to the curriculum development process.

Improving the quality and relevance of research

Hargreaves argues for more systematic research and documenting of good practice in schools, in order to improve the knowledge base available to teachers. This research should be collaborative and rooted in practice, jointly carried out by practitioners and academics (ibid.). Participatory approaches in the production of knowledge through research will promote dialogue, reflection and negotiation, and lead to the growth of organizational learning (Reimers & McGinn, 1998). They will also result in a better understanding of the process of change in various contexts of educational practice (Hargreaves, 1999).

Such a knowledge base would clearly be of great value to curriculum developers, who need to know what works in schools in order to design appropriate programmes. They should be key partners in such research initiatives, which would enable the sharing of human and technical resources in the research process. Moreover, with school-based curriculum development increasingly advocated as possibly the most effective means of curriculum design, teachers as curriculum designers will need to possess such a source of well-documented knowledge (Kelly, 1999). All parties would have to be trained in how to develop and maintain such collaboration so as to make it genuinely fruitful, with an adequate support structure established.

Improving the dissemination of information

The issue of dissemination must be central to efforts to improve the use of information in curriculum development. Information needs to be better packaged and marketed, with appropriate exploitation of ICTs. Reimers and McGinn (1995, p. 28) state that, for effective reporting, research information should be *relevant to real problems, practical, useful, credible, understandable* and *provided in a timely fashion.* State-of-the-art reviews and digests of selected research and outcomes, such as those produced by the ERIC database, are potentially useful ways of selecting and synthesizing research.

Anderson (1992) recommends that a prototype communications strategy be designed by researchers to communicate the results of research and innovation effectively in relation to curriculum reform. She recommends that research teams have a staff member responsible for communicating and also that they should hire a professional writer familiar with educational issues and with the various audiences to prepare reports and brochures disseminating research results. She suggests that, for dissemination to be effective, it should seek to use communication channels that are already familiar to/popular with users, and she advocates use of a constructivist approach to information dissemination, i.e. providing opportunities by potential users for interaction with and application of the knowledge.

Dissemination cannot be effective in itself. Knowledge has to be internalized, reflected on and used in professional practice, as it appropriate. Relevant training and networking structures will assist this process of knowledge transfer (OECD, 2000).

Managing information and knowledge

OECD argues for a clearly defined knowledge management policy within educational institutions. From the perspective of this paper, this may include curriculum development centres and ministries of education. Knowledge management is defined as 'management of the intellectual capital' of an institution (OECD, 2000, p. 70). Some of the elements considered necessary for managing knowledge include: (a) effective use of networking and of ICTs; (b) defining and establishing a new relationship between educational research and practice that would involve joint production and dissemination of knowledge; and (c) designing an infrastructure to support the process at national, regional and local levels. Such an infrastructure should provide resources for networking, training, information services and other aspects of the process, and decentralize responsibility to regional and local levels (ibid.).

The information broker's role

In order to facilitate access to and use of quality information for educational development, the concept of 'information broker' or 'knowledge broker' has emerged. This role could be assumed by individuals working within education or research institutions, or operating as freelance experts, who would assist in bridging the gap between research, decision-making and practice. They would identify and select relevant research, summarize/synthesize the findings in an easily readable style to the targeted users, and make it regularly available to them. They would be able to provide comparative state-of-the-art reviews and analyses of relevant research, and inform and report on the progress of ongoing studies. They should have the ability to assess the validity of research findings and present alternative findings on particular issues.

Information brokers should have the capacity to anticipate information needs. Those working with curriculum developers would need to be well informed about existing curriculum practice and knowledgeable about international as well as local educational trends. One of their functions could be to co-ordinate training seminars to discuss and analyse leading new trends and research findings of relevance to educational practice.

In some cases, the profile of knowledge broker has been seen as that of a policy analyst, a researcher trained to communicate research-based information to the public (Reimers & McGinn, 1998). The report of the International Meeting on Educational Reform and Educational Research (1995), on the other hand, identified the need for such a profile to be developed within the profession of documentation/information workers.

The role of information broker is being increasingly played by national and international institutions. These may be research and development institutions, national or regional information networks, such as ERIC in the United States or the Asian Pacific Programme of Educational Innovation for Development (APEID), or international organizations, such as the IBE.

Notes

1. The various requirements for learning to learn include:
    - being motivated to learn throughout life;

- being skilled at identifying one's own learning needs or knowing how to get help with this task;
- being able to identify the kind of education and training to meet those needs and how it is assessed;
- being able to acquire a range of meta-cognitive skills—thinking about ones own thinking, learning how to be flexible with learning styles and strategies;
- being able to think independently and in a range of contexts (work, leisure, home) other than formal educational organizations;
- learning how to access information and knowledge form the new world of the information and communication technologies (OECD, 2000, p. 74).

2. An important observation of Reimers and McGinn (1998) is that, while the current educational discourse relating to preparation for the job market originated in the developed world to reflect changes in economic production, it is also the driving force for educational reform in the developing world often without research having been carried out to show that such change is really necessary or viable for these countries.

References

Anderson, B. 1992. *Successful curriculum reform: sharing the knowledge with policymakers and practitioners in ways that influence practice.* Boulder, CO, Colorado University.

Delors, J., et al. 1996. *Learning: the treasure within.* Paris, UNESCO, (Report to UNESCO of the International Commission on Education for the Twenty-first Century.)

Hargreaves, D. 1999. The knowledge-creating school. *British journal of educational studies* (Oxford, UK), vol. 47, no 2. pp. 122-44.

Husén, T., et al. 1998. *Education: the complete encyclopedia*—CD-ROM (version 1.1). Elsevier Science.

International Bureau of Education; National Institute for Education Research of Japan. 1995. *International Meeting on Educational Reform and Educational Research: new challenges in linking research, information and decision-making: final report.* Geneva, Switzerland, IBE.

Kelly, A.V. 1999. *The curriculum: theory and practice,* 4th ed. London, Paul Chapman Publishing.

Organization for Economic Co-operation and Development. 2000. *Knowledge management in the learning society*. Paris, OECD.

Reimers, F.; McGinn, N.; Wild, K. 1995. *Confronting future challenges: educational information, research and decision-making*. Paris, UNESCO.

Reimers, F.; McGinn, N. 1998. *Informed dialogue: using research to shape educational policy around the world.* Westport, CT, Praeger.

Skilbeck, M. 1998. Curriculum renewal. *In:* Husén, T., et al. *Education: the complete encyclopaedia*—CD-ROM. Elsevier Science.

Role of Communication within the Framework of Curricular Reform

Liliana Jabif

Introduction

Globalization and its implications, as observed in the Delors Report,[1] has not only consequences for the economic dimension of human activity but also for the socio-cultural and ethical dimensions with regard to the growing inter-dependence and inter-relationships between peoples and cultures. The need for human beings to strive towards a deeper understanding amongst themselves has never been greater. The augmentation and reform of school curricula has hence become an ever more relevant preoccupation.

In this context, the training seminar organized by the International Bureau of Education (IBE) and the UNESCO Principal Regional Office for Asia and the Pacific (PROAP) in Bangkok, Thailand, from 12 to 15 December 2000, focused on capacity building in fundamental skills for effective curriculum development.

One of the seminar's objectives was to develop wide-ranging competencies related to systematic process of curriculum reform, within the perspective of 'learning to learn.' In this framework, a workshop on relevant communication skills to the curriculum development process was organized. The main goal was to discuss, reflect and draw guidelines related to some of these questions: What do we need to communicate? To whom? In which way? The process of the workshop design and implementation will be discussed in this paper.

The Design Stage

The demand

Within the broad framework of the seminar, the concrete demand was for the design of a workshop that would provide an opportunity for discussion and analysis of problems linked to the strategies for communicating educational policies in the process of curriculum change.

The first step

To start with, information on shared experiences in similar contexts was collected. In this regard, documents[2] were studied and interviews carried out with key informants[2] were studied and interviews carried out with key informants[3] with the aim of understanding the context better and obtaining a deeper appreciation of the details of some of the experiences that had been carried out by IIEP[4] in the framework of the development of communications skills for educational policy-makers.

This preliminary exploration led to a decision to go beyond the case study, which would already provide the participants with a concrete experience, and to make the workshop methodology even more experiential, using the activity to unify the heterogeneous group of participants.

The questions

The process of selecting an appropriate case suitable for adaptation to the didactic objectives of the seminar was indeed a challenging one. It was deemed that the following criteria be taken into account: that the context be so chosen as to make the case readily comprehensible to the target audience and thus fully serve the pedagogical ends of the seminar; that the presentation be concise and clear, presenting critical elements of vital aspects of the curriculum reform.

It was therefore decided to construct a case study from a variety of experiences garnered from different countries. A review of newspaper articles was carried out and interviews with key informants undertaken. From this emerged a scenario wherein the development and implementation processes of curriculum reform were characterized by conflicts and tensions. The communication strategy used within and outside of the education system was empirically causing and contributing to these tensions.

The definition of thematic areas and methodology

The thematic areas of the workshop were developed out of the problem situation that in this case represented the 'lessons to be learned'. Once the thematic areas were defined from the empirical evidence, the next step was to design the methodological sequence and the learning activities.

This phase involved taking a number of decisions given the existing relationship between the theme of the workshop and the recipients of the training. Since there is a strong link between communication and culture, the dilemma was: what activities should be chosen? What level of acceptance would games have with this audience? Would the objective of learning be affected? It was decided to combine the practical exercises with didactic games. These would serve as triggers for generating discussion, while the analysis would take place jointly with the theoretical presentation of those aspects found to call for further development.

The expected results

It was hoped that the workshop would generate a premeditated space for reflection and analysis in order to:

- visualize the complex network of variables which affect the processes of change;
- get to know in greater detail the communication strategies which are used in the reform processes in the countries concerned;
- learn if these had generated conflicts and tensions and at what levels, magnitude and range;
- elaborate some general guidelines on communication strategies which should be taken into account in the process of curriculum reform;

- apply this knowledge to develop competence in communication.

Carrying out the workshop

The following are the presentation of the sequence of workshop activities:

1. *Objectives were presented to participants, who were informed that by the end of the workshop they would have:*
   - reflected upon the importance of communicating policy in curriculum development processes;
   - applied and developed the necessary skills for communicating educational processes within a context of change.
2. *Participants' expectations were requested in order to align objectives with their own expectations and to verify if they had been achieved at the end of the session. Their expectations were related to two main problems.*
   - the need to discuss and analyze the focal points of the curricular reforms with the teachers *before* implementing the changes, so as to increase understanding, clear doubts and allow for a sense of ownership of the changes that were being envisaged;
   - the need to discuss *how* to disseminate information on reforms to teachers, politicians, parents and the wider society.
3. *With the objective of introducing the theme and initiating a discussion in relation to problematic issues at the workshop, the work groups were asked to answer two questions in a word or a phrase.* The first question, 'What does the expression "communicating educational reform", suggest to you?' evoked the following phrases;
   - 'Deliver ideas of changes through participation and co-operation with stakeholders.'
   - 'Understanding change.'
   - 'Interactive way of bringing about changes in education.'

- 'Sharing experiences.'
- 'Multiplier effects.'

The second question, 'Do we need to build a strategy for communicating educational reforms? Why, for what purpose? To whom, to what audience? If not, why not?' brought forth the following responses:

- 'We need a strategy because it is difficult to communicate reforms, they are wide ranging and we need to transmit and discuss ideas with large audiences. We want to be efficient in communicating change.'
- 'Educational reforms are complex and all actors need to understand the change. We cannot proceed without them. The audiences are parents, teachers, students, administrators, supervisors, communities, mass media, industries, employers.'
- 'We need to communicate reforms because we need a wider acceptance and enhancement of participation of varied stakeholders.'
- 'We need effectiveness in understanding concepts, ideas, rationale, problems and issues as well as effectiveness in the implementation process.'
- 'We need a strategy to ensure that the public will share a common under standing of changes and encourage their co-operation in reform.'
- 'We need to communicate in order to make the direction clear, to help people understand, to get feedback, to mobilize all stakeholders to take an active part and contribute to reforms. To whom? To policy makers, practitioners, each and every one in society,

4. *The context of the particular secondary education reform and its principal aspects were then explained:*

The reform of secondary education involved certain changes in administration, teachers training and curriculum development, in three main areas, namely, *content, strategy,* and *implementation.* With reference to the content of change, the main aspects were that:

secondary education was divided into two stages, a basic (first, second, third grade) and a further stage (fourth, fifth, and sixth); instructional hours increased from 3.5 to 5.5 hours a day; number of subjects was decreased, being merged into integrated areas of knowledge. Thus, for example, as a result of integrating biology, physics and chemistry into natural science, teachers with knowledge in chemistry had to also teach biology; English became compulsory as a foreign language instead of French and many teachers feared losing their jobs; computer studies was added as a new subject. With reference to the strategy and the implementation of change, expert teams, from outside the system, were specially hired through the National Board of Education to help plan the reform.

5. *Once the reform and its context were explained, the information obtained from the research was distributed to the work groups, Participants were asked to analyze the texts and respond to the question: 'From the evidence you have, which are the problems that appear to be most relevant?'*

The principal problems cited by the participants were the following:

- lack of information;
- poor communication;
- rumours distorting the communication process.

Quotations from press articles and interviews with members of teachers' unions

- 'This National Board of Education never developed communication strategies with teachers, inspectors and directors (...); the president of the National Board of Education met with Teachers Union only on one occasion, but not to listen to us.'
- 'We see it as extremely difficult to establish a dialogue on the educational reform with the authorities, we speak different languages.'
- 'We demand the educational reform to be stopped at the end of the year and at the same time to have

a national debate with the participation of everyone involved.'

- 'It is not possible that teachers learn what is going to happen with the reform only through the media. If there is a reform plan, there has to be at least a written document or a video...'

Quotations from press articles and TV interviews with teachers

- 'Teachers discontent is not due to "resistance to change" as the authorities say.... The problem is that we are not clearly informed about the content of changes... We see it as a threat to our work security.'
- 'The new curriculum decreases the number of subjects, merging them into integrated areas of knowledge and as a consequence of that, many teachers were left without hours to teach...we are worried about our jobs....,
- 'Even though they say that this is a transitory situation, too many teachers were left without hours of teaching.'
- 'The communication strategy was achieved through informal channels, we must eliminate the rumours and begin a dialogue where all parties can express their opinions.'
- 'Authorities take relevant decisions in curriculum development which are communicated through memos'...
- 'In this reform we are not the actors, everything happens without previous agreements... communication works in one direction.'

Quotations from press articles and interviews with students

- 'The National Board of Education stated that they are not willing to continue with the dialogue until we leave the occupied schools... but we want to start debates and workshops in order to know the content of the reform and the counter proposals of the teachers.'

- 'Government officials are the ones who have to take the first step in creating an atmosphere of participation and communication.'
- 'This reform is imposed by international organizations and it is not a result of a national debate with all the parties involved.'
- 'Because we did not receive the whole document, the reform is a kind of Pandora's box: every day we find out something new.'
- 'We are not against the reform, because we do not know what it is about. This is against not having information, against the authoritarian style used to put the reform into practice.'

Quotations from press articles and interviews with teachers on TV programmes

- 'The most serious problem with this reform is the lack of an institutionalized dialogue with the different hierarchies. There cannot be an educational reform without the actors being convinced of what they are doing.'
- 'It is obvious that there are different visions. It is essential to have a organized framework of discussion so that everyone can give his or her opinion. I do not believe this would stop the functioning of the system; on the contrary, it could prevent the conflicts that endanger the effectiveness of the process of change.'

---

6. *The next step was to present the problems that the investigation had revealed and relate them to the problems detected by the participants, identifying the similarities:*
   - a directive leadership style that could not prevent conflict;
   - failure of internal communication process;
   - no social marketing programmes were developed 'to sell' the reform;

- leaders did not adapt communication styles according to situations.

7. To begin with, the problem—'a directive leadership style that could not prevent conflict'—was explained and this was related to three simple communication models. Figure 1 was used to introduce the conceptual framework and to relate the three elements available: the empirical material, the theoretical explanation, and the actual experience of the participants.
8. *Participants were asked to engage in an activity in order to relate the case to their personal experiences by asking them to think about an innovation they have to communicate. Which of these models would they use? In what sorts of situations? Keeping what purpose in mind? To what kind of audiences? And why?*
   The participants presented in plenary the results of these experiences. There were many cases where the different countries had experienced problems of communication related to educational policies. Although Laos and Indonesia are working in this area and showed explanatory leaflets on distinct aspects of their curricular reforms, they indicated that much more sill needed to be done and the efforts had to be continued in order to inform all sectors of the society.
9. *In order to initiate analysis of the problem:* 'of failure of internal communication processes' *a communication game was played to demonstrate the distortions and barriers to communication.*

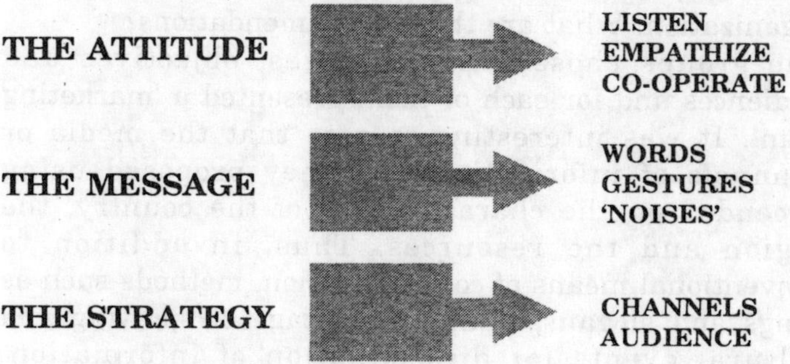

Figure 1: Three important communication elements

With a view to relating the problem to the experiences of the participants, they were asked to carry out the following exercises:

- to think about situations in which they experienced 'distortions' in communication;
- What was the situation? How did it appear? What was the impact? To think about their future work in the curriculum development process. Which are the most important elements they must take into consideration in order to avoid 'distortions'?

The teams related anecdotes of similar situations. They cited problems of distortion due to lack of written communication and those caused by poor interpersonal communication.

In this regard, they offered some advice as to some measures that could be taken in such situations: to listen empathetically, give and request feedback and use language that is clear to the interlocutor. This last aspect was considered very important. The importance of the careful use of technical language for communicating with non-specialized audiences was also stressed.

10. *In the presentation of the problem* 'no social marketing programmes were developed "to sell" the reform', *participants were asked to do an exercise, responding to the following situation:*

They are in a meeting with their team. They are planning the strategies for communicating the new curriculum's main guidelines inside the organization (ministry, district, university, etc.) and outside the organization. What are their recommendations?

The groups chose different cases, objectives and audiences and for each of them presented a 'marketing plan'. It was interesting to note that the media or channels of information that they proposed using depended on the characteristics of the country, the region and the resources. Thus, in addition to conventional means of communication, methods such as songs and slogans, taking advantage of sporting and cultural events for dissemination of information, designing of posters, etc., were proposed. From the presentation of cases, a series of recommendations that were deliberated upon are summarized below:

- 'Try to persuade: If you use persuasion, conflicts with teachers, parents and students can be diminished. People who understand the way others think are better persuaders. They try to keep actors informed.'
- 'Consider the characteristics of the audience before sending the message.'
- 'Consider the following aspects, before implementing an innovation: who is our target audience, and what are their needs? What are we trying to accomplish? Is the project we propose clear and comprehensible? Has the target audience clearly understood the explicit benefits?'

11. *To illustrate the problem of leaders not adapting their communication styles to the needs of the situation:* Participants were trained in applying the four styles of leadership according to the situational leadership model, which uses the interaction of two variables, relationship and task. Participants were asked to identify different situations in which they had to apply different styles, depending on the circumstances.
12. *They were presented with three important communication elements while working on curriculum development processes:*
    - attitudes—listening, empathizing, co-operating;
    - message—words, gestures and distortions;
    - strategy—audience, channels.
13. *To summarize the main points discussed in the workshop, they were asked to generate a communications policy by doing an activity in which they had to communicate the main guidelines of new curricula to different audiences by planning a strategy in which they had to answer the following questions:*
    - Why do we need to communicate?
    - To whom?

- How will the message be communicated?
- What would the channel be?

The results of the working groups summarize the main concepts that were arrived at during the workshop:

- 'Educational reforms imply a great number of actors: teachers, pupils, unions community, parents, administrative and technical staff.'
- 'To establish communicational forms and channels for these audiences is important in order to manage to the policy.'
- 'This transformation implies, among other things: Making the policy explicit, informing very clearly about the purpose of the project, generating consensus, leading and organizing activities, promoting compromises, following, and ensuring others follow the new legal framework.'
- 'The communication process has to be executed in *"stages"*:'

First stage: The announcement—The policy is publicly announced. It is transmitted from the education authority. *It is informative, generic and strategic. It is given through mass media channels.* It is 'a one direction message'.
Second stage: The internal communication—The message is presented to those actors involved in implementing the policy. The objectives are to inform, to obtain understanding, to orient and guide, to detect needs, to get commitment.
Third stage: The social communication—The message is transmitted through mass media (radio, TV, written press, posters), meetings, congresses, etc. to the community. The objective is to inform, consult, get consensus, introduce demands.
Fourth Stage: The moment of feedback—The objective is to get information about the impact of the message on those who received the information in order to make the necessary adjustments.

Main Conclusions

The examination of problems related to communication in a seminar organized for the discussion of relevant aspects of curriculum reform was an interesting innovation that showed the limited analysis and importance that educational managers give to this variable, at the stage of the elaboration of the design and implementation of change.

The case presented, the research undertaken to carry it out and the reaction of the representatives of the countries present at the seminar is a significant example. Although it would be naïve and nearly absurd to suggest that the communication aspect is the determinant factor in the success or failure of a reform, empirical data indicate that poor communication can obstruct, slow down and distort the progress of a project. Nevertheless, it is important to point out that the reforms studied in the process of the elaboration of the case study were successful, that is that in spite of the problems posed, the changes were finally implemented.

Although the 'costs' that had to be paid were high: many actors were excluded from the process and the teams which supported the reform had to invest much time and effort repairing the damages caused by poor communication, the reforms went ahead and today represent an important milestone for those educational systems.

The factors that made this development possible can be linked to specific variables, that is to say those that define each context. The reforms studied took place in a context of administrative and functional transparency, with a total absence of curruption. While the management style of the reform was that of directive leadership, it received great academic approval and strong support from the Prime Minister, as well as additional financial resources.

All things considered, it is important to point out that the success and failure of the reforms and the role that the communication variable plays in them, depends to a great extent on economic, political and socio-cultural aspects which are the factors that in the final analysis, determine the course of events.

It should also be noted that both the expectations of the participants, as well as the objectives of the activity were achieved, as indicated by the presentations and recommendations from the working groups.

The most interesting conclusion can be summed up in the sentence of a participant at the end of the workshop: 'we must all be conscious that poor communication can cause a curricular reform to fail. We have the obligation to contribute to making communication clear, to ensure it targets all actors and that appropriate methods and strategies are used which lead to understanding and bring about support and co-operation'.

Notes

1. Delors, J., et al. *Learning: the treasure within.* Paris, UNESCO, 1996, p. 22. (Report to UNESCO of the International Commission on Education for the Twenty-first Century.)
2. UNESCO: IBE, India, Ministry of Human Resource Development; Central Board of Secondary Education. *Globalization and living together: the challenges for educational content in Asia.* Geneva, 2000.
3. Director and personnel from IBE.
4. International Institute for Educational Planning.

35

Networking for Curriculum Development and Renewal

Isabel Byron

IBE and PROAP: Building on Networks for Development

The International Bureau of Education (IBE) and the UNESCO Principal Regional Office for Asia and the Pacific (PROAP) see the promotion of networking as essential to their role and functioning mutually beneficial to themselves and to the countries which they serve. Without direct active links with experts and institutions, they cannot adequately respond to the needs of Member States. In order to fulfil its role as an international centre for capacity building for curriculum change, the IBE needs to benefit from the ideas and expertise of education professionals in the different regions of the world and to have access to the technical resources of their institutions. PROAP must maintain similarly close working ties with individuals and institutions in the countries of the Asia-Pacific region. At the same time, both the IBE and PROAP desire to make their resources available to relevant institutions in Member States. Networking is arguably the most satisfactory way to achieve this.

Both the IBE and PROAP have considerable experience with the mechanisms and modalities of networking: the IBE, through its International Network for Educational Information (INED),[1] and its close involvement with the establishment of other international networks of educational innovation for development (APEID, CARNEID, NEIDA, EIPDAS);[2] PROAP as the headquarters of APEID, its close links with the South-East Asian Ministers of Education Organization (SEAMEO) Network,[3] and similarly with network in East Asia. Both institutions see it as essential that their future networking activities in curriculum development in the large and diverse region of Asia learn from and build on the experiences of existing networking structures working in this field, seeking to collaborate with and strengthen them, rather than compete with them.

Defining Networks

The New Oxford Shorter English Dictionary defines networks as 'a chain or system of interconnected or intercommunicating things, points or people' (Browne, 1993, p. 1909). Dubbeldam (1996, p. 11) quotes Hanks, 1979, in describing networks as 'a large number of people, groups or institutions, etc., that have a connection with each other and work together as a system'. He later describe a network as 'the pattern of social contacts of an individual through which she or he can achieve information, support, credits, power and other essentials needed for survival or for improvement of one's position', stressing that 'individual' may be replaced by 'institution' (ibid.). While this short paper is principally concerned with the development of institutional networks, it recognizes the importance of networks which function in a more *ad hoc* manner, comprised of individuals with common interests. A useful definition of an educational network is that given at the World Conference on Education for All (Jomtien, Thailand, 1990): 'An educational network is essentially the interactions among individuals and groups of individuals to share information, and thereby increase the potential for utilization of this information to improve the quality of education'. However, the IBE's and PROAP's vision of networking goes beyond the simple sharing of information.

Networks should ideally develop as systems for support and mutual assistance. Dubbeldam (1996, p. 12) writes: 'Essential to the proper functioning of a network is the participants' belief that they have something worth sharing and that they may call upon the others in the network when a need arises.' Networks provide wonderful opportunities for the sharing of resources: knowledge, ideas, opinions, expertise, technical and sometimes financial capacities. They can reduce problems of isolation of professionals and their institutions, by putting them in contact with persons of like-minded interests and concerns. One writer thus describes networking as 'catalytic to development as it provides for cross-fertilization of ideas for better productivity' (Nyati-Ramahobo, 1996, p. 80). However, their successful functioning depends on the commitment of the members and effective means of, and strategies for, communication.

As Reimers and McGinn, state 'networks are as old as human civilization' (1998, p. 77). In today's world, capacities for networking over long distances and across borders have been revolutionized by the development of increasingly sophisticated communications technologies. In an age of globalization, networking has become an integral aspect of the process of development, essential to the functioning of modern societies. Ideally, collaboration and sharing through networks will permit developing countries to advance by providing them access to the resources of other countries/institutions and enabling them to have a better understanding of the main trends and developments in specific fields, thus facilitating their adaptation, where desirable and appropriate, to local needs.

However, the relative success and capacities for long term survival of networks varies considerably. In addition to institutional constraints, the life of networks depends on the motivation and commitment of the individuals comprising their membership. There must be a felt need for starting a network and reasons for keeping it going.

The Structure and Functioning of Networks

Networks may be loose and informal or structured and formal. The form they take will depend upon political and cultural factors related to the geographical regions and types of institutions in which they develop. The levels of autonomy of the individuals making up a network will depend on whether they are representing an institution and the degree of freedom they have within it, or whether they are operating independently. Reimers and McGinn (1998) observe that it is easier for individuals to participate autonomously in networks in societies were individualism is a common feature of life, while in societies and organizations dominated by community or collective values, networking is likely to be institution-based. Similarly, Cheng (1996) points out that in societies which are traditionally hierarchical, such as in East Asia, networking, especially autonomous individual networking, is far more uncommon, as the custom is to work within established roles and to remain within one's institutional framework. In such societies, networks, if they develop, are likely to be structured along formal institutional lines, which can hinder their effectiveness.

The way a network operates will depend on whether it is formal or informal and based on individual or institutionalized relations. Dubbeldam (1996) observes that networks of institutions normally define clear objectives and activities, while ones comprised of autonomous individuals may function in an *ad hoc* manner, being kept alive by the interests of the members in being part of a group of like-minded individuals. However, he stresses that even formal networks are heavily dependent on 'informal relations between the individuals in the participating institutions' (p. 15). Komba (1996) suggests that overformalizing of networks may diminish their effectiveness, as it will tend to restrict or suppress individual autonomy and creativity.

In addition to political and cultural influences, economic constraints may make the free flow and sharing of information among individuals and institutions difficult or undesirable. Institutions or individuals wishing to participate in networking may lack the technological and other resources needed to support their active involvement. Possibilities for cross-national networking pose linguistic challenges in a region such as Asia, where English normally has to be used as the lingua franca. This requires competence in a foreign language and adequate resources for translation of written information.

International institutions, such as UNESCO, need to be aware of and understand the factors influencing how networks develop in different counties and regions, in order to work constructively with them and facilitate greater dissemination and exchange of information and expertise on a truly international scale.

Issues in Networking for Curriculum Development

As indicated in the first section of this article, education networks already exist in the region and their fields of interest touch on many areas relating to curriculum development and change. IBE and PROAP are interested in networking as a means of strengthening capacities among curriculum professionals and the institutions they form a part of. It is for the regions and Member States to decide what form they wish future networking to take—whether they should expand the curriculum development activities of existing networks, or establish a new more specialized structure. Dubbeldam (1996) observes out that any institution or individual can be part of more than one network. Areas of interest and objectives of networks may overlap, creating possibilities for inter-relationships networking among networks. To respond to the demands for improved educational provision, it is now considered essential for institutions involved in education to network both with others in their sector and with sectors outside the education system (OECD, 2000).

Professional networks combine the intellectual and technical resources of member institutions, allowing the sharing of the knowledge, skills and experience of the individuals that work in them. Where they work in partnership with international institutions, such as UNESCO, they allow these organizations to be better informed about and understand national or local concerns, needs and ideas in the network's specific field of competence.

Meetings, conferences and seminars provide the opportunity for establishing interpersonal and institutional contacts, which may become fruitful, long-term relationships. However, curriculum professionals are typically very busy, dealing with challenging situations in their daily working lives, to which they have to return once the brief interlude of a meeting is over. Maintaining professional contacts on a regular basis requires commitment and reciprocity. It is nevertheless to be hoped, that through relations formed or strengthened during national, regional or international encounters, the foundations may be laid for developing on-going collaboration through networking. Some of the possibilities this may offer are proposed below. It is equally important that curriculum specialists from the region engage in reflection on the issue, and develop their own ideas and suggestions.

1. Networking provides opportunities for the exchange of a range of types of relevant information, such as:
   - new discoveries about the teaching and learning processes;
   - trends in curriculum development in other countries of the region and in other parts of the world;
   - research findings from local/sub-regional studies which could be of benefit to the rest of the region and the world;
   - findings from comparative studies;
   - innovative approaches from the region or outside it;
   - essential statistical data, socio-cultural data and information on teachers, students, parents, community which have implications for curriculum development, etc.;

   As international institutions, the IBE and PROAP may play leading roles in collecting, processing and disseminating information of this type to Member State, but will rely considerably on curriculum professionals in the institutions with which they collaborate to assist them in identifying, obtaining and translating such information.

2. Essentially through e-mail, participants in a network may communicate ideas and information, request assistance, propose contacts, suggest new members, etc. E-mail is also the easiest and cheapest way for the IBE and PROAP to stay in close touch with members. Through e-mail technology, a 'list-serv' can be established leading to the setting up of net fora to debate and reflect on specific themes in curriculum development and reform.

3. In addition to information sharing, networking should foster and generate knowledge production by curriculum specialists from the region. It should create a space for reflection and debate on ways for improving the quality of the curriculum development process, focusing on opportunities for professional development. Relevant areas for research should be proposed by members, and joint and comparative studies at sub-regional or regional level undertaken. In conjunction with IBE and PROAP and national and regional institutions, strategies for the effective dissemination of relevant research should be developed.
4. Networking should permit and encourage the sharing of resources and their more equal distribution within a region comprised of countries of very varied levels of economic development. The IBE and PROAP will put their technological and institutional capacity at the disposal of participants through the development of their websites, databases, documentation collections and overall knowledge based on the curriculum development process. As international institutions, they can provide valuable links and opportunities for collaboration with curriculum-related institutions and networks in other regions of the world.

Conclusion

Networking provides an alternative to the traditionally defined 'top-down' or 'bottom-up' models of educational decision-making. In a networking paradigm, all actors may be seen as collaborators. The challenge is to find ways of enabling all actors to intervene in a clearly articulated and productive manner in the decision-making process. Co-ordinating institutions, such as IBE and PROAP, must assist the member institutions of networks to achieve the means to do this through the provision of technical support and training, through fostering opportunities for exchange and dialogue, and providing guidelines and frameworks for action.

IBE and PROAP can serve as co-ordinators or catalysts in networking, providing an international perspective and possibilities for interaction on an international scale. The IBE ultimately sees its role as the hum of a network of networks, using its international position to link and provide support to national and regional institutions working in the area of curriculum development and reform.

Notes

1. The INED network was created as a follow-up to the thirty-sixth session of the International Conference on Education (1977) which had as one of its themes: 'The problem of information at the national and international level which is posed by the improvement of educational systems'. It ceased operation in the early 1990s.
2. Asia Pacific Programme of Education Innovation for Development; Caribbean Network of Educational Innovation for Development; Network of Educational Innovation for Development in Africa; Educational Innovation Programme of Development in Arab States.
3. This comprises a number of regional centres, including INNOTECH (Regional Centre for Educational Innovation and Technology), RECSAM (Regional Centre for Education in Science and Mathematics), RELC (Regional Language Centre), RETRAC (Regional Training Centre), RIHED (Regional Centre for Higher Education and Development), SEAMOLEC (Regional Open Learning Centre), VOCTECH (Regional Centre for Vocational and Technical Education).

References

Browne, L., ed. 1993. *The new shorter Oxford English dictionary.* Oxford, UK, Clarendon Press.

Cheng, K. 1996. Appreciating cultures: educational research and networking in East Asia. *In:* McGinn, N., ed. *Crossing lines: research and policy networks for developing country education,* pp. 119-23. Westport, CT, Praeger.

Dubbeldam, L. 1996. Networks and institution building. *In:* McGinn, N., ed. *Crossing lines: research and policy networks for developing country education,* pp. 11-18. Westport, CT, Praeger.

Komba, D. 1996. Problems of networking: the ERNESA experience. *In:* McGinn, N., ed. *Crossing lines: research and policy networks for developing country education,* pp. 87-89. Westport, CT, Praeger.

Nyati-Ramahobo, L. 1996. The culture of networking in educational research in Eastern and Southern Africa. *In:* McGinn, N., ed. *Crossing lines: research and policy networks for developing country education,* pp. 79-86. Westport, CT, Praeger.

Organisation for Economic Co-operation and Development. 2000. *Knowledge management in the learning society.* Paris, OECD.

Reimers, F.; McGinn, N. 1998 *Informed dialogue: using research to shape education policy around the world.* Westport, CT, Praeger.

Educational Research Network for Eastern and Southern Africa (ERNESA); Northern and European Research Review and Advisory Group (NORRAG); Information Network on Education for Latin America can the Caribbean (REDUC); Southeast Asian Research Review and Advisory Group (SEARRAG). 1990. *From research to action in basic education: the potential of networking* and North-South partnership. p. 4. (Prepared for WCEFA Thematic Round-Table 14. Available from IBE on microfiche: SIRE/02474.)

Section 3

Curriculum Changes and Reforms in East and South-East Asia

The Social Context of Curricular Changes and Reforms

Virginia A. Miralao

I came to be involved in work relating to curriculum changes and reforms because some colleagues at the Philippine Social science Council and the Social and Human Sciences Committee of the UNESCO National Commission of the Philippines and myself formed a team to review the social Sciences framework and content of textbooks that are currently being used in Philippine elementary and secondary schools. We embarked on this project mainly in response to growing criticisms and complaints about the state of our local textbooks. True enough, our review findings supported many of the complaints.

Among other findings, we found that pedagogically, many textbooks are written in a language and present their material in a manner not appropriate to the ages/development stages of students at various grade levels. Content-wise too, textbooks appear overloaded with facts, data and a variety of information which are neither systematically analyzed nor pooled together to present a coherent view of the topics or lessons at hand. In addition, our textbooks have not been rid of longstanding (class-, urban-, gender- and ethnic-) biases and stereotypes that perpetuate falsehoods and exclusionary or discriminatory practices. These are in addition to some other factual and typographical errors found in the textbooks and to their poor visual designs and layouts.

Since Philippine textbooks are developed following the guidelines and lists of learning competencies prepared by our national education department based on the existing curriculum, the poor state of our textbooks is a reflection of problems in the curriculum itself and the national education system as a whole. One notes that various sectoral reports on the state of Philippine education over the years have called attention to its deteriorating quality. We have many indicators of this, the more telling of which is the poor performance of Filipino students in standardized international and national achievement tests. Other available data further indicate that the country's impressive educational achievements in literacy (over 90%) and school enrolment rates have not been matched by commensurate improvements in the country's state of economic and human development. This situation has brought into question the quality and/or standards of Philippine education and has prompted some analysts to ask the rather embarrassing question: why, if Filipinos are so smart, is the Philippines so poor?

Problems of educational quality and relevance manifest themselves in different ways in the countries of our region, but in general, there is increasing agreement that such problems are best addressed by changes in the curriculum and its delivery than by simple increases in public investments/ expenditures on education. For curricular changes and reforms to effectively address problems of educational quality however, it is important that these are not undertaken piecemeal. As pointed out by Zhou Nanzhao, effective curricular reforms require 'radical, fundamental and comprehensive' changes in our educational views and orientations, as well as in curricular content and in teaching approaches and pedagogies, in addition to still other necessary changes in curriculum planning and implementation processes and in educational management and administration. It is quite clear that the task of pursuing meaningful curriculum reform is a complex undertaking which has been made even more so by today's rapidly changing environment. Available knowledge from the work of education experts and researchers (e.g. as those presented in the 1996 Delors Report on education) now tell us that if we are to improve, update and change our existing curriculum, we cannot rely on the same models/theories that informed our earlier work in education planning and curriculum development and design. From a social scientific standpoint in fact, the need for a fundamental shift in our educational perspectives and policies may constitute the biggest challenge in curriculum change and reform.

Earlier educational/curriculum planning, for example, was heavily oriented towards using education to service the economy and to prepare students for productive and secure employment. In recent decades however, it has become evident that there is no one-to-one correspondence between educational qualifications and today's labour markets. Economic conditions in this new century are expected to become more changeable and uncertain, with many countries likely exhibiting higher rates of un- and underemployment than previously. The increasing reliance of firms and companies on the outsourcing of goods and services, moreover, is encouraging short-team employment contracts rather than permanent ones and which, in turn, is changing the 'working life' and the meaning of 'career paths' among the youth. Today's labour markets too have become observably globalized, thus complicating the task of using education as a means for improving national economies.

Additionally, it should be pointed out that while earlier educational planning models tended to emphasize education's role in contributing to the economy, education systems themselves are as much the products of prevailing economics. Consequently, in the case of many Third World countries, their poor economies and lack of resources to improve their education system (e.g. to produce textbooks, upgrade teachers' salaries, build more schools, etc.) already reduce the likelihood that they can use education as a mechanism to make their economies grow and become globally competitive. These weaknesses in the education/economy linkage are prompting a reorientation in educational perspectives away from the heavily economic rationale of education in earlier periods. Today, regardless of the state of the economy, the provision of (basic) education is increasingly seen as a fundamental human right to be guaranteed by the state and extended to all. This shift in perspective calls for a re-examination of the educational goals and objectives.

As with the education/economy linkage, there is also a need to rethink the nation-building role of education in the face of globalization and the changing role of the state. In the Philippines, for example, the nationalistic fervour and anti-colonial and anti-foreign bent of the curriculum content forged in the 1970s and 1980s now sound increasingly anachronistic, considering that large numbers of Filipino families even among the lower classes and rural communities have members working and/or living abroad. There is thus a need to reconstruct our notions of national identity and pride away from the 'old guard nationalism' that may have been appropriate in the years following Independence.

It is also well to remember that notions about the 'nation-building' role of education may predispose governments to use the education system and the curriculum as instruments of government propaganda to foster obedience, curtail dissent and enlist popular support for the state's own political and socio-economic programmes. And here I am not referring only to so-called authoritarian and communist states, but even to freer democratic states who are not beyond similarly using the curriculum and the education system to promote certain political agendas and interests. Again, we should note that the uncritical acceptance of the nation/state-building function of education is likely to run counter to the human rights and social democracy movements that are expected to gain more acceptance in the twenty-first century.

New data and research on the lives of today's youth offer yet other reasons for re-examining current perspectives and assumptions behind educational planning and curriculum development. In the last two to three decades, various researches show no neat patterns in 'youth to adult transitions' as in the past when such transitions typically involved a sequence of going to school and finishing some basic schooling, followed by getting a job and then by getting married and beginning one's own family. At present, many of the youth are staying longer in school (with not a few seeking different kinds of training after the compulsory level), although many too are combining part-time study with part-time work. It is also no longer uncommon for the youth to drop out of school for various reasons and to resume schooling or educational training at a later point or at other periods in their lives. On-going changes in youth cultures and lifestyles suggest that it is unrealistic to plan school programmes and curricula around the same youth-to-adult transition patterns of earlier generations. There is in fact a need to diversify our educational programmes and curricula of these are to remain relevant to the needs and aspirations of the youth and if we are to adapt the education system to today's changed socio-cultural conditions.

Finally, there are several other changes occurring in various fronts—unprecedented advances in science and technology, new studies on learning processes and human capacities, new pedagogies and so forth—which similarly call for changes in our educational/curriculum models and perspectives. These changes and developments invite us to be innovative and to go beyond the content-heavy and skills-based framework that guided earlier curriculum planning and development. We are, I think, most fortunate at this point to have in the Delors Report, with its exposition on 'education for life' and its four pillars of learning (to know, to be, to do and to live with others), a most useful guide for charting new directions in education and in our school curriculum.

The Delors Report invites us to refocus our educational efforts towards enhancing personal growth and development (and away from an overemphasis on producing a trained/skilled labour force and nationalists for the country) and providing learners with a sense of rootedness or mooring so that they can 'soar above the storm' so to speak and not be caught by the flurry of changes, even as they are able to seize the new opportunities presented by unfolding social and technological developments. These kinds of 'life-skills' that allow learners to be anchored while adapting flexibly to changes in their wider environments do not conform neatly with the usual categorization of learning skills and competencies (e.g. cognitive, affective, psychomotor, etc.) but require new ways of conceptualizing learning behaviours, processed and outcomes.

But although many of us recognize and appreciate the need for changes in our educational perspectives, we are also keenly aware of the many barriers to shifting our paradigms in educational planning and in pursuing needed curricular reforms. Among the problems and barriers that we face are a shortage of resources for systematically undertaking educational and curricular reforms, and other political and bureaucratic tensions and resistances that usually accompany the introduction of change. Let each of us dare to innovate and exhibit the will to change.

37

Synthesis of Country Reports and General Trends and Needs

Virginia A. Miralao and Lucille C. Gregorio

Introduction

A Training Seminar on Capacity-Building for Curriculum Specialists from East and South-East Asia was organized in Bangkok, as a collaborative activity between the International Bureau of Education (IBE) and UNESCO-PROAP. This was hosted by the Ministry of Education Thailand, from 12 to 16 December 2000. The seminar was focused on capacity-building in fundamental skills for effective curriculum development and reform, with participants from eleven countries and one SEAMEO Centre.

To allow for informed exchange within the regional context, participants were requested to prepare written reports on their country's recent curriculum reforms, identifying the main elements and stages in the reform process. The participants were provided with guidelines for the preparation of their country presentations.

Structure of the Country Reports

The participants were requested to structure their reports, according to the following points:

1. Present the main organizations and mechanisms involved in the process of adapting curricula in the respective countries.

2. Indicate the particular philosophy(ies) or principles of education/curriculum development which inform the curriculum design and reform process in the respective countries. Outline the principal new content areas and teaching/learning methodologies introduced in recent reforms. Indicate whether any of the principal concepts of learning outlines in the Delors Report were used in the design and formulation of recent reforms.
3. Discuss the main problems faced by curriculum specialists in the country during the following three steps of curriculum reform: (i) design, (ii) implementation, and (iii) follow-up of the process. At the same time indicate the strengths and successful aspects of the reform process.

Based on the above guidelines, participants prepared their written country reports and presented the highlights to the seminar. These are presented here based on sub-regional groupings: East Asia sub-region; South-East Asia sub-region; and the Mekong sub-region.

Synthesis of Country Reports

East Asia sub-region

China

Curriculum reform in China is based on the policy of quality improvement at all levels derived from two policy documents 'The Action Scheme for Invigorating Education towards the Twenty-First Century' and 'Decision on the Deepening of Education, Reform and the Full Promotion of Quality Education.' The focus is modernization, the world and the future with the aim of preparing the younger generation with appropriate morality, intellectual accomplishments, awareness of one's responsibility towards oneself and the nation, independent personalities and lifelong learning. Guidelines for the curriculum reform provide the direction, principles, objectives, policies and strategies of the curriculum while the National Curriculum Standards set the minimum requirement for the curriculum content. These two documents provide the basis of material development that follows.

The management of the reform is a shared responsibility by the Ministry of Education and the local education authority. The development of textbooks is given to various professional institutions. Between 2000 and 2005, the curriculum reform will be experimented and modified before full implementation—between 2005 and 2010.

Japan

Japan's curriculum reform is centred around setting National Curriculum Standards based on the concept of equal educational opportunities for all. The basic philosophy of the standard is the balanced development of the child, who can think wisely and creatively and contribute to societies, equipping them to cope with change, and increased awareness as a member of the international community, as well as encourage each school to develop its own personality. Major changes brought by the new curriculum standards are: (i) The introduction of 'Life Environment Studies' which combines social studies and science at the first two levels of primary schooling; (ii) periods of integrated study; (iii) reduction of teaching hours in line with the policy of five-day school week system. The new standard will be implemented in 2002 allowing three years for the preparation of teachers and development of materials. Implementation of the new standards will be followed by nationwide survey on student achievement in certain subjects, as practiced with previous national curriculum standards.

One problem faced by curriculum specialists at the design stage is determining the scope of each subject due to the reduction of time allotted.

Mongolia

Mongolia undertook its curriculum reform in 1998, following a directive from the Ministry of Education, Culture and Science. The curriculum, outlined in the 'Curriculum Plan for General Secondary School', has two components, i.e. 'core' and 'optional'. The core curriculum is the national standard to be followed by all schools and accounts for 80% of total time. The 'optional' component provides an organizational standard and is intended to meet the needs of the schools. The Centre of Academic Curriculum and Teaching at the School of Educational Development plays a significant role in defining teaching methods.

The main aim of the curriculum is to provide knowledge, skills, cultural values to students as well as to develop individuals as responsible citizens. The development of the Mongolian curriculum is based on the spiral model, increasing in intensity as one moves up the grades. A big percentage of time is allocated to Humanistic Science al all levels. Computer education is integrated into mathematics.

Republic of Korea

Korea is undertaking its seventh curriculum reform based on the framework provided by 'The Presidential Commission of the Educational Reform' affecting all levels of schooling. It has a national curriculum, centrally, prepared, providing the general framework, subject curriculum, materials as well as guidelines for implementation. It is mandatory for all schools to use. A salient feature of the new curriculum is the differentiated curriculum with different learning content for different groups of students based on academic ability. Another feature is the 30% reduction in curriculum content and the introduction of Information and Communication Technology (ICT) at the secondary level. Superintendents at municipal and provincial levels oversee the curriculum implementation at the local level to ensure local needs are met. Schools prepare their own implementation plan in accordance with the guidelines of the national curriculum and that of the metropolitan and provincial education authorities. There are problems at both the design and implementation stages. Those at the design stage include the inability of a centralized curriculum to cater to differing local educational needs, the lack of time to undertake research resulting in low level relevance to school needs and strong pressure of interest groups over subject curriculum. Problems at the implementation stage include resistance to change among teachers, lack of teachers' ability to teach the new curricula and lack of financial resources and facilities.

South-East Asia sub-region

Indonesia

Curriculum development and reform in Indonesia are guided by the 1999 State Guidelines which emphasize the importance of a diversified curriculum to serve a diverse range of pupil abilities, available learning facilities and regional cultures. The 1999 State Guidelines lay down the 'general principles' for curriculum reform while the Ministry of National Education assumes responsibility for education policy. The Indonesian education system used to be highly centralized but this is now being decentralized with the increasing transfer of authority and responsibilities from central- to district-level bodies. Under the decentralized system, the central-level Ministry of National Education maintains the important role of ensuring the functioning of public services and the consistency of standards on curriculum design and implementation.

The major challenges of curriculum reform in the new millenium include those posed by the ongoing decentralization process; the impact of the Asian economic crisis; other changes in labour market, skills and knowledge demands as a result of advances in information and communication technology and globalization processes; and other public/political considerations aimed at addressing the uneven development of the country's regions, and popular clamour for increased choices is educational programmes and for parental/student freedom in choosing schools and educational programmes.

Curriculum reforms thus are directed to the foregoing challenges and aim to contribute to the goals of making the national economy more efficient and competitive, and Indonesian society more open and democratic and more responsive to regional cultural differences and local needs.

Indonesia's curriculum framework for the new millenium envisions the development of pupils who are healthy, independent and culturally aware, with good moral conduct and work ethics, are knowledgeable and can master technology, and show a love of their country. Curriculum development in the foreseeable future therefore is expected to become more diversified to accommodate student, environment, cultural and local differences; provide the national standards for academic and skills achievements as well as for the formation of social/personal values and morals; be flexible and relevant to current changes and future developments; integrate the four pillars of learning as proposed by the Delors Report; and enhance the participation of communities and schools in educational programmes and policy decisions.

Philippines

The Philippines is in the midst of undertaking curricular reform for secondary education. The reform initiative is contained in the development plan for the 'Twenty-first Century Secondary Education Curriculum' (T-SEC) launched in 1999.

The reform focuses on a review of the Philippine Secondary Schools Learning Competencies (PSSLC) and hopes to address issues pertaining to the overloading of curriculum content, and the need to, among others, integrate the disciplines, achieve a better balance between general and specialized education, and rationalize elective offerings.

Core study groups have been formed to work on the planned curricular reforms following the conduct of multi-sectional consultations and discussions. Results and recommendations are expected to be presented in plenary sessions with the Secretary and concerned offices of the Department of Education, Culture and Sports (DECS) which will formulate the new vision and mission, and the subjects and programme objectives of the curriculum plan. These activities are to be followed by various 'writeshops' to refine learning competencies, curriculum guides and the development of instructional materials. Several types of trainers' and teachers' training are also being planned in support of the new curriculum. Finally, a system of monitoring and evaluation is being set up to ensure way of assessing both the processes and outcomes of the planned curriculum reforms.

Malaysia

The Education Act of 1996 defined the philosophy, goals and objectives of Malaysia's national curriculum. The national curriculum is developed centrally within the Ministry of Education which maintains three main departments (the Curriculum Development Centre, the Department of Technical and Vocational Education and the Department of Religious and Moral Education) responsible for curriculum design and development, and a number of other units/divisions (Textbooks Division, Teacher Education, etc.), the directors of which comprise the Central Curriculum Committee headed by the Director-General of Education. Curricular programmes which are approved by this central committee are then discussed by the Curriculum Implementation Committee, comprised of the directors of education of Malaysia's fourteen states and Education Ministry representatives who discuss the final points bearing on the implementation of the curriculum.

Curriculum development, reform and revisions follow a cyclical model beginning with a needs analysis, followed by planning, implementation, evaluation and then back to needs assessment. Changes in the curriculum may begin with a policy directive from policy makers, or derive from weaknesses found in the existing curriculum or from observations in world trends or from public opinion.

A curricular revision was undertaken in 1996 to allow Malaysia to incorporate new elements in its curriculum design framework. The new elements draw from emerging knowledge and insights derived from the concepts of multiple intelligence and emotional intelligence, the Four Pillars of Learning in the Delors Report, developments in ICT and the country's move towards developing a K- (knowledge) economy. These new elements are reflected both in curriculum content and in teaching and learning approaches.

The process of curriculum formulation and reform is not without its issues and problems. Among other challenges, curriculum developers in Malaysia have to balance breadth and depth in determining the scope of the curriculum, and they also have to contend with differing school environments, teachers' and other forms of resistance to change, and other weaknesses and inconsistencies in the education system and structures. Nonetheless, the participation of different groups and stakeholders in the planning and implementation of curriculum changes ensures some level of co-ordination in the conduct of curriculum reforms.

The Mekong sub-region

Cambodia

The educational reforms being implemented in Cambodia are all geared towards complementing its socio-economic rehabilitation plans. The Ministry of Education, Youth and Sports (MOEYS) has drawn up nineteen programmes and seventy-two priority action plans which included prioritizing the reforms on curriculum, textbook development and the general education. These would be implemented through the education system development committees which were formed primarily for this purpose.

Values such as co-operation, environmental concern, love of country, independence, respect for human rights and diversity, etc., are being taught to and developed in the students to make them responsive to the needs of the country in terms of its social, political and economic aspects. General education goals provide the development of necessary knowledge, skills, and experiences for Cambodians to gain the tools that would enable them to function as responsible and thinking citizens. The approach taken in designing the curriculum is content/topic-based and competency-based.

The new curriculum took effect in 1996, yet the whole education system is still reeling from old problems and issues, such as poor qualifications of current teachers or the lack of capable teachers, classroom shortages that have caused student overcrowding in classrooms, and the passive and non-creative attitude of teachers and students.

People's Democratic Republic of Lao

The Ministry of Education established the National Research Institute of Educational Sciences (NRIES) to be responsible for the development of the general education curriculum, compilation of textbooks and teacher's manuals, design of prototype of teaching and learning materials for general education, and the provision of teacher training. The general education goals is to equip Lao citizens with the knowledge and skills that would ensure their active participation in family, economic, social and cultural life. It also aims to inculcate a moral and patriotic sense in the students and to foster a well-rounded education system that would seek to be at par with internation standards through educational innovations and the use of technology.

The present curriculum, a product of the educational reforms adopted in 1991, came in the light of the socio-economic transformation which the country underwent from having a centrally planned economy to assuming a liberal market system. So aside from the goals stated above, this curriculum also encourages internationalism, combination of theoretical study with practical activities, integration of political awareness and juridical awareness, and the combination of modern world education with the best of the country's traditional culture. It identified five educational pillars: moral, intellectual, labour, physical and aesthetic.

In terms of teaching methodologies, various methods and techniques are encouraged, such as use of brainstorming, role playing, games, panel discussions, debates, case study, etc. The employment of language encounter techniques has improved and sped up the acquisition of language skills by children from ethnic minority backgrounds who speak other languages than Lao. Teacher-training continues to be carried out and monitored. Through the use of different evaluation tools in assessing the quality of education—both in terms of the teachers and the students—the effectiveness of textbooks and teacher's manuals being used and the teacher-training workshops being held, the NRIES tries to gauge the effectiveness of their programmes and recent evaluation findings show satisfactory achievements with regard to the curriculum's relevance and its contribution to the improvement of learning performance and quality of education. According to this recent educational evaluation, the current curriculum reflects the national identity of the Lao people, their cultural diversity, modernity, and openness to the international community.

Yet some problems remain in the design, implementation and follow-up on the curriculum. Regarding the design, the curriculum is insufficient in adapting to the specific needs of students from various ethnic, linguistic and cultural backgrounds. Relatedly, the teaching aids and instructional materials and other classroom and school facilities to support these needs are lacking and have not been adequately addressed. Despite the introduction of new teaching/learning methods, teachers continue to teach obsolete conceptual structure using old methods.

Thailand

Thailand's National Education Act of 1999 prescribes that curriculum development be guided by the 'Conceptual Framework for Basic Education Curriculum' which contains information on the rationale for curriculum development, the characteristics of the basic education curriculum, its contents, and guidelines on education curriculum management.

Ongoing socio-economic and global changes require that the basic education curriculum be continuously revised and updated. Other than changes in the global economy and the advances in science and technology, Thai society itself has undergone dramatic changes in its demographic, socio-cultural, economic, environmental and political characteristics which also now require new adjustments in the national curriculum and educational system. Recent assessments indicate that the curriculum offered little flexibility in content to meet the varying needs and conditions of localities. It also provided inadequate learning time for necessary basic courses (e.g. as for science and math, language, etc.), and did not allow for the satisfactory integration of teaching and learning processes. In general, Thai students were assessed as lacking the kinds of knowledge and abilities necessary for seeking further knowledge and future living.

The foregoing limitations of Thai education were some of the considerations that went into the formulation of the 1999 National Education Act and the Conceptual Framework for Basic Education Curriculum, Current reforms guided by these policy documents therefore aim to improve Thai education by, among others, making the curriculum more flexible to suit specific circumstances at local levels; more diversified in terms of its contents and programmes to reach and meet the needs of different groups of learners and develop their potentials; and more decentralized in terms of administration and management to allow the participation of schools, parents, local communities and various sectors and stakeholders in curriculum development and the education system. Current reforms are also taking into account the new knowledge and information that have arisen in the areas of curriculum standards, subject matters and contents, learning approaches and pedagogy and the basic learning principles advocated in the Delors Report.

Viet Nam

In 1998, the Education Law was approved by the National Assembly which clearly defined the objectives, contents and methods of general education and institutionalization of curriculum and textbooks in the new development period of the country. This is the fourth curriculum reform following those carried out in 1950, 1956 and 1981. It set a vision for the development of the country's human resources until 2020 and is oriented towards striking a balance and complementation in the formulation of the curriculum contents for the primary and secondary education, as well as vocational education to equip the citizens with the necessary skills and competencies for Viet Nam's industrialization and modernization. It sought to have a rationalized textbook and curriculum contents that would promote learning absorption at a pace adapted to the student's capacity.

Already expected to happen between 2000 to 2005 is the wrapping up of the pilot testing of the proposed textbooks and curriculum contents and even teachers' training curriculum so as to finalize suggestions. A phased and gradual implementation of this new curriculum will be done accordingly in the primary and secondary education from 2002 to 2007. Several activities to ensure achievement of these goals have also been outlined.

Regional Trends and Needs

The regional trends and need identified from the country reports synthesized above are presented by sub-region, because of the vast diversity of the Asian region, in terms of culture, language, geography, socio-political conditions, economic dimensions, etc.

East Asia sub-region

Trends

- All four countries of the region—China, Republic of Korea, Japan and Mongolia—are at the stage of curriculum reforms, which began in the late nineties (1997-95) and planned for implementation beginning 2000 (Korea), 2001 (Mongolia) and 2002 (China/Japan).
- All countries have a national curriculum, centrally prepared, but allowing for adaptation at the school level. The curriculum consists of core subjects to be studied by all and electives at the secondary level.
- The curricular reforms focus on quality improvement, emphasizing the overall development of children, who are able to learn and think, are creative, who can play as effective members of society and be proud of their national culture. In terms of curricular content, Japan and Korea have made moves to reduce curriculum content by about 30%. However, there are also moves to introduce new subjects. Japan, for example, has introduced 'periods of integration' whereby children are allowed to study things of their choice, as an attempt to reduce academic pressure. All countries are at the stage of introducing ICT in the classroom.
- Although there is no explicit statement on the Four Pillars of Education as a principle in their curricular reform, elements of the four pillars are manifested in the countries as single subjects as well as integrated across the curriculum.

Needs

The needs expressed by countries of the region pertain to the following:

- Ways of designing an integrated curriculum;
- Addressing the issue of relevance;
- Balancing an academic with a pragmatic curriculum;

- Teaching techniques in the application of IT/ICT in the classroom;
- Ways of involving the community in the development of the curriculum;
- Ways of effectively communicating with stakeholders so that the curriculum is well understood;
- Ways of convincing parents of the intrinsic value of education and the benefits of the new curriculum and reduce the pressure form examinations.

South-East Asia sub-region

Trends

- The three countries in the region (Indonesia, Malaysia and the Philippines) are all in the process of introducing ICT in the school curriculum.
- The countries are placing renewed emphasis on the principle of 'learning to live together' in their values-moral education programmes in response to continuing challenges and threats to social cohesion, peace and national unity.
- All countries have moved to decentralize certain aspects or processes of curriculum development, implementation and administration. Central or national level authorities continue to be responsible for general policies and basic guidelines on the curriculum and for setting national standards for educational quality; while school units, parents, teachers and local communities are encouraged to participate actively in the operationalization and implementation of the curriculum.
- To ensure effective curriculum delivery, increasingly more consultations are being held between and among curriculum developers and implementers.

Needs

- The countries report a common need for teacher training on their new curriculum and curriculum reforms in order to translate these effectively into practice.

- They also need to reform their existing pre-service training programmes in light of the new changes and elements introduced in the curriculum.
- There is also a need to reform or revise existing national education laws and policies to make these consistent with the new changes in the curriculum.
- More work needs to be done to customize educational programmes in different schools and at different levels to meet varying learners' needs.

Mekong sub-region

Trends

- Curricular reforms in the four countries of the Mekong sub-region (Thailand, Viet Nam, Cambodia and Laos) follow closely the elements and spirit of the Delors Report.
- The school curricula in all countries are centrally planned but allow for flexibility to accommodate local conditions.
- All countries are conscious of improving the quality of their education systems and programmes and are setting up new standards and benchmarks to note improvements in educational quality and performance.
- Education for employment and contributing to the improvement of the national economy constitute a basic educational thrust/goal in the countries of the sub-region.
- There is also a serious move to democratize access to education in the sub-region. Viet Nam and Laos plan to increase their years of free and compulsory education from 5 to 8 years; whereas in Thailand and Cambodia, free and compulsory education stand at 9 years.
- The curricula in all four countries also emphasize the propagation of a national identity.

- All countries are active in generating popular support for education and ongoing curriculum reforms.

Needs

- Ways of designing an integrated curriculum incorporating the 'Four Pillars of Learning'.
- Addressing the issue of quality and relevance.
- Ways of involving the community in the development of the curriculum.
- Continuous teacher training on their new curriculum and curriculum reforms in order to translate these effectively into practice.
- Reform their existing pre-service training programmes in light of the new changes and elements introduced in the curriculum.

Conclusion

With the information above, the participating countries will be undertaking a detailed 'Situation Analysis of the Basic Education Curriculum' utilizing the framework and guidelines agreed upon. A documentation of eleven country studies and one regional report will be published at a later date.

Annex: List of Participants and Resource Persons

Cambodia

Ms. Ton Sa Im
Director
Pedagogical Research Department
Ministry of Education, Youth and Sport
Phnom Penh.

China

Mr. Qiao
Yuquan Basic Education Department
Ministry of Education
C/o Chinese National Commission for UNESCO 37 Damucang
Hutong, Xidan.

Indonesia

Ms. Ella Yulaelawati
Head
Curriculum Division of Primary School
Office of Research and Development
Ministry of National Education
Jalan Jenderal Sudirman—Senayan
Jakarta 10270.

Japan

Ms. Shigeo Yoshikawa
Senior Curriculum Specialist (Arithmetic)
Elementary School Division
Elementary and Secondary Education Bureau
Ministry of Education, Science, Sports and Culture
Tokyo, Japan.

Lao PDR

Mr. Khampay Sisavanh
Director
National Research Institute for Education Sciences
Ministry of Education
Mahosot Street, Vientiane.

Malaysia

Ms. Sharifah Maimunah
Director,
Curriculum Development Centre
Ministry of Education
Persiaran Duta Off Jalan Duta
50604 Kuala Lumpur

Mongolia

Mr. Dashjamts Tuvshintugs
Curriculum Specialist
Non-Formal Education Centre, MOSTEC
C/o Mongolian National
Commission for UNESCO
Ministry of External Relations
Ulaanbaatar.

Philippines

Ms. Eugenia Moraleda
Director,
Curriculum Development Centre
Department of Education, Culture and Sports
UL Complex, Meralco Avenue
Pasig City.

Republic of Korea

Ms. Nan-Sim Cho
Director General, Textbook
Research Centre
Korea Institute of Curriculum & Evaluation
25-1 Samchung-dong
Jongro-gu Seoul 110-230.

Viet Nam

Mr. Do Dinh Hoan
Director
Centre of Content and Method of
Teaching for General Education
National Institute for Education and Science
101 Tran Hung Dao Street,
Hanoi

Thailand

Mr. Chaub Leechor
Director,
Office of Education Assessment and Testing Service
Department of Curriculum and Instruction Development
Ministry of Education,
Bangkok

Mrs. Mallika Nitayaphorn
Director,
Guidance Centre
Department of Curriculum and Instruction Development
Ministry of Education,
Bangkok

Ms. Parinya Ritcharoen
Educational Officer
Book Development Centre
Department of Curriculum and Instruction Development
Ministry of Education
Bangkok

Mr. Sophon Somdee
Curriculum Developer
Department of Curriculum and Instruction Development
Ministry of Education
Bangkok

Ms. Chantra Tantipong
Curriculum Developer
Department of Curriculum and Instruction Development
Ministry of Education,
Bangkok

Ms. Watanaporn Rangubtook
Supervisor, Department of General Education
Ministry of Education
Bangkok

Mrs. Patcharee Sawangsup
Supervisor
Department of Vocational Education Ministry of Education
Bangkok

Ms. Aksara Prasitsilp
Supervisor
Office of the Private Education Commission
Ministry of Education
Bangkok

Mr. Pirach Susansuk
Supervisor
Office of the National Primary Education Commission
Ministry of Education
Bangkok

Mrs. Yawarat Tusgate
Supervisor, Bureau of Educational Standard
Office of Rajabhat Institutes Council Ministry of Education
Bangkok

Mrs. Pornnipha Limpaphayom
Secretary-General
Thai National Commission for UNESCO
Ministry of Education
Bangkok

Ms. Suchitra Chitranukroh
Deputy Secretary-General
Thai National Commission for UNESCO
Ministry of Education
Bangkok

Ms. Duriya Amatavivat
Thai National Commission for UNESCO
Ministry of Education
Bangkok

Recsam

Mr. Tan Khun
Director
SEAMEO Regional Centre for Education in Science and Mathematics
Glugor,
Penang
Malaysia

Resource Persons

Ms. Liliana Jobif
International Bureau of Education
Case postale 199
1211 Geneva 20
Switzerland

Ms. Virginia Miraloa
Secretary General
Association of Asian Social Science Councils
(ASSREC)
P.O. Box 205, UP Post Office
Diliman, Quezon City
Philippines

Ms. Cecilia Braslavsky
Director
International Bureau of Education
Case postale 199
1211 Geneva 20
Switzerland

Ms. Isabel Byron
Assistant Programme Specialist
International Bureau of Education
Case postale 199
1211 Geneva 20
Switzerland

Mr. Zhou Nanzhao,
Director a.i.
Acting Chief of ACEID
UNESCO Principal Regional Office for Asia and the Pacific
920 Sukhumvit Road,
Bangkok,
Thailand

Ms. Lucille C. Gregorio
Specialist in Science and Technology Education UNESCO Principal Regional Office for Asia and the Pacific
920 Sukhumvit Road,
Bangkok
Thailand

Secretarial and Administrative Aupport

Mrs. Amporn Ratanavipak

UNESCO Principal Regional Office for Asia Pacific (PROAP)
920 Sukhumvit Road,
Bangkok 10110
Thailand

Annex: Information Note

UNESCO's International Bureau of Education (IBE) and the UNESCO's Principal Regional Office for Asia and the Pacific (PROAP) are organizing, with the support of the Ministry of Education, Thailand, a sub-regional seminar for curriculum specialists from countries of East and South-East Asia. The seminar will focus on capacity building in fundamental skills for effective curriculum development and reform and will be held in Bangkok from 12-16 December 2000.

Background

The South-East and East Asia region is faced with numerous challenges to the provision of quality basic education to meet the rapidly changing needs of its large population. Recent economic upheavals influenced by an increasingly globalized economy, rapid advances in science and technology, immense social and cultural changes, have all led to the need for innovative reforms and renewal of primary and secondary education curricula. Under the present social and economic pressures, education policy-makers and curriculum developers face the crucial task of defining new contents of education that reflect the knowledge and skills necessary for individuals' personal growth, their functioning in an increasingly complex society and their integration into the world of work.

While reforms to address these challenges have already been taking place for a number of years in the member countries of the East and South-East Asian region, it is recognized that they have so far been inadequate to reply to the changing needs of the countries. Furthermore, reforms are most of the time not implemented effectively, Where formal educational institutions do succeed in keeping up to date with the advances in knowledge, information learned in school soon becomes obsolete in the wider society. Even in the most developed of these of these countries, governments are realizing that young people are not being properly prepared to think and act independently and creatively within a perspective of learning beyond school.

The Report of the International Commission on Education for the Twenty-first Century proposes reorientation and re-organization of education systems through curricular innovations/reforms based on the guiding principle of 'learning throughout life', building on the 'four pillars of learning', (learning to know, learning to do, learning to be, learning to live together). This has strong implications for the process of curriculum reform, taking into consideration the cultural sensitivities of each country.

Curriculum reform is a complex process, and requires curriculum developers' full awareness of the intentions of and demands made by policy-makers, an understanding of the diverse needs of students and the challenging tasks of teachers. It also requires a full appreciation of the concerns of parents, employers, other interest groups and the society at-large. Curriculum processionals need to master a number of essential competencies in order for curriculum development and reform to be carried out as effectively as possible through all stages of the process. Clarity of objectives, consistency and feasibility of plans, active participation and a sense of ownership by key stakeholders, sustainability of change, all need to be ensured.

The IBE's mission is to strengthen the capacity of UNESCO Member States as regards the content of education. It has identified the strengthening of competencies among curriculum specialists as a key area of concern. The UNESCO Principal Regional Office for Asia and the Pacific (PROAP) has long been involved in capacity-building for curriculum development in the region. Its present concern is to examine the strengths and weaknesses of the curriculum for basic education of selected countries in East and South-East Asia and to formulate a sub-regional strategy for developing a curriculum framework for the twenty-first century. Both institutions have therefore come together to organize this seminar in light of their shared aim to build national regional capacities for curriculum reform.

Objectives of the Seminar

- To exchange experiences about recent and ongoing initiatives in curriculum reform in the participating countries.
- To develop a number of competencies related to a systematic process of curriculum reform, within the perspective of "learning to learn".
- To formulate a regional curriculum framework, as defined in the Delors Report. The framework will identify criteria for curriculum analysis and will be used as the basis for the conducting of national case studies in selected countries.
- To begin a dialogue on modalities for closer regional co-operation in the field of curriculum development, leading to the establishment of a "Network of Curriculum Specialists" in the South-East and East Asia sub-region.

Participation

Participants well be invited from the following countries: Cambodia, China, Indonesia, Japan, Lao PDR, Malaysia, Mongolia, Philippines, Republic of Korea, Thailand, Viet Nam, and SEAMEO-RECSAM. The seminar is intended for Directors or other high-ranking officers of Curriculum Development Centres or corresponding institutions.

Contents and Modalities

The seminar will emphasize active participant involvement and interaction. It will be divided into country presentations, training and drafting components. Training sessions will consist of a presentation by an expect in one of the selected competencies, followed by group work and discussion. Drafting sessions will be carried out by identifying members of task groups, who will formulate the outlines of key documents.

Country Presentations

To allow for informed exchange within the regional context, participants will be requested to prepare written reports on their country's recent curriculum reforms, identifying the main elements and stages in the reform process. Participants will receive guidelines for the preparation of these country presentations.

Competency Profile Presentations

Principal elements of the selected competencies will be presented by experts in the field. Presentations will be interactive and supported by OHP or multi-media learning aids.

Workshops

During the workshops, aspects of the skills to be developed will be practised through various exercises, facilitated by the invited expert. Each session will end with a discussion of the main elements of each competency and how it may be applied actively to the curriculum development process, and in the formulation of a 'generic' regional framework.

Drafting Session

During the second half of the seminar, discussions, followed by practical drafting sessions, well take place to formulate the curriculum framework and the guidelines for the case studies to be undertaken on curriculum reform in selected countries.

Each participant will be requested to bring to the seminar, copies of the national curriculum for the basic education level. This will be the main document used in preparing the analysis of the country's national curriculum, following the framework agreed upon. (Background Document: the Delors Report.)

Concluding Session

Participants will discus plans for national follow-up action relating to the conducting of the case studies on curriculum reform. Participants will also have the opportunity to discuss the possibility of creating a regional network of curriculum specialists. This network would permit participating countries to intensify information exchange on curricular issues, and develop, under IBE and PROAP leadership, various shared activities (such as conducting studies of a common interest, organization of policy seminars for decision-makers, development of expertise in various curricular areas, etc.).

to discuss the possibility of creating a regional network of curriculum specialists. This network would permit participating countries to intensify information exchange on curricular issues, and develop, under IBE and PROAP leadership, various shared activities (such as conducting studies of a common interest, organization of policy seminars for decision-makers, development of expertise in various curricular areas, etc.).